Not Fair!

The LAW AND PUBLIC POLICY: PSYCHOLOGY AND THE SOCIAL SCIENCES series includes books in three domains:

Legal Studies—writings by legal scholars about issues of relevance to psychology and the other social sciences, or that employ social science information to advance the legal analysis;

Social Science Studies—writings by scientists from psychology and the other social sciences about issues of relevance to law and public policy; and

Forensic Studies—writings by psychologists and other mental health scientists and professionals about issues relevant to forensic mental health science and practice.

The series is guided by its editor, Bruce D. Sales, PhD, JD, ScD, University of Arizona; and coeditors, Bruce J. Winick, JD, University of Miami; Norman J. Finkel, PhD, Georgetown University; and Stephen J. Ceci, PhD, Cornell University.

***

Not Fair!

The Typology of Commonsense Unfairness

Norman J. Finkel

American Psychological Association, Washington, DC

Published by
American Psychological Association
750 First Street, NE
Washington, DC 20002
www.apa.org

To order:
APA Order Department
P.O. Box 92984
Washington, DC 20090-2984

Tel: (800) 374-2721, Direct: (202) 336-5510
Fax: (202) 336-5502, TDD/TTY: (202) 336-6123
Online: www.apa.org/books/
Email: order@apa.org

In the UK and Europe, copies may be ordered from
American Psychological Association
3 Henrietta Street
Covent Garden, London
WC2E 8LU England

Typeset in Goudy by EPS Group Inc., Easton, MD

Printer: Sheridan Books, Ann Arbor, MI
Cover Designer: Debra Naylor, Naylor Design, Washington, DC
Technical/Production Editor: Catherine Hudson
Project Manager: Debbie K. Hardin, New Page Publishing, Charlottesville, VA

The opinions and statements published are the responsibility of the authors, and such opinions and statements do not necessarily represent the policies of the APA.

Library of Congress Cataloging-in-Publication Data
Finkel, Norman J.
    Not fair! : the typology of commonsense unfairness / Norman J. Finkel.
       p. cm.
    Includes bibliographical references and index.
    ISBN 1-55798-752-1 (acid-free paper)
       1. Fairness.   I. Title.
  BJ1533.F2 .F56 2001
  170—dc21

                                                                    00-068943

British Library Cataloguing-in-Publication Data
A CIP record is available from the British Library.

Printed in the United States of America
First Edition

To my wife, Marilyn

For a generosity that goes beyond fairness

CONTENTS

ix

PREFACE

"Not fair!" Who has not made that claim? If a preface is part con-
fessional, then let me own up: I know I have made the claim, no doubt in
every decade and year, about all sorts of situations, circumstances, and
relationships, and even about life itself. That said, there are two important
qualifiers: First, many have faded from mind, and second, some have stayed
a lifetime.

"Not fair!" Who has not *heard* it? I know that I have heard that cry
so many times, from people I know, from people I love, from people I don't
know at all. As a professor, I also know that I have the claim hurled at
me, with an invisible finger of blame pointing my way, in every academic
year, when students disagree with my standards for papers and exams, or
with my holding them to the standards. Doing the research for this book
has made matters worse, in a sense, because I now hear that cry everywhere,
like some physicist picking up the background noise of the universe. This
may happen for the readers of this work as well, as we come to hear how
ubiquitous the cry of unfairness is.

So when and why did it begin, and what about the topic intriqued
me? The genesis and ontogeny of the topic is what a preface is also supposed to make clear. Yet I am skeptical of the clarity of most preface
"stories," because a preface, though it is many things, is always a paradox:
It comes at the beginning of the book, yet it is typically written at the
end; it recounts why the author began this work, yet, to paraphrase the
poet W. S. Merwin, it comes far from a beginning that can scarcely be
remembered. Even when the author privately introspects, recollections are
likely to be a mix of memory, fancy, and reconstruction, like some over-
priced blend of coffee, short on body yet reeking with aroma. In trying to
reconstruct it for the readership, it is like trying to tell someone a dream
you had: Without meaning to, you revise and rearrange the misaligned,
and you neatly tidy up the chaos, thereby creating a coherence to that

which had little. In these ways, a nonfiction preface comes uncomfortably close to fiction. Prefaces, then, ought to come with warning labels, and here I have affixed mine. That said, here is what I "remember."

The *in the beginning* origins remain elusive, for when I try to unearth those journalistic facts—its where or when, or how it all began—I hit rock. There was no Proustian smell of madeleine cookies to break the seal on remembrances. There was no "let there be light" moment; at lesser wattage, not even a lightbulb lighted. It certainly was not a dream or visual hallucination, for unlike Leonardo and Michelangelo, there was no bird at my lips calling me to flight and no marbled prisoner summoning me to its freeing. If not there, then where? My best guess, more a default option, is that the book began in some time out of mind.

It may be that the concept of "unfairness" simply eased its way into my psyche—as an old habit that insinuated, got comfortable, and never left, to paraphrase the poet Rilke. At home and now a familiar, the notion rested like an old dog lying on its spot, unmoved and unnoticed. Yet this sleepy picture was periodically shattered by my cat-like reactions replete with sound and fury when an unfairness sprung to mind. So the concept was not, and could not be, entirely unconscious. Still, with so many springs and opportunities for the issue to root and break ground, it did not; I would have known, surely, if it had. Rather, like a cat returning to its nap, my reflection on the "why" of unfairness did likewise. Yet this cat picture, like the dog picture, remains an unsatisfactory picture, because for research to get off the ground and for a book to begin, some rain must have stirred the dead land to life, as the poet Eliot had it. For me, and this I clearly remember, that rain came in the form of a doubt.

I was finishing a work, *Commonsense Justice: Jurors' Notions of the Law* (Harvard University Press), and I was looking over an early passage where I had defined my key term as reflecting "what ordinary people think is just and fair" (p. 2). I must have edited the paragraph dozens of times, yet I had left that phrase undisturbed. This time, though, I was disturbed.

I suddenly realized that I had so easily slipped into a locution and a way of thinking that seemed so prevalent in the field: where "just" and "fair" were either used as synonyms (e.g., "procedural justice" and "procedural fairness") or where the two were conjoined in a euphemistic idiom ("just and fair") without careful examination of whether the back end ("fair") conveyed anything of its own that the front-end ("just") did not already deliver, or where "just" was prejudged the brighter star in the binary, relegating "fair" to the penumbra. The disturbing thought grew: Perhaps "commonsense justice" was not the whole story; perhaps "commonsense fairness," neglected and dwarfed, had its own story to tell.

Being an inveterate "clipper," I began cutting articles from my morning newspaper, the *Washington Post*, where "fair" and "unfair" and "just" and "unjust" were featured. In addition, I began listening more closely to how children, and my students, faculty, and administrators, used those terms. I went back to Supreme Court opinions and philosophical writings for cites and nuances. From these anecdotal reports and informal indicia —neither the best of sources nor the surest of findings—I nonetheless sensed something distinguishable. Enough so that I began a series of studies on the topic.

In addition to the "fair" versus "just" distinction, there is another that serves to focus this work: the distinction between "fair" and "unfair." These two terms, I would argue, are neither just endpoints of a continuum nor even two sides of the same coin, for the absence of one may not, *ipso facto*, define the other, any more than the absence of "abnormality" defines "healthy." A few illustrations make the point. A young child might feel that the "bedtime" fixed by her parents, or the way her parents treat her older sister differently than she, are instances of "unfairness," although the child has little clarity about how parents ought to be "fair" in these matters; a high school teenager may feel that the school's random searches of his locker and its rules about "trash talk" unfairly violate his basic rights, yet he may have no idea how the school ought to fairly balance competing interests; a college student may believe that a professor's methods of ped-agogy and grading, and the university's methods of admitting students and distributing financial aid, are all instances of unfairness, yet she has little clarity about the fair way in these matters; and an adult may rattle off a host of rules and practices at his company that he finds unfair, yet he is stumped about what would be fair.

At least three significant differences emerge. First, our instances of "unfairness" seem to be much clearer, sharper, and more concrete than the more abstract, aerial notions of "fairness." Second, unfairness instances typically come with more heat, indignation, and moral outrage than the emotional accompaniments to fair, and these heated feelings typically press for release and response, in louder rhetoric and stronger action. Third, unfairness seems to have primacy, for children will utter that cry—"Not fair!"—long before their formal moral and civic lessons begin instructing them on fairness principles. Given clarity and concreteness, passion and insistence, and primacy, these suggest that the most yielding way into the topic is likely to come from the "unfair" end.

There. Despite my skepticism, I have told a preface story about the genesis and ontogeny of the book. It may be that stories are what we have, even what we are. This work again relies on that extensively. The cry— "Not fair!"—represents the book's title, its goal, and its method. The goal is the unearthing of commonsense unfairness, to find its substance, basis, and essence, as ordinary citizens see it. This is primarily phenomenological research, looking into the subjectivity of participants. Methodologically, we ask people to give us their "Not fair!" instances, their stories. What we get are concrete examples, unfairness narratives that stayed in mind, came to mind, and were voluntarily expressed. In proceeding this way, the landscape is wide open, because we do not steer participants toward particular directions: We do not, for example, furnish unfairness stimuli, examples, vignettes, or cases, all of which may involve issues the researcher cares about but may be of little concern to participants. Thus, in the beginning, it is their unfairness stories that drive the researcher, and not the other way around. The job for the researcher is then two-fold: First, to deconstruct the story, to find out why it is unfair to the participant; second, to find the stories within the stories, the deeper meanings, and to construct the basic categories of unfairness that house these instances.

This book was written for those who have been struck by unfairness —as an experience and as a topic—and who have, at some point, contemplated the whys and wherefores of it, and its short- and long-term consequences for individuals, relationships, law, and society. This is a vast and disparate audience, united in some personal or professional belief that the topic has import and resonance. Yet within this large audience, three groups stand out.

First, there is the broadest group, which encompasses the ordinary citizen, the politician, and the Supreme Court justice, because all deal with unfairness in one form (or forum) or another, be it by coping, legislating, or adjudicating. In presenting this work, I have tried to reduce some of the labor for the reader by writing in a nonjournalese style and by putting technical, statistical, and reference matters in notes. Second, there is an academic audience—primarily those professors, researchers, and students in the disciplines of psychology, philosophy, sociology, anthropology, theology, criminology, and political science—who are likely to find substantive links to their own work. Third, there is the specialized audience who call "psycholegal" or "sociolegal" studies their home base; whether their perspective is primarily legal, psychological, social, philosophical, or public policy, and whether their approach is empirical, normative, linguistic, conceptual, or some combination, all will find some common ground in this work.

A book is not only about some topic, for some audience. It is an undertaking that comes into being because the author has received encouragement and help along the way, from many who deserve acknowledgment. First, I wish to acknowledge the anonymous students, and their family members, young and old, who gave up their unfairness instantiations, because without the data there would be no book. Then there are other students, research assistants, who helped code the data and build the categorization schemas. To Jen Groscup, Mason Couvillon, Tarik Jackson, Lisa Faraldo, Erin Crum, Susan Tebbe, Erin Peterson, Karen Kaczynski, Jen Lafferty, John Burke, Danielle Vauthy, Christina Morgan, and Colin Huntley, my deep appreciation. My thanks to coauthors on the cross-cultural work, David Crystal, Hirozumi Watanabe, Rom Harré, and Jose-Luis

Rodriguez, for taking me and this work to places where we could not go alone. I am grateful to my colleagues at Georgetown University, Steve Sabat, Ali Moghaddam, Jim Lamiell, Jerry Parrott, and Darlene Howard, for their encouragement and insightful suggestions. To Bruce Sales, who saw the theoretical import of this work before I did, and to Sol Fulero, who recognized the deconstructive theme before I did, my deep thanks for all your encouragement. Finally, to my wife, Marilyn Zalcman, for our many talks on the topic of unfairness, for reading and editing earlier drafts, and for so much more, my thanks go beyond mere words and a dedication.

I

SITUATING UNFAIRNESS WITHIN THE PSYCHE, ANCIENT CRIES, AND A JUST WORLD

Then Eliphaz the Temanite Said:
Can an innocent man be punished?
Can a good man die in distress? (p. 21)
Then Bildad the Shuhite Said:
Does God make straightness crooked
Or turn truth upside down? (p. 25)
Then Zophar the Namathite Said:
For he knows that you are a sinner;
He sees and judges your crimes. (p. 31)

Then Job Said:
But I want to speak before God,
To present my case in God's court. . . .
For I have prepared my defense,
And I know that I am right. (pp. 34–35)

From Stephen Mitchell's *The Book of Job* (1987)

1

INTRODUCTION:
THE CRIES, AND THE CRITICS,
OF UNFAIRNESS

Quick as thought he snatched a knife from Hook's belt and was about to drive it home, when he saw that he was higher up the rock than his foe. It would not have been fighting fair. He gave the pirate a hand to help him up.

It was then that Hook bit him.

Not the pain of this but its unfairness was what dazed Peter. It made him quite helpless. He could only stare, horrified. Every child is affected thus the first time he is treated unfairly. All he thinks he has a right to when he comes to you to be yours is fairness. After you have been unfair to him he will love you again, but will never afterwards be quite the same boy. No one ever gets over the first unfairness; no one except Peter.

J. M. Barrie, *Peter Pan*, p. 127

SURFACE CRIES AND DEEPER SOUNDINGS

In the epigraph, Hook's bite leaves Peter speechless, though luckily for the reader, J. M. Barrie is not.[1] In the author's account and commentary, a root word recurs: "fair," "unfairness," "unfairly," "fairness," "unfair," and "unfairness." Counting them up, that's a lot of "unfairness" in one short excerpt from a "once upon a time" fairy tale. In the present work, however, it is the count in this land that matters, though numbers matter less than meaning. With "meaning" as the primary goal, my aim is to unearth the stories of unfairness, and beneath that, the story of the stories of unfairness —that is, "commonsense unfairness."

Words such as "unearthing," "uncovering," and "beneath" suggest digging under the surface, implying that the treasure being sought is buried there. But the casual observer might question this imagery and direction, seeing, rather, the everyday surface as the subject matter's home. The surface is the obvious choice, because at the sensory, the cry of unfairness hits our ears as a ubiquitous rant. So if all we need to do is keep our ears open and our attention at the ready, why dig?

There are a number of good reasons. First, if we hear only the surface din, we are likely to miss some deeper themes and variations. For example, though ubiquitous screams may be the typical trumpeter of unfairness claims, it was "stunned silence" in Peter Pan's case, and that silence suggests that unfairness may be deeper than even the surface ubiquity bodes. Moreover, if Peter is not just a fairy-tale outlier, but the *puer aeternus*[2] who stands beside other lost boys, girls, and grownups also crying in silence, then the rant that hits our ears may significantly undercount the underlying rage. Thus if the goal is to extract the meaning, we must take its full measure, going beyond the surface's length and breadth to its depth as well.

There is a second reason for unearthing, which becomes apparent when we listen to just those surface cries above the auditory threshold that the casual observer suggests we attend to. What can we learn from these data? Put another way, what do the variables of the cry, its physical properties, tell us? The answer, I submit, is nothing. Nothing of what we really want to know. For instance, the cry's amplitude only alerts us that something is happening, but tells us nothing about its *substance*. Similarly, although the cry may be pitched in a child's whimper, a basso profundo's lament, or a soprano's tremolo, octave tells us nothing of its *essence*. Furthermore, although the frequency of occurrence and periodicity reveal the phenomenon's pervasiveness and beat, they reveal nothing of its *basis*. In sum, though we are first struck by what we hear, the answers—about the cry's substance, essence, and basis—are not to be found in those physical, objective measures.

There is still a third reason for choosing this inward direction, which can be seen when the unfairness claim is put to paper. On paper, many unfairness instances are followed by exclamation points, or multiple, histrionic exclamation points, a coda added for more than good measure, I believe. Rather, these points are added because claimants want the reader to most definitely understand that something is very, very wrong!!! But these trailing punctuation marks, however insistent and numerous they may be, are merely accessorizing flourishes. Like the objective variables of the cry, the exclamation point signals that something is important to the writer, and should be so to the reader (according to the writer)—but what that "something" is remains unknown. Thus in the end, although the cry's physical variables and the unfairness claim's punctuation marks may rivet our attention to the surface and sensory, we come to realize that the story of the story of unfairness lies in deeper ground.

SITUATING THE MATTER AND SETTING COURSE

In developing the subject matter of "unfairness" in part I ("Situating Unfairness Within the Psyche, Ancient Cries, and a Just World"), the topic is situated in a different context in each of the first three chapters. These contexts provide the psychological and social, the historical and theological, and the conceptual and empirical backdrops for the known and the unknown about unfairness. In chapter 1, unfairness is situated in the psyche of the crier, although the psyches of the critics of criers will receive attention as well; although subjectivity is given primacy, objectivity has its place, because who or what delivers the bite is located in the social world, or in nature, or in life itself. Chapter 2 accents the historical, theological, and moral grounding to unfairness; here, those ancient, "in the beginning" biblical cries of unfairness serve as backdrop for exploring Job's world and the "just world," and why both still affect us today. In chapter 3, unfairness is situated within a current literature of justice and fairness, where the relevant conceptual and empirical ground of fairness and justice is turned. From these chapters, hypotheses are developed, new questions and directions are pursued, and new ways of investigating unfairness follow.

In setting the course, there is something odd about the doing, if not "wrong-way" about the going, that requires some justification. I seek, by book's end, to have a far deeper understanding of ordinary citizens' conceptions and concepts about "fairness," yet the course I set is to "unfairness." The question, then, is why study "unfairness" instead of "fairness"?

In the preface, I put forth the view, which bears repeating, that "unfair" and "fair" were neither endpoints of a continuum nor two sides of the same coin. It is quite possible that we can be clear about one without having clarity about the other. Now I will amplify this point, which Thomas Simon calls "separability."[3] Consider the following example. A high school student believes, with great conviction, that the school's dress code, random searches of his locker, prohibitions about "hanging out" (assembling) on school grounds, and "talking trash" within the school are all unfairnesses that violate basic freedoms, yet this student has only the vaguest notion of what fairness would be or how the school ought to balance the competing interests of protecting individual rights and protecting the safety of all. I could easily multiply such examples, covering all ages and almost all situations, but one is enough.

"Separability," though it points to distinctiveness, does not tell us which distinct road to take, though the illustration suggests answers. The first answer is that our notions of "unfairness" are typically clearer, sharper, and more concrete than those of "fairness." The second answer is that the emotions accompanying unfairness have more heat and moral outrage to them than those that accompany fairness, and these typically press for release and response, in louder rhetoric and stronger action. We can labeled these "clarity and concreteness" and "passion and insistence."[4]

The third answer involves "primacy," and this reaction will take a bit of developing. It begins with the fact that individuals grow and develop (i.e., ontogeny). If we listen to children, or to psychologists who have systematically studied children,[5] the cry of "unfairness" is heard before the child reaches school or Sunday-school age. Thus the *sense of unfairness* comes long before the child first encounters those *foundational fairness doctrines* (e.g., the Declaration of Independence, *The Federalist Papers*, the Constitution), and it comes long before grownup philosophers can parse a "fairness" argument and long before grownup lawyers can write a writ of complaint. Expressed as primacy, "commonsense unfairness" comes first— headier, more abstract notions come later.[6]

Having laid out reasons for pursuing the cry inward, into the subjective psyche, and for pursuing "unfairness" rather than "fairness" as the topic, we now turn to the speculative. What are we likely to find there?

The Variables and Variability of Subjectivity

The basis of unfairness must be situated in the subjective psyche. A thought experiment tells us this. Can we not imagine a different Peter Pan, with a different history and upbringing, having a very different reaction to the same bite? Had Peter Pan been an earthly, urban street kid of today, rather than the eternal youth fathered by a turn-of-the-century Britisher, he might have reacted quite differently. It is possible that this "gangsta" Peter might have driven that knife home "quick as thought"—and without any. Can we not imagine a third child, one who has been beaten down by years of physical abuse, who seems to react not at all to the bite, or, sadly, to much of anything.

This thought experiment brings variables and variability to light. We see both in the various actors' inner reactions, which interpose between the biting stimulus and responsive cry, and which give rise to the cry. We can speculate that this inner reaction involves perceiving, construing, interpreting, emoting, and judging; it may well involve other psychological functions. But it seems most reasonable to assume that this inner reaction contains some notion of unfairness, even if in nascent form, for the judgment and cry could not arise without it.

It is doubtful that this inner reaction is hard-wired; it is also doubtful that it lodged in the psyche fully grown and remains there unswayed. Rather, it is likely to be influenced by the person's developmental history, parenting, siblings, peers, education, social background, and culture. Such influencing factors and prepotent processes are what lead to the development of the unfairness concept, and it is this judgment of unfairness, rather than the bite per se, that reveals the story and the variability. We are fairly confident of this, particularly when we consider another variation. What would have happened if Peter had grabbed not Hook's hand, but a dog's tail, and received the same objective bite, but now coming from "man's best friend"? In all likelihood, Peter, and J. M. Barrie, would not reach an unfairness judgment in this case.

When it comes to unfairness, the most interesting questions seem to lie in subjectivity. But whose subjectivity? Mine, yours, or Peter Pan's? Chances are that these will not always align. At this disjunct, we meet *variability*. We saw that form of variability that psychologists call "between-subject" variability in the thought experiment, where Peter Pan, the urban street kid, and the abused child all had differing reactions, even though the age of the bitten victims and the biting circumstance were the same. This type of variability may show when age varies as well, for the child, Wendy, may claim an unfairness around bedtime whereas the mother, Mrs. Darling, may disagree. This variability may show when gender enters the judgment, for if parents give their son a later curfew than their daughter when both reach the same age, the daughter may perceive a "discriminatory unfairness." Yet *perspective* may produce variability and determine the daughter's judgment of unfairness quite apart from gender, age, and a comparative focus on inequality; in fact, from a different perspective, she might be seeing "an arbitrary rules unfairness" in regard to her parents' decision making.

In this work, we look at a number of questions relating to between-subject variability. Will the *types* of unfairness cited change as the age of our participants increases? Will the frequency of unfairnesses change with age? Will our reported unfairnesses grow more or less severe? Will we come to focus more or less on our own unfairnesses, showing greater or lesser narcissism as we age?

In addition to "between-subject" variability, there is another type that psychologists call "within-subject" variability. To illustrate, let us recall the fact of ontogeny, that individuals grow and change. This being so, it is likely that a person's perspective on unfairness will change over time as well. By comparison to the eternal child, Peter Pan, who stays forever young, Wendy, like the rest of us, grows up—and the adult Wendy is likely to perceive unfairnesses differently than her childhood self, perhaps seeing no unfairness where the child Wendy once did.

Individual variability raises another question, which is implied in the epigraph: Do we ever get over our unfairnesses? On the question of first unfairnesses, Barrie took a position that these do not roll off our backs and into history easily: "After you have been unfair to him he will love you again, but will never afterwards be quite the same boy."[7] If Barrie is right, we are changed by the unfairness, and it is not a good change. Moreover, despite the palliatives that may be offered by our comforting parents (who may have also been the ones who delivered the bite), those bromides generally fail to restore us to the same boy or girl. In Barrie's view, the first unfairness marks us indelibly, representing the end of the innocence. But do children react as Barrie claims? Do they suddenly go from gay, innocent, and heartless, to dour and sour with one bite? Barrie's is a literary answer. But what we have is an empirical question, which remains open, to be taken up later in this work.

With a bit more reflection, we surmise that subjectivity, variability, and perspective are likely to be affected by other variables, such as time, history, geography, and culture, to name but some. For example, our current judgment of whether it is unfair for young children to be working in factories is likely to differ from judgments in Charles Dickens's best of times and those at the twentieth century's beginning;[8] so, too, are judgments about religion, segregation, and corporal punishment in schools, and women and African Americans at the voting booth. Time and history change our judgments, and if we change the geography, we likely could find countries where what we regard as unfair would not be so there. Then there are the variables of culture and subculture to consider: A certain gesture may be taken as a disrespect unfairness in Japan, but not in the United States, whereas the same curse word may evoke laughter from one group of teenagers while evoking violence from another. Then there is religious background, or one's specific views on "theodicy"[9]—the problem of reconciling God with evil in the world—as these views may determine our unfairness judgments.

In laying out a case for "unfairness" and situating it in the psyche, we have gone inward, though not forgetting the social world where the bite occurred. Moreover, though the cry's meaning is likely to be found in subjectivity, the cry's aim and consequence is toward the social world, at those who inflict bites, or seem to permit bites to others. Here we find a variable that seems to sit at the heart of the unfairness claim, perhaps being endemic to it—blame.

Unfairness claims seem to be lodged everywhere, in all sorts of situations, in all sorts of relations: they occur between equals, such as friends, strangers, neighbors, roommates, lovers, and spouses, and they occur in hierarchical relationships, between parents and children, employees and employers, patients and caregivers, students and teachers, and athletes and coaches. Although these claims root in the everyday ground and generally remain there, some litigiously migrate into the law, where they are voiced by the lowliest of defendants or written into Supreme Court decisions by our highest justices. Still, despite the various relationships and venues where they are heard, the commonality is blame.

The cry seems to be an accusation, a finger pointing. It may be directed at a particular person, be it peer, parent, or professor, or directed at a group, like the family, or broader still, at the collectivity we call society, government, or law. Going wider, blame may be directed impersonally, at nature, heredity, life, or luck. Going still higher, it may even be directed at the transcendent God. The bottom line is that someone or something has wronged the crier, or so the crier believes.

In Shaver's classic work on blame,[10] the author began by stating that after a misfortune or a moral affront, "Who is to blame?" is one of the first questions asked. According to Shaver, "people are never blamed for doing good,"[11] only for negative events, and the negative initiates an "epistemic search"[12] for an accounting, through the assignment of blame. Will we find this in our research? Do people always blame when they perceive an unfairness? If we do blame, who or what do we blame, and why do we blame?

To summarize, the case I have been building for "unfairness" goes deeper and wider than the starting cry, for its ubiquity, decibel level, pitch, and trailing punctuation marks remain enigmatic despite their objectivity, telling us little of what we want to know about the cry's underlying substance, essence, and basis. In refocusing our observations from the ear to the mind, in redirecting our search from the objective to the subjective, and in reframing the matter around the crier's inner reaction, the cry's significance mutes to a mere signal as we pursue its deeper meaning. The terrain to be followed has been sketched, with defensible reasons offered for why this road would likely get us closer to the essence of the matter. Along the way, I have touched, albeit lightly, some of the likely dimensions (types and severity) and connections (blame) of unfairness, while marking the central place that variability, perspective, age, gender, culture, and context are likely to play in its judgment.

The Critics' Howls of Foul and the Charge of Petty Whines From Whiners

Although the subject matter and direction have been defined and set, and the course has been outlined in speculative strokes, a reasonable objection can be lodged to this endeavor that would throw everything into doubt. Consider the possibility that the sound and the fury of these cries and claims of unfairness signify nothing but tempests in a teapot. Here, heat and noise are present, but such tempests typically turn out to be evanescent, evaporating, and eminently forgettable. We do not have to strain for illustrations. We may rail at unfair weather that spoils our plans, or we may loudly condemn an umpire's unfair call against our team. These "tempest" possibilities challenge the importance for study of unfairnesses: if tempests uncorked evaporate in short order, why not send the bottle back and go for something with more body?

Although "tempest" remains a possibility, we do not know if it is a probability. J. M. Barrie, of course, argues for just the opposite, that the first unfairnesses are not evanescent but have a staying power of forever. In the end, the question is an empirical one, and one we will examine. But the examination now turns to a critical backlash that has been leveled at those ubiquitous cries of unfairness and the ever-present blaming. In fact, those unfairness cries, along with the blaming, seem to incite certain critics to seeing red, ranting purple, and writing screeds, jeremiads, and howls—which all cry foul—as loudly and shrilly as those who cry "unfair."

To ignore these critics "would not be fighting fair."[13] Three specific criticisms will be examined. The first criticism, the loudest and most pervasive, is taken take up here, and it may be dubbed "petty whines." The second criticism, which is the oldest, will be taken up in chapter 2, and it may be called "so who says life's supposed to be fair?" Finally, the third, which may be dubbed "failing to discriminate," will be addressed in chapter 3.

The Social Critics

Under *petty whines*, we have a number of critics concluding that most unfairness claims are either baseless, bogus, or, at best, the petty whines of Peter Pan–types who have never grown up. This is finger-pointing criticism, but one that commands the psychological high ground, arising as it does from the superego rather than the id. Like righteous grand inquisitors pressing the miscreants to the wheel, they bring barbed words and the "rack-of-guilt" to crush a heresy that is already out of hand.

The examples are numerous, with variations ranging from the tame and traditional to the inane and incendiary, with all manner betwixt and between. At the softer end of things, within the traditional morning newspaper antidote columns of Dear Abby, Ann Landers, and Miss Manners, for example, we find this criticism growing more frequent within the queries, and within the responses from the doyennes. If we move to another section of the newspaper, or to the weekly magazines, or to the evening news, we find that traditional media sources have picked up the "petty whine" thesis, and poured it into a growing number of critical stories. This increasing criticism is not some transitory blip—like an artifact of the millennium[14] or a presidential impeachment[15]—for the criticisms have had a longer and deeper run than the blips. No, there is a real phenomenon here, but getting a clear sense of it is not so clear.

Three problems particularly cloud the picture. First, unfairness instances are frequently presented in a highly distorted way, such that what makes the news is neither the representative nor the average picture of unfairness instantiations, but extremist cases: the worst of the worst. This type of distortion, widely documented in media portrayals of crimes, criminals, crime control, and jury decisions,[16] is likely happening for "prototypical unfairness" as well. These atypical examples can distort the phenomenon and severely skew the public's perception.

The second problem goes to *how* unfairness is presented, in what context. Getting a clear and consistent picture from these criticisms becomes exceedingly difficult when the critics set "unfairness" within a highly littered landscape—among the ills of incivility, rudeness, crudeness, permissiveness, family breakdown, violence in families, violence in marriages, violence in schools, road rage, victimization, sex, drugs, alcohol, music, movies, television, self-involvement, pretensions, lack of generosity, blaming, and other assorted dysfunctions. But the problem is worse than just creating a social mélange, for the critics fail to sort out their mess or critically analyze it. Specifically, they seldom bother to pinpoint what is cause and effect, what is correlate, or what is merely coincidence. To make the point with "cause and effect," surely it makes a difference if the critic argues that unfairness claims cause a climate of incivility, rather than the reverse, that the climate of incivility causes unfairness claims. In failing to document a connection, some critics seem satisfied with simply firing shotgun blasts—as if they were on a roller coaster drive-by—content with hitting anything. In addition, there is little in this "reportage" that resembles sampling, science, or even a police spreadsheet, for these news reports round up the usual suspects and foils from convenient scapegoats. Finally, most critics never raise the possibility that there might be another side to the story, with notable exceptions to this one-sidedness standing out starkly.[17] This, as a reminder, is just the traditional end of things.

On the other extreme, in a galaxy far removed from kinder, gentler, traditional sources, we find ordinary citizens, "more than kin but less than kind," who have weighed into the fray in new ways. Armed with cordless phones and deeply bunkered in La-Z-Boys, they fire off salvos to talk radio and call-in television shows. Not only are some of the same mélange ingredients named in the callers' complaints, but callers can go from anger to irony to hypocrisy— without missing a reflective beat—by making their complaints with all the rudeness, incivility, profanity, and blaming they can muster. Perhaps the topper, on this end, is the daytime television talk show,[18] where some of the same mélange elements now do hand-to-hand combat.

In addition to *which* cases get presented, and *how* they get presented, the third problem producing confusion involves the culprits: the *who*. Some critics are quite confident here, having already put the Generation-Xers squarely in their cross-hairs. But then why not? Their hair, clothes, music, tattoos, body piercing, and general strangeness seem to send a "hell with you and your world" message that offends some; if that's not enough, add avoiding responsibility, embracing victimology, and, of course, claiming unfairness.

But there are other critics, equally confident, who aim their wrath at the parents, the baby boomers, finding their narcissistic entitlement claims particularly galling. Still other critics go in for "the two birds with one stone throw" approach, trying to fell boomers and their offspring in one causal hit, as the causes proffered run hither and yon: Boomers have passed on whiny genes, administered permissive parenting, and modeled childish self-centeredness. Then there are the critics who take aim at high-priced athletes, rock stars, models, actors, politicians, and assorted odds and ends on their prima donna list, along with those in the psychobabble professions who help with the excuse making.

Finally, betwixt traditional and incendiary sources, we have social critics who have their own bully pulpit and a point of view. In the following example, columnist George Will took aim at the narcissism of baby boomers.[19] He wrote that this group, the oldest of which is now turning 50, has discovered a "cosmic injustice"—that they are going to die, and not only is this unfair to them, but they expect that "Congress produce just one more entitlement." Going from Will's jeremiad to comedian Dennis Miller's rant, the latter asked if "anybody else noticed that civility is disappearing . . . [and that people] have simply lined the borders of their personal space with razor wire."[20] Miller hurled his examples of incivility in a language that is anything but civil, and fingers as "the fountainhead of all this bad behavior . . . the daytime talk shows."[21] Strange, that with all of the possible punch lines, culprits, and causes available to Miller and his writers, the comedian ended up with one that is both tame and familiar.

In summing up, the rant and the jeremiad begin with anecdotes, real or imagined. These raw materials are better than facts for sculpting rants and jeremiads, because they are unencumbered by nuance, unmarred by graininess, and have no contradictory hard edges to them; in their soft simplicity, they are easily honed through the author's particular ax to grind. But in the end, the point is far too pointed and simple, and the culprit all too convenient.

If we parboil these criticisms, many social critics see disorder on sociological and psychological fronts, with loss of perspective, generosity, community, and civility resulting, with a rise of permissiveness, whining, and "boomer babble."[22] On the psychological end, the critics have let loose the diagnostic labels, the dogs of this new war, as they impugn the psychological health of unfairness claimants without the Hippocratic ethic's leash. In this labeling game, the diagnosis *du jour* is "narcissism," the disease of the me-decade, which is judged epidemic by these critics-turned-psychiatrists who overlook their inconsistency of using diagnostic labels to condemn when they so frequently condemn those who use them to exculpate or mitigate. Nonetheless, once labeled, the unfairness claimant can be viewed as having little sense of proportion, little sense of the other, or just plain little sense. In the end, the critics leave us with a fairy tale, one that lacks J. M. Barrie's elegance and Peter Pan's integrity.

What cannot be dismissed, though, is the critics' underlying question: Are the unfairness claims mostly *petty whines*? This, too, is an empirical question: Where the "tempest" claim focuses on the short duration of unfairnesses, the "petty whines" allegation focuses on the triviality of the complaint. The critics may turn out to be right, when the data are examined, but not on the basis of what they have offered so far, because when their proffers are examined, it is their substance that evaporates.

The situation is actually worse, because some critics make no attempt to render either fact or analysis, as legerdemain is the tactic: Here, the voicing of a claim is used as proof that the claim must be false, which leads to impugning the claimant's mental health and character. This ends in great nonsense, as I will demonstrate, by using such a legerdemain in the following thought experiment. For my raw material, I turn to Thomas Jefferson's Declaration of Independence; specifically, I turn to that point in the document after his famous second paragraph (wherein the self-evident truths and unalienable rights of life, liberty, and the pursuit of happiness are found). What do we find next in the great document? From the critics' characterizations, Jefferson wrote 27 short paragraphs of unfairness whines[23] —which may be exactly how King George III read it. The point of the thought experiment is this: Without knowing the claimant's point of view, and investigating whether the facts indeed support the claims, it is all too easy to discount the claims as whines and the claimants as whiners.

Academic Critics

In sharp contrast with the social critics' methods of analysis, academic constructionists generally rely on solid research and scholarship, and by these, most would dismiss the pundit's jeremiad, the comedian's rant, and caricatured tautologies for what they are. Still, the common ground is the topic of "unfairness," along with the collateral mélange targets of rudeness, incivility, permissiveness, narcissism, and blaming. Caldwell wrote,

> It's difficult to pinpoint the earliest tremor of this latest, thousand-year manners panic, but Allan Bloom's surprise best-seller *The Closing of the American Mind* (1987) is a likely candidate. On the surface a denunciation of contemporary American higher education—which (Bloom

thought) had abandoned rigor in favor of moral and intellectual fads—the book was at bottom a long howl of despair over lost civility.[24]

Bloom began his work this way. "There is one thing a professor can be absolutely certain of: almost every student entering the university believes, or says he believes, that truth is relative."[25] Bloom linked the absence of absolutes (relativism) with permissiveness within the academy (and at home), and to rudeness and incivility. Yet, despite Bloom's prose and punch, his work is, as Caldwell described it, but "a howl." It is not research at all. It is one long anecdote, where the "data" are the impressions of one academic, with the field being only that part of the academy that he had direct experience with. Though erudite in places, it is quaint and simplistic in others. In hindsight, the academy and the country survived the 1960s, and, to some, the American mind is less closed now than it was in the 1950s. In its best light, Bloom's book is an alarm. What it is not is an answer.

If incivility is a bugbear of social critics, then narcissism has been their *bête noire*. On this topic, historian Christopher Lasch wrote *The Culture of Narcissism* two decades ago,[26] a "short jeremiad," according to Robert Coles, that forgets "the nonsense that *other* ages found congenial to their purposes."[27] Lasch's thesis held that America's rugged individualism had given way to conformity, adjustment, and acquiescence, which ultimately leads to narcissism. But something is different about Lasch's "narcissism," because he sees it resulting from a "conformity, adjustment, and acquiescence"—a turning away from rugged individualism—whereas most critics see it as a turn toward individualism.

Questions arise. How do we end up with same diagnosis when opposite processes are being described, and is the diagnosis being used in some catchall, careless, or carefree way? One part of the problem, quite evident to psychologists and psychiatrists, is that the diagnostic label is being used as more than a descriptor for symptomatic thoughts, feelings, and actions, for in the hands of critics it is a normative sword that cuts pejoratively. A better cut, one more likely the further the discourse than kill the patient, is to rid the discourse of pathological parlance entirely.

Exchanging sword for plowshare, many scholars have furrowed with "individualism," a view that claims that as individuals, and as a society, we have come to prize and accent autonomy, self-reliance, and selfishness to the neglect of interdependence, vulnerability, and luck.[28] Historian Charles Taylor, for one, blamed the "radical individualism" that comes with modern liberalism, creating a sense of aloneness in and detachment from the world,[29] where the accent on autonomy weakens our "situatedness" in civic life.[30] Law professor Mary Ann Glendon,[31] for another, cited the rise of "rights talk" and the corresponding decline of "duties" discourse. Similarly, a communitarian sees us pulling away from community,[32] a cross-cultural psychologist sees us specializing and pulling back from global to local/parochial concerns,[33] whereas Putnam sees us "bowling alone."[34]

Looking first at "individualism," can this be the problem? It cannot be "individualism" per se, for that notion threads its way through the cherished notions of "liberty" and "rights" as to be almost indivisible. More than just a tight package, it is a highly valued one, symbolically and constitutionally protected under the guarantees in the Bill of Rights and in judicial rulings—protected from the overreaching of the community, be it in the form of federal or state powers, or from the tyranny of a majority.[35] No, individualism per se cannot be the problem; not even individualism within the psyche, for preserving the self is so basic to what it means to be human that a person who exhibits no self-interest is likely to strike us as exceedingly odd, if such a person is even around long enough to whine.[36] What these scholars accent is not individualism or self-interest, then, but imbalance.

Similarly, it cannot be "bowling alone" that is the problem, for such a view is only embraceable if we selectively ignore all the contra-signs of involvement. Like the fact that so many citizens are deeply involved with schools, churches, community associations, and their local governance; the fact that so many are immersed, in work or pleasure, with telecommunications that take them across the information highway to a world far beyond their local parochial; the fact that many citizens, according to opinion polls, are concerned over health care and insurance for those who do not have it—even when they do; the fact that private groups, such as Save the Children or Doctors without Borders, bring care about the globe to those in desperate need—even though the caregivers are healthy and could rest quite comfortably; and then there is the growing concern for exploited sweatshop workers in third-world countries, even though I am shod in the best of sneaker wear. Again, as with self-interest, it is not solitary actions per se that are problematic, but imbalance.

The concept of imbalance brings balance to the picture, for it moves us from caricatured extremes to the center of things. Applying these lessons to "unfairness," it becomes less likely that unfairnesses are exclusively localized about our detached and self-interested selves, and unlikely that we give no thought nor have no feelings about the unfairnesses suffered by others. But ridding the story of caricature and fairy tale may be easier than ridding it of myth, for myths, burrowed more deeply, have a longer life. Around individualism, for example, we have overrated if not revered Thoreau-like tunes preaching withdrawal from society, because, in part, we fundamentally misunderstand the federalism our founding fathers were creating, as historian Gary Wills put it.[37] At the level of "unfairness," then, will we find some myths within these unfairness claims? Will we find some myths spun about such claims? To the latter question, the evidence already suggests a yes answer.

Martin Seligman, former president of the American Psychological Association, has been critical about some of today's children who seem to be "imbued with victimology," all too ready to claim unfairness, to blame others for their problems, and to avoid responsibility.[38] From a superficial read, it may appear that the academic makes the social critics' petty whines theme his own, but such a conclusion would miss his key distinctions. For example, he discriminated "blaming" (which is not only appropriate at times, but goes on all the time within American courts at least) from "victimology" (which is the inappropriate blaming of others while disavowing one's own responsibilities), and he spoke of "some of today's children,"[39] rather than generalizing to all of them. With discriminations come implications. For example, if Seligman is right that unfairness claimants are disproportionately young, then this would make the "unfairness" phenomenon less than generationally ubiquitous; if it is not all children but some, this again would lower the ubiquity; and if his distinction between those who blame and those who engage in victimology identifies two different groups, then petty whines and bogus claims are more likely to come from the latter.

Finally, another factor separates Seligman's assertions from those of most social critics, a factor that is at the center of this work: Seligman will seek data to validate his claims, as I must do. It will be empirical findings that most inform the open questions. In that light, we must assess whether today's children are imbued with victimology, and whether this is in fact a rising trend across time and generations. In terms of unfairnesses, we must see if the young are citing more unfairnesses, or more questionable ones, than older generations. Will it be they who whine and rant over tempests? Will they cite only those unfairnesses where they are at the self-centered, narcissistic center, and where the Other, let alone empathy for the Other, is nowhere to be found?

LOOKING BACK, LOOKING FORWARD

When we look at the social critics' "petty whines" howl thesis, we find fables, with simplistic caricatures, grounded on neither facts nor reasons, but that take a life of their own. These must be tested, and when the test is run, we will be in a much better position to judge whether the critics' petty whines charge is right, or whether the sharp claim falls flat.

Where critics wave an appropriate warning flag is over context, reminding us that the unfairness matter is not just psychological, for the related topics of blaming, victimology, rudeness, and incivility are socially rooted as well. Even narcissism, which seems so psychological, has a social root—in that it is insinuated so often because the civic focus seems so absent. Thus in telling the story of unfairness, the contextual net must be thrown wide and not prematurely cast just on the waters of the psyche.

We began this chapter with an epigraph featuring Peter Pan and an unfairness. Now, after all the howls, rants, jeremiads, and criticisms of unfairness, I put forth this claim: that the critics have failed to deliver anything approaching a knockout blow, as Peter Pan's unfairness claim still stands. When a boy lends a helping hand, and has the hand willfully bitten, this is not fighting fair. Nor would it be fair if one boxer bit the ear of another. I could add 27 unfairness claims from the Declaration of Independence which, I believe, would stand as well. In fact, when we look to particular instantiations of unfairness, the topic is less bruised and battered than the prototype the critics create.

In the next chapter, we begin by looking back to "in the beginning," from Genesis through Job, where Old Testament cries of unfairness wailed. Those cries, traveling across oceans and millennia, have surely reached our ears by now. Are they heard still, or are they forgotten? Are they too dated for our postmodernist world, too out of step with this generation's beat, or are they simply masked by today's all-too-frequent shrieks?

In looking forward, we turn to those who hear the ancient cries. Beyond the prophets, poets, and patients who regularly hear the hallucinatory, we meet ordinary individuals caught in extraordinary situations that can leave one trapped beneath the poet's wasteland.[40] But first we meet a biblical tale with an ancient wail, involving a just man treated unjustly; a man who will shriek his "But it's not fair!" heavenward—when the just world meets Job's world.

ENDNOTES

1. J. M. Barrie, *Peter Pan* (New York: Charles Scribner's Sons, 1950).
2. The eternal child. *See, e.g.,* C. G. Jung, *Mysterium Coniunctionis*, Series XX, trans. R. F. C. Hull Bollingen (Princeton, NJ: Princeton University Press, 1970).
3. T. W. Simon, "A Theory of Social Injustice." In *Radical Philosophy of Law: Contemporary Challenges to Mainstream Legal Theory and Practice*, ed. D. S. Caudill and S. J. Gold (Highlands, NJ: Humanities Press, 1995), 54–72. Simon made his "separability" point about "justice" and "injustice," and I believe the argument extends naturally to "fair" and "unfair."
4. *Id.* Simon made these points about injustice.
5. There is some disagreement in the developmental psychology literature as to where and when in the stages of moral development the concepts of fairness and unfairness arise. From Piaget's studies of his own and other children through Kohlberg's presenting moral dilemmas to children, the cognitive view puts the sense of fairness later in the general moral development sequence. *See, e.g.,* J. Piaget, *The Moral Judgement of the Child* (London: Routledge and

Kegan, Paul, 1932); L. Kohlberg, "Moral Stages and Moralization: The Cognitive-Developmental Approach." In *Moral Development and Behavior*, ed. T. Lickona (New York: Holt, Rinehart, and Winston, 1976); M. Siegal, *Fairness in Children: A Social-Cognitive Approach to the Study of Moral Development* (London: Academic Press, 1982).

On the other side, dating from an even earlier time, we have the diaries of Clara Stern, tracking her children, Hilde and Gunther, over 18 years. *See* W. Stern, *Psychology of Early Childhood up to the Sixth Year of Age* (New York: Henry Holt and Company, 1924). Stern presented many examples of the children showing affection, sympathy, altruism, unselfishness, and recognizing unfairness and fairness. Moreover, Robert Coles, who over his lifetime has looked at children's actions, deeds, and behavior, found many examples, even in the preschool years and in the years before words, of moral intelligence, the recognition of unfairness, and the leading of a morally courageous life. *See, e.g.,* R. Coles, *The Moral Life of Children* (Boston: Atlantic Monthly Press, 1986); R. Coles, *The Spiritual Life of Children* (Boston: Houghton Mifflin, 1990); R. Coles, *The Moral Intelligence of Children* (New York: Random House, 1997).

In another work, Coles drew the distinction between moral action and moral reflection, analysis, and argument, noting that a well-developed power of moral analysis does not "translate into an everyday willingness to face down the various evils of this world." R. Coles, *The Mind's Fate: A Psychiatrist Looks at His Profession* (Boston: Little, Brown, 1995), p. 395.

Finally, if we link the work of Clara and William Stern to the current controversy of children as witnesses in court, preschoolers are deemed competent, most of the time, to perform those moral tasks of telling fact from fancy, truth from lie. *See, e.g.,* C. Stern and W. Stern, *Recollection, Testimony, and Lying in Early Childhood*, trans. J. T. Lamiell (Washington, DC: American Psychological Association, 1999); S. J. Ceci and M. Bruck, *Jeopardy in the Courtroom: A Scientific Analysis of Children's Testimony* (Washington, DC: American Psychological Association, 1995).

In my assessment of the literature and the dispute, I believe that the better studies of children in their worlds show that the recognition of unfairness and the moral aspect to their lives emerge early.

6. E. H. Wolgast, *The Grammar of Justice* (Ithaca, NY: Cornell University Press, 1987). Elizabeth Wolgast took the view that "the concept of justice is rooted in a sense of injustice, a felt indignation, and that abhorrence of wrong is the foundation of all talk about justice" (p. 194). In her Wittgensteinian analysis of language, it is not justice that gives meaning to injustice, but the latter which gives rise to the former. "Justice comes into our speech on the occasion of some injustice or wrong, which brings us to demand it" (p. 146).

7. Barrie, *Peter Pan*, p. 127.

8. This issue, in a form, arose in one of the great Supreme Court cases, the 1905 case of *Lochner v. New York*, where the Court's decision, when measured against Holmes's great dissent, reveals the changing views position. In *Lochner*, the Supreme Court invalidated a New York statute, which limited the number of hours bakery employees could work, leaving it as a private contractual matter between worker and employer. Some employees were working 16-hour

days. Justice Holmes's famous dissent in *Lochner*, 198 U.S. 45 (1905), would later carry the day, as majority views would change on this issue.

9. *See, e.g.*, D. Birnbaum, *God and Evil: A Unified Theodicy/Theology/Philosophy* (Hoboken, NJ: Ktav, 1989); L. B. Brown and A. Furnham, "Theodicy: A Neglected Aspect of the Psychology of Religion." In *The International Journal for the Psychology of Religion* 2 (1992), 37–45; S. T. Davis, ed., *Encountering Evil: Live Options in Theodicy* (Atlanta, GA: John Knox Press, 1981); J. Hick, *Evil and the God of Love* (London: Macmillan, 1966); H. M. Schulweis, *Evil and the Morality of God* (Cincinnati, OH: Hebrew Union College Press, 1984); J. M. Trau, *The Co-existence of God and Evil* (New York: Peter Lang, 1995).

10. K. G. Shaver, *The Attribution of Blame: Causality, Responsibility, and Blame-worthiness* (New York: Springer-Verlag, 1985).

11. *Id.*, p. 3.

12. *Id.*, p. 4.

13. Barrie, *Peter Pan*, p. 127.

14. In fact, on the first day of the new millennium, this letter to the editor, by Barry R. Fetzer, appeared in the *Washington Post* under the title, "No Excuse," p. A35. It seems Mr. Fetzer was upset about two things. First, an incident in a National Football League game where a "self-proclaimed tough guy," a 6-foot-7-inch, 350-pound lineman named Orlando Brown, pushed an "unprotected referee" to the ground after the latter threw a penalty hankie, "weighted with three ounces of BBs," which inadvertently hit Brown in the eye. The second upset for Fetzer was with the *Washington Post* sports reporter Thomas Boswell, who, writing about the suspension of Brown, seemed to be urging understanding, a view that "Brown cannot be expected to be responsible for his actions, Boswell would have us believe." Now we get to Fetzer's criticism: "Give me a break. It's just this kind of 'not my fault,' 'somebody or something else made me do it,' 'I had no choice' and victim-reversing mentality—and our acceptance of these as excuses—that is at the crux of many of our nation's social ills."

15. *See, e.g.*, E. J. Dionne Jr., "Let the Deflating Begin: Talkin' Bout Our Generation Is Getting Old. And So Are We," *Washington Post* (December 26, 1999), p. B1, B4.

16. *See, e.g.*, N. J. Finkel and B. D. Sales, "Commonsense Justice: Old Roots, Germinant Ground, and New Shoots," *Psychology, Public Policy, and Law* 3 (1997): 227–241; K. T. Gaubatz, *Crime in the Public Mind* (Ann Arbor: University of Michigan Press, 1995); D. A. Grabor, *Crime News and the Public* (New York: Praeger, 1980); V. P. Hans, "Law and the Media: An Overview and Introduction," *Law and Human Behavior* 14 (1990): 399–407; H. Kurtz, "The Crime Spree on Network News," *Washington Post* (August 12, 1997), pp. D1, D6.

17. A noteworthy exception is Mark Caldwell's recent work on rudeness. This social critic not only cited evidence of the breakdown of public behavior, but he pointed to a complex dynamic having positive and historic value for society. M. Caldwell, *A Short History of Rudeness: Manners, Morals, and Misbehavior in Modern America* (New York: Picador, 1980).

18. In focusing on daytime television talk shows, I do not mean to ignore ordinary

television shows. A recent survey from the conservative Center for Media and Public Affairs (CMPA) found that "the 1998–99 television season was a veritable cesspool of verbal filth, with a whopping 2,156 instances of trashy talk. That did not even include TV news coverage of 'Monica Does the White House.'" L. D. Moraes, "'Rude and Crude': A Course Study in Trash Talk," *Washington Post* (December 13, 1999), p. C7.

19. G. F. Will, "Really 'Risky' Times," *Washington Post* (January 11, 1998), C9.

20. D. Miller, *The Rants* (New York: Doubleday, 1996), p. 84.

21. *Id.*, p. 86.

22. Dionne, "Let the Deflating Begin," p. B4.

23. The facts, for Jefferson, which he submitted "to a candid world," has the king refusing his assent to laws, dissolving representative houses repeatedly, obstructing the administration of justice, keeping standing armies without the consent of legislatures, cutting off trade, imposing taxes, and many, many more. *Declaration of Independence*, in Congress, July 4, 1776.

24. Caldwell, *A Short History of Rudeness*, p. 3.

25. A. Bloom, *The Closing of the American Mind* (New York: Simon & Schuster, 1987), p. 25.

26. C. Lasch, *The Culture of Narcissism* (New York: W. W. Norton, 1979).

27. R. Coles, *The Mind's Fate: A Psychiatrist Looks at His Profession* (Boston: Little, Brown, 1995), p. 93.

28. *See, e.g.,* L. E. Mitchell, *Stacked Deck: A Story of Selfishness in America* (Philadelphia: Temple University Press, 1998).

29. *Id.*, p. 139.

30. T. A. Spragens Jr., *Civic Liberalism: Reflections on Our Democratic Ideals* (Lanham, MD: Roman & Littlefield, 1999).

31. M. A. Glendon, *Rights Talk: The Impoverishment of Political Discourse* (New York: Free Press, 1991).

32. A. Etzioni, *The Spirit of Community: Rights, Responsibilities, and the Communitarian Agenda* (New York: Crown, 1995).

33. F. M. Moghaddam, *The Specialized Society: The Plight of the Individual in an Age of Individualism* (Westport: Praeger, 1997).

34. R. D. Putnam, "Bowling Alone: America's Declining Social Capital," *Journal of Democracy* 6 (1995): 65–78.

35. G. R. Stone, R. A. Epstein, and C. R. Sunstein, eds. *The Bill of Rights in the Modern State* (Chicago: University of Chicago Press, 1992).

36. In his review of the self-interest motive, which Thomas Hobbes enthroned as the cardinal human motive, Dale Miller stated that "people act and sound as though they are strongly motivated by their material self-interest because scientific theories and collective representations derived from those theories convince them that it is natural and normal to do so" (p. 1059). D. T. Miller, "The Norm of Self-Interest," *American Psychologist* 54 (1999): 1053–1060. As Jerome Kagan put it, "People treat self-interest as a natural law and because they believe they should not violate a natural law, they try to obey it." J. Kagan, *Unstable Ideas: Temperament, Cognition, and Self* (Cambridge, MA: Harvard University Press, 1989), p. 283.

37. G. Wills, *A Necessary Evil: A History of American Distrust of Government* (New

York: Simon & Schuster, 1999). Wills noted that such withdrawal movements have typically failed, as they did in the 1840s, in the 1960s when hippie communes played at it, and in the 1990s, when right-wing free masons and Branch Davidians had their turn.

38. M. E. P. Seligman, "The American Way of Blame," *Monitor* 29 (July 7, 1998), p. 2, President's Column; S. Martin, "Seligman Laments People's Tendency to Blame Others," *Monitor* 29 (October 10, 1998), p. 50.

39. In Robert Coles's work, he certainly found examples of self-centeredness and narcissism. In the *Privileged Ones*, he wrote that "with children of well-to-do families I have had to comment repeatedly on the self-centeredness one finds, the "narcissistic entitlement"; and in his work with the desperately poor of Brazil's slums, he wrote that "I have noticed they are often self-centered, truculently snotty, and mischievously preoccupied with their own whims and impulses. . . . Their selfishness and hauteur could be described psychodynamically as a developmental 'narcissism,' perhaps a budding species of 'character disorder.'" Coles, *The Mind's Fate*, pp. 101, 123. Yes, we can find some, no doubt anywhere along the socioeconomic scale, but that is a far cry from affixing the label to all children.

40. T. S. Eliot, *The Waste Land and Other Poems* (New York: Harcourt, 1930).

2

WHEN THE JUST WORLD
MEETS JOB'S WORLD

More than two decades ago, social psychologist Melvin Lerner proposed *The Belief in a Just World*,[1] where the underlying assumption is that people "get what they deserve." In this well-subscribed-to view, rewards and punishments are supposed to be justly related to our behaviors, attributes, and character. In simple terms, the good are rewarded and the wicked are punished. In even simpler terms, life makes sense.

The "just world" is a psychological theory that speaks directly to unfairness. A believer in a just world has certain expectations about the way people and the world ought to be, and violations of those expectations may give rise to unfairness complaints. Specifically, the believer has expectations regarding "distributive justice" (i.e., the basis on which rewards are doled out) and typically will use some version of equity theory's inputs and outcomes to explain why the haves and have-nots have earned it. The believer also has expectations regarding "retributive justice" (i.e., about why some are punished and to what the extent), explaining why punishment fits the individual's blameworthiness. Likewise the believer has expectations regarding "procedural justice" (i.e., fairness or due process in adjudication). Overall, just-world expectations relate to just about all the major theories of justice.

The "just-world belief" is not simply speculative, because it is grounded in a large body of research findings. For example, a "just-world scale" has been developed that discriminates believers from nonbelievers;[2] other studies have investigated the "antecedents, correlates, and social consequences of the belief in a just world."[3] Although this body of research is extensive and substantial, I shall focus not on causes (i.e., whether this belief is "socially determined,"[4] indicating a nurture explanation, or whether "our brains attempt to maintain a unifying harmony,"[5] indicating an immanent justice, nature explanation[6]), but on consequences—where the theory links with other theories and where nonobvious predictions result.

Regarding its ties to other psychological theories, Fritz Heider tied the just-world belief to the more general principle of "cognitive balance," where emotional states (e.g., happiness and unhappiness) come to be linked to moral traits (e.g., goodness and wickedness). The linkage is through a conception of justice as a harmonious fit between state and trait, such that if we know the state we can attribute the trait. Heider gives the following example of the linkage and attribution: "misfortune, sickness, accident are often taken as signs of badness and guilt. If O [the other] is unfortunate, then he has committed a sin."[7]

One consequence of holding to a just-world belief, and it is no small consequence, is that it makes the world more predictable and less frightening because things are as they ought to be. But what happens when cognitive imbalance results, because things are not as they ought to be? Specifically, what happens when bad things happen to good people? Here is where the just world generates nonobvious predictions, for it says that believers are apt to either deny that suffering is occurring or, more perplexing, that they are apt to blame the victim for it. The perception that either "the innocent are not really suffering" or "the person is not really innocent" removes the imbalance and restores the just world. We will shortly come to see how these answers play out in what may just be the grandest unfairness drama of all. Before we do, though, we must meet the second of the three broad challenges to unfairness claims, one with very close ties to the just-world view.

Who Says Life Is Supposed to Be Fair?

In chapter 1, we met the first challenge, dubbed "petty whines," which we will further differentiate. There are two distinct challenges under this rubric. One challenge is more extreme—that unfairness claims are simply bogus. This "bogus" view grants no legitimate basis to these claims, because it sees these claimants as making much ado over nothing. If these critics are right about these claims having no legitimate basis in fact, then these claims are delusions. The second view, which appropriately earns the petty whines label, sees these claims as loud whining over small infractions, where claimants make much ado over little. In this true petty whines version, the critics grant some legitimacy to these claims but give nothing but their ire for their hysterical shrillness.

The second broad challenge, which is putatively the oldest and certainly the broadest of the challenges, typically arrives on the family scene this way. If the child first serves a "But it's not fair!" complaint at a parent, the parent is likely to rip the following backhand return: "So who says life is supposed to be fair?" Now, what are we to make of this return? Pejoratively, this appears to be a parent on the defensive, who is more than a bit testy, using the backhand to get off the hook, put the kid on the run, and charge the net. Although it may look, sound, and feel that way to the child, who is now on his heels, there is another characterization that is more generous to the parent and more interesting from an American vantage point. With a different spin, this challenge can be seen as sending an important educative and socializing message to the child—aimed at debunking the child's naive expectations and idealizations of people and the world. If a parent's job is to prepare the child for the adult world (and for the adult he or she will one day become), then the child must come to understand that unfairness is part of life. If driving the lesson home means delivering a *who says?*—a challenge that seeks to weed these childlike, delusional just-world notions out at their roots and infancy—then so be it, for it is better to learn this hard-but-necessary socializing lesson early than whine evermore.

This "who says?" challenge feels like an earthy kick in the pants, hard and pointed in its delivery, pragmatic in its goal. Like the "bogus" challenge, it regards unfairness claimants as essentially deluded, for the supporting facts and the underlying psychology are empty. If this challenge needed further support, the critic could find it in the subtitle of Lerner's work, where Lerner calls the just-world belief A *Fundamental Delusion*, a strong judgment from the theory's founder.

Yet despite appearances, this "who says?" rejoinder turns out to be broader and more conceptual than the "bogus" response or petty whines. To explain, the "petty whines" response grants that there may be some basis in fact to the claim, whereas "bogus" and "who says?" grant nothing of the sort. But the "bogus" advocate grants nothing because the supportive facts are not true, whereas "who says?" is a challenge to the ontological or deontological expectation of fairness, arguing that the very notion of fairness the child is relying on is only a construction, one that has no sacred status to it. Put another way, this challenge regards unfairness claims *and the just-world view on which they are founded* as false views of human nature and the cosmos, far more pernicious than those other childhood illusions of Santa Claus, the tooth fairy, and Peter Pan, which most children naturally outgrow. If these "who says?" advocates are correct—that nothing is fair or unfair on earth (the ontological argument), and that no one has listened in at God's keyhole and gotten the transcendent truth (the deontological argument)—then there is no "certainty" whatsoever to unfairness claims. Thus unfairness claims fall not because they are factually false (like "bogus" claims)—but because they are necessarily false.

Looking at this "who says?" challenge critically, we see that it is open to counterattack. One comeback, strategically targeted at the psychological and everyday levels where most parents live, begins by doing and saying nothing, just patiently waiting for that moment when the "who says?" parent now hears "But it's not fair!" coming from his or her own grownup lips. This is the comeback of the judo master, letting the *who says?* advocate be hoisted on his or her own petard, as hypocrisy topples the challenge.

But if that sort of "gotcha" fails to impress, there are more serious comebacks we could aim at the "who says?" challenge, starting with Lerner's evaluative subtitle, A *Fundamental Delusion*. First, if this just-world belief is only a delusion, then it may be the most pervasive one we have, because if it is as widely held as the evidence suggests, then this by itself raises questions about whether a "delusional" diagnosis fits. Then there is logic to consider. For the diagnostician to call this belief a delusion means that the clinician knows the truth of the matter. But as we saw earlier, the advocate of "who says?" claims that we do not know (and cannot know) the truth, which means that the advocate must be less than certain about its falsity.

Finally, we can take aim at this challenge on psychological, legal, historical, and philosophical grounds. First, most individuals who believe they have an unfairness complaint are not likely to be dissuaded by "there is no such thing as 'fair' and 'unfair.'" They strongly believe otherwise. In fact, they are likely to get quite angry when someone claims that they are deluded, or engaging in denial, or both. If this psychological point–counterpoint ends in a stubborn stalemate, the individual could move to legal grounds.

The unfairness claimant can surely point to American law, which recognizes and codifies certain fairness and unfairness expectations. Here, the claimant's views of what is fair and unfair are not the subjective, delusional products of one mind, for we have broad societal consensus for these fairness notions, with long, supportive, historical lines running back to the Bill of Rights, the Constitution, the Declaration of Independence, the common law, natural law, and the Ten Commandments. These laws and legal rules value and validate those expectations, and when the people's representatives pass new laws, they are generally in accord with those expectations. Although these laws may not be the deontological truths, their secular standing is sacred enough for most people, and it is doubtful that the "who says?" advocate wants to disavow this base, leaving only anarchy. Finally, we can turn to modern political philosophers, with H. L. A. Hart and John Rawls as eminent examples, who have invoked the principle of "fair play" as answer to a fundamental question, "Why should people obey the law?"[8]

The ones who first challenged us with "who *says?*" —our parents— were clearly in the power position: Quite beyond making us, they created our worlds and dictated the rules we would live by, maintaining control and dominance for years. They were our first gods, as the Freudians would have it, and with all the time, control, and power they had, and with all the conditioning opportunities they had to extinguish our fairy-tale fairness notions, you would think that the just world would have gone the way of the tooth fairy. But the endurance of these notions, their psychological realness to believers, the passion they arouse, and the conviction they inspire, suggest that our unfairness notions are deeply foundational and powerfully resistant to extinction. We now turn to the exemplar Job, because if anyone has an unfairness claim, he does.

JOB'S CLAIM AND BLAME

It began this way. Once upon a time in the land of Uz, this man of perfect integrity learned in quick succession that the Sabeans attacked and took his 500 yoke of oxen and his 500 donkeys, that the Chaldeans attacked and took his 3000 camels, that lightning fell from the sky and burned up his 7000 sheep, and that all his slaves were killed or burned up as well. Those losses were just possessions, yet Job's day was not done. Where "death of a child" ranks as a catastrophic stressor in the *Diagnostic and Statistical Manual of Mental Disorders* of the American Psychiatric Association,[9] Job will hear that his seven sons and three daughters, all ten of his children, perished, as "a great wind came out of the desert and knocked down the walls of the house and it fell on them and they're dead."[10] In colloquial terms, although that day "was the day from Hell," his next day was not so great either: adding proverbial salt to his wounds, Job finds himself covered with boils. The prologue and the curse end and the first round is about to begin, we hear Job's lament:

> my nightmares have come to life.
> Silence and peace have abandoned me,
> and anguish camps in my heart.[11]

From our millennia distance, we could quibble as to whether all of these calamities were "injustices," inflicted with intent, for which Job would have a case, or whether some were merely the "misfortunes"[12] of nature, life's randomness, or what insurance adjusters call "acts of God," for which there is neither coverage nor blame. Job, however, makes no such hair-splitting distinctions, nor do his three friends (Eliphaz the Temanite, Bildad the Shuhite, and Zophar the Namathite); none of this can be written off as "random," and no one tries, as all agree that these calamities were inflicted by God.

Yet Job and his three friends part company over *who* is to blame. For the friends, Job the victim must be Job at fault, not a victim at all. This is the "blaming the victim" effect that Lerner's just-world theory predicts. As Stephen Mitchell has written, the friends construct a syllogism: "Suffering comes from God. God is just. Therefore Job is guilty."[13] The syllogism flows directly from a just-world view, and it puts Job on the hook, a man somehow deserving of the punishment he received. Job will counter with another syllogism, also from the just-world view, where he agrees on the major premise that suffering comes from God but disagrees about the minor premise and the conclusion. Job's minor premise is "I am innocent." His conclusion is then inescapable: "Therefore God is unjust."

Job will not let God off the hook. God cannot be some "well-intentioned bungler,"[14] making an "oops." It is preposterous to think that God "would allow a good man to be tortured because of a bet." For if God is all-knowing, all-seeing, and all-good, as Job-before-the-day-from-Hell believes, then the day-after Job has a few major problems. One is with God, whose "interpersonal" dealings with Job now seem anything but just and fair. A second is intrapsychic: God has inflicted on Job *in reality* what the God in his mind (in his *psychic reality*) would never do.

From the friends' perspective, Job's "blaming God" is more than just blasphemy: On the psychological level, they see Job engaged in denial, displacement, and other assorted defense mechanisms. As Bildad says, "How long will you go on ranting, filling our ears with trash?"[15] Bildad offers a hypothesis that makes the punishment a just dessert: "Your children must have been evil: he punished them for their crimes." This is an inversion of "the sins of the father visited upon the sons," and it works to keep God's punishment just and Bildad on safe ground, for "God never betrays the innocent or takes the hand of the wicked."[16] With PR work like Bildad's, no wonder God does not have to defend Himself.

But Job does not accept Bildad's excuse-making for God or his blaming of Job, and in a remarkable passage, tough-talking Job takes it right to God:

> I will take my complaint to God.
> I will say, Do not condemn me;
> why are you so enraged?
> Is it right for you to be vicious,
> to spoil what your own hands made?
> Are your eyes mere eyes of flesh?
> Is your vision no keener than a man's?
> Is your mind like a human mind?
> Are your feelings human feelings?
> For you keep pursuing a sin,

trying to dig up a crime,
though you *know* that I am innocent
and cannot escape from your grip.[17]

Here, if anywhere, is Job's problem, and the problem of so many who feel victimized at the hand of God. At Auschwitz and the other concentration camps, the cry was "Where was God?" "How could God let this happen?" Job's friends, caught in their just world, have a comforting answer that eliminates existential anguish: For the friends, their moral world and God continue to make sense, for a crime is being punished.

Job is caught in a profoundly torturous and paradoxical way. He knows he is being punished, yet knows it is not deserved. His experience is totally at odds with his just-world belief, as he chides God to shape up. He is in torment with two contradictory images of God: His just world God is supposed to be wise, fair, and, above all, *just*, yet the God of his recent experience seems enraged, vicious, and all too human. Job wants the old God back, the just-world God. But his entanglement grows deeper: for although he knows he cannot escape God's grip, he must appeal to his tormentor to become his rescuer.

Returning to the friends, if they can get Job to doubt his certainty, then their syllogistic version of the just world remains intact, and their own discomfort vanishes. In their arguments, they use a variety of ploys, and what better psychological ploy is there to engender doubt than the "unconscious" ploy? Zophar delivers it:

But if God were to cross-examine you
and turned up your hidden motive . . .
you would know that your guilt is great.[18]

If the unconscious ploy does not take, there is still another, "the earthly human doubt" ploy, which is offered by Eliphaz, who asks Job how he can be so certain:

What do you know that *we* don't?
What have you seen that we haven't?[19]

Though Job has neither seen the divine plan nor listened at God's keyhole, Job does not relent.[20] His belief in his innocence does not change, but what does change is his belief in a just world. As the third round nears its end, and before the voice from the whirlwind speaks, Job speaks of a world without meaning and hope, where injustice and malevolence seem to thrive. His words are laced with his deepest despair, his almost unendurable disappointment with the God he believes in:

In the city the dying groan
And the wounded cry out for help;
but God sees nothing wrong.
At twilight the killer appears,

stalking his helpless victim.
The rapist waits for evening
and roams through the darkened streets.
The thief crawls from the shadows
with a hood pulled over his face.
They shut themselves in by day
and hate the sight of the sun.
Midnight to them is morning;
they thrive in the terrors of night.[21]

This is a nightmarish landscape, a hell on earth, and the speech has the clinically depressed tone of hopelessness and helplessness, as evil roams, stalks, and thrives. This is a world without God to rescue the innocent or punish the sinners. Why is God not there to aid the needy and punish the wicked? The answer is not that God has absented Himself from the scene and is no longer interceding in the world, because we have, and Job has, far too many Old Testament instances of God being Johnny-on-the-spot. In Genesis,[22] God is there to confront Adam and Eve when they take the forbidden bite, and then to serve them with an eviction notice and mark them with mortality; God is there for the next generation, hearing the blood of Abel crying out from the ground, and He is there to confront and mark Cain; He is there again for Noah, as He threatens to bring the whole show to a close; and God not only has a running dialogue with Abraham but makes a covenant with him and his descendants yet to come. No, the answer cannot be that God does not involve Himself with the world and the creatures He created, for this is contradicted by "in the beginning" evidence and Job's personal experience.

The answer that Job comes to, an answer more frightening by far, is that God has lost His moral way here by seeing nothing wrong. This is far worse than an indifferent God: For if suffering is one way of defining evil in the world, and He purposefully inflicts suffering on an innocent, then God is doing evil. This is a crushing conclusion for Job, and for others across time who have reached the same bottom line. It means that God seems to have lost what we most want Him to have—a sense of justice.

The Legacies of Job

The legacies of Job are best developed by considering what Job might have done but did not. Before God, he might have relented, saying, in effect, "You've convinced me. I suffered no unfairness." With his friends, he might have yielded, saying, in effect, "You're right. I'm to blame." Within his own psyche, he might have questioned himself into peace, with "Who says life is supposed to be fair?" Had Job done any of these, there would be no legacy, for there would be no story worthy of the biblical.

Job fights. He went three rounds against three opponents throwing punches above and below the belt, fighting for what he knows and what he experienced. In this fight, he brings passion and persistence, aspects that mark unfairness. There is moral outrage as well, not just for what he experienced, but for what he saw happening to others, which defiles that which he holds sacred about fairness and justice. His moral outrage, his passion and persistence, and his views of justice and fairness lead him to fight for a better world. He also wants answers, some meaning to come from a madness that seems so unfair. Through all of this, he wants some comfort for his grief and anguish.

Theodicy

There is a branch of theology called "theodicy,"[23] a word that links the Greek words for "God" and "justice," which deals with the problem of evil in the world and reconciling this apparent evil with God. The theodicy problem runs throughout the Old Testament, where we meet questions of unfairness and calls for answers. As Birnbaum stated, "From its beginning, Israel has never yielded its right to call for a rational Divine justice, to ask God's justice be morally justifiable and answerable, as well, to the standard He has set for man."[24] Abraham (Genesis 18:23–25) asks God, "Wilt Thou indeed sweep away the righteous with the wicked?" when learning of the cases of Sodom and Nineveh, and asks "shall not the Judge of all the earth do justly?" The prophet (Isaiah 59:9) also protests, "Therefore is justice far from us, Neither doth righteousness overtake us; We look for light, but behold darkness, For brightness, but we walk in gloom." In Jeremiah (12: 1–2), we hear the unfairness question, and the call: "Right wouldest Thou be, O Lord, Were I to contend with Thee, Yet will I reason with Thee: Wherefore doth the way of the wicked prosper? Wherefore are all they secure that deal very treacherously?" The psalmist laments (Psalms 44:24– 27), "Wherefore hidest Thou Thy face, And forgettest our affliction and our oppression? For our soul is bowed down to the dust; Our belly cleaveth unto the earth. Arise for our help. And redeem us for Thy mercy's sake."

The problem of theodicy has attracted theologians and scholars of all faiths,[25] who invoke sacred texts and commentaries, along with historical, theological, and philosophical arguments to rationally reconcile the co-existence of God and evil. Some of this literature is aimed at ordinary people who have suffered extraordinarily. As Schulweis put it,[26] "Jobian boils have reappeared in our times more massively spread than before. It is now the comforters, not Job, who feel constrained to place their hands upon their mouths in disbelief."

Yet speak we must, for ordinary people want answers that make sense, like Job wanted answers. Most citizens are not likely to find sustenance in answers floating from monism to dualism, or those mined from gnostic, mystic, or Kabbalistic tomes, for such answers comfort only a few. No, ordinary men and women who have suffered the extraordinary, and who come to their priests, pastors, ministers, and rabbis, seek answers more concrete and touching to fill the hole in the heart.[27] It is here that Job may be an exemplar, in his fight and faith, for those who suffer. There are other sources that people may turn to from a literature that is personal and poignant, written by those who lived the nightmare, like Holocaust survivors and writers,[28] and those who faced years of imprisonment in their country's Gulags for political or racial reasons,[29] all of whom offer their own Jobian experiences and, at times, their hard-won answers, if answers they be. They may also turn to writers and mystics,[30] the afflicted and the blessed, who have wrestled with God in the dark nights of their souls.

At the risk of oversimplifying, the theodicy problem comes into focus when we try to take as givens the following theistic beliefs,[31] which I slightly amend to fit the Job situation: (a) there is one God (which Job and his friends believe); (b) God created the world (this, too, they believe); (c) God is omnipotent (they not only believe this, but they stand in awe of His power); (d) God is omniscient (He surely sees all); (e) God is personal (this fits Job's prior experience and all of Genesis); (f) God is perfectly just (this is Job's position just prior to his suffering, and it is the position of his three friends before and after Job's day). Now, when we try to add another—(g) that there is evil in the world, even gross, gratuitous evil, typically seen as suffering, which may be perpetrated by man ("moral evil") or nature ("natural evil")—logic tells us that something must give, because all of these "givens," apparently, cannot be true.

How, for example, can we reconcile that God is just and compassionate if He lets human beings, particularly innocent human beings, suffer, and worse, if He inflicts the suffering? How can we reconcile our view of God as all-powerful, capable of doing what He will—which includes preventing, interceding, and reversing the suffering—when He does nothing? Where is Job's personal-but-now-AWOL God, the God who made a contract with Noah, a covenant with Abraham, and had a personal relationship with his perfect servant Job? Given the evidence at hand, God has let the roof fall in on Job and no longer answers his pleas.

Such contradictions can lead some to reconcile by challenging the very existence of God—that this is proof that God does not exist. Others come close to that quandary. Martin Buber, who has written extensively on this topic,[32] posed the question for a post-Auschwitz world:

> How is a life with God still possible in a time in which there is an Auschwitz? The estrangement has become too cruel, the hiddenness too deep. One can still "believe" in a God who allowed those things to happen, but can one still speak to Him? Can one still hear His word . . . Dare we recommend to the survivors of Auschwitz, the Job of the

gas chambers: "Call on him, for He is kind, for His mercy endureth forever"?[33]

In his *Faith after the Holocaust*, Berkovits stated that

> there were really two Jobs at Auschwitz: the one who belatedly accepted the advice of Job's wife and turned his back on God, and the other who kept his faith to the end, who affirmed it at the very doors of the gas chambers, who was able to walk to his death defiantly singing his "Ani Maamin—I Believe." If there were those whose faith was broken in the death camp, there were others who never wavered. . . . Those who rejected did so in authentic rebellion; those who affirmed and testified to the very end did so in authentic faith.[34]

The original Job does neither of these two extremes: he neither turns his back on God, nor blindly goes forth without question; rather, Job struggles with the Jobian problem.

Other reconciliations attempt to reconstrue the suffering (evil) as not really suffering at all. This is another prediction that the just-world theory generates. In this vein, we may reconstrue suffering as a "teaching," a lesson that brings us greater wisdom, deeper spirituality, and leads us, in the end, to a greater closeness with God. Job's friends do not go in this "higher good" direction: they reconstrue by trying to make the suffering deserved and hence not evil at all. Job rejects their reconstrual, seeing this as undeserved suffering dished out by God.

Still other reconciliations try to link suffering to "free will," the great gift God gives, and this ties back to a limitation on God's omnipotence: If God gives us free will, He may no longer be free and all-powerful Himself anymore, for if God kept interceding or reversing misfortunes and injustices with every prayer, He would negate the very free will He gave.[35] Some reconciliations would seem to require jettisoning the notion of God being all-good and all-loving, whereas others seem to require a reevaluation of God's justice or some reinterpretation of His omniscience.

One answer to Job was offered by Carl Jung.[36] Jung's *Answer* starts with a

> contradictory picture of Yahweh—the picture of a God who knew no moderation in his emotions and suffered precisely from this lack of moderation . . . [and who] admitted that he was eaten up with rage and jealousy and this knowledge was painful to him. Insight existed along with obtuseness, loving-kindness along with cruelty, creative power along with destructiveness.[37]

This is a God who is not all-loving and all-compassionate; nor is this an omniscient God, for He apparently fails to see His own "divine darkness"; nor is it a moral and just God, for the contradictions within God, the *complexio oppositorum* of good and evil within the one, can be described as "amoral," says Jung.

About God's raw power and omnipotence, there is no doubt. Job is confronted by a savage ruthlessness that has him "a half-crushed worm, groveling in the dust,"[38] who better be very careful about how he confronts a God "who is personally most easily provoked,"[39] and who will brook no moral judgments of Him at all, and who would smash this imprudent child into oblivion, even if Job had a point. Job's evidence of "divine arbitrariness"[40] and unfairness are overwhelming: God has committed crimes (e.g., "robbery, murder, bodily injury with premeditation, and denial of a fair trial"[41]), violating "at least three of the commandments He Himself gave out on Mount Sinai,"[42] and there is nothing to stop Him from destroying Job completely, if the latter gives Him any "lip." So when Job questions, "How can a man be just before God?" the answer may be, "very carefully and very quietly."

Jung argued that Job sees the contradiction

> that God is at odds with himself—so totally at odds that he, Job, is quite certain of finding in God a helper and an "advocate" against God. As certain as he is of the evil in Yahweh, he is equally certain of the good. . . . Because of this knowledge Job holds on to his intention of "defending his ways to his face," i.e., of making his point of view clear to him, since notwithstanding his wrath, Yahweh is also man's advocate *against himself* when man puts forth his complaint.[43]

To Jung, God is neither just nor recognizing his own shadow side, whereas His creature, Job, beholds the "backside" of God. If the man sees more than God, then Yahweh has suffered a "moral defeat" at "Job's hands."[44] Whether Job is as "certain" as Jung suggested is debatable.

In the end, Jung's *Answer* is more of an answer *to the God question* than an answer *to Job*. To tell Job that he has achieved a moral victory over God is unresponsive to Job's plaint, and trying to comfort Job by making him aware that he now sees the backside of God will not comfort . . . as long as that backside is unjust. Moreover, the text itself offers little validation for Jung's claim, for there is nothing of Job sensing moral victory. If anything, Job's suffering grows more acute, not less, through the three rounds, and in his silence to God's harangue Job shows nothing that would indicate joy and moral triumph; if his suffering eases, it is only out of the frightful realization that God could have made it worse.

Jung's answer is not likely to bring comfort, any more than telling a child who is violently beaten by his father each day that "your father really loves you, but he's just having a bad day" day after day. These trite words may give the child an ounce of hope, an illusion to hold on to, or a bit of succor within the reign of terror, but this is far from justice, and such pap is not likely to convince the child that his or her dad is being fair.

Remembering and Fighting

Elie Wiesel has been called "the Job of Auschwitz,"[45] and in his book *Legends of Our Time*, he stated, "I prefer to take my place on the side of Job, who chose questions and not answers, silence and not speeches."[46] Whereas Job is with him in the beginning[47] and through so many of his works, Wiesel also reserves some distance, for though "he admires Job's passionate rebellion," "the man who refused to surrender," Wiesel is troubled by Job's "hasty abdication."[48] Moreover, Wiesel is deeply angry with God's answer, which "did not answer," but "merely overwhelmed" Job.[49] The implications for Wiesel's theodicy are immediate. As Berenbaum wrote,

> Wiesel is unwilling to preserve the sacred theodicy of his youth if its cost is a denial of the individual and the reality of his pain. The defeated Job is not a man Wiesel admires. Wiesel would prefer that Job transcend his weakness and allow his accusations to define his individuality and personality to those people robbed of it by an overwhelming universe. He seeks to teach us to begin again with an affirmation of life despite the overwhelming reality of death and despair.[50]

It is overwhelming. If "death is the marginal experience *par excellence* which threatens to reveal the innate precariousness of all socially constructed universes,"[51] then Job has the deaths of 10 children leaping from the margins to shatter his world,[52] and "the death of six million Jews in the Holocaust is the marginal experience *extraordinaire* which has undermined the socially constructed universe of normative Judaism."[53]

Wiesel's account involves "void" and "silence," the trials of man and God, and the madness of both,[54] an account that "undercuts almost all positive images of God,"[55] as Wiesel will not "relieve God of His responsibility"[56] that stretches back to Moses at Sinai. Despite the enormity that cannot be captured, and despite all of his words and works, Wiesel seeks not only to remember and give witness, but to make meaning out of it all.

The search for meaning can be thwarted by enormity of the unfairness. Still, only a small percentage of unfairnesses, as our research shows, are directed at God, and the Holocaust's enormity is an off-the-scale phenomenon. To see Job's legacy, then, it is best to scale down the unfairness to the individual level, where the alleged harm is inflicted by someone or something in this world. What we find are particular, concrete, individualistic instances. They are unfairnesses and injustices that carry with them strong emotions, "a felt indignation, and the abhorrence of wrong."[57] These are not cool sentiments, but "powerful and passionate, typically angry and impatient, and sometimes able to move one to heroic efforts."[58] When harnessed and directed, these emotions, allied with the rhetoric of claims for fairness and justice, may be a powerful force for change. When moral outrage is present on a collective scale, it may lead to broad social change, or even revolt; when absent, grave social injustices may be endured.[59] Although it may turn out that some just-world beliefs are worth jettisoning, and Job gave up a few, he fervently held on to his core beliefs. So it seems for ordinary citizens, whose hold is neither out of delusion nor denial but to preserve and work for what is best and moral—what is just and fair.

Comparisons That Give Succor

By comparative standards, if we put our unfairnesses up against Job's, there is no contest. Yet Job's "win" may be our win, in a psychological sense. As a growing body of psychological literature suggests,[60] many people, as a way of coping when traumas befall them, go about finding a comparative Job-like individual who has it worse: by making this "downward social comparison," their own sufferings appear less so, making their crises more manageable and less overwhelming. Comparing yourself with someone worse off is a way of gaining perspective on your unfairness, even if you selectively abstract a "comparison-other" who has it worse; being fair in this downward social comparison is not to one's psychological advantage.

To make this downward comparison we do not even need a particular person—like Job—for the "average person" can work as well. Take the student who studied hard for an exam and gets a score of 65. He feels crushed. Then he asks the professor what the class average was and finds out it was a 60. Aha, he's above the average! Knowledge of the mean grade, a "central tendency" measure, helps, even if there was no other student in the class who actually got a 60. It could in fact be that most students did better than our lad's 65, but that one or two stunningly low scores brought the average down to 60. Yet the mean, an abstraction that may adhere to no one in particular, can nonetheless ease the pain.

At still other times, however, we may not want a measure of central tendency at all, for these measures may lead to mistake and despair. That mistake, says Stephen Jay Gould, is viewing "a measure of central tendency as the most likely outcome for any single individual."[61] Gould uses his own case, where he learned, at age 40, that he had abdominal mesothelioma, "a rare and 'invariably fatal' form of cancer (to cite all official judgments at the time)."[62] He subsequently learned, through his search of the literature, the "brutal message" of the central tendency, that the median mortality rate for this disease was eight months. For Gould, the key comparison involved neither a person nor a central tendency measure, but the concept of variance. As he stated,

> I then had the key insight that proved so life-affirming at such a crucial moment. I started to think about the variation and reasoned that the distribution of deaths must be strongly "right skewed" in statistical

parlance—that is, asymmetrically extended around a chosen measure of central tendency, with a much wider spread to the right than to the left.[63]

He found that this was so, and then realized

that all factors favored a potential location on the right tail—I was young, rarin' to fight the bastard, located in a city offering the best possible medical treatment, blessed with a supportive family, and lucky that my disease had been discovered relatively early in its course. I was therefore far more interested in the right tail (my probable residence) than in any measure of central tendency (an abstraction with no special relevance to my case).[64]

As Gould noted, "I had used knowledge and gained succor."[65]

By using knowledge of another person, or of the average, or of variation, we can shift the focus and situate our unfairness in a different context. Creating a new context and comparative framework may lead to a widened perspective and a new picture whereby our misery may be muted, or even transmuted. If this is so, then Job-the-exemplar can serve.

In picking someone who had it worse, Job is a good choice. Yet, in one way, victims may envy Job, for he *gets an answer*. For most, to the contrary, God seldom answers a *subpoena duces tecum*, and we never get Him on the witness stand to cross-examine and uncover motive and meaning. Even for the few who do hear a voice in the whirlwind, this message is not likely the answer. Job gets the victim's wish, but curiously he falls sheepishly silent.

Many who read the answer from the whirlwind find it to be an answer that "answers nothing," an "unsatisfactory harangue" an "eloquent browbeating."[66] It may be an answer that is hard to simply hear, for Job says that he feels and *sees* the answer, which is an odd locution for a strictly auditory message; more than words are conveyed, and more than words are received. But if we stay with the words, there is more than a hint of a way out of the dilemma between the friends' view and Job's view—where the two choices seem to be "God is just and Job is guilty" and "Job is innocent and God is unjust." When God asks him, "Am I wrong because you are right?"[67] a third possibility is being presented, different from the friends' syllogism and different from Job's. This third possibility may be out of the just world entirely. As Stephen Mitchell phrased it, it is this: *Suffering comes from God. God is just. Job is innocent. (No therefore.)*[68]

The gods we make may not be as God is, for it is we who insist that there be no contradiction, no unfairness coexisting with fairness. But there is unfairness in the world, along with suffering that is gross and gratuitous; if we do not deny it, then the problem of theodicy is still ours to reconcile. How we try to reconcile it is likely to play some part in reaching unfairness judgments. We have already seen one way that the judgment of unfairness vanishes: Job's friends see no unfairness but do so out of the just-world view, where suffering is God's will, which is always just. Yet in the epilogue, God chastises Eliphaz for not speaking the truth, a message to these moral defenders of an always-just God that they got it wrong. Now we find a possibility not from the just world but from a different mind-set entirely, where there is blame neither for Job nor for God.

LOOKING BACKWARD, LOOKING FORWARD

In the previous chapter, starting with a bite in Neverland, the topic of unfairness was introduced and then situated in the psyche. In this chapter, I shifted the context to the historical, biblical, and theological, with Job at the center of it, a man with arguably the strongest unfairness claim of all. His three friends tried to blame and transform him from victim to villain, as the just-world belief predicts, but he held fast to his claim. If we see God as the biggest parent of all, posing the "who says?" challenge, Job holds fast to his claim again. The "who says?" challenge, then, despite its source and longevity, seems to fail. It probably fails with each generation, and it does fail, I believe, because we just know that most unfairnesses are unfair, and because we are unwilling to give up the hope, the promise, and the expectation of fairness, no matter how big the parent is.

The ancient story of Job is the exemplar, the prototype of unfairness. But it is also the most extreme case, as very few of us could stack our unfairnesses against his. Yet in spite of its outlier position, the story endures, still serving in many ways. Job's unfairnesses may serve as a succoring comparison, reminding us that the unfairnesses we deal with, no matter how severe these first appear to us, may not shatter our spirits after all. Job's constancy may also serve, for this is a story of a man holding to his faith even when his pleas go unheeded. His change may serve, for his expectations, beliefs, and his just-world views all change by story's end.

Looking more specifically at the unfairnesses he suffered, what is likely to stand out as primary may be categorized as "When Bad Things Happen to Good People."[69] Whereas the punishment of a man whose actions and attributes are right and fine may be the quintessential unfairness, less extreme but more probable variations raise their own questions. For example, if Job was not the perfect servant, but only a decent one, would this not also be an unfairness? If he was a lousy servant, does this punishment really fit the crime? Job's story also presents us with other types of unfairness. For example, in his lament about killers, rapists, and thieves, we have the bad getting away with wrongful acts, failing to get their just desserts. Then there is Job's lament about the process, for God has acted in a high-handed, underhanded, and arbitrary way, and this lack of due process is another unfairness.

We know how Job's world turned out in the end. But what of the just world? Although it took a beating, it did not shatter, as a simple illusion might. Job certainly resisted the friend's just-world attempt to frame him, and he rejected their blaming arguments and held to his innocence. He also called it as he saw it, when it came to God (who must be the deontological source of the just world), knocking the divine ground that had been upholding the just world. In his most despairing moments, he no longer held to a perfect just world, for the evidence seemed incontrovertible that some bad people get away with bad deeds. Despite these blows, much of the just world is left standing, for Job never gives up on justice and fairness.

In the next chapter, unfairness is set within the third of our three contexts, an extensive literature on justice and fairness. This context is current, and one that has been conceptually cultivated and empirically tilled. In many ways, it is a natural setting, for we so easily link "just" and "fair" in our utterances and writings, and join them even closer in that idiom, "just and fair." In trying to build the story of the story of unfairness, we might find, on this cultivated and tilled ground, a number of solid floors already in place. Good reasons to turn to "just and fair."

ENDNOTES

1. M. Lerner, *The Belief in a Just World: A Fundamental Delusion* (New York: Plenum Press, 1980), p. 11.
2. Z. Rubin and L. A. Peplau, "Who Believes in a Just World?" *Journal of Social Issues* 31 (1975): 65–89.
3. *Id.*, p. 65.
4. Lerner, *The Belief in a Just World*, p. 11.
5. *Id.*, p. 14.
6. J. Piaget, *The Moral Judgment of the Child*, trans. Marjorie Gabain (Glencoe, IL: Free Press, 1948), p. 256.
7. F. Heider, *The Psychology of Interpersonal Relations* (New York: Wiley, 1958), p. 258.
8. *See, e.g.*, W. A. Edmundson, ed. *The Duty to Obey the Law: Selected Philosophical Readings* (Lanham, MD: Rowman & Littlefield, 1999).
9. American Psychiatric Association, *Diagnostic and Statistical Manual of Mental Disorders*, 3rd ed., revised (Washington, DC: Author, 1987).
10. S. Mitchell, *The Book of Job* (San Francisco: North Point Press, 1987) p. 7.
11. *Id.*, p. 14.
12. J. N. Shklar, *The Faces of Injustice* (New Haven, CT: Yale University Press, 1990).
13. Mitchell, *The Book of Job*, p. xiii.
14. *Id.*, p. xiii.
15. *Id.*, p. 25.
16. *Id.*, p. 26.

17. *Id.*, p. 29.

18. *Id.*, p. 31.

19. *Id.*, p. 41.

20. "God has tricked me, and lured me into his trap. I call, but there is no answer; I cry out, and where is justice? . . . If only my cry were recorded and my plea inscribed on a tablet . . . Someday my witness would come; My avenger would read those words. He would plead for me in God's court; he would stand up and vindicate my name." *Id.*, pp. 48–49.

21. *Id.*, pp. 60–61.

22. S. Mitchell, *Genesis: A New Translation of the Classic Biblical Stories* (New York: Harper Collins, 1996).

23. K. Rahner, ed., *Encyclopedia of Theology: The Concise Sacramentum Mundi* (New York: Crossroads, 1982), pp. 213–217.

24. D. Birnbaum, *God and Evil: A Unified Theodicy/Theology/Philosophy* (Hoboken, NJ: Ktav, 1989), p. 48.

25. *See, e.g.,* Birnbaum, *God and Evil*; S. T. Davis, ed., *Encountering Evil: Live Options in Theodicy* (Atlanta, GA: John Knox Press, 1981); J. Hick, *Evil and the God of Love* (London: Macmillan, 1966); J. M. Trau, *The Co-existence of God and Evil* (New York: Peter Lang, 1995).

26. H. M. Schulweis, *Evil and the Morality of God* (Cincinnati, OH: Hebrew Union College Press, 1984), p. 1.

27. *See, e.g.,* J. B. Cobb Jr., "The Problem of Evil and the Task of Ministry." In *Encountering Evil: Live Options in Theodicy,* ed. S. T. Davis (Atlanta: John Knox Press, 1981), pp. 167–176; H. S. Kushner, *When Bad Things Happen to Good People* (New York: Avon Books, 1981).

28. *See, e.g.,* V. E. Frankl, *From Death Camp to Existentialism,* trans. Ilsa Lasch (Boston: Beacon Press, 1959); P. Levi, *The Drowned and the Saved* (New York: Vintage Books, 1988); E. Wiesel, *Zalmen, or, the Madness of God* (New York: Random House, 1975); E. Wiesel, *The Trial of God,* trans. M. Wiesel (New York: Random House, 1979).

29. *See, e.g.,* N. Mandela, *The Long Walk to Freedom: The Autobiography of Nelson Mandela* (Boston: Little, Brown, 1994); A. Shcharansky, *Fear No Evil,* trans. S. Hoffman (New York: Random House, 1988); A. I. Solzhenitsyn, *The Gulag Archipelago,* trans. T. P. Whitney (New York: Harper & Row, 1974).

30. *See, e.g.,* W. Blake, *Blake's Job* (Providence, RI: Brown University Press, 1966); M. Buber, *Eclipse of God* (New York: Harper & Row, 1957); M. Buber, *Good and Evil* (New York: Charles Scribner's Sons, 1952); A. Camus, *The Stranger,* trans. Stuart Gilbert (New York: Vintage Books, 1946); A. Dante, *Dante in Hell: An Account of Dante's Inferno for the Reader of English* (Roma: Edizioni Kappa, 1986); F. Kafka, *The Trial,* trans. Willa and Edwin Muir (New York: Schocken Books, 1968); Saint John of the Cross, *The Dark Night of the Soul* (Cambridge: James Clarke & Co., 1973); W. Styron, *Darkness Visible: A Memoir of Madness* (New York: Random House, 1990); W. Styron, *Sophie's Choice* (New York: Random House, 1976).

31. Davis, *Encountering Evil.*

32. Buber, *Good and Evil*; Buber, *Eclipse of God.*

33. E. L. Fackenheim, *To Mend the World* (New York: Schocken, 1982), p. 196.

34. E. Berkovits, *Faith After the Holocaust* (New York: Ktav, 1973).

35. As Schulweis put it, "Invariably, the attempted exculpation of God defends a major aspect of perfection at the expense of another. Each type of theodicy is compelled to divest itself of some vital part of monotheistic belief in order to protect what it considers to be the more valued ideal. It is around that excluded aspect that the arguments and counter arguments of theodicy are centered." Schulweis, *Evil and the Morality of God*, p. 7.

36. C. G. Jung, *Answer to Job*, trans. R. F. C. Hull (Princeton, NJ: Princeton University Press, 1973).

37. *Id.*, p. 3.

38. *Id.*, p. 5.

39. *Id.*

40. *Id.*, p. 7.

41. *Id.*, p. 14.

42. *Id.*

43. *Id.*, p. 7.

44. *Id.*, p. 42.

45. *See, e.g.*, M. Berenbaum, *The Vision of the Void: Theological Reflections on the Works of Elie Wiesel* (Middleton, CT: Wesleyan University Press, 1979); M. Friedman, *To Deny Our Nothingness: Contemporary Images of Man* (New York: Delacorte Press, 1967); R. L. Rubenstein, "Job and Auschwitz," *Union Seminary Quarterly Review* XXV (Summer 1970): 4.

46. E. Wiesel, *Legends of Our Time* (New York: Holt, Rinehart and Winston, 1968), p. 221.

47. E. Wiesel, *Night* (New York: Hill & Wang, 1960).

48. Berenbaum, *The Vision of the Void*, p. 51.

49. *Id.*, p. 123.

50. *Id.*

51. *Id.*, p. 9.

52. P. Berger, *The Sacred Canopy: Elements of a Sociological Theory of Religion* (Garden City, KS: Doubleday, 1967).

53. Berenbaum, *The Vision of the Void*, p. 9.

54. D. Patterson, *In Dialog and Dilemma with Elie Wiesel* (Wakefield, NH: Longwood Academic, 1991); Wiesel, *Zalmen, or, the Madness of God*; Wiesel, *The Trial of God*.

55. Berenbaum, *The Vision of the Void*, p. 7.

56. *Id.*, 14.

57. E. H. Wolgast, *The Grammar of Justice* (Ithaca, NY: Cornell University Press, 1987), p. 194.

58. *Id.*

59. B. Moore Jr., *Injustice: The Social Bases of Obedience and Revolt* (White Plains, NY: M. E. Sharpe, 1978).

60. F. X. Gibbons, "Social Comparison and Depression: Company's Effect on Misery," *Journal of Personality and Social Psychology* 51 (1986): 140–148; L. S. Perloff and B. K. Fetzer, "Self-Other Judgements and Perceived Vulnerability to Victimization, "*Journal of Personality and Social Psychology* 50 (1986): 502–510; S. E. Taylor, H. A. Wayment, and M. A. Collins, "Positive Illusions and

Affect Regulation." In *Handbook of Mental Control*, ed. D. M. Wegner and J. W. Pennebaker (Englewood Cliffs, NJ: Prentice Hall, 1993); S. E. Taylor, J. V. Wood, and R. R. Lichtman, "It Could Be Worse: Selective Evaluation as a Response to Victimization," *Journal of Social Issues* 39 (1983): 19–40; R. G. Tedeschi and L. G. Calhoun, *Trauma & Transformation: Growing in the Aftermath of Suffering* (Thousand Oaks, CA: Sage, 1995); T. A. Wills, "Downward Comparison as a Coping Mechanism." In *Coping With Negative Life Events: Clinical and Social Psychological Perspectives*, ed. C. R. Snyder and C. E. Ford (New York: Plenum Press, 1987); J. V. Wood, S. E. Taylor, and R. R. Lichtman, "Social Comparison in Adjustment to Breast Cancer," *Journal of Personality and Social Psychology* 49 (1985): 1169–1183.

61. S. J. Gould, *Full House: The Spread of Excellence From Plato to Darwin* (New York: Harmony Books, 1996), p. 48.
62. *Id.*, p. 45.
63. *Id.*, p. 49.
64. *Id.*, p. 50.
65. *Id.*
66. Mitchell, *The Book of Job*, p. xviii.
67. *Id.*, p. 84.
68. *Id.*, p. xiii.
69. Kushner, *When Bad Things Happen*.

3

SEPARATING "FAIR" FROM "JUST" AND "UNFAIR" FROM "FAIR"

Social scientists advance knowledge by finding facts and grounding theory on them. But that advance is impeded, I submit, by confusion and inconsistency over how the concepts of justice and fairness are understood, related, and used. This confusion and inconsistency is illustrated through three patterns relating justice to fairness, which continue to be used, which I label *identity*, *conjugate*, and *subset*.

In *identity*, the terms "justice" and fairness" are treated as synonyms, so one can interchange one for the other without changing the meaning. In their widely used text, *Psychology and the Legal System*, Wrightsman, Nietzel, and Fortune gave an example of *identity* when they stated that "justice means *fairness*."[1] Other social scientists use *identity* through their locutions, as Tyler did when he calls the same referent "procedural justice" and "procedural fairness" at different places in the same article.[2]

The second pattern is *conjugate*, where the two terms are paired in a common idiom, "just and fair." Although the idiom is euphemistic, it is unclear how it should be understood. For example, is the reader to treat it as a "gestalt," a whole that not only means more than the sum of its parts, but one that really means "ignore the parts"? Or do the parts matter, and if they do matter, what does each convey to this union? Is the placement of "just" on the front end to be taken as an indication of its primacy, and, if so, then what does the back-end "fair" convey that the front end has not already delivered? These questions remain unanswered, for the unique contributions of the idiom's components remain unspecified.

In the third pattern, one concept is the *subset* of the more inclusive, subsuming concept. In principle, either "fair" or "just" can be the subset or the subsuming term, but in practice it almost always goes one way— where "fairness" is a subset of "justice." This seems to make "justice" the brighter star of the binary, as "fairness" is dwarfed and relegated to the penumbra. This is how Tyler,[3] in the same article referred to above, portrayed *subset*, when he stated that "fairness" is a type of "justice judgment."

Finally, when social scientists do make differentiations, justice is portrayed as having dominion over outcomes (distributive justice) and most all legal matters, whereas fairness has the limited domain over procedure and games. We see this division of labor in Wrightsman, Nietzel, and Fortune's text,[4] where they stated that "justice is an outcome of the process in which people receive what they deserve or are due." But the confusion grows worse, being compounded by inconsistency, because some social scientists switch patterns within the same work and even within the same paragraph. Even when seeming to be using one pattern, say *identity* or *conjugate*, they may slide into *subset*, for a "just bias" often creeps into the language and the research.[5] That "just bias" is evident even when "fairness" appears to take center stage, for these studies are typically dubbed "procedural *justice*,"[6] a locution that implies that justice still has primacy.

This continuing confusion is no impediment for *identity*, where "justice" and "fairness" are one and the same, and where research findings of one would apply fully to the other. But this affords little comfort, for *identity* is the pattern that is least likely to be true. The confusion remains an impediment for *conjugate* and *subset*, where the two terms appear to have some distinctiveness, though their meanings, respective domains, and their relationship remain undifferentiated.

Now I add a fourth pattern, a complication that it is hoped will clarify. This pattern, which I dub *overlapping and separate*, holds that "fairness" and "justice" are likely to overlap in certain areas yet remain distinct in other areas. If *overlapping and separate* is the more accurate portrayal, then we would have no justification for generalizing justice findings onto fairness, or vice versa, unless we first knew what was common ground and what was distinct.

A "JUST" AND "FAIR" CONFUSION

At this point, with four patterns now in play, the confusion directs us toward seeking clarity. If the social scientists' use of "justice" and "fairness" remains inconsistent and confused, turning directly to their research findings would leave us with severe interpretative problems. Our direction, then, is toward first getting greater clarity on the concepts of justice and fairness, and their relationship. That being the goal, I turn to prominent legal, moral, and political philosophers, along with political scientists, historians, and jurisprudes, whose forte it is to analyze fundamental and fuzzy concepts. In that regard, political philosophers, especially, have highlighted "justice," giving considerable thought to how it relates to other fundamental concepts. But to introduce this conceptual work, I begin with a phrase and precept chiseled into marble atop the Supreme Court building, "equal justice under law."

It seems a simple phrase, but a mere four words. Yet there is doubt about the meaning of each of these words, their combination, and the whole. For example, in Weinreb's discussion of the concept of equality, he stated that it can mean (a) an equality before the law, (b) an equal humanity, (c) an equality of opportunity, and (d) an equality of result.[7] Dworkin picked up the first two meanings, as he conceives equality to be a fundamental right "to equal concern and respect."[8] Dworkin's "equal concern" (political equality) is Weinreb's "equality before the law," and it means that characteristics by which people may be classified (race, gender, age, looks, nationality, etc.) should not be determinative before the law; put another way, the least advantaged members of society should be entitled to the same concern and respect before the law as the most advantaged. In the second sense, equality involves "the vague but powerful idea of human dignity,"[9] which Kant and many other philosophers have defended and which coincides with Weinreb's equal humanity. In Weinreb's third meaning, equal opportunity focuses on procedures and processes, such that the rules of law and the rules of the game apply equally to all. Finally, his fourth meaning, equality of result, speaks to the distribution of outcomes. As for long-running trends, McKeon[10] noted two—that there is an "increase in the number of those who are considered 'equal' and diversification of what is sought as 'equal.'"

This short sampler by no means exhausts the possibilities, but it is enough to show that "equal" has multiple meanings. Regarding the last word of the phrase, "law," the same can be said, as even a cursory read on the central questions in jurisprudence—What is "law"? What is *Law's Empire?*[11] What principles sustain it? Which principles serve in its interpretation?—reveals varied answers. For example, a legal positivist account of law is going to be a very different account than one deriving from natural law,[12] as Weinreb showed in his work.[13] As Dworkin demonstrated, laws (and a society) founded on utilitarian goals are going to be different from ones founded on duties or from ones founded on rights.[14]

Returning to that chiseled phrase, even the lowly preposition, "under," produces doubt. Is justice really *under* law, as the phrase has it, or does justice stand behind, beneath, above, or beyond the law, to toss out a few prepositional possibilities? To a natural law advocate,[15] or to an ordinary citizen-turned-juror who believes in the right of the jury to nullify the law,[16] such proponents believe that justice is higher than the law.[17]

Putting further pressure on the "under" preposition is the matter of how law is adjudicated and by whom. Supreme Court justices routinely decide cases where there is doubt about the law (or the "justice" under the law) or where the law conflicts with other law (one justice notion conflicts with another). This means, according to Dworkin, that justices "must answer intractable, controversial, and profound questions of political morality that philosophers, statesmen, and citizens have debated for many centuries, with no prospect of agreement" and that we "must accept the deliverances of a majority of the justices, whose insight into these great issues is not spectacularly special."[18] That unelected judges have this power produces bipartisan resentment, for it "seems unfair, even frightening."[19] Yet in doing the adjudication, by which they will pass judgment on whether the lower court's ruling was just or unjust, the justices may draw forth a new justice, fairness, or integrity principle (which stands outside the law) as the deciding factor,[20] or they may apply "some measure, standard, yardstick, or norm" (which leaves open the question of whether the norm is "just" or not),[21] or they may reconstrue the law, finding a new principle hidden within.[22] This new principle or standard, which was outside the law or never seen within the law to begin with, cannot properly be said to be *under the law* until its discovery or incorporation. Thus, in regard to how the justices go about deciding, we may add another preposition and speak about justice of the law itself.[23]

From this second sampler, the appropriate preposition changes with perspective, situation, and task, as does the justice–law relationship itself. But when we put the complexities aside, a simple truth seems to emerge. Whatever the apt preposition is for the particular situation, "justice" is firmly embedded in marble, political philosophy, and etymology, for as Knight put it, "justice is a legal term (*jus* meaning 'law')."[24]

In contrast, "fairness" is absent from the marbled phrase, which raises some familiar questions. Does this omission indicate a secondary status for "fairness," a sign that it occupies the back end of the *conjugate* for good reason, such that the front-end "just" conveys all that is needed? Or are we to assume *identity*, where "fairness" is really there, expressed by its synonym? Or are we to assume *subset*, where it is subsumed under the wider orbit of "justice"? With the absence of "fairness" from the phrase, and with familiar questions still without answers, it seems that this chapter's opening confusion is with us still. But this is not quite the case, for we are beginning to see clues of separate spheres of influence. For example, it seems more likely that "justice" will appear within the "law," whereas "fairness" may be more applicable to everyday life and relationships.

Fairness Behind the Veil and Beneath Justice

The preeminent political philosopher of our time is John Rawls, and one of his most influential pieces is "Justice as Fairness,"[25] a title suggesting that fairness may occupy a more fundamental position in relation to justice than either identity, conjugate, or subset would seem to permit. Rawls has asked us to consider a situation where a number of individuals come together to form a group, a social compact, or even a new government, and these individuals come to this "original position" as equal sovereigns. A reasonable psychological assumption leads to a reasonable prediction: that these individuals have self-interests (which will not align perfectly), and these interests will motivate each to favor laws that further each individual's self-interests. What is most intriguing about Rawls's hypothetical original position is that he manages to take self-interest out of the game by using the "veil of ignorance," where persons make decisions without knowing their self—without knowing, for example, whether they are adult or child, male or female, single or married, wealthy or poor—or any of those traits, attributes, or acquisitions that are part of our "self" concept.

A simple example might help. Let us say that a husband, wife, and child come together to establish a rule (a family law). They are going to set the bedtime for the child. Now if you are the husband or wife, the time you select is likely to be lower than what the child selects, whereupon there is dissent, and possibly guerrilla war. But consider what your decision would now be if you are behind the veil of ignorance, where you do not know whether you are the husband, the wife, or the child. Under these conditions, what you propose may be quite different.

Rawls certainly thinks the decision will be different.[26] He believes that each person will want the greatest degree of liberty compatible with an equal degree of liberty for all others. He also believes that inequalities of resources should not exist, unless they work for the benefit of the least advantaged members of this society. Beneath these two justice principles, at a foundational level, is a deeper principle of fairness-as-reciprocity. Thus Rawls has reversed the far more typical view of justice as the subsuming construct, putting fairness in that position. As Chapman[27] put it,

> According to Rawls, the fair is to be seen as what free and rational men could reasonably be expected to agree on in their dealings with one another. Fairness is essentially right dealing or, more precisely, reciprocity in institutionalized relationships, and it is the possibility of mutual acceptance that is the test or criterion of fairness as this standard is applied to institutions or practices. Further, according to Rawls, mutual acknowledgment and acceptance of the standard of fairness is a manifestation on the part of those concerned of their mutual recognition of one another as persons.

In Chapman's analysis of Rawls's position, "a fair practice is, or becomes, a just practice when it is authoritatively established. Justice, then, on Rawls's interpretation, is essentially the legal or political counterpart of the ethical concept of fairness."[28]

Based on what both Rawls and Chapman have said, some further differentiations between "justice" and "fairness" become evident. "Justice" is associated with the legal and political, whereas "fairness" is more connected to the ethical, be it in games (fair games), competition (fair competition), and commerce (fair bargains). Justice, then, is likely to involve formal, authoritative sanctions for violations that have a finality to them, whereas fairness is likely to involve informal, social sanctions for violations. Another distinction is that fairness seems to involve the voluntary, such that you and I come to Rawls's original position freely, as an option, and we may give our consent or choose not to. By contrast, there is much that is involuntary under justice and the law, such that a defendant cannot choose not to appear at his trial, and his consent is not needed for the trial process to happen. Justice applies to more complex matters, whereas fairness applies to simpler matters.

At this point, a social scientist might ask, "But is there any support —empirical support—for these speculative distinctions?" In Chapman's work, he tried to provide some. He put forth a linguistic analysis of how people use the two terms, and he found more differentiations (as well as more areas of overlap) than Rawls seems to have granted. Chapman began by citing H. L. A. Hart's work, where the latter made the observation that most of what could be said about just and unjust "could almost equally well be conveyed by the words 'fair' and 'unfair.'"[29] If this is so, great areas of overlap between the two terms ought to be evident. Hart went on to give some specific examples of overlap and of difference. Regarding difference, he stated that when the focus is not on the individual but "the way in which *classes* of individuals are treated . . . what is typically fair or unfair is a 'share.'"[30] As for overlap areas, these can be heard when we speak of distributions or compensations as either just or fair, or unjust or unfair. As for separate areas, we tend to speak about a trial being fair or unfair, but we speak about a judge being just or unjust and a person as being justly or unjustly convicted. Chapman believes that Hart's differentiated and overlap areas are correct.

Although "fair" again dominates when process is involved, Hart and Chapman extend this hegemony to legal processes (a fair trial), which are set within "justice's" authoritative realm and where formal sanctions and involuntariness apply. It would appear, then, that the realm of fairness grows at the expense of justice. But if this oft-cited distinction between process (fair) and outcome (just) is sound, then this leads to situations where the two terms are not only separate, but may be at odds— because we can speak about a trial being fair and the outcome being unjust, or a trial being unfair and the outcome being just.

When Chapman summed up these overlapping and separate areas, he found that[31]

> At the very least, linguistic investigation does suggest that the distinction between fairness and justice is less clear-cut and less closely tied to types of practice than Rawls's interpretation would allow. The distinction appears multidimensional in that it contains not only an ethico-legal dimension but also dimensions which may be described in terms of the contrasts between reciprocity and equality, continuity and finality, simplicity and complexity.

Chapman's linguistic analysis is not likely to impress a rigorous empiricist. Looking at how a leading philosopher uses the two terms, or his own use of the terms, is a very limited and skewed sample of participants. Based on what he reports, we have no idea whether ordinary people use the terms as Chapman suggests, nor whether these distinct and overlap areas fully map the terrain, nor whether the generalizations and conclusions he draws are supportable. Yet his notion of "multidimensionality" carries a significant implication: If fairness is interchangeable with justice when we appraise the distribution of benefits, said Chapman, then we must be using "fairness" to mean something different from game-playing reciprocity. This seems sound. When it comes to distributions, fairness expands beyond its first and primary meaning (reciprocity), taking on a second meaning where it is used like "distributive justice" (fairness-as-outcome). There is another implication as well: If the two terms were fully interchangeable (identity), we would expect to see justice expand and be used when the standard of reciprocity was invoked, but this is not the case, Chapman believes. Thus "fairness" overlaps with "justice" (distributions) while having its own distinction area (reciprocity), and "justice" seems narrowed to distributions and areas within the authoritative law. Chapman's conclusion, contrary to Rawls's, is that neither fairness nor justice is fundamental to the other, as both "are rooted in the moral nature of personality."[32]

There remains a troubling matter with Rawls's position, according to Chapman. Where in Rawls's view do we situate "need"? This problem emerges if we return to Rawls's "veil of ignorance," which allows for laws to be conceived on nobler sentiments, for self-interests are no longer known. But in the real world no one is ignorant. Moreover, the sovereigns who come to the playing field have unequal resources, such that the playing field is not perfectly level at the outset. We can see what is likely to happen in the following familial example, with a new twist.

In Lawrence Mitchell's work, *Stacked Deck*,[33] he began with an anecdote about fixing the bedtime for his 10-year-old son, Alex, at 9:30, to which the boy responded, "That's not fair." Here comes the new twist. Being fair minded, the author called a family meeting where his wife joined, and relying on the fairness of democracy, they put it to a vote. As

Mitchell wrote, "Surprise! The vote was two to one in favor of 9:30, with Alex dissenting."[34] Although formal fairness or political fairness or majoritarian fairness reigned[35]—for everyone was heard, and a vote was taken—this sort of fairness was not enough to protect Alex's interests, as the deck was stacked against him. Clearly, not everything was equal going into the family vote, as the relationships and power alliances were such that the kid got the pretext of fairness rather than the genuine article.

Mitchell took his family vote story to the societal level, where some individuals have more power, resources, and influence, and others have much less; within the latter group, there are many in need, because of fate, luck, nature, inheritance, and catastrophe, and for them, fairness as reciprocity does not seem to work. As Mitchell put it, "due process provides a somewhat limited understanding of fairness," for it is "concerned exclusively with fair *process* and thus expressly excludes concerns of substantive fairness that may exist at a deeper level."[36] As he put it, "If the metaphors are bad, the conclusions will be bad. And the game metaphor is a bad one to use in looking at fairness."[37] It is bad, in Mitchell's opinion, because it is based on "equal autonomy," a self-interest focus, which does not consider the matter at the community level or from the moral level.[38]

Chapman's criticism of Rawls is similar to Mitchell's, but with a significant addition. Chapman has already imbued "fairness" with a substantive meaning (distributive justice) beyond fair process (reciprocity), yet this addition is still not enough to make "justice as fairness" account for those in need. Recalling Hart's usage, since we are referring to a disadvantaged group needing a better share, "fairness" rather than "justice" is the appropriate term. If we are going to take this group into account on some nonequal, nonequitable basis, or by changing procedures to respond to the particular circumstances of the needy, then the concept of fairness will have to expand further in yet another direction, acquiring a third meaning. For Chapman that further direction is rooted in the "moral nature of personality,"[39] and given this moral dimension, the Other and the community of Others are going to have a major place in the picture. If that is so, then self-interest cannot be the whole of the motivational story.

Social Science Contributions to Distributive and Procedural Justice

It is best known as "equity theory," although George Homans, regarded as its founder, preferred "distributive justice." As for "fairness," Homans subsumed it under "procedural justice," "about which we do not have much to say, as it is subsidiary to decisions based on 'retributions or distributions.'"[40] Beyond the name of the theory and the subsidiary place he assigned to fairness, Homans expressed dismay over the fact that authors treat terms such as *justice, equity,* and *fairness* "as if they referred to different things. In their most general sense they do not. The special senses are the ones that make trouble."[41]

I would disagree strongly with Homans's trouble-making assessment, for his solution guarantees that the confusion will continue. As we have seen, the distinctions that political philosophers and political scientists draw help define the overlapping and separate spheres to "just" and "fair," and to provide a substantive and moral basis to "fair" beyond its primary, reciprocity meaning associated with the ethics of game playing. Yet Homans's recommendation seems to be taken to heart, for the blurring of "justice" and "fairness" and the former's subsuming of the latter occur in the very first paragraph of Greenberg and Cohen's work:

> Justice is a fundamental theme in social life. . . . one need look no further than daily social interaction to appreciate the pervasiveness of the concern for and the impact of the theme of justice. Although there may be differences in response to them, there is a universal appreciation for the appeals made for "fair treatment," "fair play," and "a fair day's pay for a fair day's work."[42]

It is ironic that these writers invoke "fair treatment," "fair play," and "a fair day's pay for a fair day's work" as their examples of "justice," when philosophers see those as reciprocity examples, the hallmark of fairness. The older, philosophic literature seems to be ignored, as "fairness" gets recast into "justice" without nary a mention, question, or justification being offered, as the fairness–justice distinction blurs into one.

The early developments of equity theory[43] and its more recent evolutions[44] have been extensively reviewed, so I will only highlight a few points. In general, equity theories give an account of the expectations people have in an exchange relationship: expectations about what they should get (outcome) given their (input), and expectations when there is another person involved, who also has an input–outcome ratio. Equity theory's expectations, explanations, and predictions cover many types of exchanges that ordinary citizens are involved in. For example, most workers are likely to want equity, such that their pay is proportional to their productivity. Likewise most students want their grade to reflect their performance, or want their admittance into college, graduate school, law school, or medical school to be similarly based. As we look around us, equity does seem to have broad coverage, being a major way of distributing rewards.

If we stand back, equity theories seem much like business, economic, and mathematical game theory models: According to equity theory, we calculate our inputs, compare it to the inputs of others, appraise our outcomes against what others get in relation to the respective inputs, and then judge whether this is equitable. Thus within this theory we are rational calculators, making rational decisions, with rational self-interest to guide us.[45] But confounding the calculations (and the expectations that derive) is the likely possibility that we are not rational calculators,[46] because our self-interests may distort our assessments and ultimately our actions.

But a deeper, more fundamental problem emerges. Equity is not the only desirable way to distribute resources. There are times and circumstances where we may want to distribute rewards equally, where equality rather than equity seems the fairer rule.[47] There are other times and circumstances where the distribution may be done on the basis of need, and where this seems to be the fairer way to go. Where rational self-interest is posited as the driving motivation for equity, it is clear that other motives must be operable, and even dominant, when equality or need solutions are enacted.

In its second decade of its development, a few equity theorists, notably Melvin Lerner[48] and Gerald Leventhal,[49] recognized that there must be other distributive rules beyond equity. Given that people have these rules (equity, equality, need) already in mind, the question becomes which rule will be selected as most appropriate in a given situation? Leventhal said that a "justice-judgment sequence" must be activated. But what activates it? One factor, said Leventhal, is that a person "occupies a role whose primary function is to evaluate deservingness or adjudicate conflict."[50] We can easily think of a judge or juror deciding a case, or an employer deciding about raises, or a parent mediating a squabble between two children. Yet we can substantially widen this group to include those who watch Court TV, or watch the evening news, or merely read their morning papers. We can widen it to include the defendant, the defendant's family, the victim, and the victim's family. We can widen it to include the workers being given raises or the students being given grades. In sum, we can widen it to include almost anybody. For what may activate the "justice-judgment sequence" for all of them may not be their formal role, but their perception that an unfairness is resulting.

As equity theory has evolved, greater attention has been given to inequity.[51] This has the advantage of giving the researcher a way into a participant's thinking through a concrete instance. In this sense, the claim of inequity is close to unfairness, where the clarity and concreteness of such instances, along with their heat and passion and primacy, were reasons for focusing on the phenomenology of "unfair" rather than "fair." In addition, equity theorists have tabbed "the nature of the phenomenological experience of inequity"[52] as requiring more research attention. To get at this, researchers will have to focus on the participants' perceptions and judgments of unfairness, while altering their typical methodology to let participants speak, and this is the methodological tack we choose for unfairness.

The groundbreaking work in procedural justice first appeared in Thibaut and Walker's *Procedural Justice: A Psychological Analysis*.[53] In one chapter, the authors reported on an experiment that tested John Rawls's "veil of ignorance" notion by having one group of participants make a decision "behind the veil," while two other groups make decisions "in front of the veil," either from a position of "disadvantage" or from "advantage." They conclude that

> although subjects in all conditions prefer fair procedures, those in different roles interpret the meaning of fairness differently. Subjects behind the veil view procedures as most fair that favor the disadvantaged party, provide opportunity for the disadvantaged party to present evidence, and provide little decision-maker control. Those in the Disadvantaged role are most concerned about their own predicament and rate procedures as most fair that favor themselves, provide them with greater opportunity for evidence presentation, do not favor the advantaged party, and maximize self-control while minimizing decision-maker and opponent control. Advantaged parties consider procedures most fair that provide opportunity for both parties to present evidence.

The importance of these results goes beyond confirming Rawls's point about a different type of decision making when one is behind rather than in front of the veil. What we further see, which Chapman felt was absent in Rawls's account, was that participants in the behind-the-veil condition did take "need" into account. Although Chapman may be right about its absence in Rawls's conceptual account, ordinary participants in the experiment incorporate need (the plight of the disadvantaged), and this factor altered their construing of fairness. This was more than equity, more than fairness as reciprocity, and more than fair outcomes. What these participants did may have been the moral thing to do, underscoring that third meaning to fairness.

The other finding of interest is that self-interest alters the construing of the two "in front of the veil" groups, as the advantaged and disadvantaged groups construed fairness in ways that were more favorable to their own circumstances. This finding is important, for in the real world (where experimental conditions and thought experiments rarely operate) we operate in front of the veil, with self-interest very much in mind. If we extend these findings to unfairness, the prediction would be that we are going to find those notions to be subjectively, situationally tinged. But there is an interesting condition that Thibaut and Walker did not test but that we will. What if the alleged unfairness in no way involves the participant, such that he or she is not the victim, and does not know the victim? Here we have a disinterested party to the unfairness, yet one who is operating in front of the veil, with self-interest, and with the facts in mind. The motivational story in this condition may not be self-interest, but something closer to the behind-the-veil condition.

The bulk of Thibaut and Walker's work concerns types of adjudicative procedures—the adversary model featured in most courtrooms in the United States, for example, versus inquisitorial models featured more prominently in Europe. Although interesting findings emerge, the studies have a number of methodological limitations. For one, the experimenters create all of the questionnaire items and all the short vignettes that they give to participants. Though these questionnaire items are clearly important to the researchers, we do not know whether these items are truly important to participants. What we have in the Thibaut and Walker work is research that is not aimed directly at uncovering the participant's phenomenology, because it is the experimenters' concerns (their phenomenology) that lead the dance.

A second point turns on the phrasing of questionnaire items or vignettes, which are likely to be very brief and abstract, denuded of nuance and specifics, like broad public opinion poll questions that are notorious for producing responses quite at odds with "flesh and blood" detailed vignettes.[54] Third, the dependent measure in this work is typically some "fairness" or "less fair" rating, where the participant circles the appropriate number. But what does that number signify to this participant? Why is he or she circling that number instead of another number? This we seldom learn, chiefly because we seldom ask. Yet we know that when we severely restrict the participants' response options, we are not getting their story as to why this is unfair. In sum, this research does not take us into the participants' phenomenology, for the participants' conceptions and concepts of unfairness remain in their minds, untapped.

In the second generation of procedural justice research, the work of Lind and Tyler brought important empirical findings about fairness to the fore,[55] although the conceptual blurring remains: They purposefully opted for the identity view, stating that "we will use the terms procedural *justice* and procedural *fairness* interchangeably in this book."[56] Yet, in fact, what is truly noteworthy about what they do is that they separate outcome (which may be seen as either just or fair) from process (which is seen as fairness) judgments. They find that people are often satisfied even when outcomes go against them because they judge the process to be fair. If a fair process can be more important to the overall judgment of fairness than the outcome, then equity models based exclusively on self-interest and "an egoistic conception of the person" are inadequate.[57] If self-interest fails, then surely the extreme of narcissism fails far more. Lind and Tyler then cast about and find alternatives to self-interest,[58] in Lerner's empathy-based theory,[59] as well as in group identification models such as Tajfel's,[60] where data show that individuals are more likely to put aside self-interest and display altruistic and cooperative behaviors when they identify with a group, which self-interest models would not predict.

One question that has been of long interest to political philosophers involves whether there is a general duty to obey the law.[61] For those who believe there is such a duty, the problem has been to conceptually ground that duty on something that holds. Is it grounded in the authority or legitimacy of the state, or the fact that we consent, or is it the duty of fair play? In Tom Tyler's work *Why People Obey the Law*,[62] he took an empirical approach to the question, looking at the "everyday behavior of citizens toward the law and examines why people obey or disobey it." His look at procedural justice is from a normative rather than instrumental perspective, for he found that people are concerned with much more than outcomes. For example, when someone goes to court, it very much matters whether the person perceives the process as neutral as opposed to biased, or whether the court displays politeness and respect for citizens' rights. Tyler found that "within the general framework of fairness, procedural concerns consistently take precedence over distributive concerns."

UNFAIR FROM FAIR

In reviewing the social science findings from distributive justice and procedural justice, we see an ever-present confusion in how the terms "justice" and "fairness" and used and conceived. Sometimes they are used interchangeably or conflated under "justice," even when distinct meanings are apparent. But when we translate what the social scientists are saying into a language of sensible and considered distinctions, "fair" is consistently linked to procedures, even legal procedures, which is its primary and first meaning of reciprocity. We also see its second meaning, which relates to outcomes, where "fair" and "just" may both apply. We see its third meaning as well, where "fair" acquires a moral sense that goes beyond the ethics of reciprocity and the fairness of the outcome, and this meaning is most evident when *need* is the distributive rule.

From conceptual and linguistic analyses, and from empirical findings, the overlapping and separate view seems more fitting than either identity, conjugate, or subset. If anything, the empirical findings from procedural justice indicate that the separation between "fair" and "just" can be quite wide, for people do judge situations as fair even when the outcome goes against them. These findings and the use of fair but nonequitable distribution rules tell us that people are not simply motivated by rational self-interest. They may prefer harmony and cooperation, for instance, when they choose an equal distribution, and they may prefer to give to the less fortunate from a moral conviction or civic duty, even when they would profit most by the equity solution. In these situations, self-interest gives way, as a larger interest prevails.

Another division is discernible in the distributive and procedural justice research and in the conceptual analyses, and this involves the distinction between "unfair" and "fair." This distinction was first suggested by some writers in the "justice" area, notably Judith Shklar, in her work *The Faces of Injustice*,[63] Elizabeth Wolgast, in *The Grammar of Justice*,[64] and

Thomas Simon, in "A Theory of Social Injustice."[65] I have extended that argument for the separateness of "fair" and "unfair," holding that the "unfair" end has concreteness, passion, insistence, and primacy, in ways that the "fair" end does not, such that our focus should profitably shift toward the "unfair" end. It is through people's instances of unfairness that their conceptions and concepts of unfairness are most likely to vividly emerge.

A Third Challenge

In the previous two chapters, we met two challenges to the "But it's not fair!" claim. There was the petty whines challenge, which hurled heated diagnostic labels, and the "who says life is supposed to be fair?" rejoinder, which had parents of every generation pounding it home. If ubiquity and decibel level are our assessment gauges, then both rejoinders have failed to quell the cry. The third challenge, which I will call failing to discriminate, does not seek to quash the indictments, only to target them correctly, and though this is the more limited of the three challenges, it is in some ways the most interesting.

It derives from Judith Shklar's work, where she distinguished between "misfortune" and "injustice." Misfortunes tend to be external events, often involving nature, events that seem natural and unavoidable and that we are resigned to suffer. Injustices, on the other hand, are more social, where ill-intentioned human or supernatural beings precipitate acts that could have been controlled or been otherwise and where indignation and outrage follow. Even though Shklar made the distinction, she recognized that it is a slippery and sliding distinction, one that changes with time and technology, value and viewpoint, and one that may not be meaningful from the victim's perspective.

I will complicate Shklar's dichotomy by adding "unfairness" to the picture, which may be different from both "misfortune" and "injustice." The challenge goes as follows: A critic might argue that a claimant's particular unfairness is not an "unfairness" at all, arguing that it is really a "misfortune." The critic says, "You are blaming what cannot and should not be blamed." If the critic is correct, then the claimant is making a thinking error, perhaps a primitive one, attributing intention when there is none. By comparison, this failing to discriminate rejoinder is less sweeping than the who says? claim, because it urges individuals to make the correct distinctions, whereas the latter urges individuals to make no distinctions. Although this challenge sees the blurring of an important distinction, it does not attribute this to narcissistic pathology, as petty whines rejoinder does.

This challenge points to a conceptual confusion but rests on an empirical assumption—that people actually do blur misfortunes into unfairnesses. But do they? Without the data, we cannot answer. There is a further problem with this challenge. Even if we had gathered unfairness instances with the purpose of looking for signs of blurring, we would have to know what are misfortunes and what are unfairnesses in order to classify the instances accurately. But as Shklar acknowledged, the line separating misfortunes from unfairnesses may slip and slide with time, technology, value, and viewpoint. Although Job and his three friends were sure that what befell Job was not a misfortune, would we be so sure today? If a modern man learns that winds from a hurricane knocked down his house and killed his 10 children, and then blames God, would his neighbors see it the same way? We can be pretty certain than an insurance company, defending in a civil action, would use that "act of God" locution to argue for "misfortune."

LOOKING BACKWARD, LOOKING FORWARD

In looking back, we began with a persistent confusion in the social science literature over "justice" and "fairness," where these two terms were either fused (identity), conjoined in euphemistic vagueness (conjugate), or arranged in a hierarchy (subset) with a "just bias" evident but with no evidence to support it. In moving to a conceptual analysis, we found areas of overlap and separateness. "Fairness" not only had hegemony over particular areas (areas that were more varied than previously thought), but it had distinctly different meanings, relating to fairness as reciprocity, fairness as outcome, and fairness as a moral response. In looking forward to an empirical investigation that is about to begin, these different conceptual meanings become hypotheses, for the question becomes whether we will find these distinctions, or others, when we examine and deconstruct participants' instantiations of unfairness.

In looking back, we also separated "fair" from "unfair," finding additional support that the "unfair" end of things is likely to be the most illuminating. Instances of unfairness (like instances of injustice and instances of inequity) have a clarity and concreteness to them; they typically come with heat and passion, anger, and outrage; and they insistently press for action or redress. These instances have primacy, coming to mind and voice before fairness concepts can be articulated. All of this suggests "unfairness" as the forward direction.

In looking forward, I will focus on the topic of unfairness. Within this topic, I will not aim high, at the conceptual level (at least not at first and not directly), because such concepts (e.g., equality, justice, fairness), as we have seen, have "contested careers,"[66] where their meanings have been construed in different ways.[67] Rather, my strategy will be to aim low, at the specifics, at ordinary citizens' concrete instantiations of "But it's not fair!"

Elsewhere, I have called this a commonsense approach,[68] by which the meanings ordinary citizens bring to fundamental notions are elucidated.

This method is phenomenological, as participants with but minimal prompting bring their unfairness instances to light, narrating and detailing their stories of unfairness, and then telling us, in their own words, why they think this instance is an unfairness. This approach derives from the pioneering work of social psychologist Fritz Heider, who considered his work on lay perceptions of the causes of behavior to be "an investigation of common-sense psychology,"[69] which later would become modern attribution theory.[70] In Heider's work, he shifted the traditional emphasis from an objective analysis of concepts to the subjective or lay understanding of them.

As I apply it, no stimulus materials (e.g., cases or vignettes of alleged unfairness) are provided for participants, because I do not want to steer them to what I find relevant but they may not. It is what they cite as relevant that is relevant. By not limiting their range of responses (e.g., through rating scales where the dimensions of the scale are set by the experimenter) as is done in typical studies and experiments, which may "flatten the way people understand and use law,"[71] I seek a fuller picture —their stories of unfairness in all their richness and messiness. By examining, deconstructing, and categorizing these instances, the participants' conceptions of unfairness ought to emerge, and through these particulars their concept of unfairness is also likely to emerge.[72] Thus in the end we do arrive at the conceptual level, but from the ground up. Curiously, by indirection, by a path that takes dead aim on "unfairness," we may end up with something substantive and solid—about fairness.

ENDNOTES

1. L. S. Wrightsman, M. T. Nietzel, and W. H. Fortune, *Psychology and the Legal System*, 3rd ed. (Pacific Grove, CA: Brooks/Cole, 1994), p. 59.
2. T. R.Tyler, "Governing amid Diversity: The Effect of Fair Decisionmaking Procedures on the Legitimacy of Government," *Law and Society Review* 28 (1994): 827.
3. *Id.*
4. Wrightsman et al., *Psychology in the Legal System*, p. 59.
5. In a fairly recent issue of *Psychology, Public Policy, and Law* devoted to "commonsense justice," the accent was clearly on justice rather than fairness in the following articles. Although this could be anticipated, given the focus of the issue, it certainly provided the room for fairness to appear and even take center stage. *See, e.g.,* J. L. Devenport, S. D. Penrod, and B. L. Cutler, "Eyewitness Identification Evidence: Evaluating Commonsense Evaluations," *Psychology, Public Policy, and Law* 3 (1997): 338–361; P. W. English and B. D. Sales, "A Ceiling or Consistency Effect for the Comprehension of Jury Instructions," *Psychology, Public Policy, and Law* 3 (1997): 381–401; N. J Finkel, "Commonsense Justice, Psychology, and the Law: Prototypes Common, Sense-

ful, and Not," *Psychology, Public Policy, and Law* 3 (1997): 461–489; N. J. Finkel and B. D. Sales, "Commonsense Justice: Old Roots, Germinant Ground, and New Shoots," *Psychology, Public Policy, and Law* 3 (1997): 1–15; C. Haney, "Commonsense Justice and Capital Punishment: Problematizing the Will of the People," *Psychology, Public Policy, and Law* 3 (1997): 303–337; I. A. Horowitz, "Reasonable Doubt Instructions and Jurors' Certainty of Guilt Standards," *Psychology, Public Policy, and Law* 3 (1997): 285–302; L. Olsen-Fulero and S. M. Fulero, "Commonsense Rape Judgments: An Empathy-Complexity Theory of Rape Juror Story Making," *Psychology, Public Policy, and Law* 3 (1997): 402–427; D. W. Shuman and A. Champagne, "Removing the People From the Legal Process: The Rhetoric and Research on Judicial Selection and Juries," *Psychology, Public Policy, and Law* 3 (1997): 242–258; C. A. Studebaker and S. D. Penrod, "Pretrial Publicity: The Media, the Law, and Commonsense," *Psychology, Public Policy, and Law* 3 (1997): 428–460.

6. Whether or not the term "justice" is in the title, when readers turn to the "Discussion" in those articles, "fairness" is likely to appear, though the discourse seldom differentiates "justice" from "fairness." *See, e.g.,* N. S. Bennett, C. W. Lidz, J. Monahan, E. P. Mulvey, S. K. Hoge, L. H. Roth, and W. Gardner, "Inclusion, Motivation, and Good Faith: The Morality of Coercion in Mental Hospital Admission," *Behavioral Sciences and the Law* 11 (1993): 295–306; R. J. Boeckmann and T. R. Tyler, "Commonsense Justice and Inclusion Within the Moral Community: When Do People Receive Procedural Protections From Others?" *Psychology, Public Policy, and Law* 3 (1997): 362–380; V. A. Hiday, M. S. Swartz, J. Swanson, and H. R. Wagner, "Patient Perceptions of Coercion in Mental Hospital Admission," *International Journal of Law and Psychiatry* 20 (1997): 227–241; R. Paternoster, R. Brame, R. Bachman, and L. W. Sherman, "Do Fair Procedures Matter? The Effect of Procedural Justice on Spouse Assault," *Law and Society Review* 31 (1997): 163–204; T. R. Tyler, *Why People Obey the Law* (New Haven, CT: Yale University Press, 1990).

7. L. L. Weinreb, *Natural Law and Justice* (Cambridge, MA: Harvard University Press, 1987), pp. 166, 167, 170, 176.

8. R. Dworkin, *Taking Rights Seriously* (Cambridge, MA: Harvard University Press, 1978), p. xii.

9. *Id.,* p. 198.

10. R. McKeon, "Justice and Equality." In *Nomos VI: Justice,* ed. C. J. Friedrich and J. W. Chapman (New York: Atherton Press, 1963), p. 44.

11. R. Dworkin, *Law's Empire* (Cambridge, MA: Harvard University Press, 1986).

12. *See, e.g.,* H. L. A. Hart, *The Concept of Law* (Oxford: Clarendon Press, 1961).

13. *See, e.g.,* Weinreb, *Natural Law and Justice.*

14. *See, e.g.,* Dworkin, *Taking Rights Seriously.*

15. Weinreb, *Natural Law and Justice.*

16. For examples, *see* N. J. Finkel, *Commonsense Justice: Jurors' Notions of the Law* (Cambridge, MA: Harvard University Press, 1995).

17. Although, in some cases, it may be "lower," grounded in "a regional code that go deeper into people's lives than the law they break." G. Wills, *A Necessary Evil: A History of American Distrust of Government* (New York: Simon and Schuster, 1999), p. 123.

18. R. Dworkin, "Unenumerated Rights: Whether and How *Roe* Should Be Overruled." In *The Bill of Rights in the Modern State*, ed. G. R. Stone, R. A. Epstein, and C. R. Sunstein (Chicago: University of Chicago Press, 1992), p. 383.

19. Dworkin, "Unenumerated Rights."

20. *Id.*, p. 393. Dworkin writes that "the idea, instinct in the concept of law itself, that whatever their views of justice and fairness, judges must also accept an independent and superior constraint of *integrity*."

21. A. Brecht, "The Ultimate Standard of Justice." In *Nomos VI: Justice*, ed. C. J. Friedrich and J. W. Chapman (New York: Atherton Press, 1963), p. 62.

22. *See, e.g.*, J. P. Stevens, "The Bill of Rights: A Century of Progress." In *The Bill of Rights in the Modern State*, ed. G. R. Stone, R. A. Epstein, and C. R. Sunstein (Chicago: University of Chicago Press, 1992), pp. 13–38. Justice Stevens notes that "the work of federal judges from the days of John Marshall to the present, like the work of the English common-law judges, sometimes requires the exercise of judgment—a faculty that inevitably calls into play notions of justice, fairness, and concern about the future impact of a decision."

23. F. H. Knight, "On the Meaning of Justice." In *Nomos VI: Justice*, ed. C. J. Friedrich and J. W. Chapman (New York: Atherton Press, 1963), pp. 1–23.

24. Knight, "On the Meaning of Justice," p. 1.

25. J. Rawls, "Justice as Fairness," *Philosophical Review* 67 (1958): 164–194.

26. J. Rawls, "Constitutional Liberty and the Concept of Justice." In *Nomos VI: Justice*, ed. C. J. Friedrich and J. W. Chapman (New York: Atherton Press, 1963), pp. 98–125.

27. J. W. Chapman, "Justice and Fairness." In *Nomos VI: Justice*, ed. C. J. Friedrich and J. W. Chapman (New York: Atherton Press, 1963), p. 148.

28. *Id.*

29. Hart, *The Concept of Law*, p. 154.

30. *Id.*

31. Chapman, "Justice and Fairness," pp. 158–159.

32. *Id.*, p. 169.

33. L. E. Mitchell, *Stacked Deck: A Story of Selfishness in America* (Philadelphia: Temple University Press, 1988).

34. *Id.*, p. 1.

35. Dworkin, *Law's Empire*, p. 164. That all things being equal, laws and cases ought to be decided in accordance with the will of the majority.

36. Mitchell, *Stacked Deck*, p. 75.

37. *Id.*, p. 185.

38. *Id.*

39. Chapman, "Justice and Fairness," p. 169.

40. G. C. Homans, Forward. In *Equity and Justice in Social Behavior*, ed. J. Greenberg and R. L. Cohen (New York: Academic Press, 1982), p. xii.

41. *Id.*, p. xi.

42. J. Greenberg and R. L. Cohen, eds., *Equity and Justice in Social Behavior* (New York: Academic Press, 1982), p. xix.

43. *See, e.g.*, J. S. Adams, "Inequity in Social Exchange." In *Advances in Experimental Social Psychology*. Vol. 2, ed. L. Berkowitz (New York: Academic Press, 1965), pp. 267–299; P. M. Blau, *Exchange and Power in Social Life* (New York:

John Wiley, 1964); G. C. Homans, *Social Behavior: Its Elementary Forms* (New York: Harcourt, 1961); E. Walster, G. W. Walster, and E. Berscheid, *Equity: Theory and Research* (Boston: Allyn & Bacon, 1978).

44. F. M. Moghaddam, *Social Psychology: Exploring Universals Across Cultures* (New York: W. H. Freeman, 1998).

45. Psychologists have been challenging the rational choice proposition with evidence that contradicts. For a recent review, *see* B. Schwartz, "Self-Determination: The Tyranny of Freedom," *American Psychologist* 55 (2000): 79–88.

46. Long before social psychologists became interested in game theory, such as the prisoners' dilemma, this was the province of mathematicians like Von Neumann, who principally worked on competitive, two-person, zero-sum games, and John Forbes Nash Jr., who worked on multiperson games, that could be collaborative as well as competitive. For his "Nash equilibrium points" and development of game theory, Nash won the Nobel Prize in economics. But the lesson I want to extract, which Nash and others found, was that people do not always behave in rational, self-interested ways. They don't always play their dominant strategies. They may base their strategies on emotions, punishing a player, being kind to a player, being fair, or splitting the difference rather than creating disharmony. S. Nasar, *A Beautiful Mind* (New York: Simon & Schuster, 1998).

47. Consider four old friends or business acquaintances who go to lunch, ordering different items. Now the check arrives. Let us say they decide to split it equally, even the person who ordered the least expensive items on the menu and who would profit more by an equity split. What motive drives this decision?

48. M. J. Lerner, "Social Psychology of Justice and Interpersonal Attraction." In *Foundations of Interpersonal Attraction*, ed. T. Huston (New York: Academic Press, 1974).

49. G. S. Leventhal, "Fairness in Social Relationships." In *Contemporary Topics in Social Psychology*, ed. J. Thibaut, J. Spence, and R. Carson (Morristown, NJ: General Learning Press, 1976); G. S. Leventhal, "What Should Be Done With Equity Theory?" In *Social Exchange Theory*, ed. K. Gergen, M. Greenberg, and R. Willis (New York: Plenum Press, 1980).

50. Greenberg and Cohen, *Equity and Justice in Social Behavior*, p. 22.

51. Adams, "Inequity in Social Exchange."

52. Greenberg and Cohen, *Equity and Justice in Social Behavior*, p. 15.

53. J. Thibaut and L. Walker, *Procedural Justice: A Psychological Analysis* (Hillsdale, NJ: Erlbaum, 1975).

54. Finkel, *Commonsense Justice*, pp. 117–122.

55. E. A. Lind and T. R. Tyler, *The Social Psychology of Procedural Justice* (New York: Plenum Press, 1988).

56. *Id.*, p. 3.

57. *Id.*, p. 223.

58. *Id.*, p. 231. Lind and Tyler call it a "group value model."

59. S. C. Lerner, "Adapting to Scarcity and Change (I): Stating the Problem." In *The Justice Motive in Social Behavior*, ed. M. J. Lerner and S. C. Lerner (New York: Plenum Press, 1981).

60. H. Tajfel, *Differentiation Between Social Groups: Studies in the Social Psychology of Intergroup Relations* (New York: Academic Press, 1978).

61. W. A. Edmundson, ed., *The Duty to Obey the Law: Selected Philosophical Readings* (Lanham, MD: Rowman and Littlefield, 1999).

62. T. R. Tyler, *Why People Obey the Law* (New Haven, CT: Yale University Press, 1990), p. 3.

63. J. N. Shklar, *The Faces of Injustice* (New Haven: Yale University Press, 1990).

64. E. H. Wolgast, *The Grammar of Justice* (Ithaca, NY: Cornell University Press, 1987).

65. T. W. Simon, "A Theory of Social Injustice." In *Radical Philosophy of Law: Contemporary Challenges to Mainstream Legal Theory and Practice*, ed. D. S. Caudill and S. J. Gold (Highlands, NJ: Humanities Press, 1995), pp. 54–72.

66. B. G. Garth and A. Sarat, "Justice and Power in Law and Society Research: On the Contested Careers of Core Concepts." In *Justice and Power in Sociolegal Studies*, ed. B. G. Garth and A. Sarat (Evanston, IL: Northwestern University Press, 1998), pp. 1–18.

67. *See, e.g.*, R. Reichman, "Power and Justice in Sociolegal Studies of Regulation." In *Justice and Power in Sociolegal Studies*, ed. B. G. Garth and A. Sarat (Evanston, IL: Northwestern University Press, 1998), pp. 233–271; S. S. Silbey, "Ideology, Power, and Justice." In *Justice and Power in Sociolegal Studies*, ed. B. G. Garth and A. Sarat (Evanston, IL: Northwestern University Press, 1988), pp. 272–308.

68. Finkel, *Commonsense Justice*.

69. F. Heider, *The Psychology of Interpersonal Relations* (New York: John Wiley & Sons, 1958), p.1.

70. E. E. Jones, D. E. Kanouse, H. H. Kelley, R. E. Nisbett, S. Valins, and B. Weiner, *Attribution: Perceiving the Causes of Behavior* (Morristown, NJ: General Learning Press, 1972).

71. S. E. Merry, *Getting Justice and Getting Even: Legal Consciousness Among Working-Class Americans* (Chicago: The University of Chicago Press, 1990), p. 5.

72. See Dworkin, *Taking Rights Seriously*, pp. 134–135, where he lays out the distinction between conceptions of fairness and the concept of fairness.

II

TAKING THE DIMENSIONS
OF UNFAIRNESS

Then the Unnamable Answered Job From Within the Whirlwind:
. . .
Where were you when I planned the earth?
Tell me, if you are so wise.
Do you know who took its dimensions,
measuring its length with a cord?
What were its pillars built on?
Who laid down its cornerstone. . . . (p. 79)

From Stephen Mitchell's *The Book of Job* (1987)

4

WHAT ARE THE TYPES OF UNFAIRNESS? TOWARD A CATEGORIZATION SCHEMA

In Part II (Taking the Dimensions of Unfairness), five studies are presented. At the heart of each study on unfairness is one of those central questions raised in Part I. Now, by drawing out the claimants' unfairnesses we seek to supplant the speculative and throw off the specious, replacing both with substantive answers grounded in empirical fact.

Although each study stands on its own, focusing on a particular dimension of unfairness, these studies are not separate set pieces. Rather, they are interlocking parts of a puzzle, as the findings of the first study affect the direction of the second, and so on, while the findings of the second elaborate the findings of the first. The interlocking continues, in that answers found in one study are tested again in another study with new samples and groups of participants in order to replicate and extend the findings. Where answers in one study are unclear, refining questions or refinements in the methodology are likely in the next study. At the end of this part, as the length, breadth, and depth of unfairness have been cumulatively added, the whole stands most visible.

In this chapter, where we begin to map the landscape, the focus is on finding the essential types of unfairness—the basic categories that house the participants' unfairness instantiations. In chapter 5, blame is the central variable, and the question is, who or what do we blame for unfairnesses? In chapter 6, severity, blame, and type are taken together, in their complexities, to see if the participants' conceptions of unfairness reveal consistency or whether they reveal a neuroticism of blaming others for what has happened. Chapter 7 examines who the victim (of the unfairness) is, as these findings allow us to gauge whether the unfairness claims are self-centered and narcissistic, as some critics have asserted, or whether an empathic focus on the other as victim is in evidence. Finally, chapter 8 examines whether people get over their unfairnesses or whether these experiences remain with us, and remain hot.

Across these studies, the age of the participant (i.e., age group) is a key variable, and we test college students, a younger "tot and teenager" group, an older adult group (30–60), and a still older group (61–95). By using these between-groups, will we find that the types of unfairness, along with blame, severity, and victim, change with age? Moreover, these groups are tested on a number of occasions to see if the findings replicate, for if they do, then the consistency adds to our confidence.

In beginning with types, we do not start with a blank slate. Some reasonable guesses can be made simply by bringing Job to mind (see chapter 2). Although his case is extreme, his type of unfairness may in fact be prototypic, for "when bad things happen to good people" is a type that springs quickly to people's minds,[1] at least from anecdotal reports. If we continue with Job, he also lamented about "wrongful behavior going unpunished" and "lack of due process," two other highly plausible types we are likely to find. We can also make predictions based on the philosophical writings and social science findings from distributive and procedural justice (see chapter 3).

Here are our questions. Will the types of unfairness identified by the participants be substantially fewer or greater than the philosophical writings suggest? Will citizens' concepts reveal the multiple meanings of fairness—as reciprocity, as outcome, as equality, as relating to need and to a moral basis? On the other hand, will ordinary citizens winnow down to some generic hodgepodge, or will they show so many conceptions of unfairness that we are flooded by particulars, unable to find concepts that draw consensus? On a specific matter, will ordinary citizens blur that outcome-versus-process distinction, or will they show an outcome bias? Most broadly, how many basic types of unfairness will emerge, and which types will be cited most frequently?

STUDY 1: AN OPEN-ENDED, NARRATIVE, AND DECONSTRUCTIVE APPROACH

As a first study, and a preliminary one at that, our participants were college students, a convenient sample. A modest number ($N = 91$) volunteered for this study, and we gave them a research booklet that featured the following introduction:

> Among children, teenagers, young adults, and older adults, a commonly heard lament is, "BUT IT'S NOT FAIR!" In this research, we are examining what people mean by "it's not fair." We are going to ask you to think about, and then write with some detail, examples of situations, events, or circumstances that would lead *you* to say that this is an instance of unfairness.

In this brief introduction that acknowledges the lament and its occurrence across the age span, the participants are not provided with a steering direction, channeling examples, or an outright definition of an unfairness, because all of these would lead or suggest. Rather, it is participants' own categorization of their instances as examples of unfairness that generates the data.

We then provided the following specific instructions:

> In this booklet, on the blank pages that follow, we want you to detail as many situations as you can where the phrase, "but it's not fair!" applies, in your opinion. The situations can be personal, where they happened to you, or to a family member, or a friend; they can also be something you heard about, or read about. For each instance, (1) briefly describe the event; (2) tell why, in your opinion, it was unfair; and (3) explain what would have to happen to make it fair. You will have a week to write these instances. If you need more paper, or prefer to use a computer and printer, you may do so, and then staple or clip those pages onto this booklet.

Consistent with the open-ended nature of the design, participants are told that they are free to respond with any and all instances that come to mind. However, there is a potential problem in the way this introduction can be construed: A participant could reasonably (but incorrectly) understand that we are asking him or her to furnish only unfairnesses *that happened to him or her*, when our intent is to keep the bandwidth wide open. If a sizable number of participants do construe the introduction in the self-limiting sense, this would not only reduce the number of their unfairness instances, but it would give their instances a decidedly narcissistic flavor —all based on misunderstanding. To prevent misunderstanding and to keep the field as wide open as possible, we added the specific instructions.

In addition to being open ended, this research design was "narrative" in that participants were encouraged "to tell the story" of the unfairness. Such an approach provides them room to richly detail their experiences, and many of their accounts ran several pages in length. Like the open-ended feature, the narrative approach avoids steering participants in predetermined directions, which would have occurred had the experimenter supplied unfairness vignettes and asked for ratings on dimensions selected by the experimenter. In our approach, the instances come *from* the participants rather than being *given to* the participants.

Although an open-ended, narrative approach has its advantages, disadvantages and problems may arise in coding the narrative. For example, a lengthy narrative may contain more than one unfairness, or the main focus may be lost within a sea of details or beneath convoluted writing. Another coding problem arises from a very brief and sketchy narrative, where crucial facts may be absent. These potential problems led us to write the specific instructions, where we asked the participants to "tell why, in your opinion, it was unfair," and we also asked them to "explain what would have to happen to make it fair," as both requests provide us with information to help us understand the essence of the instance, as the participant sees it, and thereby allow us to categorize it accurately.

In addition to being open-ended and narrative, this approach is deconstructive and constructive. As to deconstructive, from participants' instantiations we try to unpack the embedded meanings and find their conceptions of unfairness. This deconstructive phase is followed by a constructive one, where we try to create a categorization schema for these types of unfairness. In creating this schema, we set two standards. First, the schema ought to be reliable, such that two coders, working independently, will put the same instances into the same categories, most of the time.[2] Our second standard is that the schema ought to be inclusive, such that the vast majority of instances fall within our designated types, with only a low percentage falling into the miscellaneous category.[3] Being realistic, we guessed that it was unlikely that we would meet both our goals on this first run; more likely, this run will serve a diagnostic function, pointing to refinements and revisions that need to be made, and these changes would have to be tested in subsequent studies.

This methodology not only brings participants' instantiations to the surface, but it brings out the reasons that lie behind their judgments. Once their reasons emerge, we can more clearly see whether their conceptions of unfairness relate to violations of reciprocity, process, and fair play; whether they relate to violations about expected outcomes in terms of inputs; whether a moral basis, related to need, emerges; or whether their conceptions stem from some other basis we have not considered. Analyses of reasons, types of unfairness, and frequency of occurrence can give us a reading of whether participants blur "misfortunes" into "unfairnesses," a hypothesis and challenge we met a chapter ago. In addition, we are likely to find evidence on the petty whines claim, as outside, independent coders assess the participants' claims. Finally, we might find evidence for a primitive, childlike view of unfairness, a delusional just-world belief, perhaps, where participants want, expect, or even insist that life, nature, and other human beings be perfectly fair, consistent, and accurate, and to which the "who says?" advocate would intone, "I told you so."

RESULTS AND DISCUSSION

The 91 participants produced 423 instances of unfairness (4.6 instances/per participant), with wide variability from participant to participant (a range from 2 to 12 instances). This average number of instances (4.6) was sizable, despite the participants' average age of 20. However, note that this average is likely to be an underestimation of the actual number of unfairnesses in memory, for in this type of research, the participants select the instances they choose to write about, and there may well be instances that are too personal or too embarrassing, which they choose not to mention. Another indication that more instances could have been cited came in the form of many unsolicited comments from participants, telling us that they had no difficulty coming up with these instances, and some noted that they could have written about even more. These comments, and the self-selection of memories, suggest that the average number could be substantially higher. But since this is just the first study, with only college students as the participants, little will be made of either this average or the variability until further studies are run, with other age group samples, under similar testing situations.

Creating a Schema for Type of Unfairness

The completed booklets were then divided among four coders, who were instructed to read all the instances of unfairness in their assigned booklets, to identify what they perceived as the essence of the unfairness complaint, and to make notes on possible categories that might capture the experiences. The coders then met, common categories were noted, and a preliminary schema was shaped. The raters then switched booklets, trying their hand at categorizing a new set of instances with this preliminary schema; they were asked to note instances that did not fit in the preliminary categories, categories that seemed too broad or narrow, and categories that were missing and needed to be added. After this second go-round, a revised categorization schema was created, and coders switched booklets once more and then used this schema to categorize. The coders switched booklets a final time, so we had two independent codings of all the unfairness instances.

The schema had 11 specific categories plus a 12th miscellaneous category (A through L), and these specific categories were grouped into five overarching major categories (I through V). The first major category involved "the relationship between rewards (gains) and effort" (I), and it included the specific categories of when "wrongful behavior is rewarded" (I/A), when "unfair advantages or connections are rewarded" (I/B), when "no work is rewarded" (I/C), or when "hard work is not rewarded" (I/D). The second major category involved "differential or discriminatory treatment" (II) and included the specific categories of "when unequal treatment results when it should be equal treatment" (II/E) and when "equal or non-discriminatory treatment results when it should be individualized" (II/F). The third major category involved the "relationship between punishment (pain) and culpability or behavior" (III) and included the specific categories of when "good behavior or innocence is punished" (III/G), when "punishment is displaced onto one who either does not deserve the punishment at all, or does not deserve this severity of punishment" (III/H), when "punishment is disproportionate to the act and intent" (III/I), and when "wrongful behavior goes unpunished" (III/J). The fourth major category, "lack of due process" (IV), contained only the "life is arbitrary, or when people make arbitrary rules" (IV/K) specific category. Finally, a fifth major category, "items not categorizable above" (V), was the miscellaneous" (V/L) category. In addition to titles for the categories, we added defining sentences and examples for each category in order to assist the coder. The full schema is shown in Appendix 4A.

What the Major and Specific Categories Reveal

The first major category, "the relationship between rewards (gains) and effort" (I), is concerned with whether certain behaviors meet the standards or expectations for reward. In the specific categories, there are violations of the standards, as behaviors get rewarded when they should not (I/A, I/B, I/C) or fail to get rewarded when they should (I/D). These instances seem to fit closely with distributive justice's equity theory and with the just-world belief, because in these instances and theories, outcome expectancies are closely tied to inputs. Put in terms of the meanings to "fairness," this category seems to represent "fairness as outcome": if the good being rewarded and the bad being unrewarded represent fair distributions, then it would be unfair if the good are not rewarded or the bad are.

Whereas fairness as outcome is readily apparent in the categories, fairness as process seems absent. But appearances are deceiving, for fairness as process lies within these categories, though not plainly visible. To bring it to light, let us consider two very similar instances of "unfair advantages or connections are rewarded" (I/B). Two participants wrote about two different students who got into a prestigious university when they should not have, according to the participants, because they did not have the requisite grades and SAT scores: One student was the child of a faculty member, the other student was a minority applicant. Now, if both participants were focusing on the wrongful outcome (getting into school when they should not have), these would be typical fairness-as-outcome instances. As it turned out, though, one participant focused on process—that the university's admissions used impermissible criteria, or made special exceptions when they should not have—and thus the decision violates fairness-as-process.

To summarize, on the surface both instances appear basically the same, and they end up being housed in the same specific category. This category's defining tag seems outcome related, but that appearance can mask the fact that process unfairnesses are found there as well. When the two narratives are examined closely, one instance does turn out to be fairness as process, and we can easily differentiate the two instances because the participants' narratives were detailed and their foci were made clear. But when that clarity is missing in a narrative, how would we differentiate outcome from process? There is a diagnostic clue, which involves who or what they blame: When the instance is viewed as an outcome unfairness, the participant is typically angry at the one who got into the university but did not deserve to; on the other hand, when viewed as a process unfairness, the anger is directed at the one who makes the decision and unfairly bends the rules. This suggests that the variable blame, which is introduced in the next study, may help separate outcome from process unfairnesses.

Yet the main point is perspectival. Two unfairnesses that appear the same may in fact be quite different, depending on what the participant focuses on (e.g., outcome or process), whether the participant is weighing someone's actions against an internalized fairness standard, or whether the weighing is comparative, as to whether there is disparate treatment of the two individuals.[4] Multiple perspectives are fascinating, revealing the variability of participants' constructions, but they nonetheless create headaches for classifying.[5] Although this perspectival problem can lower reliability and increase the miscellaneous percentage, the emerging problem that we will have to solve is that of validity—is the category the correct one.[6]

Returning to the categories and what they reveal, we introduce the frequency data (see Table 4-1), where the number of instances cited by category, the percentages, and rankings of specific and major categories are shown. As expected, category III/G, "when innocence is punished" (the Job category), ranks high, although it ranks only second highest. The category that ranks first turns out to be II/E, "when unequal treatment results," which covers a very wide variety of discriminatory instances (e.g., where two people do essentially the same work, or have roughly equal credentials, but where one gets more, or less, without apparent justification). The discrimination may be based on factors such as race, ethnicity, gender, age, sexual orientation, looks, and socioeconomic class. As noted earlier, these instances can be viewed as an outcome unfairness, which many participants seem to do, or it can be viewed as unfair process, as some do. Thus in this major category II we find that while "outcome" appears the obvious reason for the unfairness, it may turn out to be an underlying process unfairness.

Category IV/K, "where life is arbitrary, or the rules are arbitrary," turns

TABLE 4-1
The Frequency of Occurrence (*N*), Percentage, and Rankings of the
Major (Roman Numerals) and Specific (Letters) Unfairness Categories

Major/Specific Categories	N	%	Specific/[Major] Rank	
I—Rewards to effort	108	25.5		[2]
A—Wrongful behavior rewarded	17	4.0	8	
B—Unfair advantages	43	10.2	5	
C—No work rewarded	12	2.8	10	
D—Hard work not rewarded	36	8.5	6	
II—Discriminatory treatment	89	21.0		[3]
E—Unequal treatment	83	19.6	1	
F—Equal treatment	6	1.4	12	
III—Punishment to behavior	129	30.5		[1]
G—Innocence punished	72	17.0	2	
H—Displaced punishment	31	7.3	7	
I—Disproportionate punishment	11	2.6	11	
J—Wrongful behavior unpunished	15	3.5	9	
IV/K—Lack of due process	50	11.8	3	[4]
V/L—Miscellaneous	47	11.1	4	[5]

out to be the third most frequently cited category, and these instances involve lack of due process. The rank of third is not insignificant, for process violations come readily to mind for the participants. Yet this category, alone, would underestimate the number of process claims, because as we have just seen, fairness-as-process shows up in other categories as well, categories that appear, on the surface, to be outcome categories.

Category III, involving punishment and culpable (or nonculpable) actions, ranks first in frequency. Perhaps punishment (when it is inappropriate, excessive, or is appropriate but fails to result), more so than reward rivets our attention and stays in memory as an unfairness; it is also likely that punishment, in comparison to reward, involves more harm and suffering, an element that may raise the theodicy question for some. Job's instance certainly falls within this category, as does Peter Pan's, for neither deserve the blows or the bite. Joining Job are some cases Job complained about, the bad who escape punishment. But *why* such instances fall here brings us to the participants' perspective once again, and the now familiar outcome versus process point: Some cite the unfair outcome, whereas others cite unfair adjudicative procedures—where criminals escape punishment because of technicalities, loopholes, change of venue, stacking the jury, high-priced defense teams, an incompetent judge, and the like. In fact, of the four major categories, only one (IV—lack of due process) involves process alone, whereas the other three (I—rewards to effort, II—discriminatory treatment, and III—punishment to behavior) involve both outcome and process, where an instance can go one way or the other depending on perspective.

CONSENSUS, DISAGREEMENT, AND NUANCE

We now look at these results in the light of theories of fairness and in the light of the critics' challenges. Equity and just-world beliefs are in evidence in the reward (25%) and punishment (30%) categories (I and III), where narratives reveal expectations about how, and on what basis, life's rewards and punishments should be distributed, and when participants find violations of those expectations, they apply the "but it's not fair" designation. Many of these equity or just-world expectations produce near consensus. To take one example, cheating is widely held to be wrong and worthy of punishment; so when it goes unpunished (III/J), or worse, gets rewarded (I/A), participants cry "unfair." The flip side of "wrongful behavior unpunished" are the Job-like cases of "innocence is punished" (III/G), and these show near consensus; in addition, these innocence punished narratives typically feature indignation, conviction, and moral certainty, as participants, like Job, are outraged about such treatment.

Although we are interested in areas of consensus, we are also interested in areas of disagreement and nuance, for the latter is also revealing. To understand consensus, disagreement, and nuance, the image of a category as a circle will help. In this analogy, most of the instances in any particular category lie near the center of the circle, and there we find near perfect consensus (between participant and independent coder) that the instance is an unfairness, and substantial agreement between the two coders as to its type category. In contrast, it is at the very edge of the category, or beyond its circumference, where consensus falters. To illustrate, take the category that involves those who do not work but who are rewarded nonetheless (I/C). With instances at the center, this work-ethic view garners broad support, as many would withdraw the reward from the lazy, the slacker, and the procrastinator if they could: Getting what is not earned is neither the American way nor the Biblical way, as sloth should not pay. Yet at the edges we have the case of a brilliant individual, who does very little studying, or of the gifted individual, who generates work effortlessly, quickly, and efficiently. To some participants, this is unfair, but not to some coders.

On the flip side of "no (or little) effort being rewarded" is the belief that rewards should follow effort (I/D). A frequently cited unfairness takes this form: "I studied 40 hours for that test (or really worked for weeks on that paper), but I didn't get a good grade." This extension of the work ethic is arguable, for we might well imagine a teacher, parent, or boss rejoining that it is not effort, but performance, that pays off. But let us continue this argument through a second go-round, where the claimant counters with, "I believe I did A-level work but I still did not get the A." In fact, we have instances of this sort. To continue, let us assume that what the student says is so: Perhaps the test was extraordinarily hard or unfair or the teacher was in a particularly picky mood when grading. In these examples, we discern an underlying expectation about evaluators (e.g., teacher, boss, parent, society, or God)—that they get it right! These claimants want evaluations to be just and true—each and every time. If this is the expectation whose violation triggers the claim, then it is unfair process that incites the ire.

Taking it further, this claim seems to rail against error variance per se. The claimant wants an orderly, predictable, and sensible world, where no mistakes result. This is unrealistic, for it expects evaluators to pick the good from the bad—the slackers from the hard workers—with 100% accuracy. Yet who has that kind of batting average? Perhaps it is this sort of claim and expectation that led Lerner to subtitle his work, "a fundamental delusion."[7] Perhaps this is also what leads some critics to question whether this is a child's lament.

Whether this is a developing delusion or a child's naivete there from the outset, we cannot say, for on the side of caution, we have yet to sample younger and older participants, and more college participants, to see if this finding recurs, and to what degree, and if age-group effects magnify or minimize it. In addition, we have not formally introduced blame into the analysis, as we will in the next study, which should shed new light on who or what is blamed and whether unreal expectations are evident. Thus for now what we can say is that we do see this lament in a small number of instances from our college-aged participants. The number is small, and far from a plurality opinion, which tells us that the vast majority of instances show no unreal expectations, and we do not find what the severest critics said we would find—a widespread delusional or childish wish for perfection.

Returning to the categories, similar sorts of unfairness were involved in "unfair advantages or connections were being rewarded" (I/B) and in "unequal rather than equal treatment" (II/E). When differential treatment was based on gender, race, or age, many cry "unfair," and coders concur. In categories I/B and II/E, we want justice to be blind to impermissible factors (extralegal factors) that should have no bearing on the adjudication, and thus we want what is engraved atop the Supreme Court—"equal justice under law." When rewards go to those with connections, money, or looks (i.e., factors deemed extralegal), these recipients have not earned it, and claimants cry "unfair."

Notice, though, that the principle that underlies these two categories turns out to be equality, not equity. Whether it is the formal authority of law or other authorities (e.g., boss, teacher, coach, or parent), they should treat us equally. Equity may come into the evaluation a step or two later, where a behavior is being evaluated that may lead to reward or punishment, but in the preceding categories the expectation is that all should stand equal before the evaluator. Here we have fairness as dignity, the equal worthwhileness of everyone, and this ethical aspect of fairness blends into the moral aspects of fairness.

There is also a flip-side category (II/F), where equal or nondiscriminatory treatment results, when we want Justice to take off her blindfold and make appropriate discriminations. Put another way, fairness ought to be individualized. For example, when a parent rewards both siblings equally when only one has done the work, or when a teacher gives the same grade to all seminar presenters when one did no work, or where all defendants, despite clear differences in their participation and culpability for the crime, are treated as fungible and given the same verdict and punishment as in accessory felony-murder cases, the cry of "unfair" is heard, because some individualized appraisal has not resulted when it should.[8]

Also in evidence in this category are instances involving those with special needs. When a student has a special handicap (learning disabled, blind, deaf), but the teacher refuses to give that individual more time on an exam, for example, this is unfair to participants. When a parent with a disability that does not prevent him from doing a job is not given the opportunity, the participant cries "unfair." When the lack of wheel chair ramps is all that prevents those with special needs to have equal access schools, jobs, housing, and so on, then this is seen as unfair, and the expense ought to be made, even when most, including the participant, will not directly profit from it. Thus this category seems to be where *need* is taken into account, going beyond the equity and equality categories we have discussed. Fairness as responding to the needy brings the moral aspect into the assessment.

Many of the instances of "unequal treatment" (II/E) are prototypic, and these generally lead to substantial agreement between claimants and coders that the instance is an unfairness; these prototypic instances also produce high interrater agreement between the two coders as to the appropriate category for the instance. Once again, it is the outlier instances that produce the disagreements. One such outlier that we saw in another category involved the brilliant student who did little or no work yet was rewarded. Other questionable examples maintain that the better-looking student who gets the guy or the gal or gets the job has an unfair advantage. A small number of participants extend looks, which are in some part inherited, to attributes such as height, weight, and athleticism, which have a significant inherited component.

It can be strongly argued that participants making these inherited inequality claims are either crossing the line from unfairnesses to misfortunes (i.e., blaming what cannot be blamed) or demanding an impossibility from nature and life. Nonetheless, a few seem to hold to these expectations, which can lead to some odd unfairness claims. For example, if I held to an unreal expectation about athleticism, would I have an unfairness complaint because I lacked the vertical leap to jump to the NBA and to have my feet land in a lucrative sneaker deal? Most would surely disagree with my claim, as the outside coders disagree with those few participants claiming inherited inequalities as an unfairness.

But there are nuances here that make the picture less black and white, and less absurd. For example, more than a few participants cited inherited birth defects as an unfairness, which may be coded under "unequal treatment" (II/E) or, more frequently, under "innocence punished" (III/G), where the child's life is severely limited. With these instances, inheritance is again the culprit, but now the coders generally agree that it is an unfairness. Some misfortunes, then, if that is what they are, may slide on that slippery slope, such that they are now regarded (or also regarded) as unfairnesses by some.

Overall, it seems that these outlier examples push the just world toward something of a uniform world, whereby the Declaration of Independence's "all men are created equal" is taken quite literally. If we take these expectations to their extreme, people would start life exactly equal—equal in terms of IQ, looks, height, weight, athleticism, health, and more; perhaps some would want to go beyond inherited physical dimensions and eliminate socioeconomic differences as well. In this new cosmology of no differences, we have a non-Darwinian starting line where neither variation nor natural selection are in the game, and where everyone is the same. This is a futuristic cloned world, but not our world, at least not yet. Still, a few participants are angry about inherited differences, enough so that they say that they lead to unfairness.

Turning to categories III/H (displaced punishment) and III/I (disproportionate punishment), both of which deal with punishment and its severity, we find that participants frequently endorse the rule of proportionality—where the one meting out punishment is supposed to weigh the criminal act and the intent in a culpability assessment (the input) and then fit the severity of the punishment (the outcome) to the culpability —such that equity results. In the abstract, the "rule" is easy to formulate, but in practice, it is not always easy to apply. To highlight the problematic, sometimes it is not clear who is meting out punishment or even whether "meting out" is apt. For example, as one participant noted, consider a drunk driver who crashes his car into another car and kills an innocent. Although the facts are clear, can it be said that the drunk driver is meting out punishment when he intended no harm? Similarly, there is a mother with AIDS, as a participant pointed out, whose baby suffers from AIDS and dies. Can it be said that the mother is meting out punishment? Although we may attribute culpability to the drunk driver and the AIDS mother for the lethal harm they do, there is nonetheless a troubling disparity between what they did and what they intended. In these instances, a judgment of displaced or disproportionate punishment may be contested.

LOOKING BACKWARD, LOOKING FORWARD

In looking back to the very beginning of this study, before the narratives were even written, we wondered what "commonsense unfairness" would look like. Would the concept of unfairness be a generic, undifferentiated catchall? In terms of our variable, would we find far fewer types of unfairness among our participants than the array philosophers conceive and social scientists research? On the other extreme, would we find so many idiosyncratic conceptions as to make categorizations unintelligible? As it turned out, neither extreme resulted.

We found 11 specific categories (setting miscellaneous aside), which housed 89% of the unfairnesses. Moreover, when the vast majority of instances that fell at the categories' center are examined, it is difficult to object to these as instances of unfairness. Said another way, nothing about these instances, or the 11 categories that house them, would support the criticisms that these claims are bogus. To the contrary, we found all of the meanings of fairness that philosophers have discussed and social scientists have researched, but with even more distinctions and nuances.

For specifics, we found fairness as process (fairness as reciprocity), the so-called first meaning of fairness, with variations and nuance. For example, many complain about an unfair standard, rule, or law, which seems wrong, bad, or unjust on its face, or they complain that the standard (be it right or wrong) has been arbitrarily set, without due process, such that either the bad law or the arbitrary law stacks the deck or tilts the playing field from the outset. In addition to fairness around the standard, there is also fair process in adjudication, in how the standards, rules, or laws are applied, or in how treatment is administered. There is also fairness as dignity, where all individuals (sovereigns) stand equal before the law, before any adjudication actually begins. Thus one's standing before the law, the law that is to govern, how that law was established, and the application of that law to the person, all reflect different aspects of fairness as process, and they are difficult to take issue with.

When we turn to fairness as outcome, "outcome" instances are numerous in every category (save IV/K—lack of due process). In these outcome instances, equity notions and expectations were evident, as were just-world beliefs. That outcomes ought to be related to inputs, such that the good (and those who follow the work ethic) ought to be rewarded and the bad ahould not, and that unfair advantages and discriminatory treatment should not determine rewards, are all evident. Moreover, equity notions go beyond their initial domain of distributive justice rewards to situations involving punishment. That the innocent should not be punished (III/G) and that wrongful behavior should not go unpunished (III/J) are the easy categories, but a rule of proportion, an equity rule of sorts, seems to govern

punishment per se, even when the latter is displaced (III/H) or disproportionate (III/I).

But equity's explanatory range, though broad, nonetheless falls short.
There is much that equity cannot account for. We also see in "equal treatment when it should be individualized treatment" (II/F) an aspect of fairness that relates to those in need—rather than our needs, our inputs, and
our self-interest. In doing "right" by those who are less fortunate, self-
interest is overruled as the determining motivation, being replaced by a
moral concern for the other, even if the specific outcome or broad social
policy actually costs us. In the category of "unequal treatment when it
should be equal" (II/E), it is equality, and not equity, that rules, with three
aspects of equality evident: as dignity before the law, as treatment under
the law, and as outcome from the law.

Moving to the broadest level, I highlight four key findings. The first
was that when we examine the vast majority of instances at the proverbial
center of each category, we see two types of agreement: an agreement between coder and participant that these instances are unfairnesses, and an
agreement between the two coders as to its type. Focusing on the first
agreement, coders are saying, in effect, "that we see these instances as
unfairnesses as well, that they are not bogus claims in our eyes." This
finding is not what the severest of critic would predict; rather, it strongly
contradicts the social critics' challenge that we examined (see chapter 1).
Such a critic might not be content with this interpretation, however, and
might argue that these coders share a bias (or delusion?) with participants,
since they come from the same environment and population. This "shared
delusion" notion, however, is an unlikely explanation, and one that is
contradicted by other data: If coders fully shared some delusion with the
participants, as the critics contend, then they would not disagree even at
the fringes, over the outliers, which they do.

Our second broad finding was that all of the meanings of fairness
were represented across the categories. In addition, these meanings revealed
finer nuances than we typically see in the philosophical and social science
literatures. If "commonsense unfairness" was idiosyncratic, quirky, bogus,
delusional, or highly distorted, these underlying concepts should either not
be found or not be this prevalent. Thus, although the philosophic, social
science, and commonsense positions on unfairness do not perfectly align,
they do comport to a fair degree.

Where they do not align is our third finding, where outlier instances
engender disagreements. Some outliers, around the brilliant or gifted or
beautiful person, raise questions about inheritance and arguable unfairness
claims about whether or not these traits are unfair advantages, and whether
the lack of such traits constitutes an unfairness, a misfortune, or neither.
With some of the outliers in the "hard work not rewarded" category, we
find confusion over effort and effective performance, disagreements over

standards of performance, and see unreal expectations regarding those doing the evaluations—that they get it right all the time. If some participants hold evaluators to an unreal standard of perfection, most participants will permit one-sided errors by the evaluator, as an example by a colleague of mine makes clear. Professors routinely hear from students when the students believe that their exam or paper was graded unfairly; yet most professors, even those on the job 20 or 30 years, are still waiting for a student to complain that his or her exam or paper was graded unfairly high, and we cannot report any such instance in this study. Thus it is in the small percentage of outliers, which occur in each category, where the critics have their best ammunition.

The fourth finding is that perspective matters. Two individuals can look at basically the same instance but focus on different unfairness aspects: One may focus on outcome, whereas the other focuses on process; one may focus on the perpetrator of the unfairness, the other may focus on the victim. Moreover, these different foci are likely to be related: Focusing on the perpetrator is more likely to lead to process unfairnesses, whereas focusing on the victim is more likely to lead to outcome unfairnesses. From perspectives on the instance to the categories that house them, we find that almost all the categories contain both process and outcome instances, and at this preliminary point, we cannot say with certainty whether participants focus more on distributive than procedural justice (i.e., whether there is an outcome bias), or vice versa. In fact, we cannot say that most claimants even make the outcome-versus-process distinction, for it is possible that their conceptions of unfairness may seamlessly blend the two.

In looking forward, there are issues that await further testing. In moving toward a second study, we certainly want to extend the age range of our participants, because based solely on this first study with college student participants, we cannot say whether these categories would capture the unfairness instances offered by older adults, seniors, or a tot-and-teen group, or whether different categories would have to be added. As the sample expands up and down in age, a host of new questions arise. Will we find that more categories are needed for the older population because their conceptions of unfairnesses are likely to be more varied, or do older participants need fewer categories because they "home-in" on the essence of the matter, no longer distracted by shadings? If the same categories did seem to work as we sampled higher and lower ages, would we find different distribution patterns across the categories for the different samples?

In looking forward, there is work to be done on the categorization schema. Based on two independent categorizations for every instance of unfairness in this study, we computed the interrater reliability, and although it (*Kappa* = .63) fell in the fair agreement range, it was less than what we hoped. In addition, too many (11.1%) instances fell in the miscellaneous category (L). The reliability and inclusiveness problems may mean that we need a new category or two, or need to combine some categories, or need clearer definitions for the categories overall. These problems have brought to light a third problem, that of validity.

To illustrate the problem and how we plan to address it, I turn to a children's book, "A Sesame Street Start-to-Read Book," aptly titled, *It's Not Fair!*[9] In the story, Ernie has an idea to sell lemonade and of course hooks Bert into the project. Bert ends up doing all the work, while Ernie makes messes and mistakes and slacks off. Yet it is Ernie who gets the praise in the end, and Bert gets none. Bert blows,

> "IT'S NOT FAIR!" Bert shouted. "I did all the work. I ALWAYS do all the work. Ernie makes a mess. Ernie makes mistakes. But he has all the fun. And everybody expects me to do everything." Then Bert burst into tears.

The story appears simple, until we try to code it into our type categories. Is Bert's unfairness claim that his "hard work was not rewarded" (I/D) when it should have been, or is his claim focused more on Ernie's "no work being rewarded" (I/C) when it should not have been? Is the claim a more comparative one, that "discriminatory treatment" (II/E or I/B) is resulting, or is the claim a process one, such that Ernie, once again, has not accorded him "due process" (IV/K)? Two outside coders may reliably agree about the appropriate category, but is this the category that Bert-the-victim would have picked? For that question, we would have to ask Bert, for he is in the best position to determine if the category chosen is valid or not. This, in essence, is the approach we will follow in Study 2 —to have the participant (the insider) be one of the coders.

Still, the "errors" between coders were not random across the categories; rather, certain categories were clearly creating the greatest difficulty, and this suggested making a number of modifications now. First, there was confusion between categories B and E, where unfair advantages are rewarded and where unequal treatment results: Coders reported that they could go either way with some instances, and too often they had difficulty discriminating the two. It was decided that these two categories would be combined. A second confusion resulted with categories H and I, where excessive punishment and punishment disproportionate to the act also proved difficult to discriminate; again, we decided to combine these two categories. These changes necessitated new major categories. Our second schema is shown in Appendix 4B.

Presentiment

Before turning to Study 2, we turn back to our exemplar Job, for the debate between Job and his three friends suggests where we are going. One classification of the type of unfairness that happened to Job is "innocence is punished," although Job and his friends disagreed about this: Job's friends saw it not as an unfairness at all, but rather as a punishment deserved. Apart from this disagreement, there was a second disagreement—over who was to blame. Job's answer was God; the friends' answer was Job himself. These entangled issues of type and blame need to be teased apart.

As we move to Study 2, blame will take center stage. It does so because from reading the unfairness instances of the participants in Study 1, it may be all but impossible for people to write about unfairnesses without the issue of blame arising.[10] If blame is situated at the heart of unfairness claims, as it was so for Job and his friends, then a more systematic analysis of blame appears warranted. There is still another reason for analyzing blame: Blaming others (while embracing one's victimization) has been a perennial criticism of unfairness claims in general, and this is an opportunity, once the data are in, to evaluate the criticism against the substance.

APPENDIX 4A

IT'S NOT FAIR! CATEGORIZATION SCHEMA

Major categories are designated by roman numerals; specific categories are designated by capital letters. For each account of an unfairness, put both the roman numeral (for the major category) and the letter (for the specific category) that you believe best categorizes this instance.

I—THE RELATIONSHIP BETWEEN REWARDS (GAINS) AND EFFORT

It is unfair when . . .

A. Wrongful Behavior Is Rewarded

Here, the reward should not be forthcoming, because the person used illegal, unethical, or immoral means to get it. Here, there is an underlying view that rewards, whether they come from people or life, should not go to those who cheat at the game of life (e.g., one who cheats on a test and gets an A; one who lies on his resume and gets the job).

B. Unfair Advantages or Connections Are Rewarded

Here, such things as looks, money, knowing someone, family connections, and so on are seen as unfair advantages or unfair connections, for they are not earned. Also included are "affirmative action" cases where rewards go to an individual or group based on a status factor. The rewards of life should be doled out based on legitimate factors—namely, earning it (e.g., someone who gets into a school, club, or job because of such an unfair advantage).

C. No Work Is Rewarded

Here, the reward should not be forthcoming because the person did not have to work for it. The underlying view, based on a work ethic, is that rewards should be directly proportional to the effort expended. When people do not work, they should not get life's rewards (e.g., the student who does not study but gets an A; the worker who does not do the work but gets the promotion or raise).

D. Hard Work Is Not Rewarded

Here, the belief is that when you make the effort people or life should reward you, each and every time. There should be a proportional relation between work and reward (e.g., the student who really studies but does not get the high grade).

II—DIFFERENTIAL OR DISCRIMINATORY TREATMENT (INVOLVES A COMPARISON BETWEEN PEOPLE OR GROUPS OF PEOPLE)

E. Unequal Treatment Results When It Should Be Equal (equal protection or blind justice, along with the Golden Rule)

Here, the belief is that treatment, be it rewards or punishments, should be equivalent and not different. Differences based on gender, race, age, and so on are discriminatory and unfair. There should be equal protection of all. Not only should groups be treated equally, but individuals should be treated equally as well. For example, a roommate should not use, rip off, or take advantage of the goodness of the other roommate, but ought to treat the roommate as the roommate treats him or her—a "do unto others as they would do unto you" perception of fairness. This includes situations where one person is selfish or inconsiderate, threatening another in an unfair way (e.g., when parents treat siblings differently; gender discrimination; racial discrimination; two people follow the same diet but one loses more weight; one roommate never cleans up his or her messes, leaving it for the other to do; even in matters of love, there is love unrequited, when one loves another but the feelings are not mutual and equal).

F. Equal or Nondiscriminatory Treatment Results When It Should Be Individualized and Different (justice not blind, but seeing the individual and making the just discriminations)

Here, people are treated equally when, for example, the guilt is not equal. Instead of individualized treatment, people are treated as fungible (e.g., siblings are given the same reward or punishment, when different treatment would be fair; the whole class is punished when John did the talking; one worker puts out greater effort than coworker but both are given the same raise; two siblings are given the same curfew even though there is an age difference).

III—RELATIONSHIP BETWEEN PUNISHMENT (PAIN) AND CULPABILITY OR BEHAVIOR

G. Good Behavior or Innocence Is Punished

Here, the belief exists that the "not guilty" should not be punished. Thus innocent people ought not to suffer. Pain and punishment not warranted. Also here, the individual does the right thing, takes the proper precautions, yet pain and punishment strike anyway. When it comes to the pain other people inflict on the subject, this seems to involve being taken advantage of, being used by others, being ripped off, others being inconsiderate or selfish: here, though, the focus is on the "good one" getting unfairly punished and not on the comparative inequality (e.g., life's random illnesses, deaths, etc. when the person does not deserve it; punishing the innocent; poverty and malnutrition inflicted on innocent people; child abuse; getting sick despite taking good care; cancer despite not smoking and eating right; getting pregnant despite taking precautions; getting ripped off by others; doing the right thing, but others take advantage; roommates take advantage; getting punished despite doing the right thing.

H. Punishment Is Displaced Onto One Who Either Does Not Deserve the Punishment at All or Does Not Deserve This Severity of Punishment

Here, punishment that should go to the person most deserving of it gets displaced onto another. The negligent actions of others bring one undeserved pain (e.g., the AIDS baby who suffers for the behavior, choices, sins of the mother; the less deserving sibling gets punished for what the other did; accessories getting the same punishment as the principle; punishing the (innocent) class for the actions of one student; a drunk driver causes harm to an innocent).

I. The Punishment Is Disproportionate to the Act and Intent

Here, there is some guilt, but the punishment is excessive to the crime (e.g., harsh punishments; felony-murder-like situation where the one who accidentally kills is punished as harshly as one who premeditates and kills; being kicked out of a dorm for one beer).

J. Wrongful Behavior Goes Unpunished

Here, the person "gets away with it"—but should not. The one who cheats, or does the dirty deed or crime, goes unpunished. As rewards should follow good behavior, punishment should follow wickedness (e.g., student cheats and does not get caught).

IV—LACK OF DUE PROCESS

K. Life Is Arbitrary, or When People Make Arbitrary Rules

Here, the person has no control, as when one is the youngest rather than the oldest, or when parents make rules that seem unfair and non-negotiable. There seems to be a lack-of-due-process complaint here (e.g., being subject to other people's [parents'] rules, which are judged unrealistic, yet they remain inflexible).

V—ITEMS NOT CATEGORIZABLE ABOVE

L. Miscellaneous

Score under this category any instances of unfairness that do not fit in any of the preceding categories.

APPENDIX 4B

IT'S NOT FAIR! CATEGORIZATION SCHEMA

Major categories are designated by roman numerals; specific categories are designated by capital letters. For each account of an unfairness, put both the roman numeral (for the major category) and the letter (for the specific category) that you believe best categorizes this instance.

I—THE RELATIONSHIP BETWEEN REWARDS (GAINS) AND EFFORT)

In this major category, the judgment of unfairness typically involves an evaluation of the actions and efforts of a single person against some standard of fairness. Here, people or life seem to reward someone for actions that do not deserve reward, or people or life fail to reward someone who truly deserves reward. Thus this category involves reward (whether it is given or fails to be given) in relation to a person's effort (not deserving or deserving).

It is unfair when . . .

A. Wrongful Behavior Is Rewarded

Here, the reward should not be forthcoming, because the person used illegal, unethical, or immoral means to get it. Here, there is an underlying view that rewards, whether they come from people or life, should not go to those who cheat at the game of life (e.g., one who cheats on a test and gets an A; one who lies on his resume and gets the job).

B. No Work Is Rewarded

Here, the reward should not be forthcoming, because the person did not work for it. The underlying view, based on a work ethic, is that rewards should be directly proportional to the effort expended. When people do not work, they should not get life's rewards (e.g., the student who does not study but gets an A; the worker who does not do the work gets the promotion or raise).

C. Hard Work Is Not Rewarded

Here, the belief is that when you make the effort people or life should reward you. There should be a proportional relation between work and reward (e.g., the student who really studies but does not get the high grade;

the person who makes high grades but does not get into medical, law, or graduate school).

II—RELATIONSHIP BETWEEN PUNISHMENT (PAIN) AND CULPABILITY OR BEHAVIOR

In this major category, the judgment of unfairness again involves an evaluation of the actions and efforts of a single person against some standard of fairness. Here, people or life seem to punish someone for actions that do not deserve punishment, or people or life fail to punish someone who truly deserves punishment. Thus this category involves punishment (whether it is given or fails to be given) in relation to a person's effort (not deserving or deserving).

D. Good Behavior or Innocence Is Punished

Here, the belief exists that the "not guilty" should not be punished. Thus innocent people ought to suffer not. Also here, the individual does the right thing, takes the proper precautions, yet pain and punishment strike anyway. When it comes to the pain other people inflict on the subject, this seems to involve being taken advantage of, being used by others, being ripped off, others being inconsiderate or selfish, though the focus is on the "good one" getting unfairly punished and not the comparative inequality (e.g., life's random illnesses, deaths, etc., when the person does not deserve it; punishing the innocent; the AIDS baby; poverty and malnutrition inflicted on innocent people; child abuse; getting sick despite taking good care; cancer despite not smoking and eating right; getting pregnant despite taking precautions; a drunk driver killing an innocent; getting ripped off by others; doing the right thing, but others take advantage; roommates take advantage; punished despite doing the right thing).

E. The Punishment Is Disproportionate or Excessive to the Act and Intent

Here, there is some guilt, but the punishment is excessive to the crime (e.g., harsh punishments; felony-murder-like situation where the one who accidentally kills is punished as harshly as one who premeditates and kills; being kicked out of a dorm for one beer; a teacher fails student because the paper was one day late; a parent grounds the child for a week for not straightening his or her room).

F. Wrongful Behavior Goes Unpunished

Here, the person "gets away with it"—but should not. The one who cheats, or does the dirty deed or crime, goes unpunished. As rewards should follow good behavior, punishment should follow wickedness (e.g., student cheats and does not get caught).

III—DIFFERENTIAL OR DISCRIMINATORY TREATMENT (INVOLVES A COMPARISON BETWEEN PEOPLE OR GROUPS OF PEOPLE)

Here, people are either treated differently when they ought to be treated alike, or people are treated alike when they legitimately ought to be treated differently.

G. Unfair Advantages or Connections Are Rewarded When Justice Should Be Blind and Equal Protection Ought to Hold

Here, when rewards are based on such things as looks, money, knowing someone, family connections, gender, race, and so on these are seen as unfair advantages or unfair connections because they are not earned. Also included here are "affirmative action" cases where rewards go to an individual or group based on a status factor. The rewards of life should be doled out based on legitimate factors—namely, earning it (e.g., someone who gets into a school, a club, a job, because of one of these unfair advantages; when parents treat siblings differently; gender discrimination; racial discrimination; two people follow the same diet but one loses more weight; one roommate never cleans up his or her messes, leaving it for the other to do; even in matters of love, there is love unrequited, when one loves another but the feelings are not mutual and equal).

H. Equal or Nondiscriminatory Treatment Results When It Should Be Individualized and Different (justice not blind, but seeing the individual and making the just discriminations)

Here, people are treated equally when, for example, the guilt is not equal. Instead of individualized treatment, people are treated as fungible (e.g., siblings are given the same reward or punishment when different treatment would be fair; whole class is punished when John did the talking; one worker puts out greater effort than coworker but both are given the same raise; two siblings are given the same curfew even though there is an age difference).

IV—LACK OF DUE PROCESS

Here, the focus is not on the outcome, which may be fair or unfair, but on the process—how things were decided or done—and whether the person felt she got "her day in court" or whether she felt she did not get a fair shake.

I. Life Is Arbitrary, or When People Make Arbitrary Rules

Here, the person has no control, as when one is the youngest rather than the oldest, or when parents make rules that seem unfair and non-negotiable. There seems to be a lack-of-due-process complaint here (e.g., being subject to other people's [parents'] rules, which are judged unrealistic, yet they remain inflexible; student gets thrown out of school without a fair hearing; parents punish without even listening to the child).

V—ITEMS NOT CATEGORIZABLE ABOVE

J. Miscellaneous

Score under this category any instances of unfairness that do not fit in any of the preceding categories.

ENDNOTES

1. H. S. Kushner, *When Bad Things Happen to Good People* (New York: Avon Books, 1981).
2. If, contrary to our goal, low reliability results, this could mean that the category definitions are imprecise, or that some categories overlap and are really one category, or that a category may be missing from the schema.
3. If, contrary to our goal, the miscellaneous percentage is high, this could mean that our designated types are too vague and poorly differentiated from one another, or the schema is missing a category or two.
4. That perspective matters has been known and developed in various "story models." Jurors, for example, focus on the central act, the crime, and the central actor, trying to weave facts and inferred motives into a coherent story. *See, e.g.*, W. L. Bennett and M. S. Feldman, *Reconstructing Reality in the Courtroom: Justice and Judgment in American Culture* (New Brunswick, NJ: Rutgers University Press, 1981). If our participants focus on different actors, or different actions, it would not be surprising that stories similar on the surface would be dissimilar at base.
5. To classify accurately and reliably, we need to know the participant's perspective (or vantage point or focus), which may not be clear from the narrative.

In addition, any diagnostic help that we might get from who or what they blame may not be there, for "blaming facts" may also be absent from the narrative. As a further complication, if coders are in doubt as to the most appropriate category, they may reach for the miscellaneous category, a catchall waste basket. These problems work against our goals of developing a reliable and inclusive schema.

6. To illustrate validity and distinguish it from reliability, consider two coders agreeing with one another almost all the time, such that they place most of the instances in exactly the same categories and use the miscellaneous category sparingly (and for the same few instances). If this occurred, we would obtain high interrater reliability and inclusiveness. But now consider the possibility that a fair number of their codings turn out to be wrong, even though the coders agree with one another. In judging whether the coders' classifications are right or wrong, let us assume that we had the participants who wrote the instances making the judgment, and where these participants say, in effect, "I didn't mean that, I meant something else, a different type of unfairness." Where reliability involves the agreement between coders, validity refers to the accuracy of the categorizations, and we would certainly like our categorizations to be accurate. In future studies, we will add validity as a goal along with reliability and inclusiveness.

7. M. Lerner, *The Belief in a Just World: A Fundamental Delusion* (New York: Plenum Press, 1980).

8. N. J. Finkel, *Commonsense Justice: Jurors' Notions of the Law* (Cambridge: Harvard University Press, 1995).

9. D. Hautzig, *It's Not Fair!* (Illustrated by T. Leigh, featuring Jim Henson's Sesame Street Muppets) (New York: Random House/Children's Television Workshop, 1986).

10. K. G. Shaver, *The Attribution of Blame: Causality, Responsibility, and Blameworthiness* (New York: Springer-Verlag, 1985).

5

WHO OR WHAT DO WE BLAME
FOR UNFAIRNESSES?

When something bad happens to one who is innocent, we can predict how just-world believers may reconcile this dissonance: by making the innocent blameworthy. Even when there are no outsiders to do the blaming, victims may blame themselves, transforming self-doubts into self-blaming conclusions: "Did I do enough?" "Did I do wrong?" "Did I unconsciously want this to happen?" Self-blame is not far-fetched, for a literature on rape trauma syndrome has documented that some victims do come to blame themselves,[1] and similar findings occur for battered women's syndrome.[2] On an even broader level, understood by parents and therapists alike, is the often seen phenomenon of children blaming themselves for the divorce of their parents.

Whatever the mode—be it others blaming or self-blame—the effects of blame may turn the matter topsy-turvy, making victims into villains and making the unsettling dissonance of a just world seem all right. These are profound, prestidigitation effects for blame, but it does not end there. Blame may transform an event that is not initially considered an unfairness into one, or the reverse transformation might occur, where an event initially considered unfair becomes "not an unfairness"— when blame enters the game. Either way the transformation goes, the link between blame and unfairness is obviously a close and sometimes determinative one. Perhaps this is a reason why social critics of unfairness frequently cite blame in the same sentence.

Still, blame's effects on the story of unfairness are even greater than just described. It can affect the participant's perspective on the instance and how he or she judges the instance. If, through blame, perspective is altered, this may shift the unfairness from one type category to another. Even if the type category remains the same, the shift of perspective will give the unfairness a different focus and meaning. Taking all of the above together, the justification for adding blame to the analysis is obvious. Said another way, had we omitted blame from the unfairness picture, something crucial would be missing.

Overall, blame seems to be a constant in unfairness claims. This was how the coders in Study 1 saw it, for it appeared to them that blame was ubiquitous and endemic to unfairness, regardless of their type categorization. Yet these are the coders' impressions, a general sense of things; they are not careful and systematic observations that result from any coding or classifying of blame.

To do a systematic analysis, we had to create a categorization schema for *who* or *what* is to blame, one that would be reliable and inclusive. We did not have to look far to find our first two items for the blame schema, as The Book of Job gave us the individual (e.g., Job) and God. Although these two are of considerable interest, we nonetheless expected that they would be cited infrequently. Our expectations come from Study 1, where God was blamed in only a small fraction of the unfairnesses, almost all falling in one specific category, "innocence punished." In addition, narratives where the participant blamed the individual at the center of the unfairness, or blamed himself or herself (individual/self), were even rarer than blaming God. Although it is possible that we might find a higher percentage of God and Self citings in the bigger and broader sample we plan to use here, it was clear that we needed to round up the more usual suspects and extend the list.

From many citings in Study 1, there were numerous people who acted unfairly and inflicted suffering (human agency); this is a large group that needed to be broken down more finely. In addition there were impersonal sources, such as inheritance, nature, and life (impersonal agency), which also showed frequently in study 1. This human versus impersonal division leads to some predictions. For human agency instances, we would expect the Jobian theodicy problem to be moot.[3] If God is going to be blamed, it is more likely for the impersonal agency instances (e.g., natural disasters, unexplained deaths). If it turns out that a minority of participants do take a Jobian view on these natural disasters and blame God, they have the troubling theodicy issue to deal with, and these unfairnesses have to be reconciled somehow. On the other hand, if a majority of participants see these instances in a secular way, then they are close if not identical to misfortunes, and these participants need to explain why they are calling them unfairnesses.

Our goal for an inclusive schema was particularly challenging in this Study 2, because the participants' ages ranged from 4 to 60; we had a tot-to-teen group (4–17), a college group, and an adult group (30–60). We wanted items that would be inclusive for each age group, yet we wanted broader categories so that we could compare groups. Because all participants had parents (parents), this was a natural category that spans the age groups. We also included a separate category for people in authority (excluding parents), such as teachers, bosses, coaches. Whereas a particular item, like coaches, would not be used much by adults, and though an item like bosses would not be used much by tots and teens, both represent someone in authority, and in that way comparisons among groups can be made. We also included categories for equals, such as siblings, friends, spouses, and romantic significant others, along with the individual/self category. We had categories for "underlings," such as children. Going in the direction of greater authority, a collective authority, society became a category, which included the government and its agencies and representatives. Moving toward the impersonal, we had that category representing life, nature, or heredity, and at the transcendent level, the God category.

Although the specific categories (see Appendix 5A) for blame are numerous (11 categories), and many will be grouped when doing the analyses, we decided to be detailed at first, so as not to omit possibilities. By using this schema, we can ask (and answer) a series of questions. Is the ubiquity of blame really so, and if so, who or what do participants blame? Do we blame parents, as an all-too-obvious pop psychology prediction would have it? Or do we blame anyone in authority, or over 30, as a generation once had it? Is blame aimed even higher, at the collective we call society, or do we aim squarely at ourselves? Do we blame impersonal factors, or the transcendent God, and do we blame misfortunes— that which cannot be blamed but which are nonetheless transformed into unfairnesses?

In this study, blame is the key variable we add to our type variable, but it is not the only new variable added in this study. We will be testing three age groups: a new student group (S), a tot and teen group (T), and an adult group (A). Finally, we added a severity variable, where we ask all of the participants, after completing the booklet, to rate the severity of each unfairness.

We also have a number of questions that involve interactions: blame × type, and blame × age group, and blame × type × age group. We expect that who or what is blamed varies by the type of unfairness, although we do not know specifically how this will display. We also expect that who or what is blamed will significantly vary by the age group, for it seems reasonable that adults will focus their blame differently than tots and teens.

But how different will it be? Also, because different age groups are likely to experience and cite different types of unfairness (type × age group), and if differences there produce different blame patterns, we ought to see a blame × type × age group effect. But what sort of patterns will show?

The data, and the way they are analyzed, are likely to shed light on the accusations of many social critics regarding a culture of blaming, victimology, narcissism, and more. In addition, by using a severity rating for unfairnesses, we may be able to provide a more substantive assessment of the petty whines challenge. By connecting blame with type of unfairness, we can see to what extent blurring misfortunes into unfairnesses occurs.

STUDY 2

Participants were divided into three groups: college students (S), an adult group (A), and a tot and teenage group (T), and all came from the same family or extended family.[4] Although this was not a random sample (i.e., it was more female, more Catholic, and more highly educated), having participants from the same family, culture, and socioeconomic group where religion was likely to be similar and with arguably similar values, allowed us to hold some variables fairly constant and afforded us the opportunity to study type of unfairness and blame by age group.

The research booklet added a new dependent variable, severity.[5] When the booklet was completed, the students (S) then received the categorization schema for type of unfairness and for who or what is to blame, and they had to designate both type and blame for each instance of unfairness.[6] Regarding the adult (A) and tot and teen (T) participants,[7] when they finished their booklets, the student participant used the categorization schema to code type and blame for each unfairness instance for both the A and T subjects. To get a second rating of type and blame for the S, A, and T groups, independent coders were used.[8]

RESULTS AND DISCUSSION

The 175 participants generated 1159 instances of unfairness, or more than 6.2 instances per participant.[9] As in Study 1, the concept of "unfairness" and its instantiations came readily to mind, and here that was true for all age groups. As expected, there were age group differences in the average number of instances, though the differences did not order neatly by age: Rather, the S group averaged the most instances, 8.0; the A group produced the next most, 6.5 instances; and the T group produced the fewest instances, 4.8.[10] If the number of unfairnesses had been a direct function of age, we would expect the highest average from the A group, because they have lived more than twice as long as the S group. It obviously was not. But why was the average number for the A group not higher?

One possibility is that the adult participants were less motivated or less patient with this task. But this hypothesis fails to explain why we see so many instances (6.5 on the average) and so many pages filled with detailed accounts. A second possibility is that unfairnesses are forgotten, contradicting Barrie's assertion that "no one ever gets over the first unfairness." But this hypothesis is contradicted by the finding that many of the adults cited instances from their childhood years. A third possibility is a Peter Pan–like one: that new unfairnesses crowd out the old so that only recent ones come to mind. But again, a recency explanation is contradicted by the many early unfairness experiences cited.

There is still another possibility: perhaps our perspective on unfairnesses changes as we age. This hypothesis argues that our subjective conceptions alter with experience, such that instances we once regarded as unfair (at earlier ages) now seem less so or not at all (in the gloaming). If, to use an analogy, age acts as it does on wine, then we become discriminating connoisseurs of unfairness, so to speak, no longer willing to cast some gripes as grapes. If our conceptions do change, we are likely to reconstrue the meanings and boundaries we give to the type categories, dilating some while constricting others. If this hypothesis has validity, we might find evidence for it in the type × age group analysis.

Specific Type Distribution

The distribution of these instances across the revised schema type categories is shown in Table 5-1. There are significant differences among age groups,[11] and with further testing we find that the A and S groups (not significantly different from one another) are both significantly different from the T group. Looking across age group, we find that categories D (innocence punished) and G (discriminatory treatment) are cited most frequently, which is consistent with what we found in Study 1. If we look only at the S group (since there was only an S group in Study 1), we find evidence of replication, as the four categories that are cited most frequently in Study 2 were the same most frequently cited categories in Study 1.

When looking at the type patterns for the age groups, we see categories that are cited more frequently with age, some that are cited less frequently with age, and some that stay the same. For the arbitrary rules, due-process category (I), this is one that grows less frequent with age: It is cited most frequently by the T group, but its rate drops by half for the S and A groups. The explanation seems obvious: It is the youngsters who chaff most under arbitrary rules, as they have more arbitrary rules placed

TABLE 5-1
The Number and Percentage of Unfairness Instances by Category for the Adult (A), Student (S), and Tot and Teen (T) Groups

	Groups								
	A		S		T		Totals	
Major/Specific Categories	n	%	n	%	n	%	n	%
I.A—Wrongful rewarded	14	3.4	27	5.2	4	1.8	45	3.9
I.B—No work rewarded	18	4.4	20	3.8	9	4.0	47	4.1
I.C—Hard work not	39	9.4	62	11.9	14	6.3	115	9.9
II.D—Innocence punished	102	24.7	116	22.2	31	13.9	249	21.5
II.E—Disproportionate	8	1.9	23	4.4	8	3.6	39	3.4
II.F—Wrongful unpunished	24	5.8	30	5.7	7	3.1	61	5.3
III.G—Discriminatory	83	20.1	110	21.0	52	23.3	245	21.1
III.H—Equal treatment	12	2.9	27	5.2	5	2.2	44	3.8
IV.I—Arbitrary rules	59	14.3	63	12.1	53	23.8	175	15.1
V.J—Miscellaneous	54	13.1	45	8.6	40	17.9	139	12.0
Totals	413	35.6	523	45.1	223	19.2	1159	100

on them. Two categories that show constancy across the age groups are categories G (discriminatory treatment) and B (no work rewarded).

Our greatest interest, though, were categories that increased with age, and category D (innocence punished) was one. Previously, we called this the Job category (for its most notable exemplar), and we also found this category to be closely linked with that aspect of the just-world view for which a consensus occurs. But the category is also the repository of impersonal agency instances, where misfortunes, if they are to be miscast as unfairnesses, will show up. The fact that the A group cites this category slightly more frequently than the S group and almost twice as frequently as the T group could mean that with age we increasingly see impersonal agency cases as unfairnesses. On the other hand, it could mean that we grow more sensitized and upset by just-world infractions when human agents do the inflicting. At this point, we cannot distinguish, because this type category mixes and confounds human agency and impersonal agency instances.

The picture may sort out if we move to categories without this confound and where the rate increases with age. There are three such categories: A (wrongful rewarded), F (wrongful unpunished), and C (hard work not rewarded), where the A and S groups cite these at almost twice the rate of the T group. These categories reflect just-world and equity violations, and these seem to grow stronger with age, such that violations are more vexing.

If we put these dilating or constricting effects together, the results do add support for the notion of perspectival changes with experience that produce threshold or salience changes for certain types of unfairness. For example, if we make a reasonable assumption—that the A and S subjects were exposed in their childhoods to roughly the same number of arbitrary rules unfairnesses as our T group—then the drop for the A and S groups to half the rate of the T group could indicate that these experiences no longer fit a category that has constricted. In the other direction, our conceptions seem to dilate around certain types of unfairness, becoming more sensitized and attuned to punishment cases generally and particularly when the innocent are punished or the bad escape punishment or, worse, get rewarded.

A few findings relate to our schema and the goals of validity, reliability, and inclusiveness. One finding is an age group difference regarding the miscellaneous category, with the S group showing significantly lower usage. This is likely the result of having members of the S group categorizing their own instances, making it easier for them to find the valid category, whereas outsiders did the coding for the A and T groups; in addition, the T group tended to write the briefest narratives, which gave the coders the greatest difficulty, which may have caused them to use the miscellaneous category when they had little to go on, producing the highest usage of that category. We then tested the reliability of the coding, and while interrater reliability slightly improved over Study 1, it was still in the fair range,[12] and not yet what we had hoped. Moreover, there were age group differences, with reliability being higher for the S and T groups than for the A group. Had it been higher only for the S group, we would have attributed this to the insider factor (i.e., that the S participants were one of the coders), but the T group was also higher than A, and outside raters were used for both groups.

Finally, there is the issue of individual variability, which I can make clear through a question. If a participant gives eight unfairness instances, do all eight fall within the same type category, or does the participant cite unfairnesses from different type categories, showing variability and thus a variety of conceptions of unfairness? The latter occurs. In fact, it is extremely rare to find an S, A, or T participant who only serves up instances from just one category. At the group level, the average number of type categories cited for the A, S, and T groups was 3.4, 4.4, and 1.9, respectively, but these results are a bit deceiving because the S group gave the most instances and the T group the least. When we compute separate ratios for the A, S, and T groups, where the number of different type categories cited is the numerator and the total number of instances given is the denominator, the resultant fractions for the three groups are .67 (A), .66 (S), and .58 (T). Interpreting, it does seem that the two older groups see or express more types of unfairnesses. But still, even at our tot and teen level, there is variation, as the youngest of participants recognize different types of unfairness.

Who or What Is to Blame Categories

In our blame schema, we started with 11 categories. Although 5 of those categories (e.g., bosses—B, parents—P, life—L, society—S, and equals—E) were frequently cited by all three groups, some categories were either infrequently cited overall (underlings—U, God—G, family/siblings —F, and the individual—I), or were so differentially cited (child—C was cited only by the A group; romantic significant other—R was cited mainly for the A and S groups), that statistical tests could not be legitimately run. Therefore, we combined categories.[13]

We analyzed the blame pattern for age groups and found large significant differences.[14] The frequency and percentage of blame citings by age group are presented in Table 5-2, and some trends are discernible. For instance, Parents (P) are blamed most by the T group and least by the S and A groups; this difference is great, with the T group blaming parents four times more frequently than the other groups. Perhaps unfairnesses blamed on parents are forgiven with age, or the category constricts, or both. On the other side, society (S) was blamed more with age, ranking first for the A and S groups, but ranking only third for the T group. Similarly, though the effect is smaller, A and S groups blame equals (E) slightly more than the T group. Finally, the categories of bosses (B) and life (L) seem constant over the age span.

There were no significant differences by gender overall, or at each of the age ranges. There was a significant difference by religion, which is shown in Table 5-3. All three religious groups blame society the most, with Jewish participants having the highest percentage. "Life" ranks second for the Jewish participants (28%) and ranks third for Catholics and Protes-

TABLE 5-2
The Number and Percentage of Citings for the Blame Categories by Group

| Blame Categories | Groups | | | | | |
| | A | | S | | T | |
	n	%	n	%	n	%
B—Bosses	71	17.4	116	22.1	43	18.7
E—Equals/underlings	79	19.4	107	20.4	36	15.7
L—Life	75	18.4	103	19.7	40	17.4
P—Parents	27	6.6	41	7.8	70	30.4
S—Society	156	38.2	157	30.0	41	17.8
Totals	408		524		230	

TABLE 5-3
The Number and Percentage of Blame Instances by Religion

| Blame Categories | Religion | | | | | |
| | Catholic | | Jewish | | Protestant | |
	n	%	n	%	n	%
B—Bosses	134	20.8	18	14.5	42	16.8
E—Equals/underlings	119	18.5	13	10.5	56	22.4
L—Life	122	19.0	35	28.2	45	18.0
P—Parents	67	10.4	12	9.7	38	15.2
S—Society	201	31.3	46	37.1	69	27.6

tants. Catholics blame bosses more than the other two religious groups, and Protestants and Catholics blame equals more than do Jewish participants, whereas Protestants blame parents the most. Recalling that there was no significant difference by religion when it came to type of unfairness, we now find a significant difference when it comes to blame. Why this is so remains speculative. It may turn out to have little to do with religious denomination, and more to do with one's theological and cosmological views or perspectives we have yet to tap.

Major Categories of Type of Unfairness × Blame

What we were most interested in analyzing was the relationship between type and blame.[15] The analysis shows significant differences across the groups.[16] The results are presented in Table 5-4. Looking first by type, in major category I (relating rewards to efforts), people blame bosses the most, followed by equals and society, with parents the least. When it comes to punishments (II), it is life closely followed by society that are blamed the most, with parents again blamed the least. For discriminatory treatment

TABLE 5-4
The Number and Percentage Citing Who or What Is to Blame
by Type of Unfairness

| Blame Categories | Type of Unfairness Categories | | | | | | | |
| | I— Rewards | | II— Punishments | | III— Discrimination | | IV— Due Process | |
	n	%	n	%	n	%	n	%
B—Bosses	67	33.2	46	13.5	62	21.7	32	18.5
E—Equals	49	24.3	69	20.2	39	13.6	17	9.8
L—Life	33	16.3	100	29.2	34	11.9	21	12.1
P—Parents	7	3.5	30	8.8	32	11.2	44	38.9
S—Society	46	22.8	97	28.4	119	41.6	59	34.1

(III), society is blamed almost twice as frequently as bosses. For lack of due process (IV), parents and society are blamed first and second most frequently.

Looking at the same results by blame, bosses are mainly involved when the rewards are not fairly distributed, when discriminatory treatment results, and when arbitrary rules are made. Equals are cited most frequently for the reward and the punishment types of unfairness. Life is blamed largely when the punishments are perceived as unfair. Parents dominate the lack of due-process unfairnesses. Society is cited in all categories quite frequently, but particularly so when discriminatory treatment is perceived.

We know from our earlier analyses that there are age group (A, S, T) differences by type of unfairness and by blame. We now tested for type × blame by age group differences and found significant differences,[17] and these are presented in Table 5-5.[18] It is clear that blaming parents declines with age but blaming society increases. Adults seem to forgive their parents for their arbitrary rules and lack of due-process unfairnesses; students also forgive, but to a lesser degree than other adults, whereas tots and teens forgive the least. Yet there is a countervailing trend with society, which is blamed more for lack of due process (arbitrary rules) and discriminatory treatment cases as the participant's age increases.

TABLE 5-5
The Blame Percentages for the A, S, and T Groups,
by Each Type of Unfairness

Blame Categories/Group	Major Categories of Type of Unfairness			
	I—Rewards	II—Punishments	III—Discrimination	IV—Due Process
B—Bosses				
A	34.3	13.0	18.1	13.6
S	32.7	13.0	25.0	19.4
T	32.0	16.7	19.6	23.1
E—Equals				
A	22.9	16.0	9.6	13.6
S	29.0	24.3	14.7	9.7
T	8.0	16.7	17.9	5.8
L—Life				
A	10.0	31.3	9.6	15.3
S	19.6	26.6	11.8	11.3
T	20.0	33.3	16.1	9.6
P—Parents				
A	1.4	5.3	7.5	15.3
S	1.9	7.7	5.9	24.2
T	16.0	23.8	30.4	38.5
S—Society				
A	31.4	34.4	55.3	42.4
S	16.8	28.4	42.7	35.5
T	24.0	9.5	16.1	23.1

These trends powerfully suggest perspectival shifts with age. With increasing age, we become the bosses and parents and are less controlled by them. When the rewards of life are doled out unfairly, adults are more likely to blame equals and society, and when punishments are unfair, society is blamed more. When discriminatory treatment results, it is blamed more on society, and less on parents, life, and equals. Due process unfairnesses are blamed more on society, life, and equals, and less on parents and bosses. Thus being exposed to different types of unfairness at differing ages with differing sources of blame does seem to change our sensitivities and thresholds and the salience of some types of unfairness. The only exception to the pattern of change across the age groups is the life category, where the rate remains constant.

Severity of Unfairness Ratings

In this study, we asked participants to make a severity rating, on a 1-to-100 scale, for each unfairness. We analyzed these ratings, using major categories of type (I, II, III, and IV) and age group (A, S, and T) as independent variables. There was no significant age group effect, and no significant age group by type of unfairness interaction effect; the lack of significance here indicates that A, S, and T participants perceive the severity of their unfairnesses at similar levels.

There was a significant effect for type of unfairness, however.[19] The means for the unfairness types were 67.0 (I), 74.9 (II), 66.6 (III), and 62.8 (IV). Further testing revealed that type II unfairnesses,[20] when punishments are inflicted in unfair ways, were rated significantly higher than the other three types of unfairness. Type II unfairness, to recall, includes the Job-like condition, when innocence is punished. Thus while the Job-like category does not predominate among unfairness types in frequency of occurrence, when it does occur it is regarded as significantly more severe than the other major types of unfairness on average.

LOOKING BACKWARD, LOOKING FORWARD

In Study 1, we tested and then revised our type schema. Now, in Study 2, we have replicated the type findings and extended them to participants older and younger than before. Though there are still improvements to be made in terms of the schema's validity, reliability, and inclusiveness, slight gains along these lines were noted, and a promising direction seen: Having participants do the coding (which was done only for the S group) improved validity, reliability, and inclusiveness. But overall, we found that the type schema worked for the older and younger participants.

In finding that age groups cited significantly different numbers of unfairnesses on average, significantly different types of unfairnesses, and a significantly different number of types of unfairnesses suggest that our conceptions of unfairness undergo change with age and experience. Said another way, our perspective undergoes refinement such that whether we call an arbitrary rule instance an unfairness may change with age. For some categories, like arbitrary rules, we see constriction with age, whereas for some other categories we see dilation with age. The innocent punished type is one that appears to dilate, as the S and A groups cite this category far more frequently than the T group. But this does not necessarily mean that we increasingly turn misfortunes into unfairnesses, for the increase could be coming from human agency instances.

The major variable in Study 2 was blame, and blaming did seem ubiquitous, endemic to unfairnesses. For example, not one participant wrote anything resembling "there's no one to blame for this." Regarding who or what is to blame, we found self-blame instances to be almost non-existent.[21] Our interpretation after reading the narratives closely is that this finding reflects neither denial nor projection nor avoidance of responsibility; rather it points to unfairness being an other-directed phenomenon. These participants, we believe, are not steeped in victimology, for they do blame themselves for other matters in their life, but they would not designate those matters as unfairnesses. Unfairnesses, then, as they are conceived and blamed, seem to come at us rather than from us.

In looking back, we found blame to significantly differ by age group and to significantly differ by type of unfairness, and we also found a blame by type by age group effect. Some effects about parents were not surprising (lessening with age), whereas some effects about society (increasing with age) were surprising. These effects further suggest that our conceptions undergo refinement, in both type and blame, and their interaction. As we age, we seem to forgive parents their imposition of arbitrary rules and due-process violations when we were under their rule, realizing, now, that such rules were probably necessary. But when students and adults cite that arbitrary rules and due-process category, they hold a bigger parent—society—to blame.

In comparing our prototype Job with these results, we find only a few participants who blame God for "innocence punished" cases; so few, in fact, that we had to lump blaming God under the blaming life category, with the impersonal agency items. Perhaps our modern world is just more psychiatric and secular than Job's: Sins give way to disorders,[22] confession gives way to medication, and God evaporates into meteorology, geology, and DNA (life). But the data on blame, when coupled with type, do give a better read on the question of whether people are turning misfortunes into unfairnesses. As it turns out, approximately 30% of these "innocence punished" cases are blamed on impersonal factors, with approximately 70%

blamed on human agency factors, and this is fairly consistent across A, S, and T groups. So there appears to be evidence that in a minority of cases, what some may call misfortunes are considered unfairnesses, and this percentage, apparently, does not constrict with age, nor does it expand.

Although we may live in a more secular world, our modern participants want it to be an equitable and just world, even though participants of all ages recognize the sad fact of unfairness in our midst. Perhaps this is why society looms larger and guiltier with age. After all, it stands midway between persons and the impersonal life and transcendent God.

But I believe it goes deeper than some central positional point on a blame scale. Society is the community. In a narrow sense, it refers to those who are elected to make our laws and carry them out or those selected to interpret them. In a wider sense, society embraces "we the people," encompassing norms and values; it is what we permit in our world or inflict on some. We see evidence for this wider meaning. The standards we use when judging an unfairness reveal our ideal, yet unfairnesses confront us with the real, and the disparity. The disparity brings home what we have not become, and society's flaws loom large.[23]

At Job's most despairing point,[24] when he is referring to rapists, thieves, unsafe streets, and terrors in the night, he might be some modern TV newscaster delivering the nightly news. Our adult participants make similar claims, substituting society for God in their laments. Although this substitution may be a comedown in the dramaturgic sense, in another sense it is a source we can address and affect. It is a source from which answers are probable.

Finally, in Study 2 we introduced severity ratings as a new variable. Severity is a measure of our anger at life's unfairnesses (an arguable but defendable inference, we believe). The results indicate that we do not get less angry with age about unfairnesses, at least for the unfairness instances participants chose to write about. The mean severity ratings for all types of unfairness are quite high, indicating that participants of all ages were selecting not only their salient instances but their more severe and important instances rather than the trivial. Said another way, the unfairnesses that are offered up to us did not turn out to be petty whines.

We can also infer that these unfairnesses have staying power in that the anger experienced when the unfairness first happened has stayed quite hot, sometimes over decades. This staying power is most notable for the adults and visible in their severity, particularly for those who wrote about unfairnesses from decades ago that still earn high ratings now. This inference must be hedged, though, for we do not have severity measures at two points in time (immediately after the unfairness occurred and years later) and thus cannot say if there is diminution or not. What we can say is that these unfairnesses still rile, still resonate in memory, and participants do not seem to get over them with age.

In looking forward, one broad question concerns memory. Participants write their instances in some sequence, choosing which comes first and so on. This sequence may be an indicator of how unfairness memories are ordered. Do the memories unfold chronologically, or does recency determine order? Do certain types of unfairness or certain blame designations come before others? Or do we remember by severity, where the hottest comes first or last?

In looking forward, we seek to solidify and extend our findings. Study 2 was the first time that adult participants were used, and we want to run another sample to see if what we found recurs. We also want to extend what worked—having the participants code their own instances. Now, new samples of students and adults will code not only for type, but for blame, as the latter allows us to answer a question about blaming and neuroticism. If participants inappropriately blame outside factors rather than themselves (i.e., a neurotic reason for the very low individual blame citings), then we can see whether disinterested outsiders view it the same way, or whether they blame participants much more, an indication that defensiveness, avoidance, and neuroticism may be operating.

APPENDIX 5A

IT'S NOT FAIR!
CATEGORIZATION SCHEMA FOR WHO OR WHAT
IS TO BLAME

These blame categories run from the impersonal (e.g., God), the broad and abstract (e.g., life), and the general (e.g., society) to the personal; and within the personal the focus of blame ranges from those individuals of higher status or age (e.g., bosses, parents), to those of equal rank (e.g., peers), to those of lower rank (e.g., children).

Note: Each category begins with a letter, which is the code for that category, and this letter should appear on your scoring sheet.

Code

G—When God is (blamed) cited
L—When life, or nature, or heredity is cited
S—When societal laws, values, or social norms are cited
P—When parents or grandparent are cited
B—When a boss, a teacher, or a coach is cited
F—When a family member (not parents), particularly a sibling, is cited
E—When an equal—like a peer, coworker, friend—is cited
R—When a romantic significant other, boyfriend, girlfriend, spouse, or lover is cited
I—When the individual blames himself or herself
C—When a child is cited
U—When an underling is cited

Note: Most often, there will be just one citing, and so the one letter that best reflects who or what is to blame should be entered. However, there may be an instance where you feel the subject is pointing the blame at two sources. To take an example, let us say you believe the subject is blaming a coach for the unfairness but is also citing himself as partly to blame. Then enter both codes, with a slash separating: in the example I just gave, it would be B/I.

ENDNOTES

1. *See, e.g.*, A. W. Burgess and L. L. Holmstrom, *Rape: Victims of Crisis* (Bowie, MD: Robert J. Brady, 1974).
2. *See, e.g.*, L. Walker, *The Battered Woman* (New York: Harper & Row, 1979).
3. An exception to this might be if a few participants believe that God actually pulled the strings, directing humans to commit unfairnesses.
4. Once again we had a college student (S) sample ($N = 65$), and this group had a mean age = 19.8 and a mean education level = 15.5. These students,

who volunteered for an extra-credit research project, had the opportunity to recruit up to two more participants with the following guidelines: one participant had to be an adult (A) between the ages of 30 and 60, and the adult could be either a parent, an aunt or uncle, or an older sibling; the second participant had to be a tot or teenager (T) between the ages of 4 and 17, and this participant could be a younger sibling, or a niece or nephew. There were 64 adults, with a mean age = 44.1 and a mean education level = 18.1, and there were 46 tots and teens, with a mean age = 13.5 and with a mean education level = 8.8. Overall, then, there were 175 participants in the total sample, 112 females and 63 males, and the religious breakdown was 56.6% Catholic, 23.2 % Protestant, 10.7% Jewish, 3.6% other, and 5.9% none (or none listed).

We modified the method so the youngest members of our T group, those below 7-years-old, did not have to write out their unfairnesses but could talk them out to the college participant who recruited them, and the college participant would take down the oral narrative.

5. We asked that "When you have finished detailing *all* your instances of unfairness, we want you to go back over them and rate each one on a scale of 1 to 100, where 100 would be the most unfair of unfairnesses, and 1 would be the most minimal of unfairness. Write the number you assign in the left-hand margin."

6. The students were given a week to complete the booklet and their categorizations.

7. The students were given booklets for the A and T subjects, to be completed over the spring holiday.

8. In proceeding this way, we could not only compute interrater reliability for the three groups, but we had one group, the S group, where one of the raters was the "insider"—the one who recounted the unfairness experience and who presumably knew it best. If we make the assumption that the subject's coding of his or her own experiences is the most valid, we then can compare insider/outsider versus outsider/outsider reliability.

9. There was, once again, variability. At the upper end, one adult detailed 20 instances, one student detailed 18 instances, and one 16-year-old detailed 12 instances. Looking at the average number of instances for only the student group (8.0), this average was considerably higher than the student group in study 1 (4.6).

10. It is not surprising that the T group produced the lowest average number of unfairnesses. The very youngest of that group, with limited attention span and the least stamina for the task, produced the fewest instances, which brings down the T group average considerably. Stamina and fatigue may have affected the adult group as well.

11. Chi-square test ($X^2[N = 175, df = 18] = 61.2, p < .001$).

12. The contingency coefficient and Cramer's V, two measures of association, were .859 and .559, respectively, for the overall distribution. Looking first at the A group, the associative values were .853 and .544; for the S group, they were .872 and .593; and for the T group, they were .870 and .587.

13. We put the infrequent God citings with the "life" (L) category and put U, C, F, I, and R together in the E category, making that equals and/or underlings.

14. $X^2[N = 175, df = 8] = 108.8, p < .001$.
15. To assess this relationship, we first dropped the miscellaneous category from the analysis, as we were unclear what that heterogeneous category represents and thus unsure how to interpret any significant results that might follow. Moreover, in looking at types of unfairness, we decided to use the major rather than the specific categories, to ensure the integrity of the statistical tests. The major categories were the relationship between rewards and effort (I—containing specific categories A, B, and C), the relationship between punishment and culpability or behavior (II—containing specific categories D, E, and F), differential or discriminatory treatment (III—containing specific categories G and H), and lack of due process (IV—containing the specific category of arbitrary rules, I).
16. $X^2[N = 175, df = 12] = 130.3, p < .001$.
17. For the A group, the Chi-square was significant ($X^2[N = 64, df = 12] = 53.1, p < .001$), as it was for the S group ($X^2[N = 65, df = 12] = 74.1, p < .001$), though it was just marginally significant for the T group ($X^2[N = 46, df = 12] = 19.8, p = .07$).
18. When it comes to blaming bosses (and teachers and coaches), the results for the three groups are quite similar for rewards (I), punishment (II), and discriminatory treatment (III) cases; however, there is a declining trend over the age ranges for the lack of due process (IV) cases, where the tots and teens group (T) cites bosses the most, and the A group cites them the least.

    When it comes to blaming equals, the pattern is much more variable: When rewards are unfair (I), the S and A groups blame equals much more so than the T group; when it comes to unfair punishments (II), the S group blames equals more than the A or T groups; for discriminatory treatment (III) cases where the blame falls on equals, we see a declining age trend (e.g., T > S > A), but for lack of due process (IV) cases where the blame falls on equals, there is an increasing age trend (e.g., A > S > T).

    When it comes to blaming life (plus God, nature, and heredity), there are significant differences by group. When rewards are unfair (I), the A group blames life at only half the rate of the S and T groups; for unfair punishments (II), the three groups are quite close in their citings of life; then there are the opposite age trends for the discriminatory treatment (III) cases (T > S > A) and the due process (IV) cases (A > S > T).

    Regarding blaming parents, the T group dominates, citing parents more than 10 times as frequently as A and S groups for unfair reward (I) cases, and 3 to 4 times more frequently for unfair punishment (II) and discriminatory treatment (III) cases. For the lack of due process, arbitrary rules (IV) cases, the percentages show the declining age trend (T > S > A) once again. When it comes to blaming society, there is a clear age trend across types of unfairness (A > S > T). The adult participants blame society much more, whereas the youngest participants direct their blame at parents.
19. $F[N = 175, df = 3,948] = 13.0, p < .001$.
20. Using the Scheffé test.
21. Participants blaming themselves, or the person on the receiving end of the unfairness (individual/self), turned out to be a small fraction of 1%.

22. For an entertaining and enlightening view of the transformation of the seven deadly sins, *see* R. C. Solomon, ed., *Wicked Pleasures: Meditations on the Seven "Deadly" Sins* (Lanham, MD: Rowman & Littlefield, 1999).

23. Here new questions arise about which we can only speculate. Are our standards of unfairness American standards, rather than universal standards of unfairness? If we lived in other cultures and countries, perhaps those that are far less free and democratic, would we see many of these *instances of unfairness as unfairness at all?* Do we, because of our cultural context, expect far more from parents and society than we would find elsewhere? These questions point toward a larger one: What is universal and what is local regarding unfairness? That cross-cultural question will be taken up in Part IV.

24. S. Mitchell, *The Book of Job* (San Francisco: North Point Press, 1987), pp. 60–61.

6

SEVERITY, BLAME, AND TYPE OF UNFAIRNESS: DO WE FIND CONSISTENCY OR NEUROTICISM?

It is time to take stock—to see where we are, by seeing where we've been, to see where we are going. Study 1 (with just an S group) produced our first type findings, which generally aligned with aspects of fairness that philosophers have distinguished and social scientists have researched, although there were more distinctions, gradations, and nuances found in this participant sample. These findings were then used, along with the inter-rater analysis, to modify the type schema to improve its reliability and inclusiveness. In Study 2, we added younger (T) and older (A) participants, a blame schema, and severity ratings. We also made a coding change (for the S group), where participants served as one set of coders, and this produced positive results in three ways: It addressed the validity question, as these participants knew best what their narratives meant; it increased the interrater reliability for this group above the other two groups; and it reduced the use of the "miscellaneous" category to an acceptable level, much below the other two groups.

Apart from the changes we added, the constants were revealing as well. The distribution of unfairnesses across the type categories for the S group remained very similar from Study 1 to Study 2, a replication of results. Moreover, the type schema seemed to work for the A and T groups as well, as these categories housed the vast majority of their instances. Although fine-tuning was needed, the results told us that we were on the right track.

There is clearly work remaining. For example, we have no replication for the A group as of yet, and without it we cannot say whether the Study 2 A group was odd or average. But doubts can be erased and confidence increased if the findings recur with a new A group, which we now intend to add in Study 3. Beyond adding a new sample, further changes will be made in how the coding is done. Because having the S group code their instances by type worked well in Study 2, we intend to have the A group do likewise in Study 3; in addition, we plan to extend this change to the blame categorizations by having both A and S participants code their own instances on this dimension, along with the outside coders. By making this latter change, we can test the interreliability of the blame schema, which is important to assess.

More important, though, having the participant and an outside coder both making independent blame categorizations presents us with a way of assessing a set of criticisms that have been leveled at unfairness complainants. A number of critics (see chapter 1) claim that those who cry "unfair" blame others for what they themselves have brought about. In the eyes of the critics, this is victimology, a defensive and neurotic reaction, which avoids responsibility. Critics might even find support for this victimology view in Study 2, where the extremely low percentage (less than 1%) who cite the individual or self as a blame designation may be seen as bolstering this "blame others" victimology view.

But now we can put this to a cleaner test. If the critics are right, then the outside coders (who have no defensive self-interest) ought to blame individual/self far more frequently than the alleged neurotic participant. On the other hand, if we find a high rate of agreement between participants and outsiders, including only a few who cite individual/self, then the distorting, avoiding victimology view would be contradicted.

To further replicate and solidify the findings, we will once again use severity ratings, looking at how these ratings relate to our type and blame variables, and to the type by blame interaction. Which types of unfairness are rated as most or least severe? Which blame designations are rated most or least severe? Which of the various type by blame combinations are regarded as most or least severe? This part of the data set will either replicate the findings in Study 2 or challenge them.

We also seek to break new ground by using severity as a rough gauge of memory. We are looking at how unfairnesses are selected from memory —in what sort of sequence the instances emerge—as participants set their unfairness narratives to paper in sequential order. Will the most severe unfairnesses emerge first with small ones coming at the end, or will the reverse sequence hold? Will the Job-like "innocence punished" types emerge first or last? Will blame designations of God or society or parents come first or last? Perhaps the order will have nothing to do with severity, type, or blame, but everything to do with chronology? If so, will the sequence be chronological, or will the most recent (a recency effect) show first?

We also plan to refine our type schema. Although achieving some movement toward our goals in Study 2, as interrater reliability increased and the miscellaneous percentage dropped for the S group, the results were not nearly as promising for the A and T groups. After analyzing the interrater reliability error pattern for type and interviewing S group participants and our outside coders, we found a number who complained that two categories were particularly confusing: "when wrongful behavior was rewarded" (I/A) and "when wrongful behavior was not punished" (II/F). Many commented that they could go either way on these categories, as some saw the latter (not getting punished) as a reward. We decided to combine these two into one specific category (under its own major category) called "Wrongful Behavior Is Rewarded or Not Punished" (II/C).

Finally, we did a major rewrite of the schema, replacing cryptic language with more specific language, replacing ambiguous instructions with more direct ones, adding illustrative examples and clearer definitions of specific categories, and, most of all, using "differential diagnosis-like hints,"[1] which would help raters decide on the close calls.[2] The new schema is presented in Appendix 6A.

STUDY 3

There were 162 participants, 82 students and 80 nonstudent adults, with 64% female and 36% male.[3] The participants produced 1082 instances of unfairness, with an average of 6.7 per participant (an average that accords closely with that of Study 2).[4] There were no significant differences between the A and S groups in the number of instances generated, with these averages showing closer accord than they did in Study 2. In addition, there were no significant differences between the A and S groups in either the severity ratings or the type distribution (see Table 6-1),[5] a closeness we observed in Study 2 as well. With no significant age group differences, the two groups were combined in the subsequent type and severity analyses.

How Severity Adds Complexity to the Type Picture

Looking at Table 6-1, on the low frequency end are "disproportionate punishment" (III/E) and "equal treatment when it should be individualized" (IV/G),[6] two categories that reflect differences in degree rather than kind: In the latter case some reward has been given (but the participant

TABLE 6-1
The Frequency and Percentage of Type Unfairness, Along With the Mean Severity Ratings

Major/Specific Categories	n	%	Severity Rating
I/A—No work rewarded	44	4.0	75.5
I/B—Hard work not rewarded	123	11.4	61.8
II/C—Wrongful rewarded or not punished	86	7.9	64.8
III/D—Innocence punished	345	31.9	77.8
III/E—Disproportionate or excessive	42	3.9	54.5
IV/F—Unfair advantages	253	23.4	61.6
IV/G—Equal treatment	40	3.7	42.1
V/H—Arbitrary rules	111	10.3	50.3
VI/I—Miscellaneous	38	3.5	53.8

believes it is not enough), and in the former case some warranted punishment has been given (but the participant believes it is too much). Because these two categories reflect fine-tuning errors, where the evaluator did not get the dosage right, as opposed to fundamental unfairnesses that never should happen, the severity scores for E (54.5) and G (42.1) are at or near the bottom.

At the top end of the categories in terms of frequency is "innocence punished" (III/D) and "unfair advantages" (IV/F),[7] ranking first and second, respectively, although the gap between D and F is now wider (31.9% versus 23.4%) than it was in Study 2 (21.5% versus 21.1%). The gap grows wider still when we examine severity: The mean rating for category D (77.8) is the highest of all the categories, whereas the mean for category F (61.6) is considerably lower but by no means low. We know that severity ratings are significantly different by type,[8] but why the significant difference between D and F, the two most frequently cited types of unfairness?

A plausible explanation involves a "reluctant accommodation." To explain, an "unfair advantage" instance appears to violate the *ideal* of what is fair. However, a number of participants seem to make a reluctant, but not total, accommodation of their ideal to the real world: They acknowledge that many people believe that it is who you know that counts in getting ahead, though they believe that this should not be. Although still embracing *their* ideal world, they give a bit of ground by acknowledging that their views are not universally held. This grudging accommodation is in sharp contrast with what they do for "innocence punished" cases: Although participants acknowledge that such unfairnesses sadly happen, claimants do not grant any legitimacy to that sad fact, for this type of unfairness seems to defy a universal ideal in *every* just world.[9] It is wrong, no matter what and no matter how many people seem to accept it.

Bringing severity into the type picture changes the picture because it adds complexity and displays the nuances of people's conceptions of particular types of unfairnesses. It certainly does so in the next illustration. Here we have a curious finding: "No work rewarded" (I/A) is rated more severe (75.5) than (II/C) "wrongful behavior rewarded or unpunished" (64.8) or (I/B) "hard work not rewarded" (61.8). We call this a "curious" finding because we expected, based on a work ethic or an equity view, that B would be greater than A, and we expected C to be greater than both B and A. For an instance in category B, the actor complies with the work ethic, yet the reward fails to come, whereas in A the actor does not work; in measuring the outcomes against the inputs, B has arguably the stronger case. For an instance in category C, there is a double insult in play: A wrong has been committed (which may reach the criminal level in some instances), and it is not only not punished, but it is rewarded. Surely, in terms of equity's outcomes to inputs, a grave violation occurs in C. So what accounts for these counterintuitive findings?

The answer is best understood if we view A, B, and C from two different perspectives: The first perspective, the typical one, focuses on the victim (who obtains what she should not have, or fails to obtain what she should); the second perspective focuses on the evaluator, the one doing the rewarding or punishing. From this victim–outcome perspective, B and C ought to arouse the most anger, because one does good (and gets nothing) and one does bad (and gets rewarded), whereas the no-work (A) case would seem to fall between the good and the bad, and a reward should not be seen as a severe infraction.

But let us see where the second perspective leads. Regarding the evaluator, that individual has made a mistake in all three cases, according to the participants. But the mistakes are not equal, for two of the mistakes are understandable and forgivable to a degree whereas the other one is not. For example, we understand that teachers can be fooled by a student who cheats (II/C): Teachers are not detectives. The realization that it is unrealistic to expect perfect detection mutes the participants' anger and mitigates the teacher's mistake. Regarding an I/B instance, participants understand that not all teachers subscribe to "effort should be rewarded," as some will not weigh the quantitative 20 pages of a student's paper one whit, but will grade quality only. Although the student might not like the teacher's standard and might see it as too harsh, there is, nonetheless, a recognition that the teacher is on the job, applying a standard. These two possibilities in II/C and I/B cases—lack of omniscience and valuing different aspects of work—add up to the fact that the teacher is on the job, which mitigates the unfairness and reduces severity.

By contrast, it is harder to forgive teachers who reward for *nothing* (I/A), because the lack of effort is right there under their noses. The conclusion for these stories seems to be that the evaluator is not on the job, as the teacher simply fails to do what should be done. This, I believe, is the perspective that makes sense of this curious finding, and in this perspective, the focus shifts from victim to evaluator and from outcome to process.

Agreements, Disagreements, Blame, and Perspectives

The interrater reliability of this new type schema was examined, and it proved more reliable than that used for Study 2.[10] In examining the error pattern, we did note a trend: Category V/H, "arbitrary rules," produced the highest percentage of disagreement between raters than any other category. This is a familiar finding by now. One participant sees a corruption of process, whereas the outside coder sees it as an outcome violation. This disagreement over what is our purest process category, along with its modest use overall, suggests two possibilities. First, the findings from all these studies to date suggest that people have an outcome bias when it comes to judging an unfairness, and that bias may grow with age. Along these lines we found that the tot and teenage group cited process unfairness more than the students and adults. The second possibility is that process unfairnesses are embedded in almost all the categories, and they may be more difficult to spot when outcome violations loom so large. Perhaps, as the story model has it, we are predisposed to focus on the central action, the harm, the crime, the unfair outcome, as we then construct its meaning. On the other hand, the findings concerning evaluators making mistakes or not being on the job point toward process, where participants are angrier about this lack of process than they are about the outcome unfairness. Clearly, these different findings point to different conclusions, and further testing will be needed to see which explanation is more consistent with the overall findings.

We are clearer about the blame findings. For the first time we had two independent codings on the blame schema, which allowed us to compute interrater reliability, and this turned out to be quite respectable.[11] Raters indicated that the blame categories were easier than the type categories to code, because they were more distinct and had less overlap, and thus it was not surprising that the reliability was higher. We combined the blame categories, as we did in Study 2, with the exception being that this time the God category was not combined with the life category but left to stand on its own, as raters blamed God for 6.2% of the instances, a significant increase over Study 2. The frequencies and severity ratings for blame are shown in Table 6-2.

Consistent with Study 2, we again find that society is blamed most frequently and quite hotly (69.8). Although the severity ratings for society are high, they do not reach the level when God is blamed. Although God is blamed less frequently than all the other designations, when God makes a mistake in the eyes of participants, it's a big one. If lower severity ratings indicate that we are more forgiving,[12] then participants let parents and

TABLE 6-2
The Frequency and Percentage by Blame Category, Along With Severity Ratings, Across Groups

Combined Categories	n	%	Severity Rating
B—Bosses	187	17.1	65.3
E—Equals	200	18.3	55.4
G—God	68	6.2	82.2
L—Life	171	15.6	66.1
P—Parents	97	8.9	55.8
S—Society	370	33.9	69.8

equals off the hook more readily than bosses, life, and society, and do not let God of the hook at all. This makes strange sense: God, in his Omniness, cannot cop to an "oops, I made a mistake" plea, and we saw that Job would not let Him off the hook.[13] But such mistake pleas receive a more sympathetic response when equals or parents are to blame.

If equals or parents are at the low end of severity, and God is at the high end, let us consider the in-betweens. Bosses have risen to that level of authority because of education or experience, presumably acquiring a higher competency along the way, whereas parents acquire their status in a most earthy way. With this distinction, it makes sense that participants blame bosses far more than parents, holding them to a higher standard, though not the omnistandard of God. Using this logic, it makes sense to hold society to an even higher standard than bosses, if society is seen as a collection of bosses, elected and elevated because of competence: Multiple heads should be better than one, and a collective failure would be more severe, warranting less understanding and forgiveness than a sole individual's error, and this is what we find as well.[14]

We can now be a bit more precise about the life designation, for we have factored out the God designations, leaving just impersonal agency cases. Life is cited approximately 16% of the time, which is no small percentage, and its average severity is 66.1, just below society and just ahead of bosses. This is the category that would house the alleged misfortune cases that are perceived as unfairnesses, if in fact they are that.

The Sequence of Unfairnesses and Unfairnesses in Mind

Because participants write their unfairnesses sequentially, questions arise about whether the sequence tracks severity, type, blame, or chronology in some systematic way. The surprising results, for all the variables examined, are no differences across the instances as the sequential patterns hold constant. To illustrate with severity, we categorized these ratings as either low (i.e., a rating of 1–25), medium (26–50), high (51–75), or severe (76–100) and counted the frequencies falling in those categories for the first eight instances; in addition, we computed the mean ratings for instances 1 through 8, and both means and frequencies are shown in Table 6-3. Severe instances dominate overall (41.0%) and dominate at each instance in the sequence, but the instances get neither more nor less severe, holding fairly constant.

The results are the same for the other variables. There is no chronological pattern—neither the older ones first, nor the most recent—and no type or blame patterns. If the overt sequential recording metaphorically mirrors our memories of unfairness instances, we might say that memories of unfairnesses do not exist in some neatly organized file drawer—ordered by type, blame, severity, or chronology. Rather, they seem jumbled together, all designated as unfairnesses, and what gets pulled out in which order reveals no obvious pattern.

Severity by Type by Blame

To assess the type by blame interaction, we again used the combined categories (e.g., B, E, G, L, P, S) for blame, and the major categories (e.g., I, II, III, IV, V) for type, dropping the miscellaneous category. The results, replicating Study 2, were again highly significant,[15] with this significant effect recurring at every instance level (i.e., 1 through 8). The percentages of who or what is to blame at each major level of type of unfairness are shown in Table 6-4.

Looking by type, when rewards do not match the efforts (I), bosses are predominately blamed, with God and parents getting little or no blame and with equals, life, and society falling in between at moderate levels.[16] When wrongful behavior (II) is rewarded or not punished, participants blame society and equals more than bosses, while God, life, and parents get nary a mention. Putting severity into the picture, the results show that

TABLE 6-3
The Frequency of Low, Medium, High, and Severe Ratings, Along With the Mean Severity Ratings of Unfairness, for the First Eight Unfairness Instances

Rating	Instance Number								Total	%
	1	2	3	4	5	6	7	8		
Low	33	19	26	17	17	16	15	9	152	14.6
Medium	32	44	32	41	27	22	15	12	225	21.6
High	37	45	35	45	33	20	16	7	238	22.8
Severe	88	78	75	50	54	42	21	19	427	41.0
Totals	190	186	168	153	131	100	67	47	1042	
Means	65.2	66.3	65.5	62.6	65.4	63.0	56.5	61.9	65.0	

TABLE 6-4
The Blame Percentages for Bosses (B), Equals (E), God (G), Life (L),
Parents (P), and Society (S) for Each of the Major Types of Unfairness,
Along With Severity Ratings

Major Categories of Type of Unfairness	Blame						Rating
	B	E	G	L	P	S	
I. Reward/effort	44.4	19.4	2.8	16.7	0	16.7	60.1
II. Wrongful behavior	13.3	40.0	0	0	0	46.7	71.5
III. Punishment/behavior	8.8	14.7	11.8	23.5	10.3	30.9	75.0
IV. Discriminatory treatment	18.2	18.2	1.8	10.9	14.6	36.4	58.3
V. Lack of due process	52.6	5.3	0	10.5	15.8	15.8	52.3

Note: The percentages are calculated across the rows (for each major category), rather than down the columns, by blame designation.

equals are more readily forgiven when they fail to deal with wrongful behavior in the right manner, but not so for society. When punishment is undeserved or excessive (III), blame is distributed widely. Discriminatory treatment (IV) is blamed predominantly on society, with bosses, equals, and parents coming in for some blame. Lack of due process (V) is blamed predominantly on bosses, indicating that these situations involve authority–subordinate relationships.

Looking at the same data by blame, bosses are blamed most in reward (I), followed by discrimination (IV) and due-process (V) cases. Equals get blamed at a moderate rate at every category except due process, arbitrary rules (V). God is blamed almost exclusively for punishment of the innocent cases (III), with 80% of the designations for God falling in this category. Life is blamed most in this category (III) as well, even more here than God. Parents are blamed most for the discrimination category (IV), followed by punishment (III), and then lack of due process (V) cases. Society is again blamed most overall, but especially for excessive or unfair punishment and for discriminatory treatment.

As of yet, no mention has been made of cases where the participant blames the self (which we code as "Individual"). In Study 2, these citings were infrequent, occurring less than 1% of the time. We find the same result here. Previously I raised the possibility that unfairness may just be an outward looking phenomenon where the experience appears to be inflicted on us and we do not think that we caused it. This outward attribution holds that blaming is not victimology, neurotic, defensive, or some avoidance of responsibility, but fitting and appropriate to the reality of unfairnesses. However, our evidence was less than convincing.

Study 3 provides more solid evidence for rejecting the defensive, neurotic view of blaming. For the first time, we have independent coders who have no neurotic need, no self-interest, and who should blame the person if they see it that way; but they do not. Its rare use by participants, now a recurrent finding, coupled with consistency between participants and outside coders, supports the view that unfairnesses are widely perceived as being externally caused.

Returning to the type categories, "innocence punished" (III) cases are rated as the most severe (which replicates Study 2 findings), and when God is blamed for these, severity is higher than all other blame designations. Two interacting factors seem to be working to push the ratings up. First, this type of unfairness strikes many as the quintessential unfairness —the most unfair of the unfairnesses. Second, there seems to be a theodicy effect or backlash where the One who is blamed has no excuse and therefore gets the full force of human fury: God not only knows better but knows all, yet He lets it happen; God, being all-powerful, could have intervened but did not; God, who is the transcendent standard of justice, has fallen down on the job. In this part of our data set, when "innocence punished" is blamed on God, our modern participants echo Job.

Finally, we found a significant gender effect in this study regarding the distribution of types of unfairness,[17] but not for the blame distribution; however, on the severity ratings, the gender effect occurs for both type and blame. To summarize the findings for type, females cite the rewards (I) and discriminatory treatment (IV) categories more frequently than males. Men cite the lack of due process (V) category more frequently than women, focusing on the "rules of the game" and objecting when those rules are violated. Regarding the severity ratings for type, the ratings from females are higher when innocence is punished (III) and when discriminatory treatment (IV) results, whereas males rate due-process (V) unfairness as more severe. When it comes to blame, females blame life and society at significantly higher levels than do males, whereas for the other blame categories, male and female ratings are equivalent.

LOOKING BACK, LOOKING FORWARD

We now have a fairly reliable schema for both type and blame, as the revisions we made to the type schema appeared to work. In addition, the schemas appear comprehensive, as only a very low percentage of instances fall in the miscellaneous category. Moreover, having participants code their own instances for type and blame also contributes to reliability and to increasing the likelihood that the valid categories are found.

We also have a growing and stable set of findings relating to type and blame and severity, how these variables interact, and how these variables relate to age and gender. Our methodological search for a reliable schema and our empirical search for the essence of unfairness begin to converge, as each search points to *complexity*. Based on more than 3000 instances of unfairness from studies 1, 2, and 3, the complexities show in the findings that type, blame, and severity are not only separate variables, but interacting ones. Who one blames and why one blames can affect one's perspective on the instance, which may move the unfairness from one type category to another (e.g., if outcome or process is the focus) or may change its severity ratings dramatically (e.g., if evaluators' mistakes can or cannot be forgiven). When perspectives differ, it is not surprising that type, blame, and severity vary as well.

In Study 2, we saw that unfairness judgments did change with advancing age, but the difference was between the T group and the A and S groups. In Study 3, without a T group, the A and S groups look quite similar in the type of instances they cite, though the particulars reflect age differences. But the conceptions and the concepts of unfairness look like they are in place for college age onward. Both the A and S groups seem more forgiving to parents and equals, though society is increasingly blamed, perhaps because greater competency is attributed. Finally, when blame is directed at the Omni-One, the most competent of all, the ire is hottest.

We used the interrater reliability on blame to assess the charge of victimology and neurotic avoidance and found that neither participants nor outside coders blamed the participant in more than 1% of the instances, evidence that refutes the view that participants are blaming in defensive, avoidance ways; if that neurotic view had substance to it, then disinterested raters ought to see the source of blame differently. But they do not.

These findings refine, replicate, and extend those of the prior studies, and as the findings grow, so does our confidence. But these findings do not erase all doubts and suspicions about unfairness, some of which have been with us from the outset. Our main objective in the next chapter is to address another of those suspicions: that we are a nation of narcissists, seeing our own unfairnesses as so paramount that others are dwarfed in the background.

In looking forward, the focal question is this: Do we relegate the unfairnesses of others to the wings while keeping our own center stage? To answer this question we go back to our general instruction—where we ask participants for unfairness instantiations that occurred to them, to those they know, and to those they do not know but have heard about. Now, we plan to code and analyze this personal variable, which speaks directly to the question.

APPENDIX 6A

IT'S NOT FAIR!
CATEGORIZATION SCHEMA FOR TYPE OF UNFAIRNESS

Major categories are designated by roman numerals; specific categories are designated by capital letters. For each account of an unfairness, put both the roman numeral (for the major category) and the letter (for the specific category) that you believe best categorizes this instance.

I—THE RELATIONSHIP BETWEEN REWARDS (GAINS) AND EFFORT (WORK) (THIS MAY BE DUBBED, "THE REWARD AND THE WORK DO NOT MESH")

In this major category, the judgment of unfairness typically involves an evaluation of the actions and efforts of a single person against some standard of fairness. Here we find instances where rewards come to some-one (A) who does not do the work, is therefore undeserving of reward, yet gets rewarded anyway. There is a second category here (B), where someone works hard, but his or her efforts are not rewarded. Thus this category involves reward (whether it is given or whether it fails to occur) in relation to a person's effort (not deserving or deserving).

Note: Someone might see the second (B) category as an instance of punishment and thereby place this in category IIID, where innocence is punished. But in this schema, you are to consider "no reward" as not a punishment, for we are reserving "punishment" for actual harms, pain, or some negative outcome: When it is an actual punishment, code it IIID; when the person expects reward but it does not come, code it IB.

It is unfair when . . .

A. No Work Is Rewarded

Here, the reward should not be forthcoming, because the person did not work for it. The underlying view, based on a work ethic, is that rewards should be directly proportional to the effort expended. When people do not work, they should not get life's rewards (e.g., the student who does not study but gets an A; the worker who does not do the work but gets the promotion or raise).

B. Hard Work Is Not Rewarded

Here, the belief is that when you make the effort, people or life should reward you. There should be a proportional relation between work and reward (e.g., the student who really studies but does not get the high grade; the person who makes high grades but does not get into medical, law, or graduate school; the employee who works hard and does more than expected but does not get the raise or the promotion.

II—WRONGFUL BEHAVIOR THAT EITHER GETS REWARDED WHEN IT SHOULD NOT, OR FAILS TO GET PUNISHED, WHEN IT SHOULD (THIS MAY BE DUBBED, "THE BAD GUY GETS THE GOODIES OR GETS AWAY WITH IT")

In this major category, the judgment of unfairness involves an evaluation of the actions of a person, where the evaluator judges the person's behavior to be wrongful, bad, criminal, and so on by some reasonable standard of fairness. It then follows that such action ought to be punished in some way. What seems unfair is when such wrongful behavior either is not punished or, worse, seems rewarded.

Note: In IA, "no work" is rewarded, while here, in IIC, "wrongful behavior" may be rewarded. This can be confusing and a close call, so here is the distinction we are trying to make. "No work" can be when the lazy person, the slacker, profits; but here, in IIC, we mean something worse by "wrongful behavior"; the person is not merely lazy, but engages in criminal, immoral, or unethical behavior.

C. Wrongful Behavior Is Rewarded or Not Punished

Here, the reward should not be forthcoming, because the person used illegal, unethical, or immoral means to get it. Here, there is an underlying view that rewards, whether they come from people or life, should not go to those who cheat; rather, the cheater gets away with it, and the dirty deed or crime goes unpunished (e.g., one who cheats on a test and gets an A; or one who cheats and does not get caught; one who lies on his resume and gets the job; one who does a crime and does not get caught).

III—RELATIONSHIP BETWEEN PUNISHMENT (PAIN) AND BEHAVIOR (THIS MIGHT BE DUBBED "JOB'S PUNISHMENT" OR "HEY GOD, LIGHTEN UP")

In this major category, the judgment of unfairness again involves an evaluation of the actions and efforts of a single person against some standard of fairness. Here, people or life (D) seem to punish someone for actions that do not deserve punishment, as when they are innocent, or

(E) punishes someone who deserves some punishment but punishes excessively, such that the punishment is too harsh for the crime. Thus this category involves punishment, whether it is given disproportionately or whether it is given when it is not deserving.

D. Innocence Is Punished

Here, the belief exists that the "not guilty" should not be punished. Thus innocent people should not suffer. Also here, the individual does the right thing, takes the proper precautions, yet pain and punishment strike anyway. When it comes to the pain other people inflict on the subject, this seems to involve being taken advantage of, being used by others, being ripped off, or others being inconsiderate or selfish, though the focus is on the "good one" getting unfairly punished and not on the comparative inequality (e.g., life's random illnesses, deaths, and the like when the person does not deserve it; punishing the innocent; the AIDS baby; poverty and malnutrition inflicted on innocent people; child abuse; getting sick despite taking good care; cancer despite not smoking and eating right; getting pregnant despite taking precautions; a drunk driver killing an innocent; getting ripped off by others; doing the right thing, but others take advantage; roommates take advantage; punished despite doing the right thing).

E. The Punishment Is Disproportionate or Excessive to the Act and Intent

Here, there is some guilt, but the punishment is excessive to the crime (e.g., harsh punishments; felony-murder-like situation where the one who accidentally kills is punished as harshly as one who premeditates and kills; being kicked out of a dorm for one beer; a teacher fails student because the paper was one day late; a parent grounds the child for a week for not straightening his or her room; a worker arrives late to work for the first time, because his car broke down, and is fired).

IV—DIFFERENTIAL OR DISCRIMINATORY TREATMENT (THIS MAY BE DUBBED, "LOSING OUT, FOR ILLEGITIMATE REASONS")

In categories I, II, and III, we may make the judgment of unfairness based just on the person's behavior and what happened to him or her (reward or punishment), against our standard of fairness, and what we believe ought to have happened. In category IV, we typically have cases that involve a more direct comparison between what happened to this person and what happened to another person, or between the treatment of one group or class of people against another group. Here, people are either (F) treated differently when they ought to be treated alike or (G) treated alike when they legitimately ought to be treated differently.

F. Unfair Advantages or Connections Are Rewarded or Irrelevant Differences Are Punished When Justice Should Be Blind But Plays Favorites, and When Equal Protection Ought to Be the Rule but the Rule Is Broken

Here, when rewards are based on such things as looks, money, knowing someone, family connections, gender, race, and so on, these are seen as unfair advantages or unfair connections because they are not earned. Also included here are "affirmative action" cases where rewards go to an individual or group based on a status factor that is judged illegitimate. The rewards of life should be doled out based on legitimate factors—namely, earning it (e.g., someone who gets into a school, or a club, a job because of one of these unfair advantages; when parents treat siblings differently; gender discrimination; racial discrimination; two people follow the same diet but one loses more weight; one roommate never cleans up his or her messes, leaving it for the other to do; even in matters of love, there is love unrequited, when one loves another but the feelings are not mutual and equal).

G. Equal or Nondiscriminatory Treatment Results When It Should Be Individualized and Different (Justice Should Not Be Blind but Should See the Individual and Make Just Discriminations)

Here, people are treated equally when, for example, the guilt is not equal. Instead of individualized treatment, people are treated as fungible (e.g., siblings are given the same reward or punishment when different treatment would be fair; the whole class is punished when John did the talking; one worker puts out greater effort than a coworker but both are given the same raise; two siblings are given the same curfew even though there is an age difference).

Note: In category V, dealing with arbitrary rules, discriminatory treatment may also result, but there the focus is on the unfair *process*; when the focus is on the unfair *outcome*, it is coded under IV.

V—LACK OF DUE PROCESS (THIS MAY BE DUBBED, "I DIDN'T GET MY DAY IN COURT" OR "I WAS RAILROADED")

Here, the focus is not on the outcome, which may be fair or unfair, but on the process—how things were decided or done—and whether the person felt she got her day in court or whether she felt she did not get a fair shake.

H.   Arbitrary Rules, Objections Overruled

Here, the person has no control, as when they are the youngest, rather than the oldest, or when parents make rules that seem unfair and non-negotiable. There seems to be a lack-of-due-process complaint here. It is as if one did not get his or her day in court, really could not argue his or her side of the case, or had one's arguments brushed aside and were forced to accept some rule or decision (e.g., being subject to other people's [parents'] rules, which are judged unrealistic yet they remain inflexible; student gets thrown out of school without a fair hearing; parents punish without even listening to the child; a judge silences the defendant and hands down a decision).

VI—OTHER

I.   Items Not Fitting Any of the Preceding Categories

If the instance of unfairness does not seem to fit any of the preceding eight categories (A through H), then this category, VI,I, should be used. Please do make sure none of the others is appropriate before using this "other" category. If you believe this is the correct category, attempt to give some descriptive title that suggests the basic unfairness principle being invoked by the subject.

ENDNOTES

1. *See, e.g.*, American Psychiatric Association, *Diagnostic and Statistical Manual of Mental Disorders*, 4th ed. (Washington, DC: Author, 1994).
2. For example, if getting a high grade without studying may be either a case of "no work being rewarded" or an instance of "unfair advantage" (person has more IQ points), when the writer seems to be using a more comparative standard (comparing that person to another), then "unfair advantage" is the category; if it is to a standard in the writer's mind as to what level of work should be forthcoming, then the "no work being rewarded" category is more appropriate.
3. The students volunteered for course credit, and they recruited their older relatives, as in the previous study. The mean age for the S group was 19.8, ranging from 18 to 28, and the mean education level was 15.0; the mean age for the A group was 46.3, ranging from 30 to 67, and the mean education level was 18.8, indicating a highly educated group. The religious breakdown of the par-

ticipants was 74.5% Catholic, 18.8% Protestant, 4.7% Jewish, and 2.0% other. The research booklet was the same as in Study 2. The categorization schema for type was modified (see above), and the categorization schema for blame was identical to the earlier study. As before, participants detailed their unfairness instances and made severity ratings for each instance. The adult participants' booklets were completed over the students' holiday break.

4. Our modifications of the type schema proved successful in reducing the "miscellaneous" percentage, as it drops from 12% (in study 2) to 3.5%, a far more acceptable figure.

5. The mean severity rating was approximately 64, which falls in our "high" category, but the standard deviation was large, about 28. Put another way, the range of the ratings was from 1 to 100. But the most frequent (17.7%) value given was 100.

6. The arbitrary rules (H) category is also at the low severity end, and it is cited less frequently here than in Study 2 (10.3% vs. 15.1%). This lowering, we believe, is artifactual, attributable to the absence here of the tot and teen group, who used that category at a higher rate in Study 2 than did the A and S groups; in fact, the A and S groups in both studies use this category at about the same rate.

7. Because we modified the schema, condensing two separate categories into one, the letters and tags do not correspond to tables in chapter 5. Although "innocence punished" is still D, now it is III/D rather than II/D, and what was called "discriminatory treatment," III/G, is now called "unfair advantages," IV/F, though they are the same.

8. $(F[N = 162, df = 8,170] = 3.01, p = .0035)$.

9. If participants engage in some inner comparison where they weigh both "innocence punished" and "unfair advantages" cases against their normative standard, the former are likely to be seen, in colloquial terms, as more wrong.

10. The Cramer's V was .620, whereas it was .567 for Study 2.

11. The Cramer's V was .736.

12. This is an assumption, for which I have no support as of yet. It is plausible that low scores do indicate a willingness to forgive, but it may be wrong.

13. Job will ask a series of questions, but they are not questions at all. Using questions as a challenge, Job asks, "Are your eyes mere eyes of flesh?/Is your vision no keener than a man's?/Is your mind like a human mind?/Are your feelings human feelings?" Job believes that the answer to all of these questions is no, for such pleas for mitigation or exculpation for human failings cannot be made by God.

14. There are findings from civil law areas that dovetail here. For example, though there is no evidence that Americans hold antibusiness attitudes, if corporations lose negligence cases that individual defendants might win, this may be because corporations are perceived as having a greater capacity for avoiding harms. *See* V. P. Hans, *The Illusions and Realities of Jurors' Treatment of Corporate Defendants*, 48 DEPAUL L. REV. 327 (1999); R. Lempert, Why Do Juries Get a Bum Rap? Reflections on the Work of Valerie Hans. 48 DEPAUL L. REV. 453 (1998).

15. $X^2[N = 162, df = 20] = 56.2, p < .001$.

16. Earlier, when we looked at the specific rather than the major types of unfairness, we noted that participants rated "no work rewarded" (A) as a much more severe unfairness than "hard work not rewarded" (B). Here we have an interaction effect: Category A is associated far more with bosses, whereas equals play a much higher role in category B; when these two categories are combined into major category I, with category B dominating, severity ratings now fall.

17. $X^2[N = 162, df = 4] = 10.7, p = .03$.

7

VICTIMS OF UNFAIRNESS: A NARCISSISTIC OR EMPATHIC STORY?

Before describing Study 4 or stating its central question, two narratives from this study are given, the import of which will soon become apparent. The first narrative comes from one of our youngest participants, a 6-year-old boy, and the second comes from a 90-year-old man.

The 6-year-old was one of three siblings who served as participants. By way of context, his older sisters, ages 11 and 12, wrote about unfair advantages and discriminatory treatment instances over and over again; instances where one got a bigger birthday present than the other, or one had a more lavish party, or one got to do something the other did not get to do. "Squabbling sisters" seemed to characterize these narratives. The 6-year-old was different. He talked about his baby brother, who was not quite 2 years old, who repeatedly had to be taken to the hospital or doctors for some painful and persistent condition in his stomach that seemed to be there since birth. On some occasions, while the boy baby-sat his brother, the child would begin to scream in pain. The boy said that no matter how much he loved his baby brother, no matter how he hugged and cuddled the baby, no matter how soothing his words, he could not make his brother's pain go away. It seemed unfair that a baby should suffer so much.

The 90-year-old man talked about how the world and this country had changed during his lifetime. He focused on the fact that in a country as wealthy as the United States, one that exports food around the world and contributes food to humanitarian relief efforts, he found it unfair that there were still pockets of poverty in this country where people were hungry and malnourished. This, he said, was a tragic failure of society, a failure to attend to the most needy. Because we have not evolved to a point where we attend to others who have needs they cannot meet and eliminate hunger in our own country, which we surely can do, this shows him how much further we need to go to be a civilized people.

CONCERN FOR THE OTHER

In both of these examples, the participants are not the victims. In the boy's case, the victim is someone he knows, his brother. In the older man's case, the victims are people he has never met. In both examples there seems to be concern and empathy for the other. In neither example is there narcissism. Are these examples typical or atypical? Will we find, contrary to the boy's narrative, many more narratives like those of his older sisters, where "what have you done for me lately" is the theme, a rather narcissistic-like theme at that.

Based on the findings from our first three studies, we are fairly certain that the critics have it wrong in a number of ways. First, unfairnesses almost never turn out to bogus claims, because objective and independent coders consistently find them to be legitimate. Second, participants neither create dubious entitlement claims nor reveal dubious conceptions of unfairness, for the coders agree about the type of unfairness in the vast majority of instances and these type categories map nicely onto philosophic distinctions about fairness. This interrater agreement and close mapping with the analytical literature should not happen if the critics had a valid point. Third, from the blame codings of participants and outside coders, we find no evidence to support the critics' claims of victimology, neuroticism, and defensive avoidance of responsibility. To the contrary, the interpretation that best fits the findings sees unfairness as coming from the outside, not from within.

But the critics still have the narcissism arrow in their quiver. Narcissism, as a charge or a disorder, reflects a marked imbalance between the self and others, where self-importance and self-absorption are so excessive that the needs, feelings, and concerns of others are seldom considered, and if they are considered, "they are surely of less importance and significance than my own." For the narcissist, empathy is all but nonexistent, and perspective is directed from and to the all-consuming self. In their universe, narcissists are fixed at the center, as others are props and supports for the one and only bright star. It is not a pretty picture.

Critics may claim that the narcissistic picture described here fits our data, pointing to recurrent findings of voluminous numbers of unfairnesses, which, they claim, indirectly attest to the pervasiveness of narcissism, or at least to a hair-trigger readiness to cry "unfair." Perhaps it does. But in fairness, mere numbers are not a good gauge of narcissism, and they may be no gauge at all. Fortunately, we have more direct ways of testing the narcissism possibility, along with its opposite, an empathy possibility.

In Study 4, a variable particularly revealing of narcissism, involving who the victim is (called personal) enters the analysis. This variable has been in our general instructions and embedded in the participants' narratives all along, but it has remained unanalyzed, until now. From our reading of participants' narratives in the earlier studies, our unsystematic impressions were that this personal variable produces differences, depending on whether the victim is the participant, or is someone known to the participant personally (e.g., a friend, spouse, sibling, parent, neighbor), or someone unknown (e.g., those one reads about in the morning newspaper or hears about on the evening news). The 6-year-old boy's narrative about his brother in pain is an example of when the victim is known personally, and the 90-year-old man's narrative about hunger in America is an example of victims unknown. Given the critics' charge of narcissism, this personal variable ought to be dispositive.

Are people more focused on unfairnesses when they are the victims, indicating a "culture of narcissism,"[1] such that they write about these far more than any other personal type? If this is so, then participants of all age groups ought to put their own unfairnesses at the center of their unfairness galaxy, dwarfing all others. The narcissistic effect, if it shows, should also be evident in severity ratings, in addition to the frequency with which they cite their own unfairnesses. Not only should their unfairnesses be situated at the center of the galaxy, but they should shine brighter and hotter than the unfairnesses that affect others.

This "me as victim" or "me generation" focus, if there is one, may not be uniform across age groups, but it may be localized at particular ages or generational groups. Will it be most prevalent in the very young, the very old, or the Generation-Xers in between? On the other hand, perhaps this self-focus, if we find it, changes with age. Will we see evidence of developmental change toward an "other focus," such that our empathy grows and extends to those we do not know yet share a human kinship to as our concern for self wanes? In coding and testing this "personal" variable, we also plan to relate it to our familiar variables, of severity, type, and blame.

STUDY 4

In addition to our main focus and set of questions about the personal variable and whether narcissism or empathy shows, there were secondary questions aimed at increasing the confidence in our earlier findings and extending their range. Overall, three methodological changes were made in Study 4. The first was aimed at extending our age range and increasing our sample sizes. Given earlier findings (Study 2) about unfairness judgments changing with increasing age (i.e., the A and S versus T group differences), the question now was this: Will this pattern continue if we add a sample of older participants (i.e., over 60), a group we have not looked at before? To test this, we asked a new sample of college students to recruit their grandparents for this study. We also wanted to increase the overall sample size of our tot and teen (T) sample above what we had in Study 2, which was not very large, and we wanted to see if those results would replicate here. To increase this sample, we asked our students to recruit a younger sibling, niece, or nephew.[2]

Our second methodological change was aimed at a finer analysis of participant and coder disagreements. We knew that some of those disagreements revealed perspectival differences. Specifically, we wanted to know if those disagreements could be reconciled, and how they would be reconciled. To explore this, we had the participant and the independent coder meet face to face, after their independent ratings had been made, to "talk out" how each perceived the unfairness, what each focused on, why each came to the judgment that a certain type and blame category fit, and whether reconciliation was possible. By adding this phase, we were able to determine the percentage of disagreements that reconcile and the direction of the reconciliation.

There were a number of possibilities. The obvious guess is that the reconciliation ought to go in the participant's direction, as we generally grant the participant primacy over his or her experience. The less likely hunch favors objectivity over subjectivity and predicts that participants may yield to the disinterested outsider, as the latter is more objective. Still a third hypothesis would predict that each might see something valid in the others' perspective, such that the reconciliation would blend both views. Of course, the final possibility is no reconciliation at all, as each participant stays fixed in the view that he or she originally had.

The third change we made in Study 4, and the major one, was aimed at discriminating unfairness instances along a personal-to-impersonal dimension, which we called "personal." We asked all participants to indicate if this experience happened "to you" (Y), "to someone you know" (K), or "to someone unknown that you heard about" (U).[3]

RESULTS AND DISCUSSION

The 172 participants detailed 1638 instances of unfairness (with a mean of 9.5), which was higher than previous studies.[4] Looking at the personal dimension, the Y category ranks second across age groups, accounting for 35.8% of the instances; ranking first is the K category, accounting for 38.6% of the instances; and the U category ranks third, accounting for 25.6% of the instances. This finding—where Y experiences do not dominate the landscape—contradicts the prediction of those who claim that narcissism is at the center of unfairnesses. Furthermore, when the K and U experiences are combined (as these both involve others), this total represents more than 64% of the unfairness instances, which looks nothing like narcissism.

However, looking by age group, we find a significant difference,[5] which adds complexity and nuance to the picture. Regarding age group differences, the T group gives the highest percentage of Y experiences, whereas the E and S groups give a higher percentage of U and K experiences, and this is shown in Table 7-1. Further testing reveals that the difference is between the T group and the S and E groups combined. Almost half (48.6%) of the T group's instances are Y, with only 17.5% being U; using those figures as a baseline for the E and S group, the latter's Y percentage falls to one third, whereas the U percentage almost doubles.

What are we to make of such differences? If we assume that the E and S participants once upon a time had roughly the same percentage of Y experiences as our current T group, then the lower percentage of Y experiences may indicate greater forgetting of Y instances, or that newer, impersonal U experiences have crowded out the older and more personal Y ones, or that both forgetting and crowding out are occurring. Whichever hypothesis we opt for, all are consistent with an interpretation that if narcissism exists at the early ages, it seems to wane with age. This is not the finding that the critic predicts.

If the attribution of narcissism is to be made based on these age group findings, it would be pinned on the T group, for one could construe its

TABLE 7-1
The Number and Percentage of Unfairnesses for the E, S, and T
Groups, by Whether the Experience Happened to You (Y),
to Someone Known (K), or Someone Unknown (U)

| Group | Personal-to-Impersonal Dimension of Unfairness | | | | | | Totals by Group |
| | Y | | K | | U | | |
	n	%	n	%	n	%	n
E	42	32.1	51	38.9	38	29.0	131
S	403	33.2	482	39.7	330	27.1	1215
T	142	48.6	99	33.9	51	17.5	292
Totals across groups	587	35.8	632	38.6	419	25.6	1638

Note: The percentages are calculated across rows.

high Y percentage as reflecting an egocentric train of thought, with narcissism being but a few stops further along on that train. But there are less pejorative ways of viewing this finding that we must consider. For example, perhaps the high Y percentage simply reflects the psychological fact that the T group's world is smaller than that of E and S groups, which is thus naturally composed of a higher percentage of Y experiences. In this developmental rather than pathological view, our world will then naturally expand as we age, as we come to know more people and their stories through personal communication (K), or because we read more newspapers or watch more television news (U). Thus the significant effects (e.g., more Y experiences for the T group, more K and U experiences in the E and S group) may simply represent naturally higher Y percentages at the younger age and naturally higher impersonal experiences accruing with age.

Furthermore, this natural accrual may be enhanced by an accessibility bias,[6] where recent, highly dramatic unfairnesses portrayed by the media[7] come readily to mind, but not to all minds equally. Older participants read newspapers and watch television news more than the youngsters do, and this accessibility bias should favor the older participants.

Whether it is egocentrism, natural accrual, or an accessibility bias affecting our selection, or some combination, we cannot say at this time. Although our conclusions are more modest, they are telling in their own right. First, Y experiences are not repressed: There is no shortage of Y experiences at any age-group level. Second, Y experiences neither dominate nor predominate at the higher age levels. These facts contradict allegations that the "me generation" has arrived, where "whiners" decry their "victimhood" over trifles. Third, the findings that the Y percentage drops with age while empathetic concern for others increases (reflected in the higher K and U percentages) support the view that empathy grows stronger than narcissism, if it is narcissism at all.

Severity Ratings

Now let us put severity into the picture. The mean severity ratings for the personal categories for the age groups are shown in Table 7-2, and there are significant differences. One difference is the age group effect, with the means for the E and S groups being significantly higher than the T group overall. Higher severity rates for the E and S groups suggest that we do not become jaded to unfairnesses as we age (accommodating to them), because if age produced greater acceptance we would expect the reverse findings.

The picture is actually more complex than the overall age effect indicates. For example, the overall lower rates for the T group result from lower ratings for Y and K experiences, but not for U experiences. The age group differences for Y and K may reflect the experiential reality of E and

Mean Severity Ratings for the E, S, and T Groups, for Instances That Happened to the Participant (Y), to Someone the Participant Knows (K), or to Someone Unknown (U)

Group	Personal-to-Impersonal Dimension of Unfairness			Means by Group
	Y	K	U	
E	67.5	67.8	77.8	71.0
S	65.9	70.9	79.6	72.1
T	58.9	56.7	75.4	63.6
Means across groups	64.1	65.1	77.6	

S participants: Perhaps the Y and K experiences that occur later in life turn out to be more severe than the ones in the tot and teen years. On the other hand, we cannot rule out the possibility that memories are culled: when we learn about new unfairnesses; if these are more severe than our current stock, they may crowd out the old. These possibilities point to a caution when comparing across groups, for even though we may be comparing a set of experiences all designated as Y, this does not mean that they are equivalent: The ones experienced and culled by the E and S groups may be qualitatively different as well as quantitatively hotter than those reported by the T group.

Regarding the Y severity ratings that E and S groups report, we see no evidence that these instances roll off our backs as we age or that some accepting perspective—which comes with age, time, and distance—mutes their formerly intense coloration. We also see that the U experiences are rated more severely than Y and K experiences—for all groups. As we speculated, these U instances may reflect unfairness in *extremis*, prototypical in readily staying in mind and inflaming the passions, but not necessarily representative of the ordinary and customary unfairnesses.[8] The high severity ratings for the U experiences coupled with the higher percentage of U experiences cited by the S and E groups give added support to the view that empathy for others increases with age. If severity, as I have argued, is some measure of our anger, then we are hotter about unfairnesses that happen to unknown others (U) than those that happen to us (Y), a finding quite at odds with what the narcissist displays.

Types of Unfairness

Now let us add type to the emerging picture. The data for major types of unfairness are presented in Table 7-3. We again see that the Job-like category (III) is cited most frequently (38%). Ranking a close second and

TABLE 7-3
The Number and Percentage of Instances Where the Experience Happened
to You (Y), to Someone Known (K), or Someone Unknown (U), for the
Major Type of Unfairness Categories

| Type | Personal-to-Impersonal Dimension of Unfairness | | | | | | Totals by Type | |
| | Y | | K | | U | | | |
	n	%	n	%	n	%	n	%
I + II. Reward/effort + wrongful behavior	157	43.1	144	39.6	63	17.3	364	23.5
III. Punishment/behavior	126	21.1	253	43.1	208	35.4	587	38.0
IV. Discriminatory treatment	155	40.1	142	36.7	90	23.3	387	25.0
V. Lack of due process	99	47.6	71	34.1	38	18.3	208	13.5
Totals across type	537	34.7	610	39.5	399	25.8	1546	

Note: The percentages are calculated across the rows, except for totals by type.

third are the discriminatory treatment (IV) and the combined rewards/effort and wrongful behavior (I and II) categories (25% and 23.5%, respectively); and cited least frequently was the lack of due process (V) category (13.5%).[9]

When we analyzed type by the "personal" variable, we found a significant effect.[10] Looking at the Y category first, this category is overrepresented for the I and II, IV, and V type instances, but underrepresented for III. Put another way, Job-like unfairnesses (III) occur less frequently to the participant than other types. This means that when participants are the victims, they are most likely victimized by rewards not being gotten, seeing wrongful behavior going unpunished or rewarded, being on the receiving end of some sort of discriminatory treatment, and having arbitrary rules imposed on them without due process. For the U instances, the disparity is in the other direction, where "innocents being punished" (III) are cited more frequently, and thus Job is more likely to be the other rather than the self.

Now let us bring severity back into the picture. Severity was significantly related to type in Study 3, and that finding is replicated here. "Innocence is punished" (III) is rated as significantly more severe than the other types. Now we find a severity × type × personal interaction that is significant. To explicate, first there are no significant differences in severity among Y, K, and U experiences in the discriminatory treatment (IV) and lack of due process (V) categories; but there is a significant difference for the I and II and the III categories: When these occur to unknown others, the ratings are significantly higher than when such experiences befall those we know or ourselves.

TABLE 7-4
The Frequency (*n*), Percentage, and Severity Ratings of Those Blaming
Bosses (B), Equals (E), God (G), Life (L), and Society (S), for the Elderly
(E), Student (S), and Tot and Teen (T) Groups

	Blame Categories											
	B		E		G		L		S		Totals	
Group	*n*	%	*n*	%	*n*	%	*n*	%	*n*	%	*n*	%
E	24	18.6	19	14.7	6	4.7	14	10.9	66	51.2	129	7.9
S	390	32.2	282	23.2	81	6.7	163	13.4	305	25.1	1213	74.5
T	153	53.5	49	17.1	15	5.2	27	9.4	42	14.7	286	17.6
Totals across groups	567	34.8	350	21.5	95	5.8	204	12.5	412	25.3	1628	
Severity ratings		69.6		70.3		89.1		79.5		81.0		

Of all the findings to date, this is perhaps the most powerful rejoinder to the "me generation" claim, for these results show that we are more angered and outraged when the unknown other is Job than we are when we see ourselves as Job, and we have greater anger when the unknown other rather than the self does not get the rewards that are rightfully earned by efforts. If participants distort by (a) magnifying their own importance and centrality, (b) relegating others and their claims to the background, and (c) concluding that their own victimizations were the more egregious, then the results should have been opposite to what we found.

Blame

Now we add blame to the picture. In this study, we made one change to the blame categories: We lumped "parent" into the bosses category on the grounds that parents are the bosses of tots and teens. The blame by age group data are presented in Table 7-4, along with the severity ratings. Looking at the totals, we see that the newly combined bosses category ranks first (34.8%);[11] the society category is cited frequently (25.3), though at a lower rate than in Study 3;[12] and the God category is again cited least. Looking by age group, there is a significant difference in the blaming pattern,[13] which is most notable for the bosses and society categories. With increasing age, bosses (and parents) are blamed less frequently, while the reverse is true for society, a finding that replicates earlier results. For equals, God, and life, the blaming pattern is fairly stable across the age ranges.

The severity findings replicate what we found in Study 3, with significant differences among the blame categories.[14] Once again, although

God is cited least frequently in terms of blame, when God is cited, the ratings are significantly higher than the other categories. If lower scores indicate a willingness to forgive, then our forgiveness is extended to bosses and equals more easily and charitably than for life and society, which repeats the earlier findings. About God, we remain least forgiving.

There is also an age group effect on severity ratings. Although the E and S groups give higher severity ratings than the T group in general, the effect is not uniform across the blame categories: When we analyze by blame categories, the E and S participants (taken together) give higher severity ratings than the T participants only for bosses (70.4 versus 63.0) and God (90.7 versus 56.2), whereas there were no significant differences for equals, life, and society. For the category of bosses (which includes parents), although the T group cites this significantly more frequently than the E and S groups, the latter groups feel more anger and outrage when bosses produce the unfairnesses. For the God category, we see that the E, S, and T groups cite God with a similar frequency, but when they do, the E and S groups judge God much more severely than the T group. If anger over unfairnesses does mute with age, we see no evidence of muting when we examine the ratings for bosses, God, and society.[15]

The Complexities of the Emerging Unfairness Picture

We only note in passing some type $\times$ blame findings, for these again replicate earlier findings,[16] and the number of significant three-way and four-way interaction effects attest to the complexity of the unfairness picture.[17] These replications add to our confidence that effects are solid and sound, at least for this population,[18] a population that has broadened in Study 4 with the inclusion of an older age group. The personal variable, which was new to this study, was significant as a main effect and significantly related to both age group, type, blame, and severity.[19]

In Study 3, based on severity ratings, we categorized instances into one of four classes (low, 1–25; medium, 26–50; high, 51–75; and severe, 76–100) and then analyzed the results. In Study 4, we decided on a different break—looking at the extremely high (90–100)[20] instances versus all the rest—and we found significant differences by personal, type, and blame categories. The impersonal (U) experiences, the punishment type experiences, and blaming of life (including God) and society were over-represented in the extremely high group.

Finally, we end with findings regarding the categorization schemas, where the interrater reliability was higher for both type and blame here than in Study 3, adding to our confidence in these schemas. We did add a new methodological feature in this study, having the participant sit down with the objective coder to reconcile categorization differences. For type of unfairness, 73% of the time the participant and outside rater agreed; 1% of the time they both saw merit in the other's perspective, and the reconciliation reflected the views of both; 5% of the time the disagreement could not be reconciled; most interesting was the finding that 8.3% of the time the disagreement was reconciled by the participant agreeing with the outside rater, whereas 12.7% of the time the outside rater switched and agreed with the participant. This finding did surprise us, for we thought the vast majority would have been reconciled in the participant's subjective direction.

For the blame data, 83.3% of the time the participant and outside rater agreed; 3% of the time they both saw merit in the other's perspective, and 4.6% of the time the disagreement could not be reconciled. When we looked at the reconciling switches, going either in the participant's direction or the outsider's direction, the findings surprised us even more: 6.2% of the time the disagreement was reconciled by the participant agreeing with the outside rater, and 5.9% of the time the outside rater switched and agreed with the participant. Though the numbers get small, we did see a good number of what we call "God versus life" disagreements between participant and outside rater. Sometimes the two agreed to disagree, and these disagreements were not reconciled. When they were reconciled, the person claiming that God is to blame would more often yield to the one claiming that "No, it's not God, but life."

LOOKING BACKWARD, LOOKING FORWARD

With four studies now completed, we have data on some 5000 instances of unfairness. We have tested, modified, and retested our categorization schemas for type and blame, and both appear inclusive, reliable, and valid. Moreover, in Study 4 we took a different approach to disagreements between participants and outside coders, having each articulate the perspective they took to each other, and we then explored the possibility of reconciliation and the direction of reconciliation. For both type and blame disagreements, participants were more open than we predicted to reconciling in the outside coder's direction. But a repeated disagreement was noted on the blame categories, which generally did not reconcile, where the participant blames God but the coder blames life. It is likely that views on theodicy and misfortunes come into play here, and we mark this as an open question for further investigation.

In looking back, the findings for the main effects of type and blame and the type × blame interaction yield a consistent picture across the studies, and though these effects did change with age group, those changes appear consistent across the studies. Regarding our age groups, we bolstered our overall numbers in tots and teens (T) while replicating earlier findings, and with a new group (E), we were able to extend the results. The type and blame and personal patterns were similar for the E and S groups, where previously we found similarity between A and S groups. Based on this work, the conceptions and concepts of unfairness seem to hold steady from college age onward.

When the quantitative variable of severity was added to the picture, the landscape of unfairness took on more detail, color, and complexity, but, most important, greater clarity. With the personal dimension added to the picture, its main effect and interaction effects (with type, blame, age group, and severity) show consistency. Substantively, the results point much more strongly to empathy rather than to narcissism as the answer to our chapter's question. Even at the youngest of ages, a time when egocentrism is most strong, we did see, as the example that starts this chapter reveals, that individuals can feel for and feel about another. With increasing age, our "me as victim" focus moderates sharply, and empathic concern for the "other as victim" increases in frequency and intensity as our perspective changes. At all age groups, even the T group, participants are angriest about unfairnesses that happen to unknown others (U), a finding that contradicts the narcissism prediction.

In looking forward, we know that there is a significant severity × blame × age group effect, such that some are less angry with bosses, parents, and equals than with God, life, and society. But what do these differences mean? Are we less angry with the former group when the experiences first occur (an "initial" effect), or does our anger fade faster for the former group (a "getting over" effect)? At this point, the evidence suggests that both possibilities are operating, but we can say very little in general about how unfairnesses change over time. We may infer that they do change, but this is speculative, for we do not know for a fact that muting has occurred. What we need to answer the question are measures at two points in time. Such measures, if we had them, could speak to a question that has been lingering since the outset of this work, about whether we get over our "hot" unfairnesses. This is the question we turn to next.

ENDNOTES

1. C. Lasch, *The Culture of Narcissism* (New York: W. W. Norton, 1979).
2. There were 172 participants overall, 103 females and 69 males, with 59.5% Catholic, 20.9% Protestant, 7% Jewish, and 12.7% other. There were 100

participants in the student (S) group (58 females, 42 males), with a mean age of 20.1 and a mean education level of 14.4. There were 23 elderly (E) participants (12 females and 11 males), with a mean age of 71.0 and a mean education level of 16.1. There were 49 participants in the tot and teen (T) group (33 females and 16 males), with a mean age of 13.3 and a mean education level of 7.9. Although teenagers predominated in the T group, we did have the younger tots as well, which called for us to make a methodological change, as we did in Study 2. When these tots could not write or preferred talking out their unfairnesses, the student participants who recruited the tots would read them the instructions several times and then wrote down their narratives as fully and accurately as possible.

3. There are findings in the discrimination literature that may relate to the frequency and severity of unfairness questions we have raised. One finding is that individuals who are members of a group believe that more cases of discrimination occur to the group as a whole than what individual members report suffering personally. Likewise, maybe more unfairnesses and more severe unfairnesses will be reported in regard to others, rather than having occurred to the person. *See, e.g.*, F. M. Moghaddam, *Social Psychology: Exploring Universals Across Cultures* (San Francisco: W. H. Freeman, 1998).

4. The explanation for this higher mean can be found in the size of the specific groups comprising our overall sample and the rate of instances produced by each group. The small (n = 23) E group produced 131 instances, with an average of 5.7, whereas the T group (n = 49), approximately twice as large as the E group, produced 292 instances, with an average of 6.0. However, the S group (n = 100), which was approximately twice as large as the T group and four times as large as the E group, produced by far the most instances, 1215, with an average of 12.1. It was this S group increase that accounted for the overall rise.

5. $X^2[N = 172, df = 4] = 27.02, p < .001$.

6. A. Tversky and D. Kahneman, "Judgment Under Uncertainty: Heuristics and Biases," *Science* 185 (1974): 1124–1131.

7. V. P. Hans, "Law and the Media: An Overview and Introduction," *Law and Human Behavior* 14 (1990): 399–407.

8. *See, e.g.*, N. J. Finkel, "Commonsense Justice, Psychology, and the Law: Prototypes Common, Senseful, and Not," *Psychology, Public Policy, and Law* 3 (1997): 461–489.

9. Unlike Study 2, where there was a significant type by age group effect, with the adult (A) and student (S) groups being significantly different from the tot and teen (T) group, in Study 4 we find that the differences among our age groups failed to reach significance. However, though not significantly different there were, again, the same trends we saw in Study 2: The T group shows a higher proportion of lack-of-due-process (V) claims than the E and S groups, and the E and S groups show a higher proportion of "when innocence is punished" (III) claims than the T group.

10. $X^2[N = 172, df = 6] = 92.5, p < .001$.

11. Although this appears different from Study 2 and Study 3, we must keep in mind a number of differences among these three studies that, when taken

together, show that there really is no significant difference. First, in Study 4 we combined the former parent category into the bosses category, thereby increasing its frequency and percentage. Second, in Study 2 we found that the T group participants cite parents far more frequently than S and A group participants, and they do so again in Study 4, citing parents (now coded in bosses) far more frequently than the E and S groups, whereas in Study 3 we did not have a T group, which lowered the frequency. When we factor in these differences among the studies, the results appear quite similar.

12. However, this lower rate can be accounted for by the presence of the T group in this study and its absence in Study 3, because we found that the T group cites society far less frequently than S, A, and E groups.

13. $X^2[N = 172, df = 8] = 99.6, p < .001$.

14. $F[N = 172, df = 20,521] = 1.6, p = .04$.

15. We do report, with caution, a significant age group personal interaction effect for one category—that of God. The caution involves the low number of citings of God to begin with, and we will have to see if this finding recurs with a larger sample. But what we found is this: For the T group, the average severity ratings for God in the three personal categories were 84.7 (U), 54.5 (K), and 49.7 (Y), whereas for the combined E and S groups, those ratings were 78.4 (U), 69.0 (K), and 63.3 (Y). It is our youngest group, the T group, that seems angriest when God causes an unfairness to someone unknown, though they are less angry than the E and S groups when the unfairness occurs to someone they know or when it occurs to them.

16. Bosses are blamed predominantly (60.5%) in the lack of due process category (V) and most heavily (48.1%) in the reward/effort and wrongful behavior categories (I and II), though they are significantly cited (30.1%) in the punishment/behavior (III) and the discriminatory treatment (IV) categories (37.2%). Equals are cited for rewards (I and II), punishment (III), and discrimination (IV) moderately (16–25%), but infrequently (5%) for lack of due process (V). God is cited almost exclusively (95%) in the punishment (III) category. Life is cited most (20%) in the punishment category (III), occasionally cited in reward and lack of due process categories (10–12%), and only rarely in the discriminatory treatment (5%) category. Society is most frequently cited (41%) in the discriminatory treatment category, cited frequently in the lack of due process category (23%), and moderately in the reward and punishment categories (15–18%).

17. There are significant interaction effects with age group (e.g., age group $\times$ type $\times$ blame), with the T group overrepresented in the lack of due process category, and the E and S groups overrepresented in the punishment category. We find severity significantly relating to age group, type, and blame as well.

18. We also replicated the sequence effect found in Study 3. There were no significant differences when we tested the order of unfairness instances, as type, blame, and severity remained fairly uniform.

19. There are also variables that have mixed results, such as gender and religion, sometimes showing significant effects, sometimes not. We are less confident, clearly, when results are mixed. The findings with these variables in Study 4

were not easily interpretable. For example, the gender effect we found in Study 3 was not significant in Study 4. For religion, we found a significant effect regarding type of unfairness, but not for blame.

20. To recall the results of Study 3, the most frequently assigned severity rating, the modal value, was 100. With that finding, we wanted to focus in on the upper end.

8

DO WE EVER GET OVER UNFAIRNESSES?

The focal question is easy to ask, though hard to answer, as a hypothetical example makes clear. If a group of adults fill out a "But It's Not Fair!" booklet, how would we know if they got over some of their unfairnesses? If they got over some so completely that they were forgotten, we would never know this because those instances would not appear in their booklets. Thus the best evidence (i.e., a severity of zero) we could find would be the least likely evidence we *would* find. Let us go to second best evidence—low level unfairnesses. The problem here is that if people report low level unfairnesses, we could not determine if once upon a time these were big unfairnesses that they are getting over or whether they are just what they are reported to be, low-level instances. To assess change, we would need two severity measures, reflecting different points in time.

The best way of doing this work, which takes time and persistence, is through longitudinal research. This involves taking one group, following the group members over time, and taking unfairness narratives at various points in time. By contrast, our methodology involves testing multiple groups at the same point in time. Is there another way, less than first best, which would yield an answer?

STUDY 5

In this study, adult and student participants do the task and make type and blame categorizations, but now we ask them to make two severity ratings: The first one reflects how they see the unfairness now; the second asks them to think back to when the experience first happened and to make a severity rating for how it felt then. The number they come up with for "then" (which could be decades ago) is a bit problematic, for it may be little more than a guess. On the other hand, the participant is the best (in fact, the only) person who can make that guess. For our purposes, the exactness of the number is not the point; the ballpark in which these numbers fall is enough.

The now and then ratings are designated sevnow and sevthen, and by subtracting the former from the latter, we have a difference score, designated as sevdiff. But time must be taken into account in assessing change, because a large sevdiff score occurring in a 1-year period is not equivalent to one that occurred over 20 years. To bring time into the analysis, we asked participants to record the approximate year when each unfairness happened, and we designate this as agewhen. Because we know their current age, by subtraction we get an age difference score (age − agewhen), which we designate as agediff. Finally, by dividing sevdiff by agediff, we get a measure of change, called rate of change. By then analyzing the rate of change scores, we can assess "getting over" in general, as well as look for differences on the variables of age group, type, blame, and personal.[1]

Results and Discussion

The 168 participants generated 1984 instances of unfairness, with an overall mean of 7.5 per participant, ranging from a low of 1 to a high of 34.[2] Regarding the type findings, there are significant differences overall, and between age groups (see Table 8-1). Once again, the "innocence punished" (III/D) and the "unfair advantages" (IV/F) categories rank first and second, respectively, as they do in almost all the studies, and this 1/2 ranking occurs for both the A and S groups.[3] Regarding the sevnow ratings across the type of unfairness, there is a significant difference: "Innocence is punished" (III/D) is again rated most severe, whereas "arbitrary rules" (V/H) and "no work rewarded" (I/A) are rated significantly lower.[4]

The blame results are presented in Table 8-2, and there are significant differences, according quite closely with previous work. More than twice as many blame society than any other category, with God and individual being cited least. Students blame parents more than adults do, but adults blame society more than students do; both groups blame God, life, and society at higher sevnow levels than parents, individual, equals, and bosses.[5]

TABLE 8-1

Frequency (*n*), Percentage (%), and Mean Severity Ratings (Sevnow) for the Major and Specific Type of Unfairnesses, for Adult (A) and Student (S) Age Groups

| Major/Specific Categories | Age Groups | | | | | |
| | A | | | S | | |
	n	%	Sevnow	*n*	%	Sevnow
I/A—No work rewarded	25	2.9	56.4	47	4.3	47.3
I/B—Hard work not rewarded	81	9.3	63.0	124	11.4	59.2
II/C—Wrongful not punished	117	13.5	62.4	105	9.7	59.9
III/D—Innocence punished	272	31.4	74.2	373	34.5	81.3
III/D—Disproportionate	33	3.8	65.6	59	5.4	68.0
IV/F—Unfair advantages	151	17.4	64.3	192	17.7	63.1
IV/G—Equal treatment	32	3.7	62.2	34	3.1	51.9
V/H—Arbitrary rules	86	9.9	57.9	104	9.6	55.3
VI/I—Miscellaneous	70	8.1	63.0	47	4.3	61.1

Once again, there is a significant type × blame interaction effect, which can be seen in Table 8-3. Bosses are blamed most frequently (33.2%) in the "reward/effort" (I) category, and second most (27%) in "unfair advantages" (IV). Equals are blamed most frequently (36.8%) in "innocence punished" (III) and next most (29.5%) in "wrongful behavior unpunished" (II). God is blamed almost exclusively (94.5%) in "innocence punished." The individual is blamed most (42.5%) in "innocence punished" (III), as is life (74%). Parents are blamed frequently in "innocence punished" (36.8%), "arbitrary rules" (30%), and in "unfair advantages" (26.4%). So-

TABLE 8-2

Frequency (*n*), Percentage (%), and Mean Severity Ratings (Sevnow) for the Blame Categories for Adult (A) and Student (S) Age Groups

| Blame Categories | Age Groups | | | | | |
| | A | | | S | | |
	n	%	Sevnow	*n*	%	Sevnow
Bosses	153	17.3	57.4	196	18.0	59.7
Equals	143	16.2	57.6	187	17.2	66.4
God	31	3.5	79.7	43	4.0	85.4
Individual	29	3.3	57.9	52	4.8	61.1
Life	121	13.7	75.8	169	15.6	76.3
Parents	51	5.8	55.9	119	11.0	60.0
Society	355	40.2	70.4	321	29.5	69.3

TABLE 8-3
Sevnow Ratings by Major Type of Unfairness by Major Blame Categories

| Major Type | Major Blame Categories | | | |
	Bosses	Equals	Life	Society
I—Reward/effort	58.1	65.0	54.2	62.2
II—Wrongful unpunished	57.1	53.9	66.7	69.3
III—Innocence punished	67.2	70.6	84.1	77.2
IV—Unfair advantages	55.8	62.7	67.4	65.9
V—Arbitrary rules	54.2	53.7	55.6	62.4

ciety is blamed most in "unfair advantages" (33.3%) and "innocence punished" (33.2%).[6]

The personal dimension is also significant, but there is no age group difference, consistent with Study 4. The overall Y, K, and U percentages are 33.1%, 40.4%, and 26.5%, respectively, and these accord closely with the percentages in Study 4. Thus participants report a greater number of instances that happen to those they know and the least to others they do not know (K > Y > U).

Shifting to the quantitative dependent variable sevnow, there is a significant main effect for "personal" and a significant personal × type interaction effect, findings that are shown in Table 8-4. Looking at the percentage columns, categories I and V (the reward to effort and arbitrary rules categories) decline sharply from personal to impersonal (Y > K > U), but the reverse is true for III (innocence is punished). The quantitative sevnow ratings show a different pattern, which is consistent at every type level: The pattern of sevnow ratings is U > K > Y, with U experiences remaining hotter than K or Y instances, on the average. Being angrier

TABLE 8-4
The Frequency (n), Percentage (%), and the Mean Sevnow (Sev) Ratings for the Personal/Impersonal Dimension (Y, K, U) by Major Type Categories of Unfairness

| Major Type Categories | Personal/Impersonal Dimension | | | | | | | | |
| | Y | | | K | | | U | | |
	n	%	Sev	n	%	Sev	n	%	Sev
I	132	21.8	56.0	106	14.3	62.5	39	8.0	64.1
II	78	12.8	53.0	75	10.1	59.9	69	14.2	71.6
III	142	23.4	60.3	340	45.9	79.1	255	52.5	83.0
IV	154	25.3	55.9	156	21.1	63.8	154	25.3	70.7
V	102	16.8	52.5	64	8.6	57.8	24	4.9	69.9
Across types	608	33.1	55.5	741	40.4	64.6	486	26.5	71.9

TABLE 8-5
The Frequency (*n*), Percentage (%), and the Mean Sevnow (Sev) Ratings
for the Personal Dimension (Y, K, U) by Blame Categories

| | Personal Dimension | | | | | | | | |
| | Y | | | K | | | U | | |
Blame	*n*	%	Sev	*n*	%	Sev	*n*	%	Sev
Bosses	176	26.6	55.9	142	18.1	60.7	31	6.0	65.2
Equals	182	27.5	54.8	172	21.9	64.4	57	10.9	77.5
God	9	1.4	70.0	45	5.7	82.6	20	3.8	89.8
Life	67	10.1	63.4	139	17.7	80.2	84	16.1	79.4
Parents	77	11.6	44.4	75	9.5	67.1	18	3.5	86.5
Society	152	22.9	57.4	213	27.1	70.5	311	59.7	75.0
Across blame	663	33.7	57.7	786	39.9	76.4	521	26.5	78.9

about the unfairnesses suffered by the other, a finding that replicates Study 4, is the empathetic finding,[7] which again refutes the claim of narcissism.

Continuing with the personal dimension, we find a significant personal × blame effect in analyzing the frequency of occurrence, and on the quantitative sevnow measure there is a significant personal × blame effect (see Table 8-5) as well. For the frequency and percentage columns, we see that bosses, equals, and parents show a declining pattern (Y > K > U) across personal, whereas society is the reverse (U > K > Y), and Life and God are greater for K and U than for Y. For the quantitative data, though, the sevnow ratings generally follow the U > K > Y pattern at each blame level; in fact, the gap between U and K, on the one hand, and Y, on the other, grows wider, a result that is similar to the type data.

These findings make more sense once we understand that sevnow reflects two types of processes: One is quick; the other is of long duration. Regarding the quick process, sevnow ratings reflect how the unfairness was initially perceived (i.e., sevthen), and we know that the correlation between sevnow and sevthen is substantial.[8] As for the longer duration process, sevnow ratings also reflect how the individual copes with that unfairness over time. Reflecting on the event and on one's own emotions may lead participants to see the unfairness in a wider and broader context and to a shift in perspective. However, although we have some degree of control over the psychological factors that affect our sevnow judgments for our own Y experiences, we have no control over what others (in K and U experiences) do with their emotions and judgments. This control component no doubt operates differentially: We have greater control of Y instances, so these should temper more over time than K and U instances.

Now we arrive at our central questions: Are the K and U instances just more severe to begin with, or are there longer term processing differences that give us greater control over our Y experiences, such that we can reduce their heat much more? Or is it some combination, where Y experiences are both less intense to begin with, and easier to process afterward?

A Second Point in Time

Sevthen is that second point in time, as far as our methodology goes. In actuality, of course, it is the first point in time for the participants—the moment just after the instance occurred—when the participant judged it unfair. Here, presumably, the unfairness is hottest. But how much hotter is sevthen than sevnow? Looking at the matter from the later point in time, we ask, Which unfairnesses "cool" the most from sevthen to sevnow, showing the highest sevdiff scores? If there are differential effects, how do they relate to type, blame, and personal?

We ran tests to assess the effects of the qualitative variables of type (I, II, III, IV, V), blame (bosses, equals, life, society), and personal (Y, K, U).[9] From our earlier analyses of sevnow, we know that there were significant effects for type, blame, and personal, type × blame, type × personal, and blame × personal. But what happens at this second point in time? The results for sevthen also reveal significant main effects for type, blame, and personal, and significant interaction effects for type × blame, type × personal, and blame × personal. To put the findings in context, we present the sevthen means in Table 8-6, along with sevnow for comparison, for the variables of type, blame, and personal. On 56 of the 59 comparisons between sevthen and sevnow in Table 8-6, the sevthen ratings are greater than or equal to sevnow, a finding we expected. Not only are the means higher, but the variance is tighter, indicating that time and processing effects are at work for sevnow, which cause both a general lowering and a spreading of scores.

The spreading of the scores is related to our variables. For example, the sevthen ratings show a main effect for the personal dimension, where the U > K > Y pattern results; although this U > K > Y pattern is the same for sevnow, the ratings on sevthen are more closely bunched. The drop in ratings from sevthen to sevnow reflects a Y > K > U pattern, where the unfairnesses that happen to us (Y) drop the most. From these findings, we see that the two hypothesized processing factors are operating: First, the instances are not equivalent to begin with, for U experiences are judged more severe than K experiences, and K experiences are judged more severe than Y experiences; the second factor that is operating is differential processing, where Y experiences cool faster than K and much faster than U.

We also see the main effect for type, as the sevthen ratings show a III > I, II, IV, V pattern. Although this same pattern occurs for both sevthen and sevnow, the gap between "innocence punished" cases (III) and all the other cases grows larger (i.e., III >> I, II, IV, V), indicating that the latter cases cool more rapidly than the type III cases. Also we see the

TABLE 8-6
Mean Ratings for Sevthen (Then) and Sevnow (Now), for the Major Categories of Type (I, II, III, IV, V), Major Categories for Blame (Bosses—B, Equals—E, Life—L, Society—S), and the Personal Dimension (Y, K, U)

		Personal Dimension					
		Y		K		U	
Type	Blame	Then	Now	Then	Now	Then	Now
I	B	74	56	71	61	71	64
I	E	73	60	64	71	78	73
I	L	65	56	58	46	63	56
I	S	69	51	72	68	69	63
II	B	90	59	68	58	45	45
II	E	61	49	63	55	68	66
II	L	80	50	70	64	87	87
II	S	74	58	76	71	80	73
III	B	80	55	76	71	84	84
III	E	65	58	79	72	90	86
III	L	83	76	89	85	89	85
III	S	68	57	78	79	83	81
IV	B	72	52	69	60	65	64
IV	E	78	60	71	63	90	88
IV	L	63	59	83	73	59	73
IV	S	69	59	70	67	71	70
V	B	73	49	67	57	81	73
V	E	72	49	67	60	—[a]	—[a]
V	L	49	48	65	55	83	83
V	S	76	63	64	59	66	65

[a] For the U experiences, under the "arbitrary rules" type (V), there were so few instances caused by equals that the means could not be calculated.

main effect for blame, where the sevthen ratings show a life > bosses, equals, society pattern. However, the sevnow pattern shows a greater spread (life > society > bosses, equals), which indicates that unfairnesses blamed on society do not cool as rapidly as those blamed on bosses and equals. Although showing significant differences in the means and variances at these two points in time, the analysis does not take duration of time from sevthen to sevnow[10] into account.

Rates of Change

The analyses of the rate of change variable show significant main effects for personal, type, and blame. For personal, the rate of change scores are 6.7 for Y, 4.6 for K, and 3.2 for U; as we suspected, the Y instances are easier to process than K, which are easier to process than U. We already know that there are initial (sevthen) and subsequent (sevnow) differences among these experiences, and now we know that there are also differences in how easy or difficult it is to get over them.

For type main effect, the rate of change scores for the five major categories are 9.1 (I), 4.1 (II), 3.5 (III), 4.9 (IV), and 7.6 (V); further testing reveals that the difference is II, III, IV < I, V. We have known that type III cases ("innocence is punished") receive the highest sevnow and sevthen scores; now we know that they are also the most difficult cases to get over as well. But type III cases are joined by "when wrongful behavior goes unpunished" (II) and "unfair advantages" (IV) cases as also difficult to get over, whereas the "reward-to-effort" (I) and the "arbitrary rules" (V) cases are more quickly gotten over.[11]

Blame also shows a significant main effect, with the rate of change scores for the four major categories being 5.8 (bosses), 7.9 (equals), 3.7 (life), and 3.9 (society), with further testing showing the difference to be bosses, equals > life, society. We sought to tease apart the blame findings a bit more, so we ran the analysis again but separated parents from the bosses category, and separated God from the life category. The results were 6.7 (bosses). 7.9 (equals), 3.3 (God), 3.9 (life), 3.7 (parents), and 3.9 (society). The low rate for God did not surprise us, given all the findings from previous studies, but the low rate for parent did surprise, indicating that we forgive bosses more readily than parents. Although the sevnow ratings for parents were the lowest for adults and second lowest for students (see Table 8-2), those low ratings now appear to be the result of much more time passing, rather than forgiving at a faster rate.

We must further qualify this finding, because we know (see Table 8-5) that there is a personal main effect and a personal × blame interaction effect, such that the severity scores generally follow a U > K > Y pattern. We see this pattern recurring for rate of change, where participants get over parent unfairnesses faster when it is their own parents who inflict the unfairness on them, but the rate of change slows appreciably when other parents inflict unfairnesses on other victims. This must be further qualified because there is a three-way type × blame × personal interaction effect: thus when a parent is blamed in a U experience it is much more difficult to get over when it is an "innocence punished" type case, as opposed to an "arbitrary rules" case.

By taking time into the equation, rate of change is a notable improvement over either sevnow or sevthen. Yet by itself this measure can be misleading, if it leads us to view change as constant across time.[12] Common sense would predict the greatest drop-off in the initial years following the unfairness and a slower drop-off in later years. To get a more accurate picture of what actually happens, we divided the unfairnesses into two groups, where experiences that occurred within the past 5 years were designated as short, whereas those that were over 5 years old went into the long category; this variable is called length of time.[13]

We next performed a number of analyses where rate of change was the dependent variable and where length of time was the independent variable, coupled with either age group, type, blame, or personal. There were significant main effects for length of time, type, blame, and personal.[14] Although mean differences tell one part of the story, the variance (standard deviation) tells another part; both are shown in Table 8-7. The length-of-time effect jumps out: The rate of change is 3 to 6 times greater in the short interval than the long, and the variance is 6 to 13 times greater. Thus most of the "getting over" occurs in the short interval.

There is great variability among participants in their processing rates during this short interval, such that some instances for some participants drop dramatically whereas others drop very little. However, once 5 years pass, the mean rates of change are low and the variance becomes almost microscopic. Once in this long period, we seem to pass the point of significant "getting over," as rates of change look remarkably uniform.[15] That variance shrinks so markedly from the short to the long period is evident for the blame and personal variables, and this is shown in Table 8-8. Specifically, U experiences continue to change least over the longer time interval, and even less so when life is blamed.

We add one final variable to the rate of change analyses. We know that the length-of-time variable dramatically affects rate of change, but what about the initial severity level? We have indirect evidence that initial severity levels matter, for we know that "innocence being punished" cases (III) are rated hotter on sevthen than "arbitrary rules" (V) cases, and the former show the least rate of change. But this is only indirect evidence.

To get a direct assessment, we went back to the sevthen ratings and found that the mean rating across all of the nearly 2000 instances of unfairness was approximately 75. We then used 75 as a rough cutoff point: Those instances at 75 or above would be designated as high, and those below 75 would be designated as low, and we called this new variable

TABLE 8-7
The Rate of Change Means (M) and Standard Deviations (SD) by Type of Unfairness, for the Adult (A) and Student (S) Age Groups, and by Length of Time (Long and Short)

	Length of Time							
	Long				Short			
	A		S		A		S	
Type	M	SD	M	SD	M	SD	M	SD
I—Reward/effort	1.3	2.0	2.3	2.9	20.4	37.3	10.1	13.3
II—Wrongful not punished	1.5	1.8	1.5	1.6	6.1	13.5	5.0	7.4
III—Innocence punished	1.0	1.5	1.3	2.1	6.3	14.3	4.4	7.9
IV—Unfair advantages	1.2	1.4	2.9	2.6	7.9	22.0	6.8	15.4
V—Arbitrary rules	1.6	2.1	3.4	2.8	12.7	31.5	10.3	19.2
Across types	1.2	1.7	1.9	2.4	9.0	22.3	6.7	12.6

TABLE 8-8
The Rate of Change Means (M) and Standard Deviations (SD) for the Blame and Personal Variables by Length of Time (Long and Short)

	Length of Time			
	Long		Short	
Blame/Personal	M	SD	M	SD
Blame				
Bosses	2.0	2.4	8.7	13.9
Equals	2.2	2.4	10.2	22.1
Life	0.9	1.5	5.7	12.5
Society	1.1	1.6	6.1	15.9
Personal				
Y	2.3	2.5	11.7	19.9
K	1.3	1.8	6.9	17.2
U	0.6	0.9	3.9	7.5

sevthen/highlow. We found a significant difference for sevthen/highlow, but the difference was not great: Instances in the high category had a rate of change score of 4.65, whereas instances in the low category had a rate of change score of 5.41, with a high-to-low ratio of 1.16. By contrast, the length of time variable of "long" and "short" produced rate of change scores of 1.66 and 8.40, respectively, and the short-to-long ratio was 5.06. Thus it is the time factor, far more than initial severity, that affects rate of change.

Predicting Severity Ratings

We began with a number of quantitative variables (e.g., sevnow, sevthen, agewhen, agediff, and rate of change), and the correlation matrix told us that some were highly correlated whereas others were not. Our final analyses focus on predicting either the sevnow or the sevthen scores from some of the remaining variables.[16] We first ran a stepwise regression to predict sevnow and found a six-variable equation that accounted for .541 percent of the variance,[17] though the variable agewhen was not significant —a finding that tells us that the age when the unfairness occurs does not affect its later severity rating. The implication is that older unfairnesses are not more difficult to get over than fresh ones, which does not support J. M. Barrie's claim that we never get over our first unfairnesses.

Returning to the model, the variable sevnow accounted for most of the variance (.455), followed by personal (.0494), rate of change (.0117), type (.010), agediff (.0085), and blame (.0063). When we turned our predictive analysis in the backward direction to predict sevthen, we found a five-variable model, which accounted for .4718 percent of the variance; here, both agewhen and blame were not significant. Accounting for this much variance (.541 and .472) is noteworthy, given that the psychological processes of judging, coming to terms, and getting over are likely to be highly complex and individualistic.

LOOKING BACK, LOOKING FORWARD

We began with a question: "Do we ever get over unfairnesses?" In this study, unlike the previous ones, we had severity ratings of two points in time, which allowed us to calculate rates of change scores and thereby answer the question in a fashion.[18] Although the answers are not simple, they do let us rule out the simplistic.

We know that Barrie's invariant answer—that no one ever gets over his first unfairness—is wrong. The rebuttal is found in our adult group's unfairnesses, particularly those that began with severe heat but now, decades later, have dropped markedly, indicating a "getting over" effect. In addition, we can also reject the Peter Pan view—that we always get over. Although some participants seem to get over some unfairnesses quite rapidly, many instances show little change from sevthen to sevnow, remaining quite hot for decades. Moreover, even for instances where the rate of change is quite rapid at first, there are many where rate of change dwindles after 5 years and where the "getting over" process enters a slower, longer phase. Thus we can rule out the extremes, because there is more variability than the literary answers of "never" and "always" allow.

We now know a good bit more about the "getting over" effect and its specifics. We know that "innocence punished" (III) cases are generally more difficult to get over than "reward to effort" (I) and "arbitrary rules" (V) cases because they are more difficult to process. We also know that unfairnesses blamed on parents, God, life, or society are generally harder to get over than those blamed on bosses or equals. In addition we know that unfairnesses that occur to others (rather than to ourselves) are generally harder to get over.[19]

After five studies with some 7000 instances of unfairness, we are confident that we are not studying some transient phenomenon that would vanish if we gave participants new booklets one year later. The best prediction is that many of these unfairnesses would show again, and from our findings we could make respectable predictions about how hot they will be. Our findings point to two types of processing that play a significant part in the "getting over" story: One type begins at the moment the unfairness happens and involves how we contextualize the unfairness; a second type occurs over time and involves how we deal with the emotions the unfairness generates, and the thoughts, beliefs, and judgments we have.

Participants believe that they have very little control over the infliction of unfairnesses; they feel "hit" by these. Yet after the hit there is some degree of control in the processing, particularly when we are the victims (Y), and this stands in sharp contrast to experiences that happen to others we do not know (U). The U instances are different from the Y instances in three important ways. First, for the U, we know so little of the story. For example, if the instance is "land mines maiming children in some far off country," we typically do not know the children, we learn almost nothing about how these children processed this unfairness, and we know absolutely nothing about how their lives turn out years later. Thus we are stuck with a short story with a tragic outcome. Second, these U stories are in steady supply through the media. Third, these stories are neither representative nor randomly drawn instances from the lives of others. All of these factors add an extremeness to the U stories and to our picture of unfairness in general.

The unfairnesses ordinary citizens hold in mind are likely to feed and affect the prototypes citizens have in mind. The relationship between instances and prototypical categories is mutual, although not necessarily logical. The prototype,[20] then, involves not only facts (i.e., unfairness stories) and abstractions (i.e., meta-stories) but judgments, construals, and interpretations; it is at the level of the prototype where we create the moral of the story. Unfairnesses are likely to affect how we come to see our parents,[21] the actions of others, and our expectations of society, life, and God. If unfairnesses affect prototypes, then the reverse is true as well: Prototypes may grow from and graft onto particular unfairnesses, as both symbiotically nourish, support, and shelter one another. This may be the way "naive psychology" works,[22] but whether the consequences are good news or bad news no doubt depends on the details.

For U experiences, we are not likely to hear about mid-range and low-range unfairnesses, and this absence may distort our picture of unfairnesses toward the severe end. When we add the fact that many may be oblivious to the ordinary and routine instances of fairness that occur daily, and the fact that these receive almost no media attention, we then realize that the picture and prototypes we construct may be very skewed.[23]

If we are off the mark, and skewed in the pessimistic direction, the consequences for individuals and society may be particularly troubling. Let us recall three findings related to society: Unfairnesses blamed on society are hot to begin with and cool very little; that the number of these instances increases with age, such that our older participants are angrier with society; and that when the blame is on society and the experience is U, this combination yields the least cooling of all. This is problematic, for although our anger with society grows, we remain members of the very society we blame. We are its citizens, voters, and taxpayers, and sometimes we serve as members of a jury ("the conscience of the community") where we are asked to uphold the law while judging an unfairness at bar (while judging whether the trial process itself is fair). During this direct exercise of citizenship, a variety of prototypes, colored by our unfairness experiences, are likely to surface. Our prototypes may lead us toward upholding black-letter law, or they may lead us toward nullifying the law as we follow "commonsense justice."[24]

On a broader scale, our anger with society may motivate us to try to make things fairer, and we may go to the polls on election day to select better leaders. On the other hand, based on their unfairness picture, some may have already given up hope, choosing to stay home on election day. Yet society, government, and its key institutions all depend—for their "institutional legitimacy"[25] and "symbolic legality"[26]—on some degree of perceived fairness. If the sense of unfairness became pervasive, this might threaten institutional legitimacy.

Still, blaming society is not necessarily all bad news. Citizens do hold society and its institutions to a higher, less forgiving standard than bosses and equals; we expect more from society because more are in charge, and we expect more of these decision makers because they were elected, selected, or self-selected for the job. Public pressure, deriving from common-sense unfairness and prototypes, keeps the feet to the fire, so to speak, as it sets the collective bar higher, wanting us to do more so that we might become more.

As this chapter closes, final thoughts focus on when life or God is blamed, because these unfairnesses cool the least. Moreover, when life or God is blamed and it is an "innocence is punished" (III) case, the cooling is even less, and when it is a U experience, the cooling is almost nil.[27] But why is this so, and what does this say? We do know that some of these unfairness instances would fit under Shklar's misfortune cases, about which she wrote, "If the dreadful event is caused by the external forces of nature, it is a misfortune and we must resign ourselves to our suffering."[28] Yet it is manifestly clear that participants do not resign themselves to the suffering. They are angry, they cry "unfair," and they stay hot. Still, it is one thing to demand of society that it should be more just and fair, but to whom do we put such a claim when it is life or God we blame, and in what court? What rascal can we turn out on election day?

Apart from the practical difficulties, there is the question of whether this demand for total justice,[29] even from life and God, is part and parcel of the just world belief, which Lerner called "a fundamental delusion."[30] If it is a delusion, it is the whopper of all delusions, for it is shared by most people. But from the insider's perspective, our participants do not regard their unfairness claims as illegitimate, misguided, or delusional; quite to the contrary. Perhaps we want a world without error variance, where chance misfortunes do not result. Perhaps it is in our psyches (or in American psyches) to blame when bad things happen, for by blaming we demand responsibility and believe that there are rules to be followed, even for the likes of life and God. This ideal world may be more comforting than accepting a ruleless world,[31] which may be too much to bear. If this ideal world is delusional or childish, the alternative—a passive and pessimistic world where we resigned ourselves to suffering, becoming first inured, and then dead to the unfairnesses—may be far worse.

But we suspect that this idealized, childish, or delusional world cannot be the whole story. Consider as counterpoint the prevalent bumper-sticker expression: "Shit happens." Although crude in syntax, people literally buy it, affix it to their car's bumper, and thereby endorse this statement— which, when we wipe away the scatological, is an acknowledgment that misfortunes and unfairnesses are a part of life. It represents a realistic side of the picture, an acceptance that contradicts childish or delusional defiance of reality. There is also some evidence from civil cases where plaintiffs bring suits for soft-tissue injuries (e.g., whiplash cases). Here, juries seem antiplaintiff, highly suspicious of their unfairness claims, to use our terms, where a persistent message from jurors to plaintiffs is "get over it, this is just part of life."[32]

In looking backward, we now know much about unfairnesses, their key dimensions, and about getting over them. Regarding the conception of unfairness, we know that it is not just one thing, as the type data, for one, consistently make clear. Still, in looking forward, there are contradictions and complexities to unravel. For instance, many of our participants apply the term "unfairnesses" to instances that Shklar calls "misfortunes." Then there is her other term, "injustices," and the question of whether this term covers the same ground of our "unfairness." We still have that question (and challenge) about whether people blur distinctions that ought to be kept separate. But given the broad ways of using "unfairness," and given the alternatives of "injustice" and "misfortune," a more profound question arises: Have we really been studying "unfairness" at all?

ENDNOTES

1. There were two groups of participants, students and adults. There were 85 students (54 females and 31 males), with a mean age of 19.5 and a mean education level of 15.2. There were 83 adults (53 females and 30 males), with a mean age of 47.9 and a mean education level of 18.0. In total, then, we had 168 participants, with a demographic and religious distribution consistent with previous participants and studies.
2. The adult group's mean was 7.1 and the students' mean was 7.9; these close results were fairly consistent with prior studies.
3. Significant differences between the age groups occur in the following categories: Students cite "rewards in relation to effort" (I/A and I/B) more than adults, but the reverse is true for "wrongful behavior going unpunished" (II/C) and "miscellaneous" (VI/I).
4. There is no significant severity $\times$ age group effect, although a significant

severity × type × age group interaction effect results, which is discernible in Table 8-1. Adults are hotter about unfairnesses in the "no work rewarded" and in the "equal treatment" (when it should be individualized) categories, whereas students are hotter about "innocence punished" cases.

5. There is a significant age group effect, but the blame × age group interaction effect just fails to reach significance. Students generally give higher sevnow ratings than adults, being noticeably higher for equals, God, and parents.

6. Using sevnow as the dependent variable, we tested for type and blame main effects, and the type × blame interaction effect. We found a significant main effect for type (which can be seen in Table 8-1), a significant main effect for blame (which can be seen in Table 8-2), and a significant type × blame interaction effect, which can be seen in Table 8-3. Looking at some of the details, for the main effect for blame, equals are lower than life and society, but equals get the hottest ratings for "reward/effort" (I). Society and life are highest in the "wrongful behavior going unpunished" (II) category, and life and society are highest in the "innocence is punished" (III) category. Life, society, and equals are highest in the "unfair advantages" category. Society dominates in the "arbitrary rules" (V) category.

7. But there is a caveat to consider before we accept the altruistic explanation, a caveat that becomes clearer when we focus on what the sevnow ratings actually reflect, for these ratings show Y to be lower than K and U at every type level. But why is that so? Are we more sensitive to the unfairnesses of others than to those that directly hit us? Although altruism is noble, it is neither consistent with the pervasive self-interest we seem to see all around us, nor is it consistent with adaptation, for self-interest can promote physical and psychological survival. Thus a simple altruism hypothesis seems too generous and not entirely plausible.

8. R = .67.

9. We also tested their interaction effects (e.g., type × blame, type × personal, blame × personal, type × blame × personal) on sevthen.

10. For example, if one unfairness for an adult participant occurred 3 years ago whereas another occurred 30 years ago, then directly comparing these sevdiff scores could be quite misleading because time duration has not been controlled. Thus we set sevdiff as the numerator in an equation, where the appropriate denominator is created by subtracting from the current age of each participant (age) the age when each instance occurred (agewhen), and this we call agediff (agediff = age − agewhen). The new variable that results when the numerator (sevdiff) is divided by the denominator (agediff) is called rate of change, and high scores would indicate faster "getting over," whereas lower reflects "slower."

11. This last finding needs to be qualified, because there is a type × personal interaction effect, such that cases in categories II and III, particularly for U and K experiences, are harder to get over.

12. To illustrate, had we graphed rate of change scores over time, we would see straight-line slopes at different angles, with a fast drop-off for Y, and a slow drop-off for U. But a straight-line representation is an unlikely reflection of what really happens, because that would indicate that the rate of change was uniform.

13. We picked five years as the cutoff point for it divided all the instances into roughly equal groups; had we picked a shorter interval, the percentage of student instances would greatly exceed adult instances, and had we picked a longer interval, the reverse would result.

14. There were a number of significant interaction effects as well: length of time × age group, length of time × type, and length of time × personal.

15. The overall type effect is most discernible in the short period but is almost absent in the long period, and this reflects a length of time × type interaction effect. Although the overall age group effect just missed significance, the A > S pattern shows clearly in the short period but is almost absent in the long period, reflecting the significant length of time × age group interaction effect.

16. It seemed reasonable to assume that if we knew how the participant rated the unfairness experience when it was happening (sevthen), and knew the rate of change score, coupled with the time interval between the occurrence of the unfairness and now (agediff), then we should be able to make fairly good predictions about how they would rate unfairness experiences now (sevnow). In addition, if we added our variables of type, blame, and personal to the mix, predictions that account for a significant part of the variance should result. Moreover, the predictions ought to work in the reverse direction: If we know how they rate the unfairness now (sevnow), plus the other variables we mentioned, we should be able to predict how severely they rated the experience when it first happened (sevthen).

17. sevnow = -3.4 (intercept) + .699 (sevthen) .292 (agediff) $-$ .229 (rate of change) + 2.58 (type) + 3.01 (blame) + 5.53 (personal).

18. Given the limitations of this method, one of which asks participants to recollect their earlier feelings and assessment.

19. These are just the main effects. When we bring interaction effects into the picture, a highly complicated answer to the simple question of "getting over" results.

20. N. J. Finkel, "Commonsense Justice, Psychology, and the Law: Prototypes Common, Senseful, and Not," *Psychology, Public Policy, and Law* 3 (1997): 461–489; N. J. Finkel and J. L. Groscup, "Crime Prototypes, Objective versus Subjective Culpability, and a Commonsense Balance," *Law and Human Behavior* 21 (1997): 209–230; N. J. Finkel and J. L. Groscup, "When Mistakes Happen: Commonsense Rules of Culpability," *Psychology, Public Policy, and Law* 3 (1997): 1–61; V. L. Smith, "Prototypes in the Courtroom: Lay Representations of Legal Concepts," *Journal of Personality & Social Psychology* 61 (1991): 857–872; V. L. Smith, "When Prior Knowledge and Law Collide: Helping Jurors Use the Law," *Law and Human Behavior* 17 (1993): 507–536; V. L. Smith and C. A. Studebaker, "What Do You Expect?: The Influence of People's Prior Knowledge of Crime Categories on Fact-Finding," *Law and Human Behavior* 20 (1996): 517–532; L. Stalans, "Citizen's Crime Stereotypes, Biased Recall, and Punishment Preferences in Abstract Cases: The Educative Role of Interpersonal Sources," *Law and Human Behavior* 14 (1993): 199–214; L. J. Stalans and S. S. Diamond, "Formation and Change in Lay Evaluations of Criminal Sentencing: Misperception and Discontent," *Law and Human Behavior* 14 (1990): 199–214.

21. J. M. Barrie gave voice to one alleged prototype, a child's expectation of the parent: "All he thinks he has a right to when he comes to you to be yours is fairness." J. M. Barrie, *Peter Pan* (New York: Charles Scribner's Sons, 1950), p. 127.

22. F. Heider, *The Psychology of Interpersonal Relations* (New York: Wiley, 1958).

23. To amplify, we know that Y, K, and U experiences are not equivalent. Thus the prototypes we extract from these types of experiences are likely to be different, and these differing prototypes are likely to have differing consequences. For example, the prototypes derived from Y instances may be more optimistic than from U experiences, because these are less extreme and we are privy to our own processing, which shows us that "getting over" is indeed possible. On the other end, from the U experiences we may draw more pessimistic conclusions about equals, bosses, parents, society, life, and God.

24. Finkel, "Commonsense Justice."

25. J. L. Gibson, "Understandings of Justice: Institutional Legitimacy, Procedural Justice, and Political Tolerance," *Law & Society Review* 23 (1989): 469–496; J. L. Gibson, "Institutional Legitimacy, Procedural Justice, and Compliance with Supreme Court Decisions: A Question of Causality," *Law & Society Review* 25 (1991): 631–635; J. L. Mondak, "Institutional Legitimacy and Procedural Justice: Reexamining the Question of Causality," *Law & Society Review* 27 (1993): 599–608; T. R. Tyler, "Governing Amid Diversity: The Effect of Fair Decisionmaking Procedures on the Legitimacy of Government," *Law & Society Review* 28 (1994): 809–831; T. R. Tyler and K. Rasinski, "Procedural Justice, Institutional Legitimacy, and the Acceptance of Unpopular U.S. Supreme Court Decisions: A Reply to Gibson," *Law & Society Review* 25 (1991): 621–630.

26. C. Haney, "The Fourteenth Amendment and Symbolic Legality: Let Them Eat Due Process," *Law and Human Behavior* 15 (1991): 183–204.

27. Thus whether we look at it as a blame main effect, or a blame × type interaction effect, or a blame × type × personal three-way interaction effect, this category burns hottest from the outset and remains so, because there is little getting over, on the average.

28. J. N. Shklar, *The Faces of Injustice* (New Haven: Yale University Press, 1990), p. 1.

29. L. M. Friedman, *Total Justice* (New York: Russell Sage Foundation, 1985).

30. M. Lerner, *The Belief in a Just World: A Fundamental Delusion* (New York: Plenum Press, 1980).

31. Shklar, *Faces of Injustice*, p. 5.

32. V. P. Hans and N. Vadino, "Something for Nothing? Citizens' Perceptions of Soft-Tissue Injury Lawsuits." Paper presented at the American Psychology–Law Society Conference, New Orleans, March, 2000.

III

TRYING TO PIN DOWN THE VARIANCE OF UNFAIRNESS

Then the Unnamable Again Spoke to Job From Within the Whirlwind:
Look now: the Beast that I made:
. . .
Go ahead: attack him:
you will never try it again. (pp. 85–86)

From Stephen Mitchell's *The Book of Job* (1987)

9

WHAT'S IN A NAME?
UNFAIRNESS VERSUS MISFORTUNE
VERSUS INJUSTICE

In Part II, we examined the dimensions of type, blame, severity, and personal in order to answer basic questions about the conceptions and concepts of unfairness. We also tracked these unfairness dimensions by age group to see if developmental trends showed, and we tracked them across time (with sevnow and sevthen), to see whether some unfairnesses still boil in memory or whether we get over some. Although these dimensional findings were highly consistent from study to study, we also found variability that we could not account for and found possible causes and explanations we could not parse, let alone validate.

A CHANGE IN COURSE, A CHANGE IN METHODS

It is the unexplained variance that drives Part III as we seek to pin some of the variance down. One portion of that variability, which is the focus of this chapter, involves equivocal findings from the studies regarding whether participants do or do not misclassify or turn misfortunes into unfairnesses, blurring a distinction that ought to be kept clear. If they do misclassify, transform, or transmute, to what extent and degree do they do so? The best evidence we have from the studies is from "innocence punished" instances of impersonal agency, and though these findings suggest that misfortunes lie within this type category, the data are less than conclusive on this point, as alternative explanations have not been ruled out. In a more broad sense, do participants' conceptions and concepts of unfairness, misfortune, and injustice overlap or separate, and which has the widest orbit? This chapter explores this broad question.

There are also equivocal findings about whether people make fewer discriminations when it comes to process rather than outcome, or whether they see outcome first and foremost and identify it with unfairness much more than they do for process. Because our type categories confound outcome with process, we could not adequately assess this question, but we will examine it in chapter 10. We also found that participants do not blame the individual/self for unfairnesses, but in chapter 11 we push this "blaming others" practice further by creating vignette variations that introduce flaw, fault, and the interaction of flaw fault, where these character (dispositional) and situational variables may alter the perception of unfairness and who or what is to blame. The question is, will the presence of "flaw or fault" information about the victim of the unfairness undercut or even nullify and individual's claim? When the fault involves another (as opposed to the victim), will this raise the severity of the unfairness? Finally, in chapter 12 we try to pin down the variance still further, looking at dispositional factors and basic attitudes (e.g., just-world beliefs, beliefs about theodicy) to see what portion of the variance these account for in comparison to current situational factors that operate.

Turning to this chapter, three questions are at its core. First, are there distinctions among misfortune, injustice, and unfairness, and which concept is the wider, more embracing one? Second, is there is an outcome bias such that outcome is what is most strongly associated with the overall unfairness judgment and process is eclipsed? Third, are unfairnesses seen from the inside view colored more hotly than when seen from the outside?

Before turning to our first experiment, a note on why the experiment is the chosen method now and why the "study method," which has served us well all along, is set aside. Our questions in this chapter specifically, and in Part III generally, seek more fine-grained answers, answers that discriminate among possibilities. Such answers could not be clearly discerned with the study method, for too many plausible answers commingled in the narrative stew, and we could not tease out from the contenders the causal ingredient; this less-than-nourishing result requires a change to a method that affords far greater control over the confounds and a way of manipulating and isolating the key factor.

EXPERIMENT 1

Injustice Versus Misfortune Versus Unfairness

When a child dies and a parent cries "unfair" heavenward, is this an unfairness or a misfortune? The concepts of unfairness, injustice, and misfortune have been uncritically mixing from the outset, and our preference, expressed in the title, portrays these as unfairnesses. But what if "unfairness" is the wrong term? If "misfortune" rather than "unfairness" turns out to be the correct term for many of these instances, then Shklar's reminder that we must be resigned to suffer "misfortunes," for there is no one or no thing to blame, leads to two conclusions:[1] first, that designations of blame are inapt (we are blaming what should not be blamed), and second, that "unfairness" is being wrongly affixed to these instances (misfortunes are being misclassified and transmuted into unfairnesses).

If there is confusion between misfortune and unfairness, it is likely to center on one type category, "innocence punished," and for only a fraction (estimated at 30%) of these, which are impersonal agency cases. On the other hand, if there is confusion between injustice and unfairness, it is likely to cut across all categories. This issue takes us back to Part I, and the distinctions I drew between "just" and "fair." But are these distinctions empty or meaningful to participants?

The importance of pinning down what it is that we have been studying is critical. The assumption that "unfairness" is the broader and better term must be put to the test, a test where "misfortune" and "injustice" compete with "unfairness" on a level playing field. Without such a fair test and a clear answer, it remains a possibility that we have been making a Ptolemaic error all along—thinking that "unfairness" is the sun and center of our universe—when it turns out to be but a small Copernican planet, dwarfed by a larger orb more centrally situated.

Outcome Versus Process

Another distinction of interest involves outcome and process. Craig Haney set the issue this way:

> Supreme Court decisions—constitutional law—serve as powerful moralizing agents in American society. It is not so much that constitutional law teaches people about good and evil or right and wrong, but more that it serves as the basis for our expectations about legal fairness and justice. The Constitution, as it is publicly understood and discussed, stands as a major source of our *symbolic legality*. By symbolic legality I mean the ideological core of values and beliefs that we associate with law and justice in democratic society. It is what we believe our legal institutions stand for, the principles upon which we believe our agen-

cies of justice operate. The Constitution is at the center of that symbolic legality.[2]

Haney then moved to outcome and process, which are captured in the phrases of the Fourteenth Amendment, "equal protection" and "due process."

> I believe that no part of the Constitution—no phrase, article, or amendment—is more important to the maintenance of our symbolic legality than the Fourteenth Amendment. What most people are thinking about when they say "I'm an American citizen; I've got rights!" are Fourteenth Amendment rights to fair and equal treatment. The Due Process and Equal Protection Clauses are absolutely central to our symbolic legality.[3]

Haney's argument, based on various Supreme Court decisions, is that the Court finesses equal protection in favor of due process, accenting process over outcome.[4] Haney stated this more forcefully in the subtitle of his article, "Let Them Eat Due Process." Yet there are Constitutional scholars and justices who argue that due process may be the most fundamental.

Our second question focuses on how ordinary citizens see and weigh "due process" and "equal treatment." Do they see "due process" first and foremost, as some constitutional scholars and justices apparently do, or do they see procedural justice secondarily, or not at all, being blinded by outcome?

Regarding this question, we do not start with a blank slate. We have evidence from the studies showing that process seems to be a youthful taste, surprisingly, as these unfairnesses are cited proportionately more by our tot and teenager group than by older groups. But as we have said before, this finding may be misleading, for our type categories do not neatly parse process from outcome, so we cannot say with certitude whether students, adults, and older participants were ignoring process or giving it second billing. Further evidence for a confounding of outcome and process comes from interrater disagreements, where one focused on the outcome and the other focused on the process, which suggests that both may be operative. Thus, the answer eludes us because we never had participants making distinct outcome and process ratings on the same set of unfairnesses. This we will now do. In addition to separate outcome and process ratings, we will have participants make an overall rating of unfairness, as this will allow us to see whether outcome or process better correlates with the overall judgment.

Point of View—Victim Versus Outsider

A third question in this experiment concerns perspective, the victim's and the outsider's. We know that unfairnesses can be seen differently by participant and outsider, leading to differences in type and blame categorizations. Moreover, in our attempts to have participants and outsiders reconcile differences, both sometimes changed their perspectives, indicating that perspective is not set in stone. We also found that personal experiences (Y) fell into differing type and blame categories than more impersonal (K and U) ones, suggesting that who experiences the unfairness affects how one sees the experience. These and other findings, taken together, point to perspective making a difference.

The question we ask is this: Is there greater heat when participants take the victim's or the outsider's view? The results from the prior studies are confounded on this question. For example, although U experiences were rated as more severe than Y ones, the instances were not identical, as the U experiences were more often the prototypical extremes. To fairly test the question, we need to give the *same* instances but ask two different groups of participants to view these instances from two differing vantage points—as if these instances happened to them or were viewed from the outsider's vantage point.

The Research Design

We are going to manipulate four variables (AIMU, view, casetype, subjecttype) in this experiment, using a two-between, two-within-subject design, with some added wrinkles. The first two variables, designated as AIMU and view, are the two-between variables, where AIMU has 4 levels and view has 2 levels, producing (4 × 2) 8 separate conditions, and each participant will be randomly assigned to one of the eight booklets.[5] The variables designated as casetype and subjecttype are the two-within variables, where casetype has 11 levels and subjecttype has 3 levels, producing (11 × 3) 33 alleged unfairness instances in every booklet, and these are presented in random order,[6] and they are listed in Appendix 9A.

The casetype variable, with 11 levels, roughly corresponds to our 8 specific types of unfairness (i.e., categories A through H, without the miscellaneous category). In addition, we added three more cases from category D (bringing the total to four in category D), for we wanted to test whether "innocence punished" cases involving human beings inflicting the punishment (i.e., injustice cases) would be rated differently from cases where nature, life, or God (i.e., misfortune cases) deliver the blow.[7]

The subjecttype variable involves the age of the person making the unfairness claim. For each of our 11 levels of casetype, we had three specific subjecttype vignettes, one involving a tot or teenager (T), one involving a student (S), and one involving an adult (A).[8]

In the two-between part of the design, our first variable was AIMU, an acronym for "all," "injustice," "misfortune," and "unfairness." For one group (I), these 33 instances were called "injustices," and the rating scale

(0 to 100) was labeled "Injustice." For a second group (M), the instances and scale referred to "Misfortune." For the third group (U), it was labeled "Unfairness." We also added a fourth group (A), where all three scales followed each instance, one labeled "Injustice," one labeled "Misfortune," and one labeled "Unfairness," and thus this A group (a within-group) allowed us a comparison with the three (I, M, U) between groups.[9]

The second between-subject variable is called view, and it had two levels. Half the participants were told to take the view of the victim and to see the instances as if they had happened to them; the other half were asked to take the view of the outsider.[10] Regarding our aim of investigating the "outcome versus process" distinction, this was done using outcome and process rating scales following each unfairness instance.

RESULTS AND DISCUSSION

We first compared the ratings of our student and adult groups, and found no significant differences on any of the dependent measures,[11] so the two groups were combined in the following analyses. We then examined the two-within-subject variables and found significant main effects for case-type and subjecttype (for the I, M, and U groups, and across groups) and a significant casetype × subjecttype interaction effect,[12] with the significant effects recurring for the within-subject A group, with the differences being even larger than the between-group (I, M, U) comparisons.[13] These findings are not surprising. Regarding casetype, we have repeatedly seen that different type categories produce significantly different severity scores, and they do so here again. That the same basic type of unfairness (though not exactly the same instance) is rated differently when the victim is a different age (subjecttype) also makes sense, though the differences do not align in some age pattern: At some levels of casetype, the tot and teen subjecttype may be rated as most severe, whereas at other casetype levels the student or adult subjecttype is rated most severe.

We turn now to the key variable, umi, for the between-subject groups. The driving question was, "What difference, if any, does the designation make?" The answer is a significant difference.[14] "Unfairness," "misfortune," and "injustice" labels clearly evoke different concepts and meanings for the participants, and thus the distinction articulated by Shklar[15] between "injustice" and "misfortune," plus our addition of "unfairness," is a factual distinction for our participants and not just an academic or speculative distinction.

For certain cases (casetype), there is a sharp rise in the "injustice" or "misfortune" or "unfairness" ratings (see Table 9-1), as some cases are seen as more "misfortune-like," or "unfairness-like," or "injustice-like"; there are also cases where there is a sharp fall in the ratings, showing that these are not seen as an injustice, misfortune, or unfairness. This case variability indicates that participants make case-by-case discriminations along this umi dimension, and we will present the details shortly, but first a note on a nonfinding.

The Victim's Subjective View Versus the Objective Outsider's View

There is no significant effect for view,[16] and no significant umi × view interaction effect, and these nonsignficiant findings occur for both the between-subject and within-subject groups. This answers our second question, "Would viewing an unfairness from the victim's as opposed to the outsider's perspective matter?" The answer is apparently not.[17] It may be, simply, that the hypothesis of greatest severity with the subjective perspective—the narcissistic view that the "me" focus ought to produce the greatest heat—is wrong, as participants rated these as moderate-to-severe unfairnesses *regardless of vantage point*.[18]

Unfairness Versus Misfortune Versus Injustice

We now return to the significant findings. Using the data from the between-groups (I, M, U), the mean severity ratings for the 33 unfairness instances, broken down by casetype and subjecttype, are presented in Table 9-1. Looking across the scores, we see the effect for casetype evident in the variability of scores: The M ratings show the greatest variability, with I ratings also being quite variable, whereas U ratings show the least variability and the highest scores on the average. This is our first piece of

TABLE 9-1

Between-Group Comparisons of Mean Severity Scores, Labeled as Either Injustice (I), Misfortune (M), or Unfairness (U) Ratings for the Eleven Casetypes and the Three Subtypes

	Casetype										
	A	B	C	D1	D2	D3	D4	E	F	G	H
Tot and teen subtype											
I	65	76	65	50	78	77	79	75	69	57	51
M	26	47	36	94	74	54	83	61	43	41	36
U	74	80	80	61	83	75	85	74	75	65	60
Student subtype											
I	63	52	73	41	63	73	61	59	41	65	72
M	29	44	37	88	85	56	87	53	27	39	48
U	72	51	78	69	73	75	73	60	55	66	75
Adult subtype											
I	70	73	78	42	86	70	42	79	66	63	70
M	33	46	50	93	73	60	87	64	54	35	43
U	80	76	79	58	86	69	65	88	68	77	86

evidence that "unfairness" is the broadest of the three constructs, the one with the widest, most inclusive ambit.

We also see variability among the four D cases (D1, D2, D3, D4), where some of those cases are high on the misfortune scale, with others much lower; similar variability is noted for injustice ratings. Although there is variability on the unfairness ratings as well, it is less than for misfortune or injustice. These findings suggest that the "innocence punished" (D) category is not unitary, but composed of different types of cases.

We already reported that the umi effect was significant. To further refine the difference, we performed two preplanned contrasts, testing "unfairness + injustice versus misfortune" (U + I versus M), and testing "unfairness versus injustice" (U versus I) for the within-group, and both were significant.[19] These comparisons indicate that the three constructs are different from one another. Overall, there were significant differences on this umi variable in 28 out of the 33 vignettes,[20] and as for the specific details, we found that the "injustice versus misfortune" comparison was significantly different on 26 out of 33 instances, whereas the "unfairness versus misfortune" comparison was significantly different on 23 out of 33 instances, whereas the "unfairness versus injustice" comparison was significantly different on just 4 out of 33 instances. These results indicate that the constructs of unfairness and injustice are closer to one another than to misfortune.[21]

Averages yield a black and white picture; variability gives coloration and chiaroscuro. Regarding variability, we find that though unfairness ratings turn out to be the highest most of the time (23 out of 33), there are exceptions. On 6 of the 33 instances, it is the misfortune rating that is the highest, and on 5 of the 33 instances, injustice ratings ranks highest. However, when injustice ratings rank highest, those ratings exceed unfairness ratings by only 5 points in total, indicating that the two were nearly identical. However, when the misfortune ratings are highest on 6 of the 33 cases, these exceed unfairness by a combined 135 points, and exceed injustice by 245 points. These variability findings suggest two things. First, if injustice is nearly indistinguishable from unfairness ratings in the few instances when the former ratings are highest overall, then "unfairness" is clearly the broader construct, and might well replace "injustice" entirely, if the latter adds little to the picture. Second, these results indicate that "misfortune" adds something distinct to the picture, a factor not captured by "injustice," and only partially captured by "unfairness."

Outcome Versus Process

The third issue driving this research involves the "outcome versus process" distinction. All of the participants made outcome and process severity ratings on every case. A new variable (called OPU—for "outcome," "process," and overall "unfairness") was tested.[22] There were significant effects overall, with a significant O versus P effect and a significant U versus O + P effect.[23] However, the O versus P comparison was significantly different on 27 of the 33 cases, whereas the U versus O + P comparison was significant on only 4 of 33 cases.

Mean ratings for the U, O, and P measures are shown in Table 9-2. Looking across casetype, and at all levels of subjecttype, the O and U ratings track one another (i.e., correlate) quite closely, typically being but a few points apart. The P ratings, on the other hand, are significantly lower than O and U ratings across cases. However, it is not a severity difference that most notably sets the P ratings apart,[24] but variability, for the P ratings range from 41 to 83, which does not correspond to the U variability pattern, and it corresponds even less with the O pattern. By contrast, the O ratings remain at moderate to high levels across cases, holding within a narrower range and tied more tightly to the U ratings.

From these findings, some reasonable inferences can be drawn. First, it does appear that participants are more outcome focused, for the O scores remain at moderate to high levels across cases. Second, this outcome focus even shows for the H cases, which deal directly with arbitrary rules and due process violations: Although the P scores are highest on these H cases, as they should be, the O scores remain quite high as well. Third, participants tend to identify the outcome unfairness as the general unfairness, as the O scores correspond with the U scores in lockstep, whereas the P scores do not.[25]

A closer examination of the outcome bias reveals that it is discernible in the low P cases (AS, AA, CS). For example, the professor has not read

TABLE 9-2

Comparisons of the Mean Outcome (O), Process (P), and Unfairness (U) Ratings for the Eleven Casetypes and the Three Subtypes

	Casetype										
	A	B	C	D1	D2	D3	D4	E	F	G	H
Tot and teen subtype											
O	77	81	73	83	84	79	89	80	76	68	56
P	60	71	54	44	75	73	77	69	76	64	60
U	75	79	76	66	84	78	85	79	77	68	58
Student subtype											
O	72	55	72	78	85	78	84	68	54	71	76
P	54	56	57	42	72	69	62	54	54	63	79
U	68	51	74	64	78	76	76	65	53	71	74
Adult subtype											
O	77	77	79	77	90	74	77	85	75	71	67
P	59	66	70	41	83	64	53	80	68	71	77
U	77	75	78	65	85	70	71	86	73	74	73

a paper carefully, yet hands out an A (AS); a company violates its own procedures for promotion (AA); and a professor fails to detect the cheating (CS). Even though process and outcome could both be cited in these cases, the participants more often and hotly cite outcome.

Cluster Analysis for Injustice/Misfortune/Unfairness

We now know that there are significant differences among injustice, misfortune, and unfairness ratings, but what do those differences mean, and what underlying distinctions are participants making? To get at finer-grained distinctions, we first took the imu ratings on the 33 instances of alleged unfairness and subjected them to cluster analysis.[26]

We found that these vignettes grouped into five clusters, and these clusters explained a very sizable proportion of the variance.[27] The cases within each cluster are shown in Table 9-3. Cluster 1 contains all of the cases dealing with the relationship between rewards and effort, such as no work is rewarded (I/A) and hard work is not rewarded (I/B), and wrongful behavior that is either rewarded or not punished (II/C). As this cluster included both major category I and II of our categorization schema for type, we called this cluster "reward or punishment failures." For these nine cases in Cluster 1, the means for unfairness and injustice are fairly high, with unfairness being slightly higher, whereas misfortune ratings were significantly lower, indicating that these are not seen as misfortune cases.

By contrast, Cluster 2 represents the misfortune cases, for here sudden death or illness, earthquakes, lightning, and famine are the triggering events for these "innocence punished" (III/D) cases. Here, misfortune ratings are the highest (i.e., ranging from 85 to 97), injustice the lowest, with unfairness falling between, although closer to misfortune.

Cluster 3 includes two sorts of cases, "disproportionate or excessive

TABLE 9-3
The Five Clusters, and the Cases Falling Within Each Cluster,
for the imu Ratings

Clusters				
1	2	3	4	5
AT	D1T	ET	FT	D2T
AS	D1S	ES	FS	D2A
AA	D1A	EA	FA	D4T
BT	D2S	D3T	GT	
BS	D4S	D3S	GS	
BA	D4A	D3A	GA	
CT			HT	
CS			HS	
CA			HA	

punishment" (III/E) and "innocence is punished" (III/D) cases, but in the D instances it is humans who deliver the punishment, and not life, nature, or God. This cluster is called "excessive human punishment," and it affirms the human versus nature or injustice versus misfortune distinction we hypothesized.

Cluster 4 contains three types of cases: unfair advantages or connections (IV/F), equal treatment when it should be individualized (IV/G), and the arbitrary rules, lack of due process (V/H) cases. For these cases, unfairness ratings are greater than injustice, which are, in turn, greater than misfortune, and thus this cluster is dubbed "unfairness."

Cluster 5 contains three (III/D) cases, involving a crack baby born to an addict mother, a violent parent who shakes and kills a crying child, and children being killed or maimed by stepping on land mines in a country in civil war. In these cases, unfairness, injustice, and misfortune ratings are all high and fairly close, indicating that both the human/injustice unfairness and the bad luck/misfortune unfairness are involved. This cluster is designated as mixed.[28]

Regarding unfairnesses delivered by human hands, we see a further differentiation (cluster 3) when punishment is excessive. This separate factor indicates a *proportionality* concern—that punishment be proportional to blameworthiness. There are now three differentiations regarding human agents who punish and reward: The first involves blaming those agents when they are either not on the job, not doing a careful job, or being slack (cluster 1); the second involves blaming them when they are being arbitrary, capricious, and discriminatory (cluster 4); and the third involves blaming them when they are being excessive (cluster 3).

Finally (cluster 5), there is a separate category, a Dante-esque circle in hell, so to speak, reserved for those humans who inflict death or serious injury on the most innocent of babes—infants and children—and this mixed cluster had the highest unfairness ratings of all. Although these cases are more outcome than process, there is something beyond outcome operating, for there are other cases in other clusters where sudden deaths occur but where the level of anger is significantly less. The additional heat for this cluster of cases involves two factors, we believe. First, there is a "who dies" distinction, for when it is the most vulnerable of our citizens, anger rises. But a second, interrelated factor is at work, which involves a duty failure to protect the most vulnerable and dependent.[29] In these cases, the grownups have failed to honor their duty, putting the most vulnerable at grave risk. This combination of a duty failure paired with the most vulnerable victim brings forth the severest condemnation.[30]

Cluster analysis ends up grouping some of our type categories together or subdividing them more finely. These differences may result because both type and blame, which we separated into different categorization schemas, are conjoined in the severity rating, which is the constituent element of the cluster analysis. This suggests that although we may parse "unfairness" into type and blame and create separate schemas for them, participants' severity judgments fuse the two together, with type and blame taken interactively, or as a whole, with both being endemic to unfairness.

LOOKING BACKWARD, LOOKING FORWARD

In looking backward, we see that perspective matters greatly in how the unfairness is viewed: Perspective is a determiner of who is seen as the central actor in the unfairness, which type category fits, and who or what is blamed. We have also learned that perspective is not always fixed, for when participant and outside coder sit down to reconcile their different initial perspectives, sometimes perspective changes. In this experiment, we again find that perspective matters, but only in some ways. It matters if citizens see the instance as an outcome or process unfairness, as that distinction produces differences in severity ratings, with outcome generally being hotter than process and much closer to the "overall" unfairness rating. Perspective also matters if one sees the unfairness as an injustice or a misfortune, as ratings and clusters change with that distinction. However, perspective did not seem to matter when it involved taking the victim's or the outsider's view. If participants did see these unfairnesses as equal in severity whether they were hit by them or someone else, then this would suggest a humanitarian view on unfairnesses, rather than a self-centered view. Said another way, these instances are bad no matter who they hit, and they are not more bad just because they hit me.

This last finding and conclusion require a caveat or two. First, although we tested many cases (33), this finding is circumscribed only to those we tested, which were all in the high and severe range. Thus, we cannot say whether this finding would also occur on the low severity end, where a victim's claim may be seen as a whine or may be sharply questioned, challenged, or rejected outright. A second caveat concerns our manipulation, which was artificial: Asking participants to imagine themselves being the victim is surely not equivalent to actually being the victim.

If all we had was the experimental evidence, these caveats would render our conclusion problematic. But we also have evidence from Study 4 and Study 5, which bring the actual perspectives to the fore, and that evidence is in line with the experimental findings. These complementary findings converge on a conclusion: It seems to be more a matter of how unfairnesses are construed, rather than the insider's or outsider's vantage point, that determines how severely they are judged.

But how is unfairness construed, and is it seen as some undifferentiated whole? The answer is both yes and no. As for the no, participants make numerous distinctions, differentiating among unfairness, injustice, and misfortune; they also differentiate among type categories, and within the "innocence punished" type category, separating those brought on by human agents from those attributed to life; and they also differentiate on the blame and personal dimensions as well. In their differentiating, participants see "unfairness" as the broadest and most inclusive term, incorporating "injustice" but adding something of its own. In addition, "unfairness" incorporates some of "misfortune" as well, but not all, for the latter adds a component of its own. In sum, when the experimental results are considered, *Not Fair!* seems to be the right title of this work.

As for the yes answer, there is evidence that unfairness may be construed as a more undifferentiated whole, where type and blame entwine into one severity rating. Although participants comply with our requests in the studies to categorize their instances using separate type and blame schemas, type and blame may naturally run together when they think about unfairness, both being part and parcel of the phenomenon.

Yet there is something new we learn in this experiment: What does not naturally come together in equal weights are outcome and process, because an outcome bias shows. In one sense, the outcome bias does not surprise us. It shows itself under a different name, the "hindsight bias," in other research. For example, it has been shown that knowing the outcome affects our judgments of the previous process, be it the procedures used by the police in stop, search-and-seizure situations,[31] or in judging a therapist's handling of a patient who threatens violence toward a third party.[32] When we know the outcome—the car's trunk contained bags of cocaine versus nothing, or the patient killed a third party versus did no harm—we judge the procedures used by the police or the therapist's handling of the patient differently. In our experiment, participants seemed to start with whether the *outcome* was bad or not and then used that information to judge the fairness of the process.

Still, there is something unsettling about the outcome bias, even though we find it in this experiment and found it in the studies, for it appears to defy common sense. From a commonsense view, we would predict that older participants ought to be more sensitive to the nuances of process (and not less), if process unfairnesses are subtler than the more obvious outcome unfairnesses, which appear so blatant. Furthermore, we would expect more educated participants to pick up on them and do so more frequently than youngsters. Yet this didn't happened in either experiment or studies. If these findings seem odd, they are supported by recent findings of Heuer, Penrod, Gefen, and Saks,[33] who sent cases involving questionable search and seizure decisions out to state appellate court judges and state trial court judges. Their findings, in our terms, revealed an outcome bias, where procedural fairness took a back seat in decision making to the outcome. When fairness was weighted in their decision-making model, it was "outcome fairness," where societal benefits are considered.

These findings were surprising, and they come from a far more legally sophisticated population than we tested. When these results are considered
with our own, it just may be that this commonsense view is simply wrong,
and that procedural fairness does become less important to outside evaluators.

There is an alternative explanation that we must consider, which
focuses on the vignettes as the source of the outcome bias problem. Perhaps
we have situated the outcome unfairness factor too dramatically in the
foreground, such that process inadvertently became background. But this
possibility would not explain why outcome shows so brightly even in the
high-process cases, where process was purposefully situated in the foreground. Moreover, even if our vignettes were skewed toward outcome, we
presented no vignettes in the studies, and participants' narratives were
dominated by outcome. Perhaps outcome is the first defining characteristic
that makes an instance an unfairness, and it is under unfair outcomes that
these instances are stored in memory. If that is a reasonable possibility,
then process may be more of a qualifier, if its violation pushes to center
stage and grabs our attention.

In looking forward, we are left to wonder about what would happen
if we used not brief vignettes, but lengthy and complex cases that brought
process and outcome to the foreground, where both grabbed our attention.
We also wonder what would happen if we asked participants to identify all
unfairnesses they find, and give reasons why each instance is unfair? That
task opens the response range wider and gives their phenomenology room
to manifest. Within a more complex task with multiple unfairnesses, would
process still be the minor chord, drowned out by the drama of outcome,
and would process turn out to be a simpler tune, one that lacks harmonies
and discriminations? This is what we plan to determine next.

The first letter indicates the specific casetype category (A through H), and the second letter indicates subjecttype (T, S, or A); where there is a number in-between the two letters (i.e., only occurring for category D), the number indicates the particular instance of that casetype category.

AT. A high school coach told the players of the girl's soccer team that the starters for an upcoming game would be determined by who came to all the practices and who worked the hardest during practice. Sara, one of the players, missed most of the practices, and when she was there she fooled around and did not work hard, yet she got to start in the next game.

AS. In a particular college course, the professor assigned a 20-page paper, which counted for 50% of the grade. The professor expected to see many sources cited. Students had most of the semester to work on the paper, but one student did no work on it; rather, he stayed up the night before it was due and turned in 20 pages of trash with no references. Yet he got an A.

AA. At a particular computer company, the policy was that promotions would go to those who showed the most initiative and made the greatest efforts toward developing new software. Despite this policy, the worker who made the least effort and showed almost no initiative received a promotion.

BT. A junior high school student started off with a C in math, so he decided to work hard to bring his grade up. He did all the homework assignments, which were all graded as "++," the top grade, and his test grades were all in the 85-to-95 range. Yet he got another C in math for the grading period.

BS. A student worked particularly hard on her paper. She did considerable research, tracking down many sources, and came up with an interesting thesis. Her paper was organized, well-written, and looked polished. Her roommates read her paper and thought she was sure to get an A. But when she got the paper back, there was not a single comment from the professor, only the grade of B.

BA. Three sales reps were competing for a promotion. One woman clearly sold more than the other two. In addition, she never missed a day, never took personal time off, and customers preferred to work with her. Yet she did not get the promotion.

CT. A sixth-grade boy forgot to do his homework, so he copied another students homework while on the bus ride to school. In the afternoon, the teacher gave a prize to the student whose homework was the best, and this boy won the prize.

CS. Although most of the students in a particular college course worked hard on their papers, one student found an old paper from a couple of years ago, typed a new cover page with her name on it, and submitted it as her own. She got an A.

CA. At an advertising agency, one guy worked hard on a concept for a client, developing the idea into a TV commercial. He and his supervisor presented the idea to the client, who loved it. The supervisor had little to do with the idea or the presentation, but when the owner of the company heard that the client was pleased, the supervisor took all the credit for the idea.

D1T. An infant who seemed perfectly healthy suffocates and died in the crib at night.

D1S. A college student who was driving home for the weekend got caught in a tornado that lifted and tossed his car; he was killed.

D1A. A 40-year-old man in good health died in an earthquake as a building fell in on him.

D2T. A crack baby born with many problems, including the likelihood of retardation because his parent was a crack addict, died from the complications in the first week of life.

D2S. A student learned that lightning struck her mother as she was stepping out of a car, and when her father called 911, the operator made a tragic mistake by sending the ambulance to the wrong address. Her father's frantic phone calls were too late, and her mother died on the way to the hospital.

D2A. A parent with a history of violence and physical abuse shook a child who was crying and the child died.

D3T. A junior high school boy went to the library after school to work on a book report, as he was a fine student; but when he left for home riding his bike, he was stopped by four bigger kids, who beat him up and took his bike.

D3S. A college student named Ellen roomed with another student in an off-campus apartment. The other student, Jane, was always crying poverty. She seemed to have money for clothes and entertainment, but not when the phone bill or rent check was due. Jane kept asking Ellen to pay her share of the bills, always promising to pay Ellen back. But Jane suddenly dropped out of school and skipped out on Ellen without paying what she owed, leaving Ellen scrambling to find a new roommate to pay half the apartment expenses.

D3A. Mrs. A liked her job and needed the income, along with her husband's, to pay the mortgage on their house. Mrs. A gave birth to a child and stayed at home for four months on maternity leave, which she believed was one of the benefits she was entitled from at the company. But the company decided to downsize, and Mrs. A was let go. She believed that the company was reneging on the entitled maternity benefit, but the company claimed it was part of their overall restructuring. Mrs. A and her husband could not make the mortgage payments and had to sell the house at a considerable loss.

D4T. In a country where a civil war was going on, innocent children have lost limbs stepping on land mines.

D4S. In a country where famine and disease were widespread, many infants were born blind.

D4A. A man in his late 30s, who ran 5 miles a day, watched what he ate, never smoked, nonetheless developed cancer. His form of cancer required frequent radiation treatments, which left him unable to do his job. He had a wife and three young children to support, but he now had only a small disability check.

ET. John, a high school student, was taking a geometry test when he heard Robert whisper to him. Robert wanted John to move his hand so Robert could see John's answers and cheat off of John's test. When John told Robert, "No way, you're not cheating off me," the teacher saw both Robert and John talking and gave both of them an F. When John tried to explain, the teacher said "I saw you talking, and that is cheating, so you're getting an F."

ES. A university has a policy of no drinking in a dorm. However, many students have defied the policy by sneaking beer into the dorm. Steve was passing a room where several guys were sharing a six pack that they had snuck into the dorm. One of them saw Steve, and said let's give a beer to Steve. Steve didn't want one, but stayed to talk for a few minutes with these guys. An RA who was walking by spotted the beer, and all the guys, including Steve, were busted and thrown out of the dorm.

EA. A man, who was at a job for 3 months, had always been on time. In fact, he usually arrived early, and did extra work to show the boss that he really cared. One day he arrived late because the Metro broke down, and his morning commute, which usually took 30 minutes, took an hour and 30 minutes this particular day. His boss did not want to hear the excuse and fired him.

FT. Tim tried out for the high school baseball team. There was one position available. Even to the guys who were on the team from last year, Tim seemed the best of the guys trying out. But the coach picked another kid. This other kid's father was best friends with the coach.

FS. There was a very popular club near the college where many students liked to go on the weekends. The club was always crowded, and there was usually a long waiting line. Bill and two of his friends were on line. Sara, a student in one of Bill's classes, passed Bill in line, said hi, and then went to the front of the line where she smiled and flirted with the club's bouncer, who let her in ahead of everyone.

FA. Mr. and Mrs. Ford saved money so their son, Edward, could go to medical school. Edward had made good grades and was recommended for medical school by his school's premed committee, but failed to get in. Mr. and Mrs. Ford were told that some of the places were reserved for minority students, even though their grades did not match Edward's.

GT. The fifth-grade class was supposed to have a pizza party on Friday, as a reward for the good work students were doing on their science projects. But on Friday morning, Al was clowning around and knocked over someone's project, breaking a piece of it off. The teacher was angry and said that because of Al, there was not going to be any pizza party.

GS. Four students were assigned to put on a seminar in class, and the seminar would count 20% of their grade. The students had two weeks to get organized. But every time they set an evening time to meet, one of students, Rachel, never showed. The other three worked on the assignment, but Rachel never did, nor did she bother to get in touch with the others, even though they left phone messages for her. The other three were organized and had done much work, and the day of the seminar Rachel showed up and asked what she should do. The other three were furious with her, but they were dumbfounded when all four of them got the same grade.

GA. A grandmother was dismayed with how her son treated his two children. The oldest son had to work a part-time job and earn straight A's before his father bought him a used car. But the second son got a car without working and despite getting poor grades.

HT. A child was punished by a parent for fighting with his brother, but the child insisted that his brother started it. The parent did not listen and sent the boy to his room. The boy shouted, "You never listen to my side!"

HS. A professor accused a student of cheating on an exam. The student claimed she did not cheat. At a hearing, a board spent 30 minutes listening to the professor and the deans, but gave the student less than 5 minutes to present her side. The board decided to throw the student out of school, although she claimed that she did not get a fair hearing.

HA. Two neighbors, Jones and Smith, were in a quarrel about a fence Jones put up, which Smith claimed was partly on his property. Moreover, in putting up the fence, Smith claimed that Jones and his workers trampled and destroyed his rose bushes. Jones claimed that Smith's dog, which ran around the neighborhood without a leash, was the problem and the reason for the fence. When the case came to small claims court, the judge seemed very sympathetic to Jones, even remarking that he was once bitten by a wild dog who ran into his yard. When it came time for Smith to tell his side of the story, the Judge told him to sit down and ruled in favor of Jones.

ENDNOTES

1. J. N. Shklar, *The Faces of Injustice* (New Haven: Yale University Press, 1990).
2. C. Haney, "The Fourteenth Amendment and Symbolic Legality: Let Them Eat Due Process," *Law and Human Behavior* 15 (1991): 183.
3. *Id.*, pp. 185–186.
4. Haney is not alone is making this argument. *See, e.g.*, D. R. Fox, "Psycholegal Scholarship's Contribution to False Consciousness About Injustice," *Law and Human Behavior* 23 (1999): 9–30.
5. There were two participant groups, a student group and an adult group. The students were fulfilling a research project requirement, and they had an extra-credit opportunity to recruit an adult participant, with the guidelines being these: The adult (A) had to be between the ages of 25 and 60, and the adult could be either a parent, aunt, uncle, or older sibling. There were 217 participants overall, 120 females and 97 males, with the religious denomination breakdown being quite similar to previous studies. There were 151 participants in the student (S) group (85 females, 66 males), with a mean age of 19.9 and a mean education level of 14.7, and there were 66 adult (A) participants (35 females and 31 males), with a mean age of 41.6 and a mean education level of 18.0.
6. The 33 instances were drawn from previous studies, and we picked only instances that fell in the "high" (51–75) or "severe" (76–100) categories; by doing so, we tried to eliminate the questionable, suspect, or borderline cases, and tried to keep severity if not constant, at least within a certain range.
7. Our aim in adding three more cases (bringing the D category instances to four, D1, D2, D3, D4) was to equally represent both injustice (human agency) and misfortune (impersonal agency) cases, and to test for differences.
8. Thus with 11 levels for casetype and 3 levels for subjecttype, we have a two-within (casetype $\times$ subjecttype, $11 \times 3 = 33$ instances) design, and this is called a "within-subject" design because all participants get all variables and levels.
9. This fourth group (A), a within-subject group, allows us to compare our three between-subject groups (I, M, U) with this within-subject-group (A).
10. Thus for the between-subject part of the design, we had a 4×2 (aimu $\times$ view) design, with 8 different groups.
11. This lack of a significant difference between S and A groups continues the pattern we generally found in the studies of Part II.
12. A multivariate analysis of variance (MANOVA) was used, revealing significant main effects for both casetype ($F[df = 10/113, N = 135] = 15.4$, $p < .0001$) and subjecttype ($F[df = 2/121, N = 135] = 15.4$, $p < .0001$), and a significant casetype $\times$ subjecttype interaction effect.
13. Although a replication with a different design adds confidence to the findings, we have reasons for believing that the less powerful, between-subject design

yields the more reliable findings. The reason for this is that the within-subject design may introduce, inadvertently, a "demand characteristic" where the key contrasts (i.e., unfairness versus misfortune versus injustice) are made all too salient, which may suggest to these participants that they make sharper differentiations than they might have otherwise done had only one dimension been rated. We see evidence that this does occur: The dimensions rated lowest and highest by between-subject groups get even lower and higher in the within-subject design.

14. $F[df = 66/180, N = 135] = 3.4, p < .0001$.

15. Shklar, "The Faces of Injustice."

16. $F[df = 33/90, N = 135] = .84, p = .71$, n.s.

17. We can rule out a "ceiling effect" operating, which might artificially mute true differences. Although the mean unfairness ratings were high (higher than either injustice or misfortune), ranging from 51 to 88 across the 33 instances, they were not so high that participants could go no higher; thus if seeing the unfairness from the victim's perspective inflames severity more than the outsider's view, there was room for the scores to rise with the additional heat. Yet they did not.

18. Still, a caveat must be considered. Perhaps our instruction to the participants —to take the view of the victim—was difficult to do. Although we cannot rule this possible artifact out entirely, we do note, to the contrary, that not one participant made note of any difficulty in role-playing the victim. To the contrary, however, in the earlier studies, we saw that severity scores were lower when the unfairness occurred to the participant (Y), whereas scores were generally higher for instances where they did not know the victim (U). The best evidence we have suggests that the artifact is not operating.

19. The U + I versus M comparison was significant ($F[df = 33/172, N = 82] = 14.7, p < .0001$), as was the U versus I comparison ($F[df = 33/172, N = 82] = 2.6, p < .0001$).

20. These were ANOVA tests, with Scheffé tests run to refine those differences.

21. If we were scaling these three constructs on a single dimension, it might be said that unfairness falls between injustice and misfortune, though much closer to the "injustice" end of things. However, this unidimensional scaling analogy falters, for the unfairness ratings are generally higher than the injustice ratings, with misfortune ratings being the lowest. The higher severity ratings for unfairness indicates that it captures more of the participants' anger and heat than does injustice. Thus this finding suggests that unfairness not only has a wider orbit than injustice, but that it better reflects the intensity of the claim.

22. However, only the A group and the U group made an overall unfairness severity rating on every case as well, and these two groups were combined for subsequent analyses.

23. The MANOVA analysis revealed a significant overall OPU effect ($F[df = 66/942, N = 127] = 5.1, p < .0001$), and the preplanned comparisons, testing O versus P ($F[df = 33/471, N = 127]$ •= $9.96, p < .0001$) and U versus O + P ($F[df = 33/471, N = 127] = 1.5, p < .035$), were also significant.

24. The P ratings are far from minimal, though generally lower than O and U, falling in the high severity (i.e., 51–75) category on average.

25. This outcome bias is not the result of some artifact—such as sensitizing participants by asking them to make process, outcome, and overall unfairness ratings—which might make one dimension more salient than it would otherwise be, for all dimensions were made equally salient. Moreover, we could argue that if there was some differential sensitizing effect, process ratings should have benefited the most, for if "process" is in the background, overshadowed by "outcome" in the foreground, a differential sensitizing effect ought to enhance the background "process."

26. We also used factor analysis and canonical discriminant analyses, and these results were highly consistent with the cluster analysis results, so we do not report those.

27. The oblique principal component cluster analysis was used, and the proportion of the variation explained by these clusters was .6629.

28. In a purely statistical way, we have established that the cases fall into groupings (i.e., clusters), and these reflect meaningful *psychological* distinctions. For instance, there is a grouping that contains what may be called "disparity cases," where the rewards and punishments do not match what is deserved, and where "human hands" deal the unfairness (cluster 1). We also have cases of discrimination and unfair advantages, equal treatment when it should not be, and arbitrary rules, and these cases cluster together (cluster 4); though these represent three different specific categories in our schema, there is an underlying reason for linking them together: We might see "equal treatment when it should not be" as discriminatory or arbitrary treatment, whereas straightforward unfair advantages cases can be seen as arbitrary treatment as well; all three categories, then, involve reward or punishment decisions where no defensible rule supports the decision and where caprice, outright discrimination, and "might makes right" seem to reign, as due process goes by the wayside. Then there are the cases reflecting the caprice of nature, life, or God (cluster 2).

29. R. Harré and D. N. Robinson, "On the Primacy of Duties," *Philosophy* 70 (1995): 513–532.

30. Cluster analysis is a *statistical* way of finding underlying dimensions. By contrast, the categorization schema for type of unfairness, developed, revised, and tested through the five studies, represents a different way of attacking the problem. If we compare the schema with the clusters, we find both similarities and differences. As for similarities, the statistical procedure did pick out and group the "reward (or punishment) to effort" disparity cases (Cluster 1); however, on the difference side, three specific categories, representing two major categories (i.e., I/A, I/B, II/C), are brought together and clustered as one, whereas we kept them distinct. For Cluster 4, three specific categories are brought together as one, whereas we kept those three distinct. The statistical approach tells us that the cases in Cluster 1 and Cluster 4 are significantly correlated, suggesting that a deeper connection links them. Going in the other direction, the cluster analysis took one specific category, "when innocence is punished," and subdivided it three ways.

31. J. D. Casper, K. Benedict, and J. L. Perry, "Juror Decision Making Attitudes, and the Hindsight Bias," *Law and Human Behavior* 13 (1989): 291–310.

32. S. J. LaBine and G. LaBine, "Determinations of Negligence and the Hindsight Bias," *Law and Human Behavior* 20 (1996): 501–516.
33. L. Heuer, S. Penrod, S. Gefen, and M. Saks, "Judicial Decision Making in Cases Regarding the Prediction of Criminality: The Role of Societal Benefits and Fairness Concerns." Paper presented at the American Psychology-Law Society Conference, New Orleans, March 2000.

10

OBJECTING TO PUNISHMENTS, SUSTAINING PROCESS

Punishment seems central in citizens' unfairness judgments, being a headliner in most type categories. The exemplar is the Job category (III/D), where punishment occurs when it should not. Although category D stands out in both its cited frequency and the anger it generates, this category by no means stands alone. The flip-side of "innocence punished" is "wrongful behavior not punished" (II/C). Although these C instances are cited less frequently and rated less severely than D instances, they nonetheless appear in substantial numbers and generate substantial heat. These two contrasting categories have commonality: In both, punishment (or lack of it) fails to align with culpability (or lack of it), and this "out of alignment" inequity is extreme.

But "out of alignment" cases do not stop at just D and C types. Citizens also cite with frequency and intensity cases where punishments are doled out in differential or discriminatory ways (IV/F), such that "equal justice under law" fails to result. In category F, "unfair advantages and/or connections" allow the impermissibly favored to escape or receive lessened punishment, whereas the nonadvantaged are punished fully. This is unfair because citizens regard those advantages as irrelevant, impermissible, or extralegal to whether punishment ought to occur and to what degree.

If category F asks the goddess of Justice to remain blind to extralegal factors, then the flip side is category (IV/G)—when "equal or nondiscrim-

inatory treatment results when the punishment should be individualized"
—is different. Here, Justice appears blind when we most want her to see.
The claim in category G cases asserts that Justice should weigh culpability
distinctions among offenders and grade punishment to fit each individual,
rather than meting out indiscriminate "one size fits all" punishment.

Categories D, C, F, and G are still not the whole of the punishment/
unfairness categories, for "punishment being disproportionate or excessive
to the act and intent" (III/E) also fits the "out of alignment" theme. In
category E, unlike D, citizens recognize that there is some degree of blameworthiness that deserves punishment, and, unlike C, they recognize that
the actor is not escaping punishment; thus, category E instances are less
flagrant than D or C instances, calling for a fine-tuning of a proportional
sort, because the punishment does not justly fit. Category E instances contrast with those in category F, for the latter center around equality, whereas
E instances, like those in categories D, C, and G, can be subsumed under
equity theory.[1] Notions of equality relate to both outcome and process,
whereas theories of equity deal largely with distributive justice.[2]

But distributive justice is not the issue in category V/H, because these
instances involve "arbitrary rules, objections overruled." To sharpen how
category H instances contrast, there are cases in H where there is guilt
(unlike D), where deserved punishment is given (unlike C) and given
proportionately (unlike E), where discriminatory factors are not used (unlike F), and where an individualized judgment is made (unlike G). Despite
all of these fairness requisites being met, which would satisfy equity theory
and distributive justice requirements, there is still an unfairness claim
grounded in procedural justice.[3] The argument is that when punishments are meted out without giving people "their day in court," without
opportunity to defend, respond, or rebut, or where arbitrary and capricious
rules reign and the game is rigged, then the required due process is absent,
and this is unfair.

FROM PUNISHMENT TO PROCESS

In moving from punishment to process, we have a clear contrast.
Punishment is situated centrally within most "types" categories and their
instantiations, an unchallenged constitutive element; in fact, punishment
is the outcome that so grabs our attention and summons the judgment of
unfairness. Process, by contrast, is centrally featured in only one category
(H), although it may sprout in other categories as well, though less visible,
as it must contend with the dominant masking effect of the punishing
outcome. Being more peripherally featured, being frequently eclipsed by
the outcome dominance of punishment, and the fact that it finds no comfortable home within distributive justice all point to an outcome bias.

But there is also evidence that runs to the contrary, or at least challenges the notion that process is eclipsed by the outcome bias. We do find process being cited throughout the studies. In categories C, F, and G, the focus may not be on the outcome but on how evaluators do their job, and the same can be found in categories A ("no work rewarded") and B ("hard work not rewarded"). Moreover, we find many intercoder disagreements about outcome versus process, which tells us that either the participant or the coder is attentive to process, whereas the other looks to outcome. In the experiment, participants did make process judgments that tracked the particulars of the cases, although their process ratings were not as highly correlated with overall unfairness as their outcome ratings were.

This review highlights four points. First, punishment is central across unfairness claims. Second, citizens make numerous outcome/inequity distinctions and some outcome/inequality distinctions regarding type of unfairness, and this tells us that their concepts of outcome unfairnesses are highly nuanced. Third, it appears that process unfairnesses cannot be subsumed easily, neatly, or at all under equity theory and distributive justice notions, and they therefore represent something distinctive from outcome, as we saw in their ratings in the experiment. Fourth, the outcome–process division is not neatly separate into our type categories,[4] such that process unfairnesses may lie hidden beneath outcome, rather than being absent. If this is so, then we may fail to see or highlight process even when it is there.

In light of the centrality of punishment, outcome's distinctiveness, process's lack of fit within equity theory, and the possibility of conflation of outcome with process, we plan a more fine-grained examination of "punishment cases," particularly those where process looms large. Methodologically, we will stay with the experimental format, as it affords tighter control over the variables, and the venue we select is the law, which is an obvious choice. Even in its iconography, where the statue of Justice is emblematically poised with sword (punishment) and balance scale (fairness) in her hands, we see the coupling. More important, in its content, the law offers a rich array of punishment cases: On one extreme, there are death penalty cases; in the midrange, there are imprisonment cases, cases involving only monetary losses, and cases involving even lesser punishments, such as probation or community service; and at the other extreme are cases where no punishment whatsoever is given.

EXPERIMENT 2: FINDING UNFAIRNESS FACTORS IN THREE LEGAL CASES

Three Supreme Court cases from the Court's 1995–1996 calendar year were selected, cases where unfairness claims regarding punishments were at the heart of these disputes. We purposefully picked open cases where the Court had neither heard oral arguments nor rendered its decision yet. By selecting open cases, we minimize the prior information participants might have about the cases and, more important, control knowledge of the right answer, because without a final decision there is none. In addition, we picked disparate punishment cases rather than one case or one type of case to see whether commonsense unfairness factors would generalize across cases.

The first case, BMW of North America, Inc., v. Ira Gore, Jr.,[5] involved punitive damages. BMW had repaired and repainted a "new" car damaged slightly during transport; operating under a 3% rule—if the damage did not exceed 3% of the sales price, BMW could repair the car, sell it as new, and not tell the buyer. Almost a year after purchase, Gore found out that his BMW had been repainted and brought the case. At trial, an Alabama jury found for Ira Gore and against BMW and set a $4 million punitive damages award (where the compensatory damages were $4000). The Alabama Supreme Court subsequently reduced the punitive damage award to $2 million, but BMW still found the damages to be excessive, and the company appealed.

The second case, Stacey C. Koon v. United States and Laurence M. Powell v. United States,[6] arose from the infamous Rodney King case, and the issue here involved the lower sentences (i.e., 30 months) given by the trial judge where ordinary application of the federal sentencing guidelines would warrant a higher range (i.e., 70–87 months). The question was, did the trial judge use permissible factors to lower the punishment, or were impermissible factors weighed in the judge's discretionary mix? The reviewing Ninth Circuit believed that the judge's sentence lowering was impermissible, whereas Koon and Powell disagreed, believing that the trial judge was right, and so they appealed.

In the third case, Coleman Wayne Gray v. J. D. Netherland, Warden,[7] the Virginia jury gave the death penalty. Gray argued that 24 hours before the sentencing hearing the prosecutors informed the defense that they were going to offer testimony linking Gray to another murder for which he was not charged. Gray's attorneys objected that they were taken by surprise and had no opportunity to rebut this damaging testimony and that the prosecution withheld evidence that the police had another suspect for that second murder.[8]

These cases involve outcome and process. The alleged outcome unfairness—a death sentence, a prison sentence of 6 to 8 years, and a $2 million punitive judgment—looms large. But behind the alleged outcome unfairnesses stand process factors. Our question is, would citizens see these process factors and to what extent?

Literally from a two-to-three-page summary of the case, we asked participants to "underline all phrases and sentences which you believe reveal or imply an unfairness." As we wanted to get at their commonsense notions, we did not provide them with a definition of what "unfairness" meant, and there was no mention of either "outcome" or "process" either. Participants were then instructed that for each underlined passage they were to give their reasons why each factor seemed unfair to them. From their reasons we developed a comprehensive and reliable schema of their commonsense unfairness factors.

Participants were randomly assigned to one of six groups,[9] and each group got a booklet containing an abbreviated version of one of the three cases (approximately two to three pages in length).[10] Two groups began with the *BMW* (B) case, two groups began with the *Gray* (G) case, and two groups began with the *Koon and Powell* (K) case.[11]

In part 1, the participant was asked "to play the part of an appellate court judge, who had to render a decision in the case and to give reasons for doing so." Their cited unfairnesses, and their written reasons categorized, gave us what we call the "commonsense perspective."

A week later, after the participants had returned their part 1 booklet, they received a second booklet, designated part 2. Three of the groups (BS, GS, KS) continued with the same case, but at a higher level, whereas the other three groups (BD, GD, KD) switched to a new case, but also at a higher level. What we mean by "a higher level" is this: We instructed our participants that they were now to play the part of a Supreme Court justice. Moreover, the cases in each part 2 booklet now ran 4 to 5 pages in length: It not only contained the brief issues and lengthy facts sections that were included in part 1, but now contained new material, including how the appellate court ruled and why, and sections designated "case analysis," where the legal arguments for and against were discussed, and a section designated "significance," detailing the implications of this case for law and public policy in general.[12]

In part 2, the participants again had to underline what they believed revealed unfairnesses and to give their reasons—but now they were getting a heavy dose of legal reasons from the appellate court's decision and reasons and from the case analysis and significance sections. Our question was this: Would these legal and often highly technical reasons (which we call the "legal perspective") come to dominate the participants' commonsense perspective (which they gave in part 1)—thereby coloring and shifting the participants' unfairness factors in significant ways in part 2? Put another way, would our naive participants now start to sound like lawyers, parroting back these legal and technical fine points, or would they essentially stick with the commonsense factors they identified in part 1?[13]

Finally, a week later, after the part 2 booklets were turned in, the participants received a new booklet, labeled part 3. The three "same" groups (BS, GS, KS) continued with their same case, while the "different" groups (BD, GD, KD) received a new case again, and thus the different groups end up getting all three cases, but at different levels of the case, never repeating the same case. The same material as in the part 2 booklet was reproduced, but the participants were now given a list of 20 "reasons" —statements, facts, arguments, or points of law that some of the Supreme Court justices were alleged to have raised (we imputed these reasons to the justices). In part 3, then, we gave the participants "designated legal reasons" attributed to highly credible sources (i.e., Supreme Court justices) and asked them to express their degree of agreement or disagreement with these reasons on a 1-to-9 scale. Last, the participants had to decide the case, making either a "reverse or remand" decision or a "let stand" decision.

Given that each participant was to make a final verdict for the case (i.e., let stand versus reverse and remand), the question we asked was this: "What factor will best predict their final verdict?" Will it be their ratings in part 3 on the reasons we selected and attributed to the justices, thus bearing a legal imprimatur? Or will it be the commonsense fairness factors that they came up with in part 1? Or will it be the heavy dose of legal arguments from part 2, which may have colored, muted, or even suppressed their commonsense factors?

RESULTS AND DISCUSSION

The participants' reasons were categorized using a 13-item schema, which proved both inclusive and reliable. Item 1, dubbed "cards up the sleeve," judged it unfair when one side withholds information from the other side, rather than playing openly and fairly with the facts. Item 2, "dealing false cards," judged it unfair when facts are manipulated to produce a distorted impression, rather than being presented in a clear, straightforward, and truthful manner. Item 3, "untrustworthy witnesses, rules, court case precedents, and deal cutting," judged it unfair when untrustworthy witnesses are cutting deals to receive lesser sentences if they testify, or when questionable rules or disputed court cases are being used to decide guilt and punishment. Item 4, "severe punishments demand greater scrutiny," found it unfair when the potential punishment is extreme and less than the most strict procedures of scrutiny are used. As Table 10-1 shows, items 1 through 4 were cited most frequently for the *Gray* (G) death penalty case, second most for the *BMW* (B) punitive damages case, and least of all for *Koon* (K) case.

Item 5, "individualized punishments," held that procedures that did not consider individual factors of the defendant in the punishment decision, but drew strict and arbitrary lines, would be unfair, for the severity of the punishment would not fit the crime and the criminal. This factor was cited most frequently in cases B and K and less in G.

Item 6, "victim's rights," held that an exclusive focus on the defendant would be unfair, and that the suffering of the victim and victim's family ought to weigh as much as the rights of the defendant. This factor was cited most in case G, then K, and least of all in B.

Item 7, "defendant's rights," held that focusing on the victim was unfair, because the defendant's rights ought to come first. There were no significant differences by case for this item.

Item 8, "incompetent attorneys," held that it would be unfair for an individual to suffer punishment simply because of failure of counsel. This factor was cited almost exclusively in G.

Item 9, "abuse of authority," held that those in authority (e.g., the police, a judge, or a jury) should not abuse or overstep their authority. Item 10, "rules, reasons, and reviews," held that rules should not bend for select people, that rulings must have cogent reasons behind them, and that cases should not be reviewed again and again to purposefully delay justice. Items 9 and 10 were cited most frequently for case K and least for G.

Item 11, "vague laws/too flexible," held that when the law is too vague or flexible then there is no precise way to assess punishment and an unfair amount of variance will result. Item 12, "variable laws across jurisdictions," held that variance from one state to another produces widely disparate and unfair verdicts. Item 13, "appellate reviews necessary to correct errors," held that it would be unfair if there were no mechanism to reverse mistakes. Items 11 through 13 were cited most frequently in case B.

The first thing to note is that almost all of the 13 items are process

TABLE 10-1
The Frequency of Participants' Reasons by Case, for Parts 1 and 2 of the Experiment

	Cases								
	B		G		K		Totals		
Reasons	1	2	1	2	1	2	1	2	Σ Total
1. Cards up sleeve	41	20	43	55	0	0	84	75	159
2. Dealing false cards	26	29	31	37	13	4	70	70	140
3. Unworthy witnesses	0	0	27	18	3	2	30	20	50
4. Greater scrutiny	4	4	7	7	1	0	12	11	23
5. Individualized	15	23	4	6	5	13	24	42	66
6. Victim's rights	7	2	25	21	17	7	49	30	79
7. Defendant's rights	9	12	11	23	9	10	29	45	74
8. Incomp. attorney	0	0	30	18	11	3	41	21	62
9. Abuse of authority	0	1	1	3	56	40	57	44	101
10. Rules & reasons	3	19	1	4	74	84	78	107	185
11. Vague laws	21	60	0	1	7	12	28	73	101
12. Variable laws	14	39	0	0	1	0	15	39	54
13. Appellate review	14	15	0	3	2	13	16	31	47
Totals	154	224	180	196	199	187	533	607	1140

items. Not only did participants see process violations, but they found numerous types. The frequency distribution of the participants' reasons for each case, for both the first and second parts of the experiment, are shown in Table 10-1. Clearly, there are significant differences in the pattern of reasons by case, though this is not surprising given the differences among the cases. Most noteworthy are the number of unfairnesses participants found, the sophistication shown in their reasons, and the case details they cited to support their judgments. For example, in part 1, participants cited an average of 6.7 unfairness factors per case, an impressive number overall. Moreover, their factors seemed apropos to the case, even though they had not received legal arguments yet. Taken together, their commonsense unfairness notions were complex and to the point.[14]

The results of part 1 reflect what we call "commonsense" factors, for they derive from the participants' construals of these cases without any legal overlay. But in part 2, participants' commonsense notions may have become colored, saturated, or obliterated by the heavy dose of legal reasons they received as the "professional" legal actors (e.g., justices, attorneys, legal scholars) weighed in. The question was, "What will the participants do?" Will they abandon their commonsense factors for the legal reasons the professionals offer, or will they stubbornly, perhaps close-mindedly, hold fast?

Legal Unfairness Factors Versus Commonsense Unfairness Factors

When we compared columns 1 and 2 (see Table 10-1), we found that the commonsense unfairness factors held up, by and large: There were no overall significant difference nor specific case differences in the pattern of reasons from part 1 to part 2. Second, when we compared the "same" versus the "different" groups in part 2, we found no significant differences. Third, the "different" groups had not seen that case before and had not made prior judgments on the case that might anchor them. Fourth, although the "different" groups in part 2 got the strong dose of legal reasons, what they found was similar to what the "same" groups found without legal reasons. These findings suggest that participants used their commonsense factors, which were not significantly altered by the legal unfairness factors.

This last conclusion needs to be tempered somewhat. We do in fact see some changes from part 1 to part 2, even if the effects fail to reach significance. For example, there are, on the average, more factors cited in part 2: 7.6 as compared to 6.7, a gain of almost one reason per case. We might simply discount this increase as artifactual—arising from the increase of material given to participants in part 2—and not necessarily arising from the legal reasons we added. But if the artifact hypothesis is correct, and the algorithm is simply "more pages = more reasons," then we would expect that all the reasons would rise proportionally, yet this does not happen.[15]

Legal reasons do seem to have subtle, modifying effects on the commonsense reasons, although the shifts are not great enough to produce statistical significance, and when we examine the subtle changes, one resultant seems to be a "boosting" effect: When the legal reasons underscore factors the participants have already found, those factors are cited noticeably more often. There also seems to be a "salient" effect, when the legal reasons accent a factor that participants have not, participants seem to take heed and then give more weight to the factor. There may also be a "muting" effect, where some factors drop; however, whether muting is an independent effect or merely a concomitant effect of other factors being boosted or made more salient, we cannot say.[16]

Even though there is evidence that legal factors do modify commonsense factors slightly, the main finding is that differences between parts 1 and 2 were small and not significant. This suggests that commonsense unfairness factors may not be all that different from legal unfairness factors in number and type, because had they been fundamentally different, we should have seen significant changes in part 2, and the changes should have gone in the legal factors direction; going even further, had the factors been very different, we should have seen significant differences between those participants who only got the legal arguments (the "different groups") in part 2 versus the part 1 participants who got the cases without legal arguments.

We took the 13 factors shown in Table 10-1 and asked, "Would these factors discriminate the cases from one another?" They did,[17] and Table 10-1 gives some indications of which factors discriminate.[18] Given the great differences among the cases, it is not surprising that there are significant case effects. What is less predictable is the relationship between these part 1 commonsense unfairness factors and the "verdict decision" (reverse and remand versus let stand) participants make in part 3: Will these commonsense factors predict the final verdict?

We first found factors that pull toward "reverse and remand" and those that load onto a "let stand" decision, and we tested whether significant factor patterns emerge. They did. Our second step was to analyze across the cases to see if there was a general factor pattern that discriminated "reverse and remand" from "let stand," and we found such factors. Our third step was to examine participants' commonsense unfairness factors of part 1 and their part 2 factors (where the legal perspective had modestly boosted, made salient, and muted some of the commonsense factors in part 1) to see if the part 2 factors better predict their part 3 verdict. The answer turns out to be "no." The commonsense unfairness factors in part 1 turned out to be more predictive of verdict in part 3 than the legal unfairness factors added in part 2.[19]

The added legal perspective ends up weakening the overall relationship between unfairness factors and verdict. Why is this so? Interpreted pejoratively, legal arguments seem to add a fuzziness to the participants' commonsense picture rather than sharpening it. But less pejoratively, one might view the participants' initial commonsense picture as naively black and white, where the legal perspective then adds shades of gray. Without some divine pronouncement of the "true verdict" and which factors ought to be determinative—a pronouncement we clearly lack—we cannot determine whether the participants' commonsense factors or their second extraction (now tainted by the legal factors) is the better.

What we can say is that the first extraction does predict verdict better. We can also say that despite some subtle movement of these initial factors, they do seem resistant to a significant shifting. That fixedness may be because the factors are on the mark to begin with, and the legal factors merely echo what most participants already found, or because we have not subjected the commonsense factors to a more vigorous shove.

This vigorous shove is what we tried to do in part 3, where we gave the participants statements attributed to most authoritative sources, Supreme Court justices. To take the *Gray* case (G) as the example, there were statements such as (11) "Using prediction of future dangerousness is unfair because predictions are unreliable"; (13) "Since the main evidence against Gray was furnished by Tucker, who wanted to save his skin, a death sentence would be unfair because of the possibility that the wrong man is getting it"; (15) "Gray should have filed his appeal earlier"; and (17) "The punishment should stand, as the jury, the conscience of the community, heard all the evidence and gave the death sentence." The 20 statements were balanced, 10 seeming to favor "reverse and remand" 10 seeming to favor "let stand," and the participants had to rate how fair or unfair they thought each statement was.

The bottom line results were that these 20 ratings were less predictive of the participants' final verdicts than their initial commonsense factors. Thus the commonsense factors, which held in the face of legal arguments (part 2), now hold in the face of arguments attributed to the justices (part 3), remaining the best predictor of final verdict.

Higher Order Factors

The 13 commonsense factors are not independent, as some correlate with others; this being so, we used cluster analysis to find the higher order factors. We ran two analyses, one for the "reverse and remand" verdicts the other for the "let stand" verdicts (see Table 10-2). For the reverse and remand analysis, Cluster 1 focuses on abuses of authority. These perceived abuses involve the jury or the prosecution. For example, in the BMW case, a significant number of participants see the jury as overstepping its au-

TABLE 10-2
The Cluster Analyses for the "Reverse and Remand" and "Let Stand" Decisions

Cluster #	Factors Within Each Cluster	Cluster Name/Description
Reverse and remand		
1	1—Cards up sleeve 9—Abuse of authority 10—Rules and reasons	Rules must trump abuses of discretion
2	3—Untrustworthy witnesses 8—Incompetent attorney	Balancing the playing field
3	5—Individualized assessment 6—Victim's rights 11—Vague laws 12—Variable laws 13—Appellate review	A Balanced System
4	2—Dealing false cards 4—Greater scrutiny	Vigilance over tainted or suspect evidence
5	7—Defendant's rights	Defendant's rights
Total proportion of the variance explained = .5620		
Let stand		
1	1—Cards up sleeve 9—Abuse of authority 10—Rules and reasons	Rules must be followed to prevent abuse of authority and promote equal justice
2	3—Untrustworthy witnesses 6—Victim's rights 8—Incompetent attorney 11—Vague laws 12—Variable laws 13—Appellate review	Laws and reviews must be followed so that violations don't over turn fair decisions and to balance rights
3	2—Dealing false cards 7—Defendant's rights	When defendant plays false cards, defendant loses certain rights
4	4—Greater scrutiny 5—Individualized punishment	Jury/judge made the decision and higher courts should not reverse
Total proportion of the variance explained = .4658		

thority in setting an outrageous punitive damages award, whereas in the *Gray* case, many participants see the prosecution sandbagging the defense. Implicit in this cluster is the recognition that justice does not always result, and that is why rules and reviews are needed to reverse such injustices.

In Cluster 2, it is the playing field of the trial that is in focus, and this cluster endorses a balanced and level playing field as an essential component of fairness. For example, lawyers for both sides need to be competent and balanced and the testimony needs to be trustworthy for the field to be level.

In Cluster 3, which we call "a balanced system," for an individualized assessment to occur, a series of factors must be balanced beyond evidence and attorneys: There must be a balancing of rights (defendant and victim's); the laws, too, must be balanced, such that vagueness and variability do not tip the scales; and the system of law needs checks and balances, where higher level reviews can correct or fine-tune lower level unfairnesses.

Cluster 4 returns to the trial's evidentiary focus and finds that possibly tainted evidence, or less than full disclosure of the evidence, should not determine the outcome, particularly when the potential punishments are high or extreme. Cluster 5, with only one factor, weighs the protection of the defendant's rights.

Moving to Cluster 1 for the "let stand" decision, we find the identical factors found in Cluster 1 for reverse and remand, although it is labeled differently. The reason for this slight change in the labeling is that although the same factors are cited, the "let stand" participants largely focus on the police abuse in the *Koon and Powell* case and believe that the trial judge's discretionary lowering of their sentences amounted to unequal justice.[20]

In Cluster 2, a different argument is forwarded. This cluster asserts that even if the law is vague or variable, or even if some testimony or the competence of an attorney is questionable, the trial is the best venue for making such determinations, not the appellate level. This cluster holds that reviews should generally not overturn lower court findings, because when appellate courts or even the Supreme Court try to rebalance what the triers of fact already balanced, the result is likely to be less justice, greater injustice, or a delay of justice.

In Cluster 3, when participants see the defendant as playing fast and loose with the facts, they are inclined to decline his subsequent claims for appeal and redress. Implicit is the argument that the defendant's rights and procedural protections are lessened when his actions are unfair.

Cluster 4 returns to the review process and argues that the required individualized punishment assessment is best done by the jury or judge, as only they hear all the testimony. Thus this cluster argues that appellate courts, including the Supreme Court, should not generally intervene.

Unfairness Principles

In the cluster analysis results, we can appreciate the levels on which participants analyze these cases and the sophistication shown. Let us first consider the level of the defendant. The defendant may have abused his authority (e.g., *Koon and Powell*), or may have done great harm (e.g., *Gray*), or may have hidden information about damage and repairs to a new car (e.g., *BMW*). If participants believe these charges, then the fairness principles are straightforward. First, the equity principle holds that these defendants ought to be punished when they are found culpable. Second, the proportionality principle holds that the punishment ought to be proportional to the intent and the harm. Third, the individualized principle holds that this culpability determination process ought to be individualized. Fourth, the equal justice principle holds that the same rules ought to apply to all, but if there is an exception to be made to equal justice, it must be grounded on some defensible reason.

Moving from the level of the defendant to the level of the trial, the metaphor of a level playing field becomes central: In this adversarial battle with serious consequences on the line, an incompetent attorney would unfairly tilt the playing field, as would tainted evidence, or evidence withheld, or untrustworthy witnesses who may lie to save their skin. The battle, then, must be fought by relatively matched principals, privy to all the cards, and operating by principled rules; falling short suggests a rigged game and an unfair process. Whereas participants whose verdicts are either "reverse and remand" or "let stand" seem to agree on this much, we now turn to unfairness claims where disagreements arise and where community sentiment seems split.

One disagreement involves the balancing of victim's rights and defendant's rights. In part 1, we found that victim's rights unfairnesses were cited almost twice as often as defendant's rights unfairnesses, a surprising ratio given the Constitution's protections of the defendant. Commonsense fairness not only places greater weight on the victim than black-letter law, but the very notion of "victim" widens: The victim may be the obvious one, like the plaintiff Ira Gore Jr., but it may well include others who thought they were buying a new car and did not know that they were getting a retouched one; the victim may be the one slain in the *Gray* case, or victim may widen to include the family of the deceased; the victim may be Rodney King in the *Koon and Powell* case, or it may widen to embrace other unnamed and unknown victims who have suffered police abuse at some point.

Championing the claims of victims runs counter to the central claims of the defendant, who, at a criminal trial in particular, is thought to be in greatest need of protection. This is where the effect of the legal arguments in part 2 did come into play, for defendant's rights were made more salient in these arguments and resulted in participants citing defendant's rights more frequently that victim's rights in part 2. Still, in the end, commonsense seems to weigh the victim's rights heavily, and there is a potential tension, if not conflict, when these rights and the defendants' rights stand in opposition.

Moving to a higher level in the process, that of appellate review, we see disagreement and division within commonsense fairness. If the sports metaphor of a level playing field served at the level of the trial, then the umpire metaphor helps here. Who should umpire the game? Some strongly feel that it is the judge or jury who ought to make the call, as they are closest to the scene and hear all the testimony; moreover, once the appellate review process begins, it can drag on, with final justice delayed interminably, in the minds of some, who generally render "let stand" verdicts. Others strongly believe that some calls are wrong calls, and there ought to be a higher umpire (like instant replay in football) who can reverse unfairnesses; moreover, it is not just the facts of the case, but the interpretation of law that must properly be decided. These participants generally favor higher review and are more inclined to reverse and remand. Thus some participants deliver a hands-off message to the appellate courts, whereas others invite review.

There is still another division that takes the matter further, and the *BMW* case is illustrative. On the "reverse and remand" side, some participants favor a much more active Supreme Court, one that is more federalist and legislative—a Court that not only sees vague and variable laws, such as Alabama's law being quite different from the law in most states, but a Court that legislates uniformity of laws such that equal justice obtains. On the "let stand" side, there is the recognition that some states have laws that are relatively unique, perhaps even quirky, but this is the law passed by the elected legislators of that state and the law the case is tried under; these participants seem to say, "Play by the rules, even if the rules are odd; it is up to the citizens and their elected representatives to change the laws, and not the appellate courts." This "federalist/legislative versus state's rights/don't change the rules during the game" dispute echoes some fundamental arguments in *The Federalist Papers*.

OUTCOME AND PROCESS REVISITED

If we return to the unfairness factors cited by case (Table 10-1) and now look at those factors in light of the outcome versus process distinction, the results suggest that the unfairness picture is more complex than we had thought. To recall, participants seemed much more outcome than process focused in the studies, particularly when the participant was college age or above, and using unfairness vignettes in the previous chapter, we also found an outcome bias. Now, however, with complex legal cases where participants extract the unfairness factors, we see that they can move beneath the obvious outcome unfairness to a thoroughgoing search of process factors.

From their explanations of their factors, participants are clearly sensitive to process, making sophisticated and numerous distinctions. One might counter by noting that legal cases, particularly those that become Supreme Court cases, are likely to turn more on process unfairnesses than outcome, and thus we may have unfairly sensitized citizens to "process" by the very stimulus materials provided. By way of a response, we do not believe that is the case: The outcomes of Gray's death sentence, Koon and Powell's initial sentence, and the $2 million punitive award against BMW are outcomes that loom large and cannot be missed. It is true, particularly in parts 2 and 3, that legal arguments over process are featured, yet our process findings occur for part 1, where those legal arguments did not yet enter the case materials. Still, the participants focused and found the process issues.

Nonetheless, as a general point we concede that certain tasks, materials, and instructions may sensitize participants to outcome or process. Our narrative task, which we used throughout part II, may have sensitized participants to outcome, but that explanation works only for the student (S), adult (A), and elderly (E) groups, but not for the T group, because the teenagers in the studies are getting the same task, yet they bring forth a much higher percentage of process unfairnesses. Thus in addition to a situational factor (which may sensitize), there may be a dispositional factor involved. Tots and teens have a recent personal history with process unfairnesses. Furthermore, situational cues are likely to interact with and excite the prototypes that the participants carry, and those prototypes are surely influenced by the participant's age and life experiences; for the teenagers, the prototypes tilt more to the process.[21]

LOOKING BACK, LOOKING FORWARD

The results in this experiment were clearly different from the earlier experiment and the previous studies. In the earlier experiment, where participants made process, outcome, and overall unfairness ratings on 33 vignettes, process seemed like an afterthought, with lower ratings that were less correlated with the overall unfairness. Outcome, on the other hand, produced much higher ratings, which were highly correlated with the overall unfairness rating. It seemed from that experiment that outcome was the unfairness. Process seemed overshadowed, like some distant relation at a wedding that no one knows what to do with. In the studies, apart from the T group finding, the story seems much the same. That is, until now.

In this experiment, participants find process unfairnesses in abundance and with sophisticated nuances to their notions. We learn that citizens' commonsense process unfairness factors, once found and articulated, hold relatively firm and remain powerfully predictive of citizens' decisions in cases. Legal arguments did have subtle effects on the commonsense factors, but overall, those initial factors remained intact. Those process unfairnesses they found were not all that different from what the lawyers and courts found, another indication of the sophistication of the distinctions they made.

The landscape of unfairness, impressionistic at first light, now becomes clearer, though more complex. Once upon a time "this unfairness business" seemed so simple to Peter Pan, who *just knew* that driving his knife into his foe when the latter was below him would not be fighting fair, and Peter *just knew* that Hook's biting his helping hand was also unfair. The fairy tale has its correspondence in the real world, where there are certain types of unfairnesses that people *just know* are not fair. But the real world presents us with far more variance than the fairy tale world.

Can we pin down some of this variance? There seem to be two profitable directions we might explore. For one, it seems reasonable to assume that unfairness judgments should correlate with certain dispositional attitudes and views, such as peoples' beliefs about a just world and their views on theodicy (i.e., reconciling God and suffering). If some participants want equals, bosses, parents, society, life, and God to make no mistakes—or want no variability in the hand we are dealt—then this attitude ought to correlate with their unfairness judgments.

A second direction involves situational sources of variability. For example, what if Job was not the man of perfect integrity? What if he had flaws, a bit of a checkered past, so to speak, or was just an ordinary fellow —but the same punishments came nonetheless? If Eliphaz, Bildad, and Zophar were participants in a new experiment, would they judge this flawed Job more harshly than they did the good Job? The blaming the victim phenomenon, which can be derived from a just-world belief, would predict yes. Background factors that speak to the character of the victim may be used by participants to judge whether or not what happens to that individual is an unfairness, and the severity of it.

Now let us add a second situational variable. What if, at the time of the alleged unfairness, the victim can be seen as having some fault for what happened? If participants can construe culpability, blameworthiness, or contributory negligence to the victim, what happens to the victim's claim of unfairness? We would expect that as the victim's culpability increased, the worthiness of the victim's unfairness claim should drop. But is this always so, or uniformly so, for the victim's contributory negligence may be small compared to the perpetrator's, or it may be remote from the unfair outcome? In the next two chapters, we will try to pin down some of this variability—first on the situational side, then on the dispositional side— to see how dispositional views interact with situational factors.

ENDNOTES

1. D. M. Messick and K. S. Cook, eds., *Equity Theory: Psychological and Sociological Perspectives* (New York: Praeger, 1983); E. Walster, G. W. Walster, and E. Berscheid, *Equity, Theory, and Research* (Boston: Allyn & Bacon, 1978).
2. M. Deutsch, *Distributive Justice: A Social Psychological Perspective* (New Haven: Yale University Press, 1985).

3. *See, e.g.*, A. E. Lind and T. Tyler, *The Social Psychology of Procedural Justice* (New York: Plenum Press, 1988); J. W. Thibaut and L. Walker, *Procedural Justice: A Psychological Analysis* (Hillsdale, NJ: Lawrence Erlbaum, 1975); T. R. Tyler, *Why People Obey the Law* (New Haven, CT: Yale University Press, 1990).

4. The interrater disagreements over type and the experimental findings suggest that "outcome" and "process" may be conflated in the categories and within the same narrative.

5. BMW of North America, Inc. v. Gore, 517 U.S. 559 (1996).

6. Koon v. United States, 518 U.S. 81 (1996).

7. Gray v. Netherland, 518 U.S. 152 (1996).

8. These very brief summaries do not convey all of the complexities, because each case had a number of alleged process and outcome unfairnesses. In addition to complexity, the cases were contentious, for the plaintiff's unfairnesses were challenged by the other side and vice versa. These cases, then, were ideal for our purposes, for it was from these "messy" cases that we asked participants to extract the unfairnesses.

9. There were 80 undergraduate student participants (56 females and 24 males), with a mean age of 19.8 (range = 18–35) and an education level of 14.2 (range = 13–18).

10. These cases were taken from the "Preview of United States Supreme Court Cases," a publication of the American Bar Association (ABA), and the specific cites are the *BMW* case (ABA, 1995, vol. 1), the *Gray* case (ABA, 1996, vol. 7), and the *Koon and Powell* case (ABA, 1995, vol. 4).

11. Three of the six groups were designated BS, GS, and KS ("S" for same); the "same groups" continued with their same case across the three parts of the experiment. The other three groups (BD, GD, KD, where "D" is for different), received a new case at the start of part 2 and a new case at the start of part 3.

12. The materials were again from the "Preview of United States Supreme Court Cases," but this time they included the whole case presentation.

13. There is another possibility we must consider. Participants in part 2 might shift their unfairness factors toward greater legal sophistication *naturally*, either because they had another week to think about the case or because they simply had more material on the case, and not because of the legal arguments. To test this, we had our "different groups" serve as a control. If the different groups' reasons in part 2 were not significantly different from the same groups' reasons in part 2, we would be confident that "more time to reflect on the case" was not producing the difference. If it also turned out that the different groups' reasons in part 2 were similar to the reasons of the same groups in part 1, then we would be more confident that the legal reasons were not causing a dramatic shift.

14. The complexity and sophistication of participants' case analyses can be seen by examining each case. Looking first at case B, the punitive damages case, the six most frequently cited factors were "cards up the sleeve" (1), "dealing false cards" (2), "vague laws" (11), "punishment must be individualized to fit the crime and the criminal" (5), "variable laws" (12), and "appellate reviews" being necessary to correct lower court injustices (13). Factors 1 and 2 deal

with the evidence: How it is presented, whether all of it is presented, and whether it is presented in distorted fashion. Factors 11 and 12 deal with the particular law governing the case: Whether it is vague or whether it varies from state to state such that unwholesome variability prevents equal justice from occurring. Factor 13 reflects neither the evidentiary facts nor the particular law—but a *system* of justice that needs checks and balances and a higher order review.

In case G, the death penalty case, the six most frequently cited factors were "cards up the sleeve" (1), "dealing false cards" (2), "incompetent attorney" (8), "untrustworthy witnesses" (3), "victim's rights" (6), and "defendant's rights" (7). Factors 1, 2, and 3 relate to the evidence that emerges or fails to emerge, and these factors are linked to both outcome and process unfairnesses in their reasons why. Factor 8 reflects that legal advocates ought to be balanced in terms of competence, and that when one side appears incompetent, fairness is compromised. Factors 6 and 7 reflect the weight and balance to be given for victim and defendant.

In case K (*Koon and Powell*), two factors stand out the most. The first is that "rules ought not to bend," and if there is bending, equal justice demands that good reasons must be offered for such exceptions (10). The second factor is that those in authority (e.g., police, judges) "must not abuse or overstep their authority" (11), for such abuse both transgresses and betrays the public trust, eroding the people's confidence in the legal system.

15. In looking for a better explanation for the increase, there is another algorithm we might try out: This hypothesis suggests that the rise in reasons ought to occur for "appellate review" (13) or "rules and reasons" (10), simply because the case has moved to this higher level, and those factors should now come into play more. Although those factors do indeed rise, as this "appellate level" hypothesis predicts, we still see other factors that increase and, more problematic, some factors that drop, which the appellate algorithm would not predict.

16. The "boosting," "salient," and "muting" effects can be seen in the following illustrations. In case B, following the legal arguments, the "vague laws" (11) factor and the "variable laws" (12) factor, which were among the top six factors cited in part 1, now get a very noticeable boost, tripling and doubling, respectively, becoming the first and second most frequently cited factors. In case G, we see a "muting" of "victim's rights" (6) and a "salient" boosting for "defendant's rights" (7), which more than double. In addition, we see a large "muting" effect for "incompetent attorney" (8), as participants hear legal arguments that make "salient" an alternative possibility—that the attorneys might have been deliberately trying to drag out the case through all sorts of appeals. Put differently, the participants' initial "incompetence" story is now being modified by a "tactic" story, the latter possibility they had not considered before. In case K, they now see the importance of an "appellate review," which had not been recognized before, and they are slightly less focused on the "abuse of authority" factor.

17. This was a canonical discrimination analysis.

18. For case K, "abuse of authority" (9) and the "rules and reasons" (10) factors are weighted heavily and separate case K from B and G, whereas "cards up

the sleeve" (1) and "dealing false cards" (2) separate B and G from K. The dimensions of "vague laws" (11), "variable laws" (12), "victim's rights" (6), and "incompetent attorney" (8) separated B from G.

19. The "reverse and remand" and "let stand" weights in the canonical discrimination analysis across the 13 factors in part 1 were .302 and .718, respectively, whereas in part 2 they were .252 and .568, respectively, showing that the distance between "reverse and remand" and "let stand" narrowed rather than widened.

20. Furthermore, these participants believe that the ninth circuit's reversal corrected the trial court judge's unfairness, thereby demonstrating good reason and the correct application of rules, and therefore they want that judgment to stand. Had the ninth circuit not reversed, with the case coming before the Supreme Court as *United States v. Koon and Powell* rather than the other way around, these unfairness reasons would be in Cluster 1 of "reverse and remand."

21. If the vignettes in the first experiment sensitized participants in the "outcome" direction, this experiment tried to create a "neutral" context in regard to "outcome versus process" in a number of ways. First, the stimulus materials were changed from simple vignettes to complex legal cases, which were rich in detail and which ran for pages. Second, these legal cases, unlike the vignettes, not only told a longer and more complex story but told a story that had two sides, where one side's facts, interpretations, and allegations were challenged by the other side. Third, the words "outcome" and "process" never appeared in the task, which might trigger more elaborated prototypes on the "outcome" side. Fourth, it was the participants who had to find the "unfairnesses" in these cases, rather than getting a vignette that already highlights the unfairness for them. Finally, the participants had to give their own reasons why each passage they underlined was an unfairness to them. These methodological changes, we believe, make for a much cleaner test of "outcome versus process."

11

WHEN THE VICTIM IS FLAWED OR BEARS FAULT

A farmer living in the Midwest knows firsthand of the destructive power of tornadoes, so when warnings are sounded, he religiously gathers his wife and children and leads them to the protection of the storm cellar. But on one deadly occasion, a tornado hits without warning, and his ten children, scattered about his land, never made it to the storm cellar and were all killed.

In two sentences, I have constructed a modern-day Job story, but one that is woefully short on details. In my version, we get little about the main character, and about his wife, children, and the relationships among them, we get nothing. Experimenters can write bare-bone vignettes, for a sound purpose: By shearing the story of its accessories and leaving but its essence, we can determine the participants' judgments about the essential story without superfluous details confounding us. By contrast, stories told by our participants in the studies tend to be rich with adorning details, so many at times that they may obscure the determination. But if the devil is in the details, or if messy details modify and qualify the actor and the action, then a story cut to the skeletal bone may have no meat to it, and though interpretations may be easier, they may end up being facile, for just too many interesting "what ifs" have been removed.

Readers of stories, even short stories, are not passive though. What the words of the story fail to convey, our imaginations may: Participants may read in, projecting certain qualities and traits onto the farmer, thus fleshing out the skeletal character. The experimenter might aid and abet these imaginative projections, for had I entitled this "A Modern-Day Job Story," participants might attribute Job-like qualities of goodness and integrity to the farmer. Even without a suggestive title, participants could take a single fact—that the farmer "religiously gathers his wife and children"—and infer that he is protective, conscientious, and loving. Thus our picture of the farmer (and of the story itself) is constructed not just from the givens, but from projections, inferences, and attributions we make as well. Once our picture is constructed, we frame it by bringing our general views about unfairness to the picture. By fitting the former to the latter, constructing and framing may occur simultaneously rather than sequentially, but once both are done, we are then ready to hang our judgments on the matter.

A Flawed Job

Now, what would happen to the picture, its framing, and the judgments about it if the farmer is no Job, but a man who lies, cheats, and steals? An experimenter can create versions where the protagonists' flaws range from none to many, but let us stay with a two-version test, where this farmer is either "good" or "not so good," and where the basic empirical question is this: Does a person's background affect our judgments of the "unfairness"?

Before addressing that empirical question, let us consider a normative question: *Should* background factors affect our judgments? Two types of unfairness principles—equal justice and individualized justice—suggest different answers. An ardent advocate of equal justice would hold that we ought to be blind to such background factors, for most are extralegal, impermissible, or irrelevant to the determination at hand. From this view, culpability should not hinge on whether the defendant is wealthy, attractive, or politically connected; nor should factors of race, religion, gender, and age be determinative. This commonsense fairness principle is amply supported by black-letter law, as constitutional and common law cites could be readily rallied in defense of this principle.

The law's support for this fairness principle is furthered by the statutory elements of specific crimes and criminal law procedures, as both minimize the intrusion of background factors into the case. Generally, the law begins and ends its culpability analysis with the act and the intent, an analysis that is tightly circumscribed around the moment of the act and where background facts are typically irrelevant or unquestionably out of bounds.[1] A participant or legal scholar who endorses equal justice would strongly object if a defendant was found guilty for a crime based on whether this defendant was an A or D student in high school, or whether he was an altar boy or stole Girl Scout cookies in the third grade, or whether he dumped his last girlfriend rather callously, had a girlfriend, or has a boyfriend. This principle holds that in the legal adjudication of guilt, background factors in the defendant's past history should not to be part of the playing field,[2] and we have learned in the studies and in the previous experiment that participants are concerned about level playing fields.

There are, however, arguments on the other side. First, other legal scholars would be quick to point out that the culpability analysis is not so tightly circumscribed to the act and the intent *in all cases*. Earlier acts that suggest a pattern of behavior may well be admitted in to prove motive, opportunity, intent, or identity.[3] Moreover, even if evidence of earlier convictions is kept off the playing field, evidence of prior acquittals may enter in a majority of jurisdictions,[4] and if the defendant's credibility becomes an issue, prior conviction or acquittal evidence may enter.[5] Finally, there are cases where past history is necessary in judging the guilt of a defendant, as in recidivist cases, or in judging a defendant's exculpatory claim, such as insanity or duress.

Beyond exceptions that would admit past history into culpability assessment, there is the sentencing phase that all but demands it. In sentencing considerations, the tightly circumscribed culpability orbit widens in time and space to embrace dispositional and situational background factors, be they of a mitigating or aggravating variety, which now have a sanctioned part to play in this determination. Was this the first offense or the third strike? Is there a criminal history that speaks to a recidivist or a history of violence that speaks to a risk for future dangerousness? The individualized justice/fairness principle holds that punishment ought to be tailored to the crime and the person, and in considering both, character and background are appropriate discriminating factors to use, lest we end up treating all as one.[6] So whether this defendant was an A or D student in high school, or was an altar boy, or stole Girl Scout cookies, or treated relationships in certain callous ways may all be germane.

Taking these two principles to the extreme, equal justice favors blind justice, a short story pointed to the act and the intent, a story that is bare bones, largely acontextual and ahistorical, whereas individualized justice favors justice without the blindfold, seeing a fuller, longer, individualized picture, where the past provides context. In reality, individuals frequently endorse both principles, as we have instantiations of both principles in the same booklets of participants in the studies. But those were different instances. The question now is what happens when two principles that most endorse appear to collide in the same instance?

The just-world view has something to say to this question. If there is a tendency to blame the victim, a tendency demonstrated by Eliphaz, Bildad, and Zophar in their reactions to Job, then background information that confirms that the victim is flawed should affect our judgments. A flawed protagonist may be seen as warranting punishment, and if a flawed victim and a good victim both suffer the same unfairness, then those who most subscribe to the just-world view ought to rate the flawed victim's unfairness as less severe. But we can also conceive of the prediction going in the opposite direction, particularly if the protagonist is not the alleged victim but the evaluator. If a flawed protagonist is seen as less capable or competent, having diminished capacity or being outright insane, then the flaw—if it raises the likely possibility of mental illness, mental retardation, or some perceived diminishment—may mitigate our judgments, and we may find this circumstance to be less of an unfairness.

A Faulty Job

Background "flaw" is our first independent variable. Our second variable is situated in the present context, and it raises issues of the victim's complicity (fault)[7] and contributory negligence in bringing about the unfairness.[8] Take, as an example, a student who studies long and hard for an exam, gets a low grade, and then claims "but it's not fair!" We might sympathize with her, until we hear more of the details. What happens to our judgment if we learn that the student overslept and had only half the allotted time for the exam by the time she got there? Might we not find her at fault? If our farmer hears the warnings of a tornado but chooses to disregard them, then do we not see that he bears some fault for the outcome, for it is no longer just what nature did, but what he chose not to do? Our second variable, "fault," should work like the variable "flaw" to reduce the severity of the unfairness rating.

From a legal perspective, we might predict a greater reduction in severity for fault than flaw, for fault is more likely to fit within the culpability orbit and more likely to appear relevant to that determination, whereas flaw, by contrast, may be distant, irrelevant, and extralegal. But the prediction of a greater effect for fault than flaw might be wrong, because unfairness is essentially a commonsense psychological judgment and not a legal one. For example, a single fault may be seen as but a momentary lapse, a sign to the poet and participants that affirms nothing more than the "to err is human" truth, a signal of no deep-seated pathology; fault, then, may be a situational misstep that any of us might make. Flaw, on the other hand, may be seen in a dispositional way, indicating a character trait that is enduring and pervasive, one that we may be much less willing to forgive. If this is how ordinary people view fault and flaw, then the latter may weaken the case more. With predictions going in opposite directions, we shall assess each variable, flaw and fault, and comparatively assess which lowers severity ratings more.

In this experiment, the variable flaw is relatively simple (i.e., the victim either has no flaw or a flaw), and the predicted lowering of the severity ratings of the unfairness for the flaw condition is straightforward; a complication may arise if participants construe the central character as not the victim, but as some evaluator or perpetrator, such that a flaw condition might actually raise the severity. The variable fault creates more uncertainty in this experiment, for we also vary who commits the fault. Consider an unfairness that falls within the "hard work not rewarded" category, where a student works hard on a paper but does not get the top grade she expects. In one variation, she fails to put the references in the form the professor asks for, and the professor lowers her grade as the fault is hers. In the second variation, the paper is perfect, but the professor fails to read it closely, and here the fault is attributed to the professor. The first is likely to weaken her claim, whereas the second is likely to enhance it.

Misfortune Versus Unfairness Cases

Finally, we will look at a number of cases, those where human agency inflicts the harm, and those where impersonal agency (e.g., nature or life) delivers the blow. This is the misfortune versus unfairness distinction we investigated in our first experiment. If most participants see nature as acting in random, unpremeditated ways, indifferent to whether the victim has flaws or faults, then any effects for flaw and fault of the victim ought to be greatly if not completely muted in nature cases.

However, we are not sure that all or even most participants actually do see nature this way. Perhaps some (e.g., Eliphaz, Bildad, and Zophar) or even most see nature as being directed by God such that hits and misses are not random. From this Eliphaz et al. position, there is no such thing as accident; rather, the punishment is targeted, and flaw and fault provide the targeting coordinates. If some see acts of nature as acts of an omniscient God, then the effects of flaw and fault may be more potent than we suspect. Therefore, depending on one's point of view, flaw and fault may be largely irrelevant or highly determinative.

In contrast to acts of nature cases, there are those where human agents deliver the blow. Even if the victim happens to be in the wrong place at the wrong time, there may be some fault on the victim's part that interacts with the harm the perpetrator delivers. Here is an example. The fact that a professor does not give the student who overslept more time to finish the exam—even though the consequence is a failing grade—is likely to be seen by the professor as an appropriate consequence to the student's fault. However, what if this usually lenient professor was particularly harsh with this student—because this was the third time this semester that this student had come late, a pattern that may suggest a flaw in the student, at least to the professor. Parents will typically react differently to their teenagers coming in after their curfews depending on whether this is the first offense or the tenth, whether there is a good excuse or not, or whether there is appropriate contrition or a disdainful attitude toward the parents and their rules. We would predict that "human agent" cases ought to be more sensitive to flaw and fault changes. In the experimental test that follows, cases, flaw, and fault are our independent variables, and the severity rating of the unfairness is the dependent variable.

In this experiment, there were 117 participants, all of them students. They were randomly assigned to one of four booklets, each booklet containing one of four versions of the 16 cases, with the cases arranged in random order in the booklet. The four versions (groups) were "no fault/ good" (NF/G), "fault/good" (F/G), "no fault/not so good" (NF/NG), and "fault/not so good" (F/NG). Participants were asked to rate the severity of each of the 16 alleged instances on a scale from 0 to 100, where "100" represents maximum severity, "1" represents the most minimal unfairness, and "0" means that you do not think this to be an instance of unfairness at all.

RESULTS AND DISCUSSION

These results will be presented on a case-by-case basis, rather than presented overall (across case, flaw, and fault), because overall effects in this experiment can be highly misleading. To explicate, there was a significant case effect, with ratings for the act of nature cases (70.6) being significantly more severe than the human act cases (55.7), but there is a confounding: The harms in the nature cases were greater than the human agent cases, and this precludes a straightforward interpretation. Similarly, the types and degrees of flaw and fault varied by case as well.[9]

Our results are best understood when the confoundings are removed, and this can be done by looking at each case separately, as though we performed 16 separate experiments. The particular case, then, whether it is an act of nature or a human agent case, becomes the contextual ground within which we assess how fault and flaw act and interact.

Case-by-Case Findings

Case 1 involves the student who works hard on her paper, expects an A, but gets a B−. The fault manipulation involved failing to follow all the instructions for the paper (f) versus following all the instructions (nf), and thus the fault, when it occurs, is hers. The flaw manipulation was that she was either a good (g) student or a not-so-good (ng) student who did very little work in all her courses. The four conditions produced the following severity ratings for the unfairness, which were significantly different: f/g = 33.9, nf/g = 67.7, f/ng = 38.6, and nf/ng = 59.8 (see Table 11-1). There is a significant difference for fault (f = 36.3, nf = 63.7), but

TABLE 11-1
Severity Ratings for the Good/No Fault (g/nf), Not So Good/No Fault (ng/nf), Good/Fault (g/f), and the Not So Good/Fault (ng/f) Conditions, Along With Whether the Main Effects for Flaw and Fault and the Flaw × Fault Interaction Effect Are Significant (Yes), Nonsignificant (No), or Marginally Significant (?)

Case	Conditions				Significant Effects		
	g/nf	ng/nf	g/f	ng/f	Flaw	Fault	Flaw × Fault
1	67.7	59.8	33.9	38.6	No	Yes	No
2	57.8	61.6	55.9	59.2	No	No	No
3	61.6	62.6	52.4	53.3	No	?	No
4	55.3	59.1	61.2	62.9	No	No	No
5	61.6	76.0	72.7	71.3	No	No	No
6	62.4	75.0	87.9	86.0	No	Yes	?
7	60.7	45.2	78.3	59.9	Yes	Yes	No
8	69.3	81.0	83.9	85.4	No	Yes	No
9	70.3	79.4	78.5	75.1	No	No	No
10	59.0	86.0	76.1	77.1	Yes	No	Yes
11	68.3	66.3	60.9	45.5	?	Yes	No
12	66.0	70.4	63.5	60.5	No	No	No
13	83.2	50.4	87.3	58.0	Yes	No	No
14	65.0	47.5	72.7	60.2	Yes	Yes	No
15	40.7	22.3	39.0	25.3	Yes	No	No
16	71.1	50.3	60.7	43.4	Yes	?	No

none for flaw, and no interaction effect. Thus in a straightforward way, the victim's fault lowers the severity of her claim almost by half, but her past track record of being either a good student or not does not affect her claim.

Case 2 is more complex in terms of the fault, flaw, and the victim. The story involves a student who cheats by turning in an old paper as his own, rather than doing the paper that was assigned, yet he still gets an A. The flaw manipulation (i.e., whether he was a good student in the past or cut corners in the past) did not matter (g = 56.8; ng = 60.4), nor did the fault manipulation, where the professor either fails to read the paper (f = 57.5) or does read it (nf = 59.7), and there was no interaction effect. In this case, the victims are the fellow students who see one of their own cheating and then profiting by it. The participants' analysis begins and ends with the fact that the student cheated, and what he did in the past or what the professor did or did not do does not matter. Put another way, the student's major fault—choosing to cheat—dwarfs the professor's fault and dwarfs the student's flaw (his past behavior) in their analysis.

In Case 3, the "victim" is again the student body, and the story involves a student who turns in 20 pages of trash as his paper, which he did the night before it was due, yet gets an A. The flaw manipulation again fails (i.e., whether or not he was generally conscientious, g = 57.0 versus ng = 58.0). The fault manipulation (f = 52.9 versus nf = 62.1) just fails to reach significance (i.e., whether the student reads the syllabus or not), as this fault is regarded as minor when compared to his bigger fault—that he waited until the last moment and turned in trash.

In Case 4, we again find no significant main effects for flaw and fault, and no significant interaction effect. One student fails to pull her weight in a group seminar, letting her three classmates down, yet gets the same grade. The three classmates can be viewed as the victims of the unfairness. Whether she was a good or a troubled student (flaw) does not increase or decrease the severity of the unfairness, and whether the professor is taken in or not (fault) does not matter either. In the participants' analysis, the professor's fault and the student's past history are dwarfed by her current fault—being inconsiderate of others and not working.

Cases 1 through 4 are all human agent cases, although they differ quite a bit. Case 1 involves a student who is conscientious and really trying to do well, whereas cases 2 through 4 are degrees of wrongful behavior getting rewarded: Put in legal terms, the actor's culpability in the latter cases is much higher than in Case 1, and the act each commits is the major fault. This major fault factor—without a significant addition or subtraction from the manipulated variables—determines the severity. Thus our manipulations of background flaws and further faults are regarded as minor or irrelevant. The exception is in Case 1, because it is her fault (for not following the instructions), which dramatically lowers her unfairness claim, as what she did or did not do is highly relevant. Still, across these four cases, we find no background effect for flaw, such that participants focus their analysis of culpability and unfairness on the act and what happened around that act.

Case 5, involving an act of nature, features a college student killed by a tornado when he decides to go home for the weekend to help out his family. Whether he is described as impulsive or not (flaw) or whether his mother neglects (fault) to call him about the tornado warnings (or not), produces no main effects and no interaction effect. In this case, nature's act solely determines the severity of the unfairness, as human failings, through flaw and fault, add or subtract nothing.

Case 6 begins with acts of nature, where drought, famine, and disease produce malnutrition, death, and blindness in the very young in a particular country. The country has either a newly elected democracy or a dictatorship (flaw), and gangs and warlords either steal or do not steal relief funds (fault). In this case, flaw produces no effect, but there is a significant effect for fault (86.9 versus 68.7), where the fault works to increase the severity of the unfairness. Here, the harm is not solely nature's doing, as human fault significantly compounds the problem.

In Case 7, an earthquake brings down a building, and a man found alive in the rubble dies before going into surgery. Regarding the background flaw, he is presented as either a man of faith or one with several outstanding crimes. Regarding fault, either the builders used inadequate materials and inspectors took bribes, or they did not. In this case, there is a main effect for flaw (g = 69.5, ng = 52.5), because the unfairness is seen as more severe for the good man. There is also a main effect for fault (f = 69.1; nf = 52.9), as the fault increases the severity ratings, but there is no interaction effect. In this case, the act of nature is seen as a tragedy for the man of faith— but as a punishment for the wrongdoer who had evaded punishment. This finding seems consistent with the view of Job's three friends and fits with the just-world view, although it is the only case so far where flaw undercuts the severity of the unfairness claim. In the fault condition, the fault belongs not to the victim but with the other, and this adds significantly to the severity of the unfairness. The harm occurs because of what nature and humans did.

In Case 8, children have lost limbs and been killed by land mines in a country where civil war occurs. The flaw condition (where families turn away from God and prayer, or they do not) was not significant. It is the fault condition, which is significant, when the government does nothing to find and remove the land mines (84.7), this makes the unfairness more severe, when compared to making best efforts to find and remove the land mines (75.1). Again, human fault adds to the severity of the tragedy.

In Case 9, a healthy child chokes on food and dies, although parents first try to give CPR and then call 911. Neither the flaw manipulation (the couple either lost another child who died suddenly or there was no prior loss) nor the fault manipulation (suggesting that is was probably a mistake to try to administer CPR instead of immediately calling 911, or not) was significant, and there is no interaction effect, as the death is viewed as a tragedy unrelated to the past flaw, whereas the so-called fault was viewed as a reasonable action.

Case 10 involves a crack baby who dies from complications during the first week of life. The flaw manipulation, which was significant, had the mother either as a crack addict (81.6) or as a crack addict who gets herself off the drug during the last 3 months of pregnancy in order to make a new life for herself and her baby (67.5), and it is the former condition that is rated as more severe. This finding counteracts the usual trend, where flaw typically mitigates severity; here, the flaw makes the unfairness more so. Why would participants not see the mother who gets off crack as being more sympathetic, which would make that condition the greater tragedy? Understanding this atypical finding requires that we see the victim as the majority of participants do—not as the mother but as the baby. With the baby being the victim, the mother's flaw—doing nothing about her crack addiction—acts like other's fault, to increase severity.

The fault (either a new intern mistakes the problem and life-saving treatment is delayed, or there is no misdiagnosis and no delay of treatment) is not significant, but there is a significant interaction effect: In the no fault conditions, g/nf (59.0) and ng/nf (86.0), we see the flaw effect clearly, but when fault enters the picture, severity increases for the "good" person (g/f = 76.1) but decreases for the "not so good" person (ng/f = 77.1), leaving both at about the same level. Thus when the outsider's fault is present, the flaw factor becomes nil, but when outsider's fault is removed, the flaw factor is highly significant. The manipulation seems to get participants to shift their view of the victim and their perspective on the unfairness.[10]

In Case 11, a man in his 30s who exercises and watches his health nonetheless dies of a heart attack, leaving a wife and three young children. There are significant effects for flaw and fault in the case, but the interaction effect fails to reach significance. It makes a difference (flaw) if the man is devoted to wife and kids (64.6) as opposed to learning that he was planning to run off with his mistress (55.9). The fault effect is also significant, for in the condition where his doctor tells him about his heart arrhythmia and tells him to stop running (53.2) is rated lower than the condition where there is no arrhythmia and no warning condition (67.3); his own fault, then, lowers the severity of the unfairness.

In Case 12, a woman dies from cancer, related to secondhand smoke (her husband being the smoker). Flaw was not significant, for it did not matter whether she had children out of wedlock or not. The fault manipulation was also not significant. Participants see a general fault that cuts through all the conditions: She chooses to marry and live with a smoker, rather than the "minor fault" of not asking her husband to smoke outside the house, as she thought of doing many times but did not.

In Case 13, a teacher sees one student cheating off another, and both students get an F. For the flaw manipulation, one student resists the other's attempt to cheat (g), whereas in the other condition both students planned to cheat (ng). Regarding the fault manipulation, the student either gets a hearing (nf) or is suspended without a hearing (f). In this case, the flaw factor is highly significant (g = 85.2, ng = 54.2), as this cuts to "intent to commit a crime." The procedural due process fault raises the unfairness level slightly (f = 72.7, nf = 66.8), but the difference fails to reach significance, and there was no significant interaction effect. The flaw manipulation changes the status of the protagonist from victim to wrongdoer, as this "criminalizing" dwarfs the process unfairness in the case.

In Case 14, students are caught drinking in a dorm room and are thrown out of the dorm. In the flaw manipulation, the victim is not drinking and does not violate the school's policy (g), or he has violated it on other occasions, although not at the moment he is caught (ng). The fault manipulation involves whether or not the school provided due process (i.e., the student either gets a hearing or is thrown out without a hearing). In this case, both flaw (g = 68.8, ng = 53.9) and fault (f = 66.4; nf = 56.3) are significant, although there is no interaction effect. That this student has violated the law in the past (flaw) markedly undercuts his unfairness claim, which is now tainted and suspect, whereas the school's due process failure (fault) significantly increases the unfairness. That the process failure is significant here but not in Case 13 is the result of how participants view the two "criminals": The cheater on the test is viewed as far more culpable than the beer-drinking offender, and that major fault dwarfs the process fault; when the fault is viewed as a minor fault, the process fault looms larger.

Case 15, the lowest level unfairness of all, involves a male student waiting on line to get into a club when a female student flirts with the bouncer and is let in. The flaw manipulation involves the relationship between the male and female student: Either the male student likes the female, or he had a relationship with her in the past and dumped her. As for the fault, the student either tries to bribe the bouncer or not. Only the flaw manipulation was significant (g = 39.9, ng = 23.8), because when the male is seen as a "cad" and a "player," then severity drops, for participants perceive that he is getting what he deserves and reduce the worthiness of his claim.

Case 16 involves an apparent reverse discrimination case of a student who does not get in to his first choice medical school. The flaw involves the fact that he only had decent grades, and gets a "barely recommended" endorsement from a premed committee, as opposed to the condition where he made good grades and got a "highly recommended" endorsement. The fault involves the student's father, who brings a suit against the top school that rejected his son: In the fault condition the father's own business has been challenged in court for not hiring minorities, thus suggesting that his legal action might be motivated by revenge or "pay-back," as opposed to the no fault condition where the father's own business is not mentioned. The flaw effect is significant (g = 65.9, ng = 46.9), but the fault effect is only marginal (f = 52.0, nf = 60.7), with no significant interaction effect. That the student only made decent grades lowers his unfairness claim almost 20 points on average, whereas the fault conditions lower the unfairness claim by 9 points on the average.

Trends Across the Cases

Having examined these results on a case-by-case basis, it turns out that uniformity and consistency are not the rule, as there is great variability (see Table 11-1). The flaw effect turns out to be significant in only 6 of the 16 cases, which is less than half, and the fault effect turns out to be significant in 6 of the 16 cases as well; of the six significant effects for both flaw and fault, four occur in different cases, whereas two occur in the same case. Thus more often then not, both variables were not significant more than they were (10 versus 6).

In analyzing trends, we see a "majority" (i.e., no significant flaw effect) and "minority" (i.e., a significant flaw effect). For the minority, where flaws in the victim's character or motivation are taken into account, the participants see these flaws as directly relevant to the alleged unfairness in question. One exception to the "directly relevant" condition occurs in Case 7, where a man dies following an earthquake and where the fact that he had past outstanding crimes (in the flawed condition) significantly reduced the unfairness, as if the death was punishment for his unpunished crimes. A different sort of exception occurs in Case 10 (the crack mother and baby), for here the flaw raises the severity of the unfairness; yet if we view the victim as the child and not the mother, the mother's flaw acts like "other's fault," to raise severity. In the "majority" cases, flaw turns out to be nonsignificant: either it is seen as too remote or irrelevant to the alleged unfairness in some cases, or in other cases it is dwarfed by the victim's "major fault"; in these cases, whether overshadowed or irrelevant, flaw does not change severity.

Except for Case 7, these results are not consistent with the just-world theory, which predicts that evidence of flaw ought to be used by just worlders to justify the punishment and to mitigate or nullify the unfairness claim, much as Eliphaz, Bildad, and Zophar tried to do with Job's claim. For most of the cases there was no lowering of the severity of the unfairness when flaw was present; for one case there was a raising (Case 10); and for the five cases where there was a significant lowering, the mitigation was modest and never a complete nullification of the claim. If people have a penchant or need to blame the victim in order to make the just world seem just, then why do we not see that sort of blaming in all 16 cases, where, after all, we have given participants the noose (flaw) with which to hang the victim? To the contrary, we see no evidence of a penchant or need to blame the victim, nor any evidence of "delusional" beliefs operating. What the data show is a pattern of discernment and discrimination, where participants turn out to be quite different from the likes of Eliphaz et al., and their ratings turn out to be quite different from just world predictions.

Refining Discriminations

Let us try to understand the discriminations participants do make. Regarding our flaw variable, we must bear in mind that our manipulations are both inexact and relative: The "good" person might be really good, or just average, or even one with flaws but having less flaws than our "not so good" character; the "not so good" character might be just that, or worse, or even a lot worse. The point is, participants make these gradation distinctions. When the flaw in the "not so good" type features past wrongful or criminal acts, participants take such flaws into account, particularly if they are seen as relevant to the unfairness in question. Thus the flaw first needs to be a "bad" one and second it must be relevant. Regarding relevance, what could be more relevant than planning to cheat on the exam, as that flaw shows culpable intent?

Fault was the more complex variable, for in six cases it is the victim who commits the fault, whereas in 10 cases it is an outsider; in one outsider instance, Case 16, the outsider is the victim's father and may be perceived as coming from the victim himself, or at least being endorsed by the victim. The trends are the following: In the cases where the fault effect is significant and it is the victim who commits the fault, severity lowers; in all cases where the fault effect is significant and where an outsider commits the fault, severity increases.

In the full context of cases, where fault was not significant in a majority, we again see a relevance standard being used, along with a relative weighting of faults. Regarding relevance, some faults, particularly when committed by the other, may not be particularly germane to the claim. Moreover, some faults, when committed by the victim, may be understandable and forgivable: Parents trying to administer CPR to their child rather than immediately calling 911 is an example of an understandable reaction; and even though the parents may second-guess themselves, participants seem to be saying, "but that's what I would have done."

In other cases, fault (whether committed by the victim or the other) may be dwarfed by the larger fault committed by the victim. For example, if a student waits until the last day to produce a 20-page paper and turns in trash, his procrastination is the major fault, whereas his failure to read the syllabus is judged inconsequential. Thus participants keep their eye on the central fault, deciding whether other faults are germane or inconsequential; if they decide that a fault is germane, then they add or subtract from the severity rating depending on *who* commits the fault, and the amount they add or subtract depends on the perceived contributory size of the fault. This sort of analysis might be performed by a judge using sentencing guidelines or by jurors in contributory negligence cases. In many ways, this sort of analysis appears as a reasonable approach at first factoring a complex situation, then making judgments about the relevance of elements, and then finally deciding about their degree of relevance in an overall culpability assessment of the unfairness.

Both flaw and fault have a greater effect in the human agent cases, as opposed to the act of nature cases. This makes good sense, for if nature acts impersonally, then nature is indifferent to flaw or fault of the victim; human agents, on the other hand, are responsive to the victim, and if some flaws and faults are relevant, then taking these into account when sizing severity would be appropriate.

Somewhat surprising was the finding that flaw and fault act independently in the vast majority of the cases, because there was only one significant flaw × fault interaction effect. The lack of interaction effects says something positive about the participants' judgments. We can understand this better if we ask, "What would it mean if there was a significant interaction effect?" Such a finding would mean that participants are rewarding the good student's claim because of her past performance and punishing the not-so-good student's claim because of her past performance—despite the current fact that both students work equally hard on this paper. Had an interaction effect resulted, one could argue that an impermissible factor had come into play when it should not have, violating the equal justice principle. Participants by and large do not make such sweeping, stereotypic judgments in these cases, but rather assess each variable on its own merits.

LOOKING BACKWARD, LOOKING FORWARD

Returning to our beginning questions, we now know that flaw seems to matter only when it is relevant to the action and intention that gives rise to the unfairness claim. This relevance determination is made not on the basis of some broad, acontextual rule that transcends case particulars, but rather it is made on a case-by-case basis, contextually, from the particulars of the case. If the victim's past flaw, such as committing the same wrongful act that she now commits herself but claims is somehow unfair, then the victim is likely to be seen as tainted, and the unfairness is judged as less so. If the victim's past flaw involves an intent that is judged as blameworthy, and this intent is seen as bearing on the alleged unfair action, then past intentions do become relevant and lower the claim. "Relevance," then, is key. When the past is seen as irrelevant, it is set aside, as equal justice will remain blind to those past indiscretions. When past actions and intentions are seen as relevant, they are included into the culpability and judgment mix, as individualized justice results.

Relevance is not the only determiner of the flaw effect. Flaws, we see, come in all sorts of shades and degrees. There are those of a minor variety, about which participants might say, "been there, done that." Minor flaws indicate errors of being human rather than deep-seated deficiencies in character, and they derive more from the situational than from the dispositional depths. On the other end, some flaws are criminal or strongly indicate wrongfulness, and these are the ones that are much more likely to be taken into account when the unfairness is assessed.

Thus in weighing the badness of the flaw and its relevance to claimed unfairness, participants seem to do no more and no less than what judges, justices, and jurors might do when they consider culpability and punishment questions. This is similar to the findings in the previous chapter regarding the legal cases, where commonsense unfairness factors were not all that different from legal factors. In this experiment, participants clearly maintain limits as to what counts and what does not, and they certainly do not throw open the door to the past at the drop of a hat, and not for peccadillos or other trivial irrelevancies, because these flaws neither enter their equations nor become dispositive in their calculations.

What they do, then, is *not* what the just-world view would predict. Among our participants, we see scant signs of Eliphaz, Bildad, and Zophar —those prototypical just worlders who grasp at any flaw to hang Job. Moreover, we have given our participants 16 opportunities to do so, creating flaws and the pretext to use them, if they had a need or a penchant to do so.

If participants remain quite selective about flaws, we can say the same about faults, and then some. Participants weigh the relevance of the fault to the unfairness, the extent of fault, whether it is understandable or not, and who commits it. Participants seem to ask and then answer some basic questions. How big a fault was it, and was it big enough to count? Does the fault connect to the unfairness, or is it tangential? Was it a fault that any one of us might make in the circumstances? If their conclusion is that the fault ought to count, then the addition or subtraction is determined by who commits the fault—if the victim commits it, we subtract, but if an outsider commits it, we add.

Again, in what factors count, and in how they do the math, participants seem to show good judgment. When they blame the victim, it is because the victim committed a fault that directly bears on the unfairness claim. Thus they blame the victim when it is appropriate to blame the victim, and their degree of blame, as it translates into a reduction of the severity of the unfairness claim, seems measured and modest, proportionate to the fault. That participants are not reacting disproportionately is evident by the fact that there was not a single case where the fault reduced the unfairness claim to the 0-to-10 level of severity, where we might conclude that participants were nullifying the claim entirely. Further evidence can be found in the lack of interaction effects, where fault is not inappropriately multiplied by flaw to drastically reduce the claim. Put another way, the process by which participants weigh flaw and fault seems to be a fair process.

In trying to pin down some of variance of severity judgments, we looked at two variables, flaw and fault, and assessed their contributions to the picture. Flaws may be of recent vintage or from the distant past of the victim, whereas faults tend to be in closer proximity to the unfairness, yet both are seen as contextual variables that may alter our construction of the unfairness picture. These variables do not operate uniformly or evenly across cases, for we see suggestive albeit questionable evidence that the "misfortune versus unfairness" distinction reappears in this experiment: In the "misfortune" or "act of nature" cases, both flaw and fault seem to matter much less than they do in human agent cases. Participants may view "misfortune" cases differently, in that there is an indifference in these cases to flaw and fault. Yet these cases continue to be regarded as unfair and their severity ratings are high, significantly higher than the human agent cases.

Why is this so? We have investigated situational variables that might affect our construal of the unfairness picture, but there is also the frame we put around the picture. In framing the picture, dispositional variables are likely to be relevant, such as our beliefs about fairness, life, nature, and God. These dispositional variables have yet to be tapped, and this is the direction we turn to in the next chapter.

ENDNOTES

1. For examples of this, and some exceptions, *see* N. J. Finkel, *Commonsense Justice: Jurors' Notions of the Law* (Cambridge: Harvard University Press, 1995).
2. However, what is part of the field and what is not part of the field is not always clear. In civil cases involving damage awards, jurors are often "blind-folded"—kept in the dark about considering attorney's fees, whether a defendant has insurance, or the unspoken trebling of compensatory damages in antitrust cases. There is also evidence, however, that jurors do know about such matters, and their verdicts and awards may take these impermissible factors into account. *See* S. Diamond and J. Casper, "What Jurors Think: Expectations and Reactions of Citizens Who Serve as Jurors." In *Verdict: Assessing the Civil Jury System*, ed. R. Litan (Washington, DC: Brookings Institution, 1992); J. Goodman, E., Greene, and E. Loftus, "Runaway Verdicts or Reasoned Determinations: Mock Juror Strategies in Awarding Damages," *Jurimetrics Journal* 29 (1989): 285–300; R. MacCoun, "Inside the Black Box: What Empirical Research Tells Us About Decisionmaking by Civil Juries." In *Verdict: Assessing the Civil Jury System*, ed. R. Litan (Washington, DC: Brookings Institution, 1993).
3. This can be admitted under Federal Rule of Evidence 404(b).
4. *See* Dowling v. U.S., 110 S. Ct. 668 (1990); U.S. v. Castro-Castro, 464 F.2d 336 (9th Cir. 1972); Wingate v. Wainwright, 464 F.2d 209 (5th Cir. Calif. 1972). *See also* M. Delao, "Admissiblitiy of Prior Acquitted Crimes Under Rule 404(b): Why the Majority Should Adopt the Minority Rule," *Florida State University Law Review* 16 (1989): 1033–1067.
5. For a review, *see* E. Greene and M. Dodge, "The Influence of Prior Record Evidence on Juror Decision Making," *Law and Human Behavior* 19 (1995): 67–78.
6. In fact, in determinations of who gets the death sentence, when North Carolina and Louisiana enacted schemas that made the death sentence applicable to conviction for certain designated crimes—without an individualized sentencing hearing—the Supreme Court struck both statutes down. *See* Woodson v. North Carolina, 428 U.S. 280 (1976); Roberts v. Louisiana, 428 U.S. 325 (1976).
7. There are some parallels to the experiment we are setting up from criminal law areas, where faults and mistakes of the actor and the victim come into play and where necessary or sufficient causality, or indirect causation, may be

in doubt. *See, e.g.,* N. J. Finkel, S. T. Maloney, M. Z. Valbuena, and J. L. Groscup, "Lay Perspectives on Legal Conundrums: Impossible and Mistaken Act Cases," *Law and Human Behavior* 19 (1995): 593–608; N. J. Finkel, "Achilles Fuming, Odysseus Stewing, and Hamlet Brooding: On the Story of the Murder/Manslaughter Distinction," *University of Nebraska Law Review* 74 (1995): 201–262; N. J. Finkel and J. L. Groscup, "When Mistakes Happen: Commonsense Rules of Culpability," *Psychology, Public Policy, and Law* 3 (1997): 65–125; E. J. Greene and J. M. Darley, "Effects of Necessary, Sufficient, and Indirect Causation on Judgments of Criminal Liability," *Law and Human Behavior* 22 (1998): 429–451.

8. The experiment we are setting up has parallels in civil law, in cases of comparative negligence, where complex factors are to be assessed and where some of those factors are supposed to be kept distinct because they are germane to one issue but not another. The law, too, is less than clear on this matter. For example, contributory negligence is the standard in only four states, and if the plaintiff had any negligence for what happened this would bar recovery of damages. On the other end of the legal spectrum, a plaintiff may get damages even if his or her negligence was greater than the defendant's, a standard used in 13 states. In the majority of states (33), the defendant may get damages if his or her negligence was less than 49% ("Wisconsin Rule") or less than or equal to 50% ("New Hampshire Rule").

Apart from the legal rule that operates, these cases ask jurors to make complex decisions. Determining liability, proportioning fault, assessing damages, and computing an overall damage award. Some research findings show a "leakage" or "fusion," whereby participants conflate issues of liability and damage, using legally irrelevant issues to assess liability and damage, and where damage awards are doubly discounted by the plaintiff's proportion of fault and hindsight biases enter the calculations. *See, e.g.,* D. J. Zickafoose and B. H. Bornstein "Double Discounting: The Effects of Comparative Negligence on Mock Juror Decision Making," *Law and Human Behavior* 23 (1999): 577–596; R. Hastie, D. A. Schkade, and J. W. Payne, "Juror Judgments in Civil Cases: Hindsight Effects on Judgments of Liability for Punitive Damages," *Law and Human Behavior* 23 (1999): 597–614; M. C. Anderson and R. J. MacCoun, "Goal Conflict in Juror Assessments of Compensatory and Punitive Damages," *Law and Human Behavior* 23 (1999): 313–330; R. L. Wissler, D. L. Evans, A. J. Hart, M. M., Morry, and M. J. Saks, "Explaining "Pain and Suffering" Awards: The Role of Injury Characteristics and Fault Attributions," *Law and Human Behavior* 21 (1997): 181–207; N. Feigenson, J. Park, and P. Salovey, "Effects of Blameworthiness and Outcome Severity on Attributions of Responsibility and Damage Awards in Comparative Negligence Cases," *Law and Human Behavior* 21 (1997): 597–617.

9. A similar counfounding is present for flaw, where the types and degrees of flaw vary from one case to the next, precluding a clear interpretation. The confounds for fault are even worse, making interpretations highly problematic. The fault variable changes not only in degree but in kind across the cases: In some cases the victim commits the fault; in other cases it is another party who commits the fault; and in still other cases both victim and others commit

faults. In some cases, fault minimizes the severity and in other cases it increases the severity, but overall these effects cancel one another, leading to an overall nonsignificant finding, which is highly misleading.

10. One might ask, why are the participants not more sympathetic to the mother who tries, and why do not they see that situation as more tragic and unfair? The answer seems to be that they do have greater sympathy, but their overall view is focused on the child, not the mother, and with the dead child as the victim and not the mother, their severity rating reflects anger more than compassion, and they are angriest about the crack mother who does nothing, for this is most unfair to the innocent child.

What then explains the interaction effect going in opposite directions when the outsider commits a fault? For the ng mother, the outsider's fault reduces her fault, and the unfairness is seen as slightly less; this is generally how "outsider fault" works. But for the g mother, who is trying, when the outsider commits a fault, participants seem to shift from the child-as-victim to the mother-as-victim, and this condition now seems like a bigger tragedy, a greater unfairness.

12

FUNDAMENTAL BELIEFS ABOUT UNFAIRNESS, LIFE, AND GOD

From a fairy-tale exemplar to thousands of real world instantiations, we have been trying to pin down the essence of unfairness. In Part III, the focus has been on the unexplained variance, starting with issues from the studies where questions produced equivocal answers, contradictory answers, or just plain curious answers at odds with common sense. From the results of Experiment 1, we now know that the concept of unfairness is different from injustice and misfortune. We also know that "unfairness" is the broader term, applicable to more cases than the other two terms. In addition, we know that the narrowest of the terms, "misfortunes," is applied to impersonal agency cases, and those cases are also considered unfairnesses by the majority of participants. Furthermore, the cluster and factor analyses of these concept ratings produced groupings, not unlike our type categorizations (but not identical either), as two different empirical methods have now produced convergent results.

We also found an outcome bias in Experiment 1, which we had suspected from the studies, where outcome unfairness closely tracks the overall unfairness, whereas "process unfairness" does not. Process ratings turn out to be lower than outcome across the cases generally, and when process severity rises, it does so over a more limited range of cases. Yet the results of Experiment 2 dramatically qualify these results. In cases where outcome and process violations both loom large, participants have little difficulty identifying such abuses, and in great numbers, and these process violations correspond closely with legal analyses of the cases.

These findings are the strongest evidence to date that process is not some vague, unrefined, undifferentiated concept, when compared to outcome. When we put the results of Experiments 1 and 2 together, along with those of the studies, it appears that the very topic and question of unfairness makes outcome particularly salient and relevant for that determination. This is much like hindsight bias research, which is, I suggest, misnamed, for the key to that paradigm is not so much the looking back (i.e., you could probably demonstrate hindsight bias by setting up a "looking forward" task as well) but making a particular outcome known; when that outcome is dramatic and strongly suggestive of culpability, then outcome overwhelms the consideration of the process violation. When the dramatic outcome (e.g., the $2 million punitive award in the BMW case) is presented as a question—Is it legitimate or unfair?—rather than as a conclusive piece of evidence (e.g., where a questionable police stop and search of a vehicle finds $2 million in the trunk, which strongly suggests wrongdoing)—participants dive into process considerations, in all their nuances.

Experiments 1 and 2 have pinned down some of the variance of unfairness and process unfairness. In Experiment 3, we introduced background factors and situational factors that bring flaw and fault (and their combination) into the judgments of unfairness to see whether the flaw and fault of the victim weakens or nullifies the unfairness claim. Put another way, when the victim is flawed or at fault or both, will participants, like Eliphaz et al., now blame the victim? The answer is not a simple one, but depends on the relevance of the fault (assuming that it is the victim's) and the relevance and severity of the flaw; if the participants' subjective standards are met, then these factors will significantly reduce the unfairness claim. However, if the claim still has some legitimacy despite the fault or flaw, participants do not nullify completely. Thus there are situational factors (faults) and background factors (flaws), which are subjectively construed as to their seriousness and relevance, which may mute, enhance, or leave the severity of the unfairness undisturbed.

GOING TO DEEPER GROUND

If we begin with our basic judgment of an experience as an unfairness—and ask why it is that we see it that way—we know that our judgment is tied in part to external factors and how they are subjectively construed. However, we suspect that our judgment of unfairness is not just tied to our construal of external reality but has roots in deeper psychic soil. This deeper, dispositional ground is where we find core beliefs and values, our expectations, hopes, longings, and sentiments, and these rise and attach like tendrils twining—affecting how we perceive, what we construe, and why we judge as we do. We can use a question to help explicate: Why did Eliphaz et al. view the same external events one way when Job saw them so differently? If the answer is, "Well, they saw flaws and faults where Job saw none," we must ask a further question: Why did they see flaws and faults? The answer may be dispositional: Their views and values, their expectations of life and God, had to differ from Job's. This would not be all that surprising. If one individual has very high expectations of others, society, life, or God whereas another has low-to-no expectations, we would not be shocked to find that the two differ sharply about whether or not something is unfair or differ about the severity of the unfairness. If one individual was a devout believer in science, believing that there is cause, reason, and explanation for everything, whereas another individual believed in chaos, randomness, and luck, these two are likely to sharply divide as well over some alleged unfairnesses.

Our focus in this chapter moves deeper into the dispositional, although in many ways, we have never left the interior, for we began with participants' instantiations of unfairness and have not strayed too far. Still, we have not gone deep enough. Perceptions, conceptions, and judgments, the layers we have been exploring, remain closely tied to the surface facts in external reality, yet these, we suspect, rest on deeper strata. Further back and further down, in what has been background until now, are the fundamental beliefs people have and how these beliefs affect the picture they construct and the frame they put on it.

Let us look at just three examples. First, two people agree about the facts of a given case, yet one reaches the judgment that it is unfair, whereas the other does not. Why? Second, two people agree about the facts and agree that it is an unfairness, yet one sees it as severe whereas the other sees it as only a mild or moderate unfairness. Again, why? Third, two people agree about the facts, agree that it is a severe unfairness, but one blames God and the other blames life. Again, why? In these examples, there is variance of one sort or another between these people, although the objective facts are constant.

It is a good possibility that these divergent judgments reflect different beliefs about unfairness. Someone who subscribes to the just-world view is likely to see some alleged unfairnesses differently from one who does not, and this belief factor may account for the first disagreement. If one person sees mistakes and variance as a part of human nature and nature, whereas another expects both to conform to expectations, the former may see a mild or moderate unfairness, whereas the latter sees severe unfairness, and this belief factor may account for the second disagreement. Similarly, individuals' unfairness judgments may differ because their views of life, God, and theodicy may be disparate, and this belief factor may account for the third disagreement. General beliefs then, which participants may unconsciously or consciously bring to the facts, may color, shade, and frame the facts such that different pictures emerge. Our basic question in this chapter is: Are these fundamental beliefs determinative of severity judgments, or are they merely a contributing factor among many, or do they not predict at all?

Measure for Measure

In chapter 2, we discussed the notion of theodicy, that branch of theology dealing with reconciling suffering, evil, and unfairnesses in the world, with God. One may reconcile the suffering by denying the existence of God. More typically, the reconstruing is done by letting go of one or another of the monotheistic holdings about God (e.g., perhaps God is not omniscient, or omnipotent, or all caring). Now, in the progression of our research, we wanted to tap participants' theodicy beliefs.

To do so, we created a nine-item measure (plus a total score) labeled "theological views," and participants indicated the extent to which they believe or disbelieve each of the statements using a 6-point scale. Three statements go to their beliefs in God, their practice of religion, and the importance of their faith to them, while the other six questions address their beliefs about God, such as whether God is all-good, all-powerful, or responsive to our prayers.

We also created a measure, which we called "unfairnesses in general," which featured 16 statements and where participants had to again make ratings on a 6-point scale, from 1 (completely disbelieve) to 6 (completely believe). Four of the items dealt with life, putting the onus for unfairnesses on life's randomness rather than on God. Four of the items put the onus on God, offering distinct reasons why this might be so. Four of the items put the onus on humans, due to free will, or because we construe things as unfair, or because we whine about such matters. One item put the onus on others, and one put the onus on society. Finally there were two other items, one dealing with whether unfairnesses are justified and the other dealing with whether there are reasons for unfairnesses. The just-world view may also relate to our judgments of unfairness, and we used the just-world scale, though we gave it a new title that did not betray to the participant what it is we were looking for. We call it "views about life," and it features 20 questions. Participants again had to make a rating for each question on a 1 (completely disbelieve) to 6 (completely believe) scale, and a total score was obtained.

Besides these measures that tap theological, unfairness (in general), and just-world views, it is quite possible that emotions—particularly those of envy, jealousy, resentment, inferiority, and the like—play some part in the judgments of unfairness. We do know that some of our type categories involve equity, equality, or need comparisons—where judgments are made regarding what different people receive and certain emotions may affect those judgments. To test this possibility, we used a short eight-item measure, called DES, where participants made ratings on a 1 (completely disbelieve) to 6 (completely believe) scale and where a total score was obtained by adding the eight scores.

Our final measure was called "ways of life," and it asked participants to rate their endorsement, on the 6-point scale from 1 (completely disbelieve) to 6 (completely believe), for five descriptions of ways to live. Way 1 stressed the social, working together with others toward a common goal; Way 2 stressed the inward, meditative, solitary path; Way 3 stressed a more passive view, letting things come to you; Way 4 stressed striving to realize ideals; and Way 5 stressed taking pleasure, a more hedonistic route.

THE FLAWS, FAULTS, AND HUMAN VERSUS NATURE CASES EXPERIMENT—CONTINUED

The experiment described in the previous chapter actually had more complexity to it than we described, for all of the measures above were given to our participants for them to rate. One of those measures, unfairnesses in general, was modified to serve as a predictor variable: We asked participants, after each of the 16 cases, to rate that specific case using this 16-item scale, which we called "case-specific unfairnesses." Thus in assessing measures that may account for significant portions of the severity of the unfairness variance, we have five background factor variables—theological views, unfairnesses in general, just-world scale, DES, and ways of life—and one scale dealing with case-specific factors, which focused on current perceptions of the case. One question we examined was, "How much of the variance can be accounted for by the deeper background factors, and how much is accounted for by current and specific factors arising in each case?"

RESULTS AND DISCUSSION

Using multiple regression analyses, the background variables (e.g., theological views, unfairnesses in general, just-world scale, DES, and ways of life) and the current case-specific unfairnesses variable were entered into a model to predict the severity ratings for each of the 16 cases.[1] Overall these factors accounted for a very sizable portion of the variance, averaging 46.7%. Yet the average hides considerable variation, for the variance explained ranged from 33.5% to 69.7% across the cases, and when we examined the particular variables and how much or little of the variance they accounted for, we find considerable variation among cases as well. We then ran the regression analyses twice more: First, we tested the past, background factors; second, we tested the current, case-specific factors. The past factors accounted for 18.3% of the variance, on the average, with a range of 11.1% to 24.8%, whereas the current factors accounted for 34.5% of the variance, on the average, with a range of 18.2% to 58.9%; thus on the average, current factors accounted for more than twice the variance of the past, background factors.

It was clear that not all of the factors were contributing significantly to the severity ratings. To identify which were, we ran three stepwise regression analyses—for all the variables (overall), for the background factors, and for the current factors. The overall stepwise analysis reduced the number of factors considerably, but the remaining factors still accounted for a very sizable portion (37.8%) of the variance on average. The current factors accounted for 30.2%, more than twice as much as the past factors, which accounted for 12.8%. Still, the past factors make a direct and significant contribution to severity; in addition, they make an indirect contribution as well, because they correlate with current factors.

Background Factors

Looking at background factors only, we focused on the participants' theodicy views and just-world scores in particular. Theodicy views tended to be a significant predictor in most "act of nature" cases, but much less so in "human act" cases. For the just-world scores, it was the opposite, with these scores being a significant predictor in most "human act" cases, but not in the "act of nature" cases. Based on these results then, the just-world scale may be a misnomer—for it appears to be a "just *human* world" scale, rather than applying to acts of nature or God.

Finally, using a canonical discriminant analysis, we took variables that were significant across many of the 16 cases and tested whether these variables would discriminate the "natural act versus human act" cases, the "good versus not so good" cases (the flaw variable), and the "fault versus no fault" cases (the fault variable). They did, as three significant equations emerged.

Staying with the background variables, we again find that "theodicy views" predict for "act of nature" cases, whereas "just world views" predict for "human act" cases, but the most powerful predictor of "act of nature" cases turns out to be the general view that there must be some reason for the unfairness, even if we cannot fathom it. When we look at flaw and its predictors, participants find reasons for the unfairnesses and believe that God has good reasons for these "human, free will failings"; in the "good" condition, on the other hand, participants put the onus on society and others for the unfairness. Finally, when the victim bears fault, participants find that the unfairness is both justified and supported by obvious reasons. When there is no fault, however, participants' ratings of free will and society predict most highly.

I have said little, as of yet, about the current factors, although they account for the major portion of the variance that is explained. I will do so in the context of how unfairness judgments seem to be reached. It is quite apparent that the judgment process begins with the particulars of a case. If this were not so, then we should see the same factors predicting from case to case and across the conditions of a given case, which we do not find.

Participants start with the facts of the case and the fact that this is an *alleged* unfairness. They recognize that there is subjectivity, relativity, and perspectival differences in this judgment, for two case-specific factors that are strongly endorsed are the following. The first is this: "'Unfairness' is a label and a judgment that individuals put on an experience, and it is subjective and relative; not everyone would agree that what some call an 'unfairness' really is an unfairness, or is a severe unfairness." The second is this: "Many people 'whine' and cry 'it's not fair,' when the suffering is no worse than what everybody else suffers." The first of these factors shows up more for the "natural act" cases, whereas the second shows up more for the "human act" cases, yet both reflect that people can take differing perspectives on the case at hand.

The facts of a case, along with the cry of unfairness, are likely to trigger memories and prototypes of unfairnesses for participants. From what is available, representative, and personal, participants are likely to cull similar instances to the one in question, which may serve as a comparative standard. Participants may also create comparatives by taking the case at hand and imaginatively permuting what-if variations; these creative variations extend the case in more and less fair directions, creating a context in which to evaluate and judge the actual claim.

There is more to this subjective, relative, and perspective-laden process. As it moves along, participants invoke unfairness memories or create comparisons to judge the person alleging the unfairness and to judge the severity of the unfairness. Adding on to the process, the vast majority of participants invoke *reasons* of one sort or another for the unfairness. The reasons may point outward, toward others or society; the reasons may point inward, toward our free will; and when the reason involves God, it is that God has a reason. *For the overwhelming majority of participants, there is or must be a reason for the unfairness.* Moreover, participants will search for the reason, the justification for the unfairness, even in cases where it may be hard to find—cases involving acts of nature, or cases where the victim is good and has no flaw, and cases where the victim bears no fault.

There is, however, a small minority who find no reason—save life's randomness—for the unfairness, and this minor chord sounds most frequently in "act of nature" cases. This small minority accepts that some things happen for no apparent reason, with no justification, and they tend to rate such unfairnesses as less severe.

For the vast majority who do cite specific reasons, these will vary by case (nature versus human) and by whether flaw or fault is present. Said another way, the reasons cited tend to be appropriate to the facts of the case. But the specific facts that trigger the participants' analysis seem to activate general beliefs and background factors as well. These background factors, such as theodicy and just-world views, account for a smaller but still significant portion of the severity rating directly, adding something that the current specific factors do not account for. Moreover, these background factors may activate the current factors that do come into play.

LOOKING BACKWARD, LOOKING FORWARD

In looking back, finding a reason seems key. For some participants, to find no reason for an unfairness—but only randomness—may be too frightening to contemplate. We can find examples of this phenomenon among patients with physical or psychiatric illnesses who would prefer to hear even dreaded labels like "cancer" or "depression" rather than to hear that the doctor does not know what is wrong. Having a label, which may not be the same as finding a cause or reason for the condition, may nonetheless serve the patient psychologically. Believing in a reason, as most of our participants endorse—even when you cannot cite the reason—brings the unfairness matter into the realm of reasonableness.

Finding reasons, however, is not the same as strongly endorsing the just-world view, for the latter variable accounts for very little of the variance of severity in this research, whereas the former predicts much more. In many of the alleged unfairness cases we used, the reasons for the unfairnesses were quite evident, particularly in the human act cases and even more so when flaw and fault were evident. Contrary to the just-world view, in our data we find that participants do not blame innocent victims. Neither do they stretch or strain the facts, nor do they engage in delusional thinking.

Yet the participants' search for reasons runs into its greatest obstacles in the "act of nature" cases and in the Job-like cases where flaw and fault seem nowhere in sight. Here, one's faith in reasons is tested. Still, "there must be reasons," say a majority of participants, even if we cannot easily identify them, and their ratings on the general background measures support this assertion. For example, they strongly endorse the following statements: "Life must have reasons, even if the relevant sciences have not unearthed them"; and "God no doubt has reasons, even if, from our earth-bound perspective, we cannot fathom them." Moreover, the various theodicy reconciliations that many endorse are themselves attempts to give reasons for why God permits unfairnesses. Finally, even for those who do not believe in God, they seem to have a very strong faith, almost a religious one, in reasons.

Regarding the "human act" cases, particularly those where flaw and fault are evident, *reasons for* the unfairness act as moral judgments, keeping someone on the moral hook. There is blame here, for sure, as the judgment is a clear statement that someone did wrong. But the judgment says even more: It insists that people, society, and civilization ought to do better and rise to the ideal. To find no reasons—and to accept that—seems to excuse all too easily what should not be excused. Had he passively accepted, this would be a Job who has given out, given in, and given up—not because he is cowering in fright before the beast God threatens him with, but because he no longer gives "a god damn" about right and wrong and unfairnesses at all. If a sizable segment ever embraced such a view, which the majority would categorize as depressing, nihilistic, and amoral, we would enter a world without standards—where "But it's not fair!" cries and whimpers would be stilled—for the underlying tendrils of fairness would wither into nothingness.

But would it be so bleak? Perhaps the small minority who accept randomness and accept that acts and actions can happen for no reason have a point. They appear to accept that unfairnesses occur in life, and that misfortunes occur for no reason, for which there is no blame. Perhaps this view is the more realistic one or the more therapeutically elevated view, although a majority of our participants would dispute that. However, from this small minority point of view, these participants do not seem to hold a grudge against life or nature for what is or is not doled out, and this may spare them grief in both the short and long term.

In trying to pin down variability, though we have made new connections between unfairness judgments and one's deeper beliefs, we end with some variability nonetheless. Whereas the vast majority of participants seeks reasons, almost desperately so, there is a small minority that seems to let "the need for reasons" go. We ask, "What if this majority/minority split was reversed?" We answer, based on the data, "not here, not now, not anytime soon."

In looking forward, perhaps it is different elsewhere, in different cultures. This cross-cultural possibility brings home the fact that all of our findings to date, from all of the studies and experiments, are based on American participants. If unfairnesses are viewed differently even by a minority of our American participants, might unfairnesses be viewed very differently, perhaps dramatically differently, across cultures? If one of our beginning questions was "What, if anything, is universal about unfairness?" it is now time to leave this soil—for the land of Uz.

ENDNOTE

1. For the background variables, there were 15 factors, and for the current case-specific variable, there were 16 factors, for a total of 31 factors.

IV

SEARCHING FOR
UNIVERSALS IN A
MULTICULTURAL WORLD

Once upon a time, in the land of Uz, ... (p. 5)

From Stephen Mitchell's *The Book of Job* (1987)

13

UNFAIRNESSES ACROSS LANDS AND BENEATH CULTURES

Across many studies, with a wide age range of American participants, certain findings recur. When asked for instantiations of unfairness, participants offer many, and these spread across personal and impersonal dimensions, where their own victimizations (Y) do not predominate. Endemic to these instances is blame, but it is not self-blame: Rather, the blame is directed externally and widely, pointing to all sorts of individuals or the large group we call society, or to inheritance, nature, life, and God. Most important, these instances can be housed reliably in our type of unfairness categorization schema, with less than a dozen type categories needed to do the job. Beyond their shear numbers and their distribution by personal, blame, and type categories, most are rated high on the severity scale, not being petty narcissistic whines, but turning out to be substantive claims that are bitter to swallow.

In taking the length and breadth of unfairness, we found that its area is extensive, overlapping injustice and partially overlapping misfortune. We also found that unfairness has depth, particularly for the hot ones, which cut deep and have a staying power (i.e., low rates of change) that may last decades, and though prescriptions are readily available and gratuitously dispensed (e.g., "let them roll off your back," "get over them," or "just forget it"), these generally fail, for we are not Peter Pan and unfairnesses do not disappear to abracadabra.

UNFAIRNESSES IN THE LAND OF THE FREE

We might conclude that unfairness is indeed ubiquitous, running from sea to shining sea, except for one small point: We have only tested American participants. This limitation brings us up short—preventing us from generalizing our findings to other lands and precluding us from proffering universals about unfairness.

America has long been described as a melting pot, where heterogeneity and variance are evident, but in a larger, cross-cultural context, American results may be only parochial and far from universal. Moreover, our American participants, despite their numbers and age ranges, are more homogeneous than the whole of the country, for they were not drawn representatively from the melting pot; yet here, even in this smaller, narrower universe, we found that fundamental values accounted for a significant piece of the unfairness variance. If fundamental values play a key role in judging and rating unfairness, then values very different from American ones might sharply alter the picture. Beyond altering the general picture of unfairness, cultural values may also shape how people construe specific situational variables, such as fault, or whether they apply notions of fault and unfairness to nature. This narrowness of our sample is a limitation, and overcoming it requires a change of course, to a cross-cultural heading.

Finding Our Bearings Amid Limitations, Variability, and Perspectives

Once upon a time the question was whether echoes of Job's claim from the land of Uz were still heard in today's secular society and in our own psyches. With "time's arrow" pointing in the reverse direction,[1] we could ask whether our modern, American findings would replicate in the land of Uz, or whether the likes of Job, Eliphaz, Bildad, and Zophar would scoff at many of our claims or sympathetically comfort us. But that question is beyond our empirical reach, because we cannot turn time around. We can, however, look elsewhere in space, to lands and peoples that have cultures and values different from our own.

Before venturing on a cross-cultural journey, we must first get our bearings. To do so, we must recognize some methodological drawbacks that limit our findings. Previously we discussed some of the limitations of the study method and why they necessitated the switch to the experiment, where fine-grained answers were sought and where potential confounds had to be controlled. But experiments, as we have also seen, have limitations as well. For one, in tightly controlling and systematically manipulating case vignettes, the experimenter may inadvertently select cases that are too few in number or that fail to cover the full domain. Second, cases may be too simplistic, failing to reflect the complexities of true-to-life cases. Third, cases may be biased in outcome or process directions. Fourth, the particular dependent variable chosen may limit the range of responses that participants can make, such that we may miss (or even preclude finding) participants' complex processing.

But now let us consider in greater depth a methodological limitation that has been there all along concerning our participants—and their representativeness. On many dimensions, our college students are not representative of their age group nationally. Whether we use their IQ or SAT scores, they are brighter and better educated than the average and their socioeconomic status is higher as well. Thus if the bell curve represents the shape of the entire distribution, our sample slice, like a golfer's, veers sharply to the right, and the conclusions that follow may be in the rough, at best, or worse, out of bounds. Yet this is not all. Although our students come from all parts of the country, the geographic distribution does not match with census data percentages, and in terms of religion, our students are even more skewed than the national population. All of these unrepresentative factors are repeated for tots and teens, adults, and the elderly group because the college students were recruiting their family members.

The slices we took, no matter how many times we sampled, do not add up to the American pie, and thus we are not able to fairly generalize to the whole. The narrowness of our sample is a troubling limitation. Despite this limitation—in fact, because of it—a number of our findings are even more telling. For example, we repeatedly find (in approximately 20% of the instances) that outside coders and inside participants will disagree in their categorizations, as their objective and subjective perspectives do not align, even among these like participants. Some of this variability results because coders focus on different aspects or see the same aspects through differing perspectives.

This is not the first time we have seen this phenomenon: We saw it in the land of Uz, in a sample of four, where Job and his three friends focused on different aspects of the alleged unfairness and took differing perspectives on the matter; we also have numerous illustrations of perspectival differences in our studies. To illustrate, if three people work hard on a project but the fourth member does no work yet gets the same reward, is it a case of "equal justice when it should have been individualized," a case of "discriminatory treatment," or "no work rewarded," or "hard work not rewarded," or "wrongful behavior rewarded," or "lack of due process"? Here, for this one instance, we have six possible type slots. If we view the same instance through outcome or process perspectives, different categorizations are again likely. If perspective is critical and produces variability even in this narrow sample, then our first prediction would be greater variability and perspectival differences if we examine countries and cultures different from our own. A second prediction holds that those disparities ought to be greater as the differences grow between the comparative cultures.[2]

Though these cross-cultural predictions seem obvious and likely, they may not turn out that way at all. Returning to our results, even though we found that a particular instance of unfairness may be slotted differently depending on how coders view the instance, *what showed repeatedly were the regularity of the categories themselves*. These type categories appear in all the studies, with frequencies that are quite consistent within age groups. This pattern might obtain across cultures as well: The particular instances may come in local colorations with cultural and perspectival variations— but the essential categories may remain the same.[3]

So two different predictions can be entertained. The first holds that if fairness and unfairness notions are solely or primarily determined by culture, then we should expect wide differences between cultures. But the second holds that if there is something universal about unfairness—such that it transcends or lies beneath culture—then we might find greater accord regarding unfairness types than the differences in culture, language, and history of the comparative countries might suggest.[4] Although we raise these possibilities about unfairness, we note that they have been raised about the concept of justice as well. Garland, for one, believes that justice lies "beyond culture and outside of history,"[5] whereas Silbey believes that it "is culturally and historically constructed."[6]

If there are universals about unfairness, what might they be? We might start with the broad findings from our American samples, which show that unfairness deconstructs in the following ways. First, unfairness is often applied when outcomes are perceived to be inequitable, and many of our specific type categories reflect this, whereas equity theory can provide an explanation.[7] Second, we also saw a category where process was the dominant focus and where equity theory seemed inapplicable. Third, we saw some categories where outcome and process are both involved, in some admixture not easily separated by participants. Fourth, we also saw the rule of proportion being applied,[8] where some punishment is deserved but where it is disproportionate to culpability. Fifth, we saw misfortune cases (i.e., where nature or life delivers the blow) under the "innocence is punished" category, which turned out to be the first or second most frequently cited category in all the studies,[9] yet where doubt and disagreement arise as to whether these are unfairnesses at all. With these American "sea to shining sea" unfairness findings in mind, we now ask, "Will they be found across oceans as well?"

CLEARING THE GROUND

Before we trek through the land of Uz, some ground needs to be cleared around the issues of justice, language, and culture. Around the concept of justice, which a number of researchers have addressed in a cross-cultural way, we need to ask ourselves, "Have the answers we seek already been found in that existing literature?" We think not. That literature focuses almost exclusively on justice or injustice, with some studies showing cross-cultural differences in regard to specific justice notions though other studies do not.[10] The problem is that those findings may not be directly relevant to unfairness, because we have shown that the concepts of unfairness and injustice are significantly different.

On the other hand, some of those cross-cultural researchers appear to bring "fairness" into their writing, under the heading of "procedural justice." This might suggest that those findings are either relevant to unfairness, or are really about unfairness albeit under a different name. However, in reading that literature, at least two confusions are evident that obscure rather than clarify and make it unlikely that those findings relate directly to, or translate into, unfairness. For one, some researchers speak of "procedural justice" in some sentences, while in others they refer to the very same phenomenon as "procedural fairness,"[11] appearing to treat the two terms as fungible and synonymous.[12] This is problematic, for we know that the two are not identical, based on our results. The second confusion involves the language of still other researchers, who conjoin the two terms in that shopworn idiom—"just and fair"—but then typically go on to focus on the "just" end. Conceptually, the problem with this idiomatic conjoining is that it leaves it unclear if the back end ("fair") carries any weight at all independent of "just," and what that weight might be. Pragmatically, the problem is that we already know that "unfairness" is not only different from "injustice" but broader, carrying its own weight, and not simply bringing up the rear.

Thus from our vantage point, the cross-cultural research findings on justice may be off point as far as unfairness is concerned. Moreover, even when *fair* is invoked as the tail end of the conjoint idiom, the failure to differentiate *just* from *fair* only confuses the issue. With much of justice work being either off point or indiscriminately mixing what ought to be parsed, there are sound arguments for following the unfairness course directly and deconstructively into other cultures.

Returning to our ground clearing, there is a second issue we must take up, involving language. Given the ubiquitousness of the "But it's not *fair!*" complaint in the American culture, one might be tempted to project it across cultural boundaries—taking it simply as a truism that unfairnesses happen everywhere. But those who make this assumption are brought up short when they try to translate the "But it's not fair!" plaint into other languages. In Spanish, for example, there is no word-for-word translation,[13] though roughly the same complaint is expressed as *"No es justo!"* which back-translated becomes "It's not *just!*" Kidder and Muller made a similar (although arguable) claim about the Japanese language,[14] finding "no word for 'fair'"; however, in the very same sentence where they make this claim, they also note the "apparent paradox," for the Japanese society is "so at-tuned to obligations and entitlements" that the absence of a word seems odd indeed. This brings to light a basic problem in cross-cultural work: Is a failure of direct translation to be explained by the absence of the concept from the target language, or is the best word in the target language poly-semic, with one of its meanings corresponding to the word in the source language?[15]

The third of our ground-clearing issues focuses on "culture" itself. A number of researchers have come to see *culture* as too vague and Rorschach-like a term, an all too easy catchall for projections, and a weak cornerstone on which to pile findings and build theory. Some argue that we ought to go beyond cultural membership, ethnicity, or nationality—to specific "value dimensions"—such as individualism versus collectivism, power distance, masculinity versus femininity, primary versus secondary control, and justice versus caring orientations—which might better differ-entiate cultures.[16] In our work, although we are mindful of such dimensions and how our unfairness findings may relate to them, we also need to be mindful of the possibility that unfairness may not fit neatly with or within such dimensions. It may well be that another preposition—beneath—may best express the relationship, for if the primacy of unfairness shows in other cultures as well and proves to be as foundational as it is here, then un-fairness may lie beneath value dimensions. We turn now to a few findings from the value dimensions literature, which provide context and clues re-garding the relationship of unfairness to value dimensions and culture.

Setting the Course by Cultural Value Dimensions?

In an ambitious experiment looking at everyday justice and respon-sibility judgments of Japanese and American samples, Hamilton and Sanders tested a number of brief vignettes involving a family situation among equals, a family situation with an authority and a subordinate, a work situation among equals, a work situation with an authority and a subordinate, and cases involving a stranger.[17] Their vignettes varied whether the actor was known or not and, if known, whether the actor was in an equal social role (solidarity) or in a hierarchical one. The cultural value dimension under examination was "individualism versus collectivism."

Before getting to their results, let us consider this "individualism ver-sus collectivism" dimension a bit further. A number of researchers have investigated this dimension, and they argue that the people in the United States can be situated on the individualism end of the dimension, in that they conceive the person as a self-contained, independent entity. People in India and Japan, on the other hand, have been situated at the collec-tivism end, where they conceive the person as interdependent, existing in relation to social context and relationships.[18] If this value dimension does capture distinct cultural perspectives, and research measures situate these cultures at distinctly different places on the continuum, then this ought to have implications for attributing the cause and responsibility for certain actions.

An early study found that it did indeed, for Americans were more likely to attribute the cause of either a job promotion or demotion to dispositional factors, whereas Indians were more likely to attribute either of those work outcomes to situational factors.[19] Yet from this finding alone, what are we to make of the difference? We cannot conclude that Americans are making the "fundamental attribution error,"[20] attributing the cause to dispositional factors (e.g., mental state, intent) when they should not, for the error might be on the Indian side, mistakenly attributing the cause to situational factors, such as blaming others when they should not. Thus without knowledge of the "true" cause, deciding whether the Americans or the Indians are correct is problematic.[21]

The second problem is conceptual: Calling the "fundamental attribution error" an "error," may be a mistake, for it may simply be a cultural bias.[22] If we think of it as a "cultural bias," then we need not be terribly concerned about the transcendent true cause of things, as our conclusions can be of a relative and comparative sort.

But this leads to a third problem: thinking that all Americans share the individualism bias and that all Indians view cases through the collectivism bias. This dichotomous thinking ends up eliminating all within-group variability, which is impossible. In addition, dichotomous thinking fails to portray the fact that the two distributions no doubt overlap, such that some Americans will be more collectivist than some Indians, and some Indians will be more individualistic than some Americans.

Returning to the Hamilton and Sanders findings, their overall results seem to support the value dimension prediction. However, when we examine their specific findings, there are anomalies. One anomaly occurs on cases involving a stranger, where the typical pattern of individualism versus collectivism differences between the Japanese and Americans suddenly evaporates; on these cases, the Japanese group acts "American," using the dispositional factor of intent, just as Americans typically do. So the particular case or context makes a difference. Said another way, the value dimension prediction does not work across all cases.

Finkel and Groscup addressed the problem of mistakes and culpability with an American sample.[23] When people claim "mistake" as either an exculpatory or mitigating factor in their defense, they are saying, in effect, "but it's not fair!" to punish me fully for what happened. In two of their experiments, Finkel and Groscup tested vignettes where another person contributes to the harmful outcome and bears some culpability along with the defendant. The researchers found that the participants' analyses clearly took the other into account, along with the defendant: As the other's culpability increased in the minds of participants, the defendant's culpability generally lessened. Put differently, the Americans were responding like the Japanese in their culpability determinations, using situational factors along with dispositional factors, making a complex assessment involving multiple variables and interactions. This finding again illustrates that a single value dimension may hold across only a limited set of cases.

In Finkel and Groscup's work, they varied the culpability of the other across three levels, from "no (or low level) culpability to moderate to high." In Hamilton and Sanders work, they used only two levels: Either the other has some culpability or does not. But in testing only "all or none" extremes, you are likely to miss the nuances in between. That is precisely what Finkel and Groscup found, because it was at the mid-range level where the interactions were most complex. Value dimensions, while denoting a continuum, can rigidify into dichotomies and stereotypes when only the two endpoints are considered.

Let us examine another value dimension, that of power distance.[24] This dimension reflects the degree to which people prefer an autocratic or consultative style of authority. Those low in power distance prefer consultation and discussion and view subordinate disagreement with authorities as appropriate and desirable. Those high in power distance prefer autocratic leadership and dislike disagreement or criticism on the part of subordinates.[25]

People with a low power distance orientation are said to have stronger personal connections with authorities, viewing them more like themselves, with stronger social bonds connecting them, and thus they would have higher expectations regarding fair due process in dealing with authorities. Such individuals, the prediction goes, would be more upset if authorities (e.g., parents, bosses, coaches, and societal agents and institutions) acted in high-handed ways without due process and personal consideration, and we would expect their "but it's not fair!" complaints to be more frequent and hot than people with a high power distance orientation. If the process is poor, these low power distance individuals would no doubt decry many of the outcomes that result. If Americans, as a group, are characterized as having lower power distance than the Japanese, for example, then the prediction from this value dimension would be straightforward: Americans should cry "unfair" more frequently and loudly than the Japanese.

But is this the only prediction we could make? Could we not make the opposite prediction? Or, less drastic, could we not make the same prediction, but based on an entirely different factor? Let us consider the less drastic possibility: the same prediction, but for different reasons. Perhaps the Japanese, if in fact they do decry unfairnesses less frequently and intensely than Americans, do so not because of a higher power distance orientation but because in their collectivistic society, where harmony (*wa*) is highly valued, they are less voluble and forthcoming about unfairnesses?[26] Using different constructs, "collectivism" or "harmony," yields similar predictions to the power distance hypothesis but for different reasons and out of a very different psychology. Lower rates and less intense ratings may have nothing to do with greater acceptance of an autocratic process style; to the contrary, it is possible that the Japanese perceive unfairnesses just as much and as intensely as Americans, but collectivism and *wa* act to suppress the expression of the claims.

Now let us consider the opposite prediction. Takeuchi has held that meritocracy is a deeply ingrained value in Japan's culture, where rewards are supposed to go to those who earn them.[27] Advancement in the Japanese educational system, for example, is based on meritocracy (equity). But if, in reality, rewards go to some who do not earn them, or rewards are not based on merit but on "impermissible factors"—such as who you know, who you are related to, your wealth, background, gender, age, birth order, and many more—then the Japanese may be more upset by such "discriminatory treatment" than Americans.

When we reflect on either the same prediction (for different reasons) or the opposite prediction, we come to realize that a single value dimension may be an oversimplification: It may not be determinative across all issues and types of decisions. Other dimensions are likely to be operating, and these have a range of issues where they apply, whereas on other issues they do not. Furthermore, some dimensions may push in the predicted direction but for very different reasons, while other dimensions may push in a very different direction altogether. Moreover, without elucidating people's reasons for why they cry "unfair" or do not cry at all, we have no way of knowing whether they are simply suppressing their discontent or actually accept the autocratic style and the arbitrary outcomes more than Americans. Finally, value dimension research can lead to another oversimplification—where cultural groups are seen as monolithic, without variance, and situated at discrete, nonoverlapping points on a continuum.

Using Distinct Types of Cultures?

In his work, Alan Fiske found four elementary forms of human relations, which he called "communal sharing," "authority ranking," "equality matching," and "market pricing."[28] Across various domains, these types of cultures differ, said Fiske. Regarding the "distributive justice" domain, communal sharing tends to regard resources as common, "without regard for how much any one person uses," for "everything belongs to all together."[29] In authority ranking, however, "the higher a person's rank the more he or she gets."[30] Under equality, each gets the same, and under market pricing, "to each in due proportion."[31] Fiske made similar distinctions across other domains—such as motivation, moral judgment and ideology, and moral interpretations of misfortune—domains that certainly relate to our "unfairness" topic.

Yet these broad distinctions may not fit *any* society and may obliterate the fact that a given culture may be highly variable, being in all four elementary models on differing occasions. The Japanese, for example, may accept authority ranking when it comes to privileges of birth order, may ask for equality when it comes to gender, may desire market pricing when it comes to the rewards of educational attainment, and may accept communal sharing when it comes to division of food within the family. Fixed distinctions, a top-down model that is prototypical in nature, may be too crude for unfairnesses.

LOOKING BACKWARD, LOOKING FORWARD

Now, after taking our bearings and clearing some ground, we set a cross-cultural course. In doing so, we put those hypothesized value dimensions on the sidelines, for those dimensions may neither be the salient ones nor the relevant and determinative ones. More important, we set them aside because in looking forward we want to hear from the participants directly, rather than seeing their responses through preselected filters. For similar reasons, we set aside fixed typologies. Thus we return to deconstructive and narrative approaches, asking participants in other countries, speaking a different language than our own, to detail their instantiations of "but it's not fair!" From the instances, we will see what categories of unfairness emerge in their cultures, how their types of unfairnesses relate to ours, and then we will examine the frequency distribution of unfairnesses across cultures.

ENDNOTES

1. S. J. Gould, *Time's Arrow Time's Cycle: Myth and Metaphor in the Discovery of Geological Time* (Cambridge, MA: Harvard University Press, 1987).
2. This view, called "relativism," sees the culture as creating a unique psychological climate where cross-cultural comparisons may be invalid. *See, e.g.,* M. H. Segall, W. J. Lonner, and J. W. Berry, "Cross-Cultural Psychology as a Scholarly Discipline: On the Flowering of Culture in Behavioral Research," *American Psychologist* 53 (1998): 1101–1110.
3. *Id.* This view has been referred to as "absolutism" or "universalism," where cultural variables, once they are peeled off, reveal some psychic unity.
4. There is still a third possibility, where the "accelerating process of globalization and the increasing interconnections between cultures" (p. 1111) work to blur cultural distinctiveness. H. J. M. Hermans and J. G. Kempen, "Moving Cul-

tures: The Perilous Problems of Cultural Dichotomies in a Globalizing Society," *American Psychologist* 53 (1998): 1110–1120.

5. D. Garland, *Punishment and Modern Society: A Study in Social Theory* (Chicago: University of Chicago Press, 1990), p. 205.

6. S. S. Silbey, "'Let Them Eat Cake': Globalization, Postmodern Colonialism, and the Possibilities of Justice," *Law & Society Review* 31 (1997): 209.

7. D. M. Messick and K. S. Cook, eds., *Equity Theory: Psychological and Sociological Perspectives* (New York: Praeger, 1983); E. Walster, G. W. Walster, and E. Berscheid, *Equity, Theory, and Reseach* (Boston: Allyn & Bacon, 1978).

8. N. J. Finkel, "Culpability and Commonsense Justice: Lessons Learned Betwixt Murder and Madness," *Notre Dame Journal of Law, Ethics & Public Policy* 10 (1996): 11–64; N. J. Finkel, M. B. Liss, and V. R. Moran, "Equal or Proportional Justice for Accessories? Children's Pearls of Proportionate Wisdom," *Journal of Applied Child Development* 18 (1997): 229–244; P. H. Robinson and J. M. Darley, *Justice, Liability and Blame: Community Views and the Criminal Law* (Boulder, CO: Westview Press, 1995).

9. N. J. Finkel, "But It's Not Fair!: Commonsense Notions of Unfairness," *Psychology, Public Policy, and Law*, in press.

10. G. Bierbrauer, "Toward an Understanding of Legal Culture: Variations in Individualism and Collectivism Between Kurds, Lebanese, and Germans," *Law & Society Review* 28 (1994): 243–264; E. Blankenburg, "The Infrastructure for Avoiding Civil Litigation: Comparing Cultures of Legal Behavior in the Netherlands and West Germany," *Law & Society Review* 28 (1994): 789–808; J. L. Gibson and G. A. Caldeira, "The Legal Cultures of Europe," *Law & Society Review* 30 (1996): 55–85; V. L. Hamilton and J. Sanders, *Everyday Justice: Responsibility and the Individual in Japan and the United States* (New Haven: Yale University Press, 1992; J. G. Miller, "Culture and the Development of Everyday Social Explanation," *Journal of Personality and Social Psychology* 46 (1984): 961–978; J. G. Miller and D. M. Bersoff, "Culture and Moral Judgement: How Are Conflicts Between Justice and Friendship Resolved?" *Journal of Personality and Social Psychology* 62 (1992): 541–554; J. G. Miller, D. M. Bersoff, and R. L. Harwood, "Perceptions of 'Social Responsibility' in India and in the United States: Moral Imperatives or Personal Decisions?" *Journal of Personality and Social Psychology* 58 (1990): 33–47; F. M. Moghaddam, *Social Psychology: Exploring Universals Across Cultures* (San Francisco: W. H. Freeman, 1998); L. Rosen, *The Anthropology of Justice: Law as Culture in Islamic Society* (New York: Cambridge University Press, 1989); T. R. Tyler, R. J. Boeckmann, H. J. Smith, and Y. J. Huo, *Social Justice in a Diverse Society* (Boulder, CO: Westview, 1997); but see L. H. Kidder and S. Muller, "What Is 'Fair' in Japan?" In *Social Justice in Human Relations (Vol. 2): Societal and Psychological Consequences of Justice and Injustice*, ed. H. Steensma and R. Vermunt (New York: Plenum Press, 1991), pp. 139–154.

11. T. R. Tyler, "Governing Amid Diversity: The Effect of Fair Decisionmaking Procedures on the Legitimacy of Government," *Law & Society Review* 28 (1994): 809–831.

12. L. S. Wrightsman, M. T. Nietzel, and W. H. Fortune, *Psychology and the Legal System*, 3rd ed. (Pacific Grove, CA: Brooks/Cole, 1994).

13. R. Harré, "Emotion Across Cultures," *Innovation* 11 (1998): 43–52.

14. Kidder and Muller, "What Is 'Fair' in Japan?" p. 140.

15. Although language differences pose problems for cross-cultural research, we cannot avoid them. Had we tried to finesse by going in English-speaking directions, this would certainly be seen as "stacking the deck," and that type of "process unfairness," as we saw, was quickly spotted by participants in the legal cases experiment, who then cried foul. Moreover, staying within Anglophone cultures would be duplicating, at the cultural level, the unrepresentative sample problem we have in the studies, which would severely limit our ability to generalize across cultures. No, the search for universals requires the harder test, where the languages in the comparative cultures are distinctly different.

16. V. L. Hamilton and J. Sanders, *Everyday Justice: Responsibility and the Individual in Japan and the United States* (New Haven, CT: Yale University Press, 1992); G. H. Hofstede, *Culture's Consequences: International Differences in Work-Related Attitudes* (Beverly Hills, CA: Sage, 1980); M. Killen, "Justice and Care: Dichotomies or Coexistence?" *Journal for a Just and Caring Education* 2 (1996): 42–58; T. R. Tyler, "The Relationship of the Outcome and Procedural Fairness: How Does Knowing the Outcome Influence the Judgments About the Procedure?" *Social Justice Research* 9 (1996): 311–325; T. R. Tyler, E. A. Lind, and Y. J. Huo, "Cultural Values and Authority Relations: The Psychology of Conflict Resolution Across Cultures," *Psychology, Public Policy, and Law* (in press); J. R. Weisz, F. M. Rothbaum, and T. C. Blackburn, "Standing Out and Standing In: The Psychology of Control in America and Japan," *American Psychologist* 39 (1984): 955–969.

17. Hamilton and Sanders, *Everyday Justice*.

18. H. R. Markus and S. Kitayama, "Culture and the Self: Implications for Cognition, Emotion, and Motivation," *Psychological Review* 98 (1991): 224–253; J. G. Miller, "Culture and the Development of Everyday Social Explanation," *Journal of Personality and Social Psychology* 46 (1984): 961–978; J. G. Miller and D. M. Bersoff, "Culture and Moral Judgement: How Are Conflicts Between Justice and Friendship Resolved?" *Journal of Personality and Social Psychology* 62 (1992): 541–554; J. G. Miller, D. M. Bersoff, and R. L. Harwood, "Perceptions of 'Social Responsibility' in India and in the United States: Moral Imperatives or Personal Decisions?" *Journal of Personality and Social Psychology* 58 (1990): 33–47; F. M. Moghaddam, *Social Psychology: Exploring Universals Across Cultures* (San Francisco: W. H. Freeman, 1998); R. A. Schweder and E. J. Bourne, "Does the Concept of the Person Vary Cross-Culturally?" In *Culture Theory: Essays on Mind, Self, and Emotion*, ed. R. A. Schweder and E. J. Bourne (Cambridge: Cambridge University Press, 1984), pp. 1–24.

19. S. Smith, and G. Whitehead, "Attributions for Promotion and Demotion in the United States and India," *The Journal of Social Psychology* 124 (1984): 27–34.

20. L. D. Ross, "The Intuitive Psychologist and His Shortcomings: Distortions in the Attribution Process." In *Advances in Experimental Social Psychology* (Vol. 10), ed. L. Berkowitz (New York: Academic Press, 1977).

21. N. J. Finkel, and J. L. Groscup, "When Mistakes Happen: Commonsense Rules of Culpability," *Psychology, Public Policy, and Law* 3 (1997): 1.

22. Moghaddam, *Social Psychology: Exploring Universals Across Cultures.*
23. Finkel and Groscup, "When Mistakes Happen," 1.
24. Hofstede, *Culture's Consequences.*
25. Tyler, Lind, and Huo, "Cultural Values and Authority Relations."
26. *See, e.g.,* Kidder and Muller, "What Is 'Fair' in Japan?"
27. Y. Takeuchi, *Nihon no meritokurashi: Kozo to shinsho* [Japan's meritocracy: structure and mentality] (Tokyo: Tokyo Daigaku Shuppankai, 1995).
28. A. P. Fiske, *Structures of Social Life: The Four Elementary Forms of Human Relations* (New York: Free Press, 1991).
29. *Id.*, p. 42.
30. *Id.*
31. *Id.*

14

FUKOHEI: COMMONSENSE
UNFAIRNESS IN JAPAN

In doing cross-cultural research, Japan[1] is an ideal contrast to the United States, both for its differences and similarities. The differences are most evident in its social structure, traditions, religion, language, geography, resources, and history. Specifically, Japan has been characterized as a "collectivistic" society, in which concern for the group takes precedence over that for the individual; this contrasts with the United States, which is viewed as "individualistic" in its social structure, where personal autonomy and self-realization are given priority over group goals.[2] The religio-philosophical underpinnings of Japanese culture, which derive from Buddhist and Confucian teachings, are quite distinct from the American culture's underpinnings, which are solidly rooted in the Judeo–Christian tradition. The sociopolitical history of Japan has featured castes, shoguns, and emperors, with democracy taking root only late in the twentieth century, and this notably contrasts with that of the United States. In terms of language, Japanese and English share no significant linguistic roots. Historically a rice-based agricultural country, Japan has a dearth of natural resources—an island nation plagued by earthquakes, volcanoes, typhoons, and tsunamis. The United States, by contrast, is a huge, resource-rich country bridging two oceans with a variety of climates and a long history of industrialization. In sum, these differences are numerous and sizable, and were we to make predictions from just these differences, we would predict very different views on unfairness in the two countries.

These differences notwithstanding, there are also similarities. Japan and the United States are comparable in terms of technology, education, and standard of living. The commerce between the two countries—in terms of the flow of dollars and yen, material goods, technology, education, travel and tourism, and more—is vast. Focusing on modern-day Japan, a country where westernization and globalization have significantly closed the cultural gap between it and the United States, we might predict fewer unfairness differences between the two cultures. Putting the differences and similarities predictions together, we would expect to find both divergence and commonality in ideas of unfairness among members of the two cultures.

To test these predictions requires that we ask Japanese (as well as American) participants to detail their "But it's not fair!" instantiations, but here we face the language problem. As mentioned previously, Kidder and Muller put forth the arguable claim that there is no equivalent word for "fair" in Japanese.[3] We believe, to the contrary, that there is a word—*fukohei*—which is defined in the revised edition of the *Kenkyusha Japanese-English Dictionary* as "unfairness," "injustice," "partiality," as used in the phrase, "to treat (a person) unfairly" (*fukoheina shogu o suru*).[4]

OVERVIEW OF THE RESEARCH DESIGN

Using our familiar deconstructive and narrative approach, we now ask a new group of American participants and Japanese participants to give their instantiations of "But it's not fair!" The basic instruction booklet is the same, only now we have translated the instructions into Japanese for those participants. In addition to our two cultures, American (A) and Japanese (J), we also had two age groups within each culture, college students (S) and adults (A), the latter being the parents of the students, and thus we have four groups (AA, AS, JA, and JS).[5]

The central question is this: Will the Japanese types of unfairness be similar to or different from the American types? To test this question fairly, we could not simply translate the American schema into Japanese and have them use it, for Japanese coders might try to force their data into unfairness categories that may not truly subsume them, which would end up biasing the data and obscuring any unfairness categories that might be unique to that culture. Using such a coding strategy would almost guarantee a yes answer to our basic question, but it would likely be an invalid answer. Therefore, using a constructive approach, we asked our Japanese colleagues to develop their own schema for type of unfairness, much as we initially did, based on their reading of the unfairness instances from the Japanese participants.

After the Japanese schema was constructed, their data were then coded using that schema, whereas the American data were coded using our familiar schema for type. The next step was to translate each schema into the other's language, and then to perform a second, independent coding of the instances using the other culture's schema.

In the assessment phase, we first look for what we call "all-or-none" extremes. Are there types of unfairness that transcend the local cultures and appear in both schemas (the "all" cases), and are there types that were not found in the other's schema (the "none" cases)? Moving from the extremes to the distribution patterns for these unfairness types, to ask another question: Are there types of unfairness that are cited significantly more or less frequently in the two cultures?

We also evaluated the two type schemas to see which is the most reliable and inclusive. For example, would one schema have a much higher proportion of instances in the miscellaneous category or would the categories in one schema be too broad or too narrow, creating reliability problems? And bringing the quantitative measure into the mix (i.e., severity ratings), we assess whether these "But it's not fair!" instances turn out to be but the petty whine plaints of noisy narcissists or something more substantive and serious, as previous monocultural work with American participants indicate. Finally, we assess how severity relates to the type of unfairness between and across cultures.

RESULTS AND DISCUSSION

In the way they are organized, the Japanese schema has 19 categories, 18 specific categories and a miscellaneous category (see Appendix 14A), but no overarching major categories, whereas the American schema has 5 major categories, containing 8 specific subcategories and an additional miscellaneous category. In terms of content, what stands out dramatically in the Japanese schema is how many categories deal with discriminatory treatment: Categories 1 and 2 deal with gender, 4 and 5 with credentials and status, 6 and 7 with birth order and age, 3 with appearance, and 17 and 14 with race and media treatment of nonfavored groups or out groups. In the American schema, by contrast, there is one category (F) where unfair advantages or connections are rewarded (or irrelevant differences are punished). Multiple categories, though, may simply indicate that the American schema is broadly constructed, whereas the Japanese schema is overly specific.[6]

Continuing with the other Japanese categories, we find a correspondence with many categories in the American schema. For the Japanese category dealing with "innate ability unrelated to effort" (11), this relates to both "no work is rewarded" (A) and "hard work is not rewarded"

(B) in the American schema. For the Japanese category dealing with "getting ahead by shrewdness" (12), this seems to closely correspond to "wrongful behavior is rewarded or not punished" (C). Categories involving luck (13) and illness (18) relate to "when innocence is punished" (D) in the American schema.

On the other hand, there are also categories in the American schema that appear to have no Japanese counterparts, at least by title. For example, we see no Japanese category dealing explicitly with "punishment being disproportionate or excessive to the act and intent" (E) and no category dealing explicitly with "equal or nondiscriminatory treatment resulting when it should be individualized" (G). But cautions must be noted regarding these two categories. In the earlier studies with Americans, the citings in categories E and G tend to be quite low, so if there is a difference between cultures it is apt to be a small difference. But there may be no difference at all or a difference that is larger for the Japanese, because these types of unfairnesses may be incorporated in the Japanese schema under headings that obscure them.

Another American category with no Japanese counterpart, this one widely used, is the "arbitrary rules, lack of due process" (H) category; here again, though, the caution mentioned earlier applies: Japanese categories that sound outcome-focused may be containing process unfairnesses, because we found that American participants do make subtle and complex outcome and process distinctions and sometimes conflate both. If the Japanese do likewise, then our initial analysis, based simply on a comparison of the titles of categories, may not be fine grained enough to pick up subtler distinctions. We next turn to percentages of instances falling within the specific categories for the American and Japanese schemas to provide greater clarity.

Frequency and Distribution Patterns

Our 542 participants generated 2073 instances of unfairness, for a mean of 3.8 per participant, which obscures sizable variance between American and Japanese groups and between students and adults. To explicate, although the Americans represented only 29% of the total sample, they generated 61% of the unfairnesses: 1262 instances ($M = 8.0$) compared to 811 instances for the Japanese group ($N = 385$, $M = 2.1$). In addition, within the American group, the means for the students and adults were quite different, 12.0 and 4.0, respectively, whereas the student and adult means for the Japanese were close, 2.0 and 2.2, respectively.

There is a caution to be noted: From these mean differences, we cannot conclude that Americans are seeing unfairnesses at much higher rates than the Japanese. There are at least two other possibilities that might account for these differences. First, our Japanese counterparts may have inadvertently limited the number of unfairnesses in their presentation of the booklets and instructions to the Japanese participants, such that this methodological artifact might account for their lower number.[7] Second, there is the possibility that Japanese participants do in fact see as many unfairnesses as Americans, but culturally they may be less forthcoming about them. Thus a methodological artifact or a cultural factor acting to suppress, or both, may be operating, rather than a true cultural difference in perceiving unfairnesses.

We turn now to the distribution of unfairness instances across the categories of the two schemas for the American and Japanese groups. Table 14-1 presents the number and percentage of instances in the specific categories for the American schema, for the participants' first and second unfairness instantiations,[8] for the two cultures. There is a highly significant difference by culture in the overall distribution pattern.[9] Looking at some of the specific categories, the American sample's percentage of "when innocence is punished" (D) cases is 10 times greater than the Japanese; category D, to recall, includes cases where human agents deliver the punishment as well as misfortune cases, where life or nature seem to deliver the blow. Three other categories find the American percentages significantly higher than the Japanese: "when hard work is not rewarded" (B), "when wrongful behavior is rewarded or not punished" (C), and for "excessive punishment" (E).

Looking at categories where the Japanese sample dominates, the first is the "differential or discriminatory treatment" (F) category, which contains approximately 60% of all the Japanese unfairnesses and which is three times higher than the American sample. At a much lower level is the "lack

TABLE 14-1
Number (and Percentage) of American and Japanese Citings for the Specific Unfairness Categories in the American Schema, for Their First and Second Unfairness Instantiation

Specific Categories	American[a]				Japanese			
	1[b]		2		1		2	
	n	(%)	n	(%)	n	(%)	n	(%)
A. No work is rewarded	8	(4)	11	(6)	26	(7)	10	(4)
B. Hard work not rewarded	28	(14)	26	(14)	13	(3)	11	(4)
C. Wrongful behavior	22	(11)	22	(12)	15	(4)	4	(1)
D. Innocence is punished	64	(33)	52	(27)	9	(2)	7	(3)
E. Excessive punishment	5	(3)	10	(5)	0	(0)	3	(1)
F. Unfair advantages	40	(21)	36	(19)	232	(60)	172	(62)
G. Equal treatment	3	(2)	6	(3)	29	(8)	27	(10)
H. Lack of due process	17	(9)	16	(8)	46	(12)	33	(12)
I. Miscellaneous	8	(4)	10	(5)	15	(4)	11	(4)

[a] The American vs. Japanese distribution pattern is significantly different.
[b] There was no significant difference in the pattern from the first to the second instance.

of due process, arbitrary rules" (H) cases, where the Japanese are somewhat higher.[10]

For the Japanese schema (see Table 14-2),[11] the cultural difference is again highly significant.[12] We see numerous differences in the discriminatory categories, such as male dominated (1), female dominated (2), appearance (3), academic credentials (4), status/social class (5), sibling/birth order (6), preferential attitudes (8), and political/international (16), where in all of these categories the Japanese percentages exceed the American percentages. On the other side, the American percentages exceed the Japanese in discriminatory categories relating to differences in wealth (9), innate ability unrelated to effort (11), luck (13), interpersonal relations (15), race (17), and illness (18). It does appear, then, that the Japanese are more focused on discriminatory treatment when human agents (or society) deliver the unfairness, whereas the Americans focus more on the unfairness of luck, misfortunes, or the fortunes or misfortunes of inheritance. Finally, we see a huge difference in the miscellaneous category, indicating that the American raters had difficulty finding the specific category to best contain many American unfairnesses within the Japanese schema.

Looking at the two schemas, the "miscellaneous" finding is one sign that the Japanese schema was less inclusive than the American. Moreover,

TABLE 14-2

Number (and Percentage) of American and Japanese Citings for the Specific Unfairness Categories in the Japanese Schema, Summed Across Their First and Second Instantiations

Specific Categories	American[a]		Japanese	
	n	(%)	n	(%)
1. Males dominant	15	(4)	134	(20)
2. Females dominant	3	(1)	19	(3)
3. Appearance	3	(1)	21	(3)
4. Academic credentials	7	(2)	36	(5)
5. Status/social class	13	(3)	79	(12)
6. Siblings/birth order	10	(3)	33	(5)
7. Age differences	10	(3)	24	(4)
8. Preferential attitudes	18	(5)	53	(8)
9. Wealth differences	16	(4)	14	(2)
10. Environmental differences	9	(2)	21	(3)
11. Innate ability	26	(7)	15	(2)
12. Shrewdness	22	(6)	47	(7)
13. Luck	45	(12)	25	(4)
14. Newsworthy discrimination	0	(0)	22	(3)
15. Interpersonal relations	45	(12)	27	(4)
16. Political/international	23	(6)	48	(7)
17. Race	20	(5)	4	(1)
18. Illness	30	(8)	3	(1)
19. Miscellaneous	71	(18)	38	(6)

[a] The American vs. Japanese distribution pattern is significantly different.

once we set "miscellaneous" aside, there were seven low-frequency categories (i.e., less than 4%) in the Japanese schema, whereas there was only one low-frequency category (E) in the American schema. Although these two schemas are significantly related, the low-frequency cells precluded running a test on the joint distributions, and we wanted to do this. Using broader categories, we could defensibly combine categories that were conceptually and statistically related: By combining categories and eliminating the miscellaneous category, the American schema reduced to five major categories, whereas the Japanese reduced to seven major categories.

Table 14-3 shows the unfairness percentages by major category when using both American and Japanese revised schemas, when each instance is jointly categorized. Overall, the two schemas are significantly related.[13] Some specifics illustrate the degree of agreement. For example, an unfairness coded as "discrimination" in the Japanese schema (1) will find that same category in the American schema (F + G) 84.7% of the time, although 6.7% of the time it is seen as a lack-of-due-process claim (H). A claim of "innate ability unrelated to effort" (11) in the Japanese schema is seen as "no work is rewarded" (A) in the American schema 74% of the time, yet it can also be seen as discrimination (F + G) as well (17%). Although the dominant conjoining categories are evident in Table 14-3, we also see evidence that members of the two cultures view similar instances of unfairnesses from differing perspectives at times.

Cross-Cultural, Age, and Gender-Related Differences

Returning to the cross-cultural findings, we broke our sample into four groups: American adults (AA), American students (AS), Japanese adults (JA), and Japanese students (JS), and compared their unfairness distributions overall (see Table 14-4). We also tested American versus Jap-

TABLE 14-3
The Percentages for the Unfairness Instances, as the Instances Are Categorized Into the Major Categories in Both the Japanese and American Schemas

	American Categories				
Japan Categories	A + B	C	D + E	F + G	H
1. Discrimination (1, 2, 3, 4, 5, 6, 7, 14, 17)	4.3	2.4	2.0	84.7	6.7
8. Preferential (8, 9, 10)	13.5	5.4	13.5	48.7	18.9
11. Innate ability	73.9	4.4	0.0	17.4	4.4
12. Shrewdness	50.0	17.7	14.7	11.8	5.9
13. Luck (13, 18)	6.0	6.0	76.0	6.0	6.0
15. Interpersonal	17.9	7.1	10.7	46.4	17.9
16. Political	2.7	16.2	13.5	51.4	16.2

Note: The former specific categories, from Tables 14-1 and 14-2, are given in parentheses.

TABLE 14-4
Number (and Percentage) of First Unfairness Instances, by Major Category
of the American Schema, for the American Adult (AA) and Student (AS),
and Japanese Adult (JA) and Student (JS) Participant Groups

| Participant Groups[a] | American Categories | | | | | | | | | | Total |
| | A + B | | C | | D + E | | F + G | | H | | |
	n	(%)	n	(%)	n	(%)	n	(%)	n	(%)	n
AA	12	(16)	12	(16)	29	(39)	13	(18)	8	(11)	74
AS	24	(21)	10	(9)	40	(35)	30	(27)	9	(8)	113
American totals	36	(19)	22	(12)	69	(37)	43	(23)	17	(9)	187
JA	21	(12)	7	(4)	3	(2)	124	(70)	22	(12)	177
JS	18	(9)	8	(4)	6	(3)	137	(71)	24	(12)	193
Japanese totals	39	(11)	15	(4)	9	(2)	261	(71)	46	(12)	370
Adult totals	33	(13)	19	(8)	32	(13)	137	(55)	30	(12)	251
Student totals	42	(14)	18	(6)	46	(15)	167	(55)	33	(11)	306

[a] There was a significant difference between American versus Japanese patterns, but not between student versus adult overall, nor between student versus adult within culture.
Note: The percentages are calculated row-wise.

anese and adult versus student comparisons. When we compared the four groups, this overall comparison showed a significant difference among them.[14] More finely, the American versus Japanese comparison was significantly different,[15] but not the adult versus student comparison.[16] The American groups clearly dominate in the "innocence punished and disproportionate punishment" category (D + E), as well as the "reward to effort" (A + B) and "wrongful behavior going unpunished" (C) categories, whereas the Japanese clearly dominate in the discriminatory treatment (F + G) category and, to a much lesser extent, in the "lack of due process" (H) category. Although the adult versus student comparison was nonsignificant overall, we do note the wider discrepancy between American students and adults, as opposed to their Japanese counterparts, who are quite consistent (see Table 14-4).

Finally, we also tested for gender effects, and these were only marginally significant.[17] Females gave more unfairness instances in "discriminatory treatment" (F), whereas males exceeded females in the categories relating "rewards and punishments to effort" (A, B, C) and in "due process" (H), with no difference in "innocence punished" (D). These findings replicate earlier work with the American samples, yet there seems to be a cross-cultural difference in degree: The gender difference is larger in the Japanese sample, showing that Japanese women cite gender inequities even more frequently than American women, and that difference is largely the result of the Japanese students, who cite gender inequities more than their parents do and more than the American students do.

Severity Ratings—Substantive Claims and Not Petty Whines

Severity is our quantitative variable, and we believe it is a measure of participants' anger and outrage over instances at the upper end of the scale; when at the very low end of the scale, however, it may reflect questionable unfairnesses or petty whines. We tested the severity ratings for the five major type categories,[18] cultural groups (AA + AS versus, JA + JS) and student/adult groups (AS + JS versus AA + JA), and found a significant main effect only for type.[19]

For the main effect for type (see Table 14-5), category D + E, which contains "the innocent being punished" cases, is rated highest in severity, and significantly higher than "reward to effort" (A + B), "discriminatory treatment" (F + G), and "lack of due process" (H), with category C, "wrongful behavior rewarded or unpunished," falling in between. The Japanese participants, like the Americans, do not just focus on instances where they were the victims of the unfairness, for others they know and others they do not know, taken together, make up the majority. Overall, the mean severity ratings are fairly high, falling in the high-to-severe range, and this is so for both the American and Japanese raters. Thus, hypotheses suggesting that petty whines and narcissistic themes dominate are not supported by the type and severity data.

Regarding interaction effects, if we focus on the A + B major category dealing with "reward to effort" inequities, it is the JA group who regard these as less severe, whereas JS, AS, and AA groups are angrier about these unfairnesses. For category C, "wrongful behavior rewarded or

TABLE 14-5
The Mean Severity Ratings (M) and Standard Deviations (SD) by Major Categories for Cultural Groups (American Adults (AA) and Students (AS), and Japanese Adults (JA) and Students (JS))

Cultural Groups[a]	A + B M	(SD)	C M	(SD)	D + E M	(SD)	F + G M	(SD)	H M	(SD)	Across Categories M
AA	69.2	(17)	65.2	(32)	79.8	(28)	53.7	(33)	61.1	(28)	65.8
AS	65.9	(20)	65.3	(27)	84.6	(13)	62.1	(25)	36.6	(23)	62.9
American means	67.5		65.2		82.2		57.9		48.9		64.3
JA	48.4	(29)	55.4	(29)	83.0	(20)	69.1	(26)	69.7	(23)	65.1
JS	75.9	(24)	79.5	(19)	67.7	(29)	69.5	(26)	64.8	(31)	71.5
Japanese means	62.1		67.5		75.3		69.3		67.2		68.3
Means by category	64.8		66.3		78.7		63.6		58.1		66.4
Adult totals	58.8		61.6		80.1		67.6		67.3		65.5
Student totals	70.9		71.6		82.3		68.2		57.7		67.2

[a] Regarding main effects, there is a significant difference by type of unfairness, but culture and age comparisons are not significant. Regarding interactions, the type × culture, type × age, and type × culture × age effects are significant.

unpunished," it is the JS group that is most incensed, JA least incensed, and the American groups (AA and AS) falling in between these extremes with near-identical ratings. For the "innocence punished" (D + E) cases, the JA group is more incensed about these than any other type, and the American groups are also angry, although the Japanese students are significantly less so. Moving to the "discrimination" cases, the two Japanese groups are highest and near-identical in their ratings, but the Americans are less so, particularly the AA group. Finally, for the "lack of due process" (H) cases, it is the AS group that is much less concerned, whereas AA, JA, and JS are significantly higher.

In sum, for certain type categories, there are Japanese versus American differences, and student versus adult differences within the specific culture, which account for the significant type × cultural group interaction effect. For the Americans, categories A + B, C, and D + E produce near-identical ratings across the generations, whereas categories F + G and H produce disparities. For the Japanese it is the reverse.

Slight Differences

The data from the Japanese participants indicate that unfairnesses are clearly in mind, as instantiations come readily when they are asked to detail them. Although we cannot say for sure why the Japanese offered fewer instances than Americans, our best guess is that the willingness to be forthcoming is the major factor—a guess supported by the extensive range of type categories in the Japanese schema and the severity ratings for those instances cited. Despite these frequency differences, there is ample qualitative and quantitative evidence to conclude that unfairness per se transcends the American boundary and crisscrosses Japan as well.

However, we were interested in much more than whether the overall concept is present. We wanted to know whether the types of unfairness would be different by culture. We found such differences, but they were more in degree than in kind: Japanese and Americans perceive the same major categories of unfairness, but their salience differs by culture. In the first major category of "reward to effort" disparities, the Japanese cite "no work rewarded" (A) slightly more than Americans, but Americans cite "hard work not rewarded" (B) much more than the Japanese. Thus, one aspect of the "work ethic" or the just-world view—that hard work (and only hard work) ought to be rewarded—is endorsed more so by Americans. Yet there is a qualifier: The Japanese students (JS) align more closely with the American students (AS) and adults (AA), whereas the Japanese adults (JA) seem more reconciled (and possibly accepting) that efforts do not always lead to rewards. This large gap between Japanese students and their parents is supported by the severity data, where the JA group's ratings are significantly lower than the other three groups (JS, AS, AA), indicating less anger over this type of unfairness.

The second major category, "when wrongful behavior is rewarded or unpunished" (C), is cited by Americans more than twice as frequently as by Japanese, and it is the AA group that cites it the most, with AS second. However, when we add the quantitative severity ratings to the mix, the picture changes: When this category is cited, it is the JS group that is most incensed, whereas the JA group is least, and here we see the widest disparity between Japanese students and their parents, but close accord for the American students and parents. If we put the results from our first two major categories together under the light of either equity or just-world theories, it would seem that the AS, AA, and JS groups are close in their categorical judgments and quantitative ratings, and when they do part over wrongful behavior (C), the JS group is the angriest about these inequities or just-world failures. For our first two major categories, then, we see a split within the Japanese participants along generational lines.[20]

BIG DIFFERENCES

When we get to the third major category of "when innocence is punished" (D + E), a cultural chasm shows: Americans cite this category more than 10 times as frequently. This difference is vast, far greater than anything we have seen in all the studies with American participants, whatever their age. But when we move from these qualitative frequencies to the quantitative severity ratings, we find that when this category is cited, the JA, AA, and AS groups are similarly incensed, whereas JS is significantly lower. Thus, in terms of severity, it is not simply a Japanese versus American difference, because the Japanese participants split along age lines, with the older participants aligning more with the Americans than they do with their children.

What might account for the huge frequency difference between Americans and the Japanese, and for the severity ratings difference between the JA, AA, and AS groups, on the one hand, and the JS group on the other? It is possible that the differences result from a fact we documented earlier: that the major category of "when innocence is punished" contains two distinct types of cases—misfortunes cases, where life and nature are blamed, and injustice cases, where human agents deliver the blow. The data clearly show a cultural split here: The Japanese are far less inclined than Americans to call misfortune or bad luck an unfairness, but there is no such hesitancy when human agents inflict the suffering. This finding might explain the huge difference, in part.[21]

The fourth major category involving discriminatory treatment also shows an extraordinarily wide cultural gap—this time going in the opposite direction, The Japanese participants cite such instances much more than the Americans, by at least a 3:1 ratio. Another indicator of a cultural gap here is the number of discriminations within the "discriminatory treatment" category found in the Japanese schema. There is also evidence of a gender gap, as Japanese women cite this category significantly more than the Japanese men and significantly more than the American women. Thus despite values of "collectivism" and *wa* (harmony) in the Japanese society, both of which may act to enjoin criticism on the social and interpersonal levels, we find that discriminatory unfairness claims boil beneath this surface. These claims are not only hot, but extensive, more so for Japanese women and particularly so for the younger women.

On the other side, there are specific discriminatory treatment categories where the American ratios exceed the Japanese, and these occur for inherited wealth, innate abilities, and race. Race, inherited wealth, and innate abilities are similar to "misfortunes," in that they are given at the start of life and are in no sense earned. Americans are angrier about factors that unlevel the playing field from the beginning of life. In more familiar terms, but with a spin our founding fathers might not have endorsed, American participants decry the fact that "all men and women are not created equal" at the start.

The Japanese, on the other hand, are far more upset when people, parents, superiors, society, and the culture discriminate by using "impermissible" factors. For instance, if a parent gives a reward to the oldest child simply because the child is the oldest or when a company promotes a worker because of family connections, these bases violate the meritocratic expectations on which those rewards in the Japanese society are supposedly given.[22]

This "discriminatory treatment" category, when severity is examined, unites JA and JS groups, who give near-identical ratings; however, for the Americans, the rating given by the AS group is lower than it is for both Japanese groups, and the rating given by the AA group is much lower. Perhaps the Japanese groups' ratings are higher because of the collectivistic nature of interpersonal relations, where discriminatory treatment would be conspicuously chafing to their sensibilities, be they young or old. The Americans' ratings may be lower because Americans see less discrimination, or less severe discrimination, than their Japanese counterparts. The ratings given by American parents may be lowest because they have seen the strides that have been made in this society to lessen discriminatory treatment.

Our fifth and final category deals with due process. Although that clause is embedded in the Fourteenth Amendment to the Constitution of the United States, it is the Japanese who cite these claims more frequently. Yet the bigger cultural divide occurs on the severity ratings, where the JA group is highest, followed by JS and AA, while the AS group is by far the lowest. This finding may indicate that the "outcome bias" seen in our American studies and experiments may be a good bit less for the Japanese. Moreover, as the parents of both cultural groups have the highest ratings, perhaps process sensitivity grows with age.

Methodologically, although our samples are neither large nor truly representative, more than 2000 instances of unfairness is no small number from which to deconstruct unfairness notions. What is more, by having students and their parents as age groups within each cultural group, we do control, to a fair degree, for socioeconomic disparities within the culture and, to some extent, between cultures, as they are like groups; similarly, we control for religious disparities within the culture as well. When viewed broadly, these findings indicate that "unfairness" is centrally situated in mind and within these cultures, although what is accented bears a local coloration.

Unfairness Beneath Collectivism

There were some unexpected findings, one of which occurs around the cultural value dimension of "individualism versus collectivism." This dimension might predict that the Japanese would keep silent about certain forms of discriminatory treatment and lack of due process if the collective and harmony were strengthened by silence. Although they may not complain outright about these forms of discrimination, our data clearly indicate that the Japanese do in fact perceive such unfairnesses. Moreover, many judge these instances of discriminatory treatment to be not merely unfair, but severely so. Given the emphasis on interpersonal harmony and cooperation instilled in collectivistic cultures like Japan, it is reasonable that discriminatory treatment by some members of the collective toward others would be particularly offensive.

We interpret these findings through a geological analogy. The cultural value dimension of collectivism can be viewed as a strata that acts to press down discontent. But beneath that strata is an irrepressible sense of unfairness, which is fueled in part by the surface's collectivism that promises equity for some decisions and nondiscriminatory equality treatment for other decisions and in part by the very primacy of unfairness itself—as both act together to break through. What we see is that the surface value dimension is neither strong enough to mask the unfairness claims, nor is it strong enough to bury them.

On the American side, two different issues are visible. One involves the first two major categories, where Americans want hard work to pay off, the slackers not to profit, and the wrongful to get their just desserts.[23] Whether this is merely a just-world view, an equity view, or something quite different is debatable; however characterized, this fairness principle acts as a persistent push and an insistent expectation—which rises to the level of an obligation and duty—that individuals be fair in their outcome and process determinations. The expectation extends beyond individuals to those elected or selected leaders of our society and its institutions, for we want society to get it right, and our anger at society generally rises higher than it does for individuals. Moreover, that anger grows as participants change from AS to AA, so that if our anger stems from overly idealistic or naive fairness notions, we see no evidence for that, for it does not dissipate with age.[24]

The second issue, more striking than the first, emerges from the "innocence punished" (D) cases, where Americans cite this category 10 times more frequently than the Japanese. When we factor out those instances where human agents bear the blame, we are left with a considerable number of misfortune cases, where nature, life, and even God is blamed and about which Americans are angriest. By contrast, the Japanese see these misfortunes as bad luck, much more a part of life, and certainly not the stuff that warrants the most anger.

Misfortune cases present Americans with a much tougher situation to cope with than cases of hard work not paying off: For the latter, we can take our complaints to *someone* in some *venue* most of the time, although whether anyone listens and responds is another matter. However, for misfortunes, we modern-day Jobs have the biblical Job's problem: "But I want to speak before God, to present my case in God's court . . . for I have prepared my defense, and I know that I am right."[25] To which courtroom do we go, and to whom do we speak, when we want to complain about what we have inherited or have not, or the calamities that nature inflicts, or the illnesses, sufferings, and traumas that life brings, or what the transcendent God may do for a bet?

Although these first and second issues seem very different, there may be an underlying common theme uniting both. Americans, in particular, seem to want to take randomness and error variance out of the game of life, not only when human agents deliver the unfairness blows (as the Japanese similarly feel), but when life, nature, heredity, and God appear to deliver the blows, and on this latter count the American and Japanese participants part company.

Yet we can question whether this latter fairness wish of Americans is Peter Pan-ish—an overly idealistic, naive, or even childish view. That characterization may be too negative and even off the mark, because other areas of inquiry suggest a more positive portrayal. For example, in the medical sciences, there are those who seek to understand all the genes and their workings, ultimately to correct illnesses, disorders, disabilities, and defects from birth in order to tame if not correct heredity. In the natural sciences, there are those in meteorology and geology who seek to understand weather, hurricanes, tornadoes, earthquakes, lightning, and volcanoes to better predict if not control some of nature's unfairnesses. Then there is the phenomenon of physicists becoming cosmologists and sounding like theologians as they seek the origins of the universe and life, as they listen "in at God's keyhole."[26] Our American participants may suffer from no greater delusions of grandeur, or be any more idealistic, naive, or childish, than other Americans with Nobel laureates to their credit and federal grants supporting this quest.

Still, on the pragmatic level, misfortune cases are the hardest to resolve (i.e., as the category's highest severity ratings suggest), for the opponent who delivers the blow, though nameable, does not enter our debate or courtroom. At this point in our cross-cultural research endeavors, we have no outcome data as to whether our Japanese participants' way of relegating bad luck to a different ontological status, and then trying to align with luck, works any better than the American take on the problem.

LOOKING BACKWARD, LOOKING FORWARD

In looking back, we see that the sense of unfairness runs deep and across the two cultures examined here and is foundational for what is built above. Some types of unfairness may yet turn out to be universal, but much research still remains before that conclusion is placed on solid footing. Still, the differentiations, shadings, nuances, and local colorations to the basic construct of unfairness are clearer now, as are the commonalities; in regard to the latter, the vast majority of type categories appear in both cultures, suggesting the possibility that they may be universal, although much more cross-cultural research needs to be done before that suggestion can be stated as a conclusion. Moreover, this research suggests that some value dimensions may not be bedrock, for they too may rest uneasily on the sense of unfairness. If unfairness is ubiquitous and foundational, as we believe our findings suggest, then its primacy and power can break through the surface strata where societal and cultural value dimensions act as a weak suppressing force. In our work, to recall a simple cue—to detail their instances of "But it's not fair!"—was more than enough to trigger the eruption.

APPENDIX 14A

THE JAPANESE SCHEMA FOR TYPES OF UNFAIRNESS

1. Males and Females—Males Dominant (e.g., when looking for a job, there are few positions for women; only women do housework; curfew for women is stricter than that for men). In this category, be it in work opportunities, in the type of work, or in certain social freedoms, women are more restricted while men are freer, having wider opportunity. Gender discrimination is clearly the complaint.

2. Males and Females—Females Dominant (e.g., physical labor is given to men; in driving to school, women are treated leniently, but men strictly; in the same class, women who come late don't get scolded, whereas men do). In this category, women are given "breaks" that men don't enjoy. Gender discrimination is again the complaint.

3. Appearance (e.g., women who are cute or beautiful are flattered; when shopping in a store, the clerk's attitude depends on your appearance; your job depends on your height, weight, etc.). "Appearance" is seen as an impermissible (unfair) criterion for basing work decisions, customer relations, and social behavior on.

4. Academic Credentials Over Competence (e.g., if you graduate from a top university, you can get a good job; your salary depends on academic credentials when it should depend on competency; during tutoring in the home, you're treated better if you're from Ehime University than if you're from Matsuyama University). This complaint finds the wrong factor (i.e., credential) determining success and treatment when competency should be the factor.

5. Status/Social Class determines rewards and treatment (e.g., you're in a traffic accident and the other person is clearly wrong, but he happens to be a relative of a local politician, so the case is dismissed; the existence of the emperor). Again, status and class are creating disparate treatment, when they should not.

6. Siblings and Birth Order (e.g., only older brother or sister gets a lot of pocket money; only the oldest male or female has to be patient; the oldest child has more pictures of himself or herself). Here we have discriminatory treatment by birth order, where the complaint asks for equal treatment.

7. Age Discrimination (e.g., if you're in a club and you're younger, the junior members are made to do all the work; if you're older, you can't accept certain part-time jobs; you have to be 20-years-old to smoke or drink alcohol). Discriminatory treatment by age, and arbitrary age lines that restrict, are the complaint.

8. Preferential Attitudes of Teachers, Schools, and Parents to Smart Children (e.g., smart children get called on; two students do the same

thing, but the better student doesn't get scolded; good students are allowed to have their ears pierced and wear makeup). Here, discriminatory favoritism is at work, where complainants feel the basis for it is unwarranted.

9. Differences in Wealth (e.g., if you're born into a rich family, you can do many things; my family was poor, and even though I wanted to go onto higher education, I could not; the sales tax is taken out despite what you make). Opportunities are not equal because of wealth differences at birth, and taxes are not proportional to wealth, creating further disadvantages.

10. Differences in Environments (e.g., there is no pool in the elementary school; compared to the city, the country has fewer events; there's a water cooler in the economics department but none in the psychology department). The complaint argues for equalism in differing life spaces.

11. Innate Ability Unrelated to Effort (e.g., even though you study the same amount, you can't measure up to someone who is bright; in archery, even though you practice the same amount, the results are different; some try hard and can't do it, whereas others don't try hard, but can). The complaint here argues for an even starting line, where inherited advantages do not dictate results.

12. Getting Ahead by Shrewdness (e.g., a person doesn't go to class, a friend turns in attendance sheet to teacher, teacher thinks the person is in class, person copies friend's report, person passes course; when you go to play, the other kids make you "manager" so you play only a little; even if a person cheats on a test, if it is not discovered, the person gets away with it). That wrongful behavior gets rewarded or goes unpunished is the complaint.

13. Luck (e.g., in the lottery, some people win, others don't; when you're driving over the speed limit, you get stopped and ticketed, while other cars passing you and going even faster don't get stopped; children can't choose their parents). The element of randomness, no choice, or fate seems to be the complaint.

14. How News Is Treated in the Media (e.g., games of popular baseball teams are broadcast on TV; only special groups are reported on; weak people are persecuted). The complaint argues that the media ought to be fair and equal in its reporting.

15. Rules for Interpersonal Relationships (e.g., even if someone does something that is blameworthy, if they are your close friend, you cannot criticize them). Certain social rules or rules of custom restrict honest expression, and this is unfair.

16. Political and International unfairnesses (no examples given).

17. Race Discrimination (e.g., discrimination toward Koreans). Using race to base decisions or treatment on is unfair.

18. Illnesses Without Fault (e.g., people who contract AIDS through blood products are discriminated against). There is a twice-suffering here,

the second time from people and society when there was no culpability for the illness.

19. Miscellaneous.

ENDNOTES

1. I would like to acknowledge my coauthors on this work, David S. Crystal, from Georgetown University, and Hirozumi Watanabe, from Ehime University, Japan.
2. C. Kagitcibashi and J. W. Berry, "Cross-Cultural Psychology: Current Research and Trends," *Annual Review of Psychology* 40 (1989): 493–531.
3. L. H. Kidder and S. Muller, "What Is 'Fair' in Japan?" In *Social Justice in Human Relations (Vol. 2): Societal and Psychological Consequences of Justice and Injustice*, ed. H. Steensma and R. Vermunt (New York: Plenum Press, 1991), pp. 139–154.
4. K. Masuda, *Kenkyusha's Japanese-English Dictionary*, rev. ed. (Tokyo: Kenkyusha, 1987).
5. Overall, there were 542 participants in this study, with 157 being American and 385 being Japanese. The American breakdown by student (AS) versus adult (AA) was 80 students (57 females, 23 males) and 77 adults (45 females, 32 males), and the Japanese breakdown (JS versus JA) was 200 students (100 females, 100 males) and 185 adults (139 females, 46 males). The mean ages of our groups were quite comparable: For the students, the means for the Americans and Japanese were 20.2 and 19.5, respectively, and for the American and Japanese adults, they were 47.9 and 46.3, respectively. The student and adult groups were not randomly drawn, but rather there was a strong relationship between them: The students in both cultures recruited their parents as the adult group members, and this allowed us to keep socioeconomic class and religious differences between the age groups from varying very much. By using the two age groups, we can compare whether cultural differences, if they do result, are uniform across age, or whether, for example, the cultural gap narrows for the younger groups.
6. The frequency data, which will come shortly, will show significant cultural differences rather than schema artifacts.
7. For the American data, however, where the method was consistent across adults and students and where these results replicate earlier findings, we are confident that the significant frequency difference is real rather than artifactual.
8. By presenting the first and second instantiations separately, rather than the totals, the American sample is not overrepresented because they gave a higher percentage of instances than the Japanese. We also compared the first and the second instantiations and found no pattern differences.
9. $X^2[df = 8] = 96.6, p < .001$.
10. The miscellaneous category, which contained about 4% of the items, a modest percentage, showed no difference by culture.

11. Because we found no significant differences between first and second instantiations, only the first instantiation is presented in this table.
12. $X^2[df = 18] = 114.7$, $p < .001$.
13. $X^2[df = 24] = 411.6$, $p < .001$, with a contingency coefficient = .67, and a phi coefficient = .906.
14. $X^2[df = 12] = 182.7$, $p < .001$.
15. $X^2[df = 4] = 176.2$, $p < .001$.
16. $X^2[df = 4] = 1.3$, $p = .86$, n.s.
17. $p = .095$.
18. These results were obtained sing an ANOVA test.
19. $F[4,522] = 3.06$, $p = .017$.
20. The Japanese students, far more than their parents, endorse the belief that equity or just-world principles should hold here. For these first two major categories, the American students and their parents align quite closely in their judgments and ratings because both endorse the belief quite strongly.
21. Unfortunately, we did not develop a Japanese blame categorization schema. Had we had one, we suspect that Japanese participants would blame nature, life, and heredity less so than Americans do, a prediction that would be in line with the notion that misfortune cases are regarded quite differently by the Japanese. We would further predict that the Japanese would blame God much less frequently than Americans, particularly for "innocence being punished" cases. This prediction would be in line with religious differences, which suggest differences toward the problem of theodicy: The Buddhist views about acceptance of misfortune and the extinction of desire are quite different from Judeo-Christian views and the Protestant ethic.
22. Y. Takeuchi, *Nihon no meritokurashi: Kozo to shinsho* [Japan's meritocracy: structure and mentality] (Tokyo: Tokyo Daigaku Shuppankai, 1995).
23. Previous blame results show that Americans are quite angry when those doing the rewarding and punishing are not on the job or are failing at their duty, because their role in a just world is to make equity theory work in practice and thus make this world fair. Although we did not test blame directly with our Japanese samples, the narratives from the JS group indicate that they too endorse this view, although the parents (JA) seem more tolerant (though very far from completely tolerant) of equity imperfections.
24. Our Japanese students (JS) appear to endorse this view at least as much if not more than the Americans, whereas their parents (JA) endorse it less so; where the Japanese parents' anger rises, along with expectations, is around fair due process.
25. S. Mitchell, *The Book of Job* (San Francisco: North Point Press, 1987), pp. 34–35.
26. *Id.*, p. 41.

15

NO ES JUSTO!
COMMONSENSE UNFAIRNESS
IN SPAIN

Under ordinary circumstances, life goes on without people paying much attention to the moral orders within which their lives unfold. We may go through an entire day, perhaps several days, without ever considering our notions of fairness or unfairness, justice or injustice, and on what principled basis we make such judgments and distinctions. This is the ordinary state of affairs.[1]

Crises may turn ordinary moments into extraordinary moments and may turn the light on what has been dark. In these extraordinary moments, we are apt to hear cries of unfairness—from news reports, acquaintances, or our own lips—and when we do hear it, we may reflect on the bases of these judgments, as to why we feel the way we do. In these introspective moments, we realize that unfairness notions, developed and prepotent, have been sprung, as a "But it's not fair!" pops out.

Introspection, though, as a method, takes us only so far. Introspection requires that we turn our attention inward, yet the processes we are trying to observe can be blocked by our own blinders and defenses or obscured by their unconscious nature. Even if we manage to overcome those formidable obstacles, what we may see may be solely, idiosyncratically our own, applicable to no one else. The particular introspecting person may be unique, or quirky, or an outlier, in many ways. These are severe restraints that handicap the introspective method. Our study method improves on a lone individual introspecting, for it tests numerous participants, of varying ages, repeated time after time, and now across cultures. In many ways, then, we know that our findings are not the result of one lone mind whose solipsistic introspections may match no one else's. Rather when thousands of instantiations are deconstructed, as they have been, consistent types emerge, and when viewed as a whole these findings illuminate some principled bases for our judgments.

PRINCIPLED AGREEMENTS AND DISAGREEMENTS

One such basis is equity. We consistently see that violations of the principle of equity underlie a wide range of "outcome unfairnesses" in the American studies, such as hard work not rewarded, no work rewarded, wrongful behavior rewarded or unpunished, and more. Moreover, through our cross-cultural work, we found equity to be a highly salient factor for Japanese students and their parents: In many of their type categorizations and in the large number of instantiations they cited, and in the severity scores they attached, this equity factor was even more salient to the Japanese than to the Americans.

In going back to our studies, process unfairnesses are of significant concern, particularly among the teenagers but not exclusively so. Using the experimental method that brought process to the fore, we further found that many college-age participants cited numerous process inequities. From our initial cross-cultural work, we found that many cite lack of due process unfairnesses (i.e., equitable processes), and these were cited even more frequently by the Japanese and even more so by the Japanese adults.

From our studies, the experiment on unfairnesses in three legal cases, and in the cross-cultural work, we find much evidence for fairness as equality. Recalling Weinreb's four distinct types of equality (see chapter 3)—equality before the law, equal humanity, equality of opportunity, and equality of result—we find all of these variations represented.[2] The Japanese participants chaffed at discriminatory treatment, which embraces all four of these equality aspects, whereas the Americans seemed to extend equality of opportunity and equal humanity into inheritance, be it of wealth or genes, that stack the deck at the outset.

To equitable outcomes and equitable processes as identifiable principles, we can add an array of "equality concerns," such as equal standing, equal humanity, equal processes, and equal outcomes. But our evidence also points to instances where these are mixed and not easily separable. This is particularly so in discriminatory treatment cases that mix outcome, process, standing, and basic humanity together, where impermissible factors intrude into the process and unfairly determine the outcome. In the cross-cultural work, we saw that both Americans and Japanese cry "unfair" about these instances, and the Japanese do so with far greater frequency.

Quite apart from the frequency differences that obtained among cultures and among age groups, there was basic agreement about what constitutes an unfairness: Both cultures, and all the ages we sampled, were in agreement that inequitable outcomes, inequitable processes, and discriminatory treatment (when it should be equal) cases, along with mixtures, were indeed instances of "But it's not fair!"

Our first sign of basic disagreement between cultures occurred in that subset of cases that fall within "innocence punished": The disagreement was over the "misfortune" cases, where nature, life, or God was blamed, with the Japanese much more likely to say "bad luck," whereas the Americans were ten times more likely to say "unfair."

In this chapter, we continue with our cross-cultural questions and research, comparing and contrasting American students with students from Madrid, Spain. As a country and a culture, the Spanish influence and involvement with the United States, in contrast to the relationship between the United States and Japan, spans a much longer period, with roots that are older, deeper, and broader. Beginning with Columbus's foothold in the new world, Spanish explorers planted their flag and cultural influence over territories that would eventually become part of the United States. In current times, where the Hispanic population is the fastest growing minority group in the United States and is predicted to constitute a majority in California sometime in the twenty-first century, that influence is considerable and enlarging. Spanish is not only the second language in this country, but a language that does share linguistic roots with English. As a "western" country, opposed to the "eastern" Japan, the history, literature, art, and politics of Spain share more in common with that of the United States. If we were to make a prediction about unfairness notions from these few facts, we might predict closer agreement between Spanish and American students than between Japanese and American students.

Predictions must be tested empirically, and to do so we will once again ask participants for their "But it's not fair!" instantiations. Their instantiations, in turn, will help us answer the following specific questions: Will we find that Spanish and American groups do cite similar instances? Will we find that these instances fall within the same type categories? If we do obtain such results, will we be able to reach the conclusion that these groups construct a similar public moral order, a principled edifice erected from the same cornerstones? But we also need to consider the possibility that the matter may not be so predictable. Perhaps we will see that the public moral orders of the United States and Spain depart in some *basic* ways and not simply in cultural colorations. Will we find, for example, type categories in the Spanish population that we do not see in the American population?

Though Absent a Word, Is There Yet a Concept?

We already cited the fact that there is no word-for-word translation of "But it's not *fair!*" in Spanish, and that roughly the same complaint is expressed as *"No es justo!"* which translated into English becomes, "It's not *just!*" But "roughly the same" is not necessarily "the same." On the one hand, maybe the Spanish say "not just" when Americans say "not fair," although both mean the same thing. On the other hand, maybe "just" is not the same as "fair" for the Spanish, such that assuming equivalence would be a mistake.[3] There is a third possibility, that "justo" is a polysemic word that has a number of meanings, one of which corresponds to "unfair" although other meanings do not, yet all meanings are conjoined and conflated in the one word?[4] The question we will put to the test, then, is whether *"no es justo!"* is polysemic, equivalent to, or divergent from, "but it's not fair!"

Our investigation begins with the now familiar study method, as we deconstruct the Spanish participants' unfairness instantiations. But here our analysis takes a different turn: In analyzing their narratives and their reasons for why this is *"no es justo!"* we will analyze in a more discursive and fine-grained way than before. In addition, we will use the experimental method, directly testing a set of the vignettes we used earlier, where now Spanish participants will make "injustice," "unfairness," and "misfortune" ratings. Using both qualitative (e.g., discursive) and quantitative (e.g., experimental) methods ought to give us a clearer read on whether the Spanish concept of injustice covers the same sorts of situations where, in Anglophone cultures, "unfairness" is the label.

THE SPANISH STUDY

A group of 26 students from the Universidad Complutense in Madrid were asked to describe an unjust episode *in which they had been involved* and were asked to provide their reasons as to why the situation was unjust. Three aspects of this method are different from what we used previously. First, we have a much smaller sample of participants. Second, we ask for only one unjust episode, asking the participants, in effect, to select from all episodes that come to mind under *"no es justo!"* the one that is most likely to be prototypic. Third, we direct them toward a "Y" episode, in which they had been involved. With a small sample and with instructions that greatly restrict the number of instances, our analytic focus was thematic—trying to identify the basic story lines of these unfairnesses—by analyzing the types of situations they presented and their reasons for judging these as *"no es justo!"*

Equality and Equity Findings

Several basic story lines emerge. One invokes versions of *justo* where fairness is an equality matter and where unfairness involves inequality. This story line was quite consistent with what we found in the American studies and in the Japanese study. To make comparisons with the findings from American studies and the Japanese study, several examples, and variants, of the equality story line versions are offered:

Equality1: Several women participants offered accounts in which the complaint *"No es justo"* expressed a perception of unfairness relative to their gender. The equality principle regarding equal treatment of men and women had been violated. Among the accounts were the following: brothers and sisters should share domestic jobs; pay scales for men and women doing the same jobs should be the same.

These accounts were thematically indiscernible from those from the American studies and the Japanese study. In refining the equality principle through an examination of their reasons, we find that some of these complaints focus on unequal outcomes, others focus on unequal processes, whereas still others focus on both, such that decisions are based on impermissible factors that may create unequal standing or unequal opportunity, which lead to discriminatory outcomes. Again, these refinements show the same sort of distinctions that result in the American studies and in the Japanese study.

Equality2: Another complaint was that the same amount of tax should attach to the same sort of property, even though they are situated in different locales, where one may be worth more than the other. To the complainant, a strict equality under taxation laws should obtain, without discriminatory differences, and an equity value—of "greater or lesser equity in property located in different areas"—is viewed as illegitimate and discriminating and should have no place in taxation policy.

Now we examine several story lines where equity is dominant.

Equity1: Several of our participants complained that examination marks should reflect effort put into study. This story line, which comes in several versions, is quite familiar to us from both the American studies and the Japanese study. It endorses the views that hard work ought to be rewarded, that no work ought not to be rewarded, and that cheating (wrongful behavior) ought not to be rewarded.

Equity2: Still another complaint held that everyone who is appointed to a job should have passed the same test of competence. This type of complaint is again familiar from previous studies, where jobs, admittance, grades, promotions, and honors are supposed to go to those who have earned them. "Competence," a level of ability and effectiveness acquired through effort (a meritocratic factor), which goes beyond merely putting out effort, should be determinative, rather than impermissible factors like nepotism.

In the two equality versions, the equality principle is expected to hold and not be toppled by impermissible gender factors or the irrelevancy of where the same amount of land is located. In the two equity versions, the equity principle is expected to hold, and this standard is not to be toppled by impermissible factors. Looking at these stories in light of the major and specific type categories that emerge from the American studies, coupled with the findings of the Japanese participants when their instances were categorized using the American schema, we find the following similar themes:

1. Reward has not matched the effort—this can be either "no work is rewarded" (category A), "hard work is not rewarded" (category B), or "equal treatment resulting when it should be individualized" to the effort (category G).
2. Wrongful behavior has been rewarded or not been punished (category C).
3. Punishment has not fit the offense (category D or E).
4. People of the same category have been differentially treated (category F).
5. Authority has been exercised arbitrarily (category H).

Although the American studies and the Japanese study reveal many subcategories and refinements, for our purposes now the generic form of each principle is sufficient to test the cross-cultural viability of the equation of "But it's not fair!" with "*No es justo!*" in certain cases. The results, so far, show that "fair" and "*justo*" track one another closely; more precisely, we do not see any divergences at all between the two, at least to this point.

Honor and Dignity Findings

Equality and equity, the first two story lines, are quite prevalent, even in our small sample. However, they were not the only story lines to emerge. The third story line invokes a different but deeply held principle involving personal honor. This principle holds that each person's honor and dignity must be respected, and this principle cannot be overridden by status inequalities. This principle appears in many of the "*No es justo!*" accounts, a few of which are now illustrated.

Honor1: One participant complained that to be subjected to a tyrannical boss was "*no es justo*"—because inferiors must be respected. In this complaint, the participant accepts the inequality of social status between his boss and himself (the employee), but he insists that the social status inequality cannot override the demand that personal dignity be respected.

In short, you can give me an order or direction, for that is your job, but you must do it and treat me in a respectful manner.

Honor2: Another participant told how he had been suspended from an exam for cheating, when in fact he had not copied his friend's answers. It is not just the accusation and the punishment that the participant responded to, which the participant insists were false and wrong. The complaint is that the teacher did not accept his explanation, which left him humiliated. As the participant told it, had the teacher accepted his explanation, this would have allowed his honor and dignity to be restored. The social status inequality of professor–student, which the participant accepts, does not override the demand that personal honor be sustained.

Honor3: Another participant complained that to have incompetent professors was "*no es justo.*" The principle here seems to be that the authorities who are responsible for appointing professors are denigrating the standing of students by appointing incompetents to teach them. The inverse seems to hold as well: Worthless students need no more than incompetent teachers.[5]

In Honor3, unlike Honor1 and 2, the issue is not personal honor, but honor that belongs to the category of persons (e.g., students) to which the complainant belongs. In Honor1 and 2, the honor is personal (i.e., it is "my honor" that is being insulted), reflecting a general honor principle, which holds that respect is due by virtue of the person's standing as a human being.

To bring out the subtleties of honor, let us begin at the broadest level. Diaz-Plaja remarked on the ubiquitous Spanish belief that each person possesses *honor y dignidad* as such.[6] But there is also, traditionally, an honor that accrues to each person and that depends on social category. Thus although each Spaniard is entitled to respect *qua* human being, men have manly honor whereas women have womanly honor, and each is entitled to have that social category of honor respected. So *dignidad* has many forms, each appropriate to the category of person whose honor is to be sustained. In discussing our Spanish cases, there is a shifting balance between *honor* and *dignidad*: In some cases, the "*no es justo*" offense is a failure to sustain *honor*, whereas in other cases it is a consequential loss of *dignidad* that is the source of psychological injury.

In addition to the three basic story lines involving equality, equity, and honor principles, there is a fourth story line involving these principles used in conjunction. In some instances, the conjunction seemed to be no more than the fact that two principles were being cited in the same account, as two independent principles operating. But we also found instances where the conjunction was tighter, where one violation leads to the other. For example, there were instances in which a violation of an honor principle is presented as making room for the violation of an equality or equity principle. On the other hand, there were cases in which the fulfillment of an equality or equity principle became a condition for the maintenance of honor.

Here is an illustration of the first pattern, where the two principles are cited independently. One of the participants told a complicated story about being passed over for a place in the swimming team in favor of the son of the trainer who had not swum in the trials. The *"no es justo"* judgment depended not only on violations of an equality principle (i.e., all individuals trying out for the team should have swum in the trials) and an equity principle (i.e., only those swimming the fastest at trials should make the team), but also of an honor principle that was not logically connected to equality or equity: The trainer had promised the place to the participant (based on his performance) and then broke his word, thus treating him disrespectfully. The status inequality trainer–team player does not override the general principle of respect for personal honor. Ironically, the trainer's son did badly in the competition, was dropped from the team, and the participant was put on the team; but this did not remedy the offense, for although equity was restored, dignity was not.

The second pattern, how a violation of honor can then lead to a violation of equality or equity, is illustrated in this account. In explaining why the treatment of handicapped people was *"no es justo,"* one participant complained that people with disabilities are presented disrespectfully in the media. She then tied this lack of respect to the equality principle, that goods should not be reserved for just the fortunate; in this linkage, the participant seems to be saying that the inequality in the distribution of goods stems from the disrespect.

The third pattern appears in a more complicated story line in the following anecdote: In planning to go out for the weekend, a group of friends agree to telephone one another beforehand to make arrangements. Only the participant does so, whereas the others do not bother. The participant interprets the lack of phone calls as being mocked by his friends, a blatant disrespect. This disrespect comes about for the participant because the equality principle was first violated: Busy or not, all should have telephoned because that was the agreement. Thus only if all are treated in an equal manner is the honor of each preserved.

These examples show three things. First, they affirm that equality and equity are important in their own right. Second, they affirm that the preservation of honor/dignity is important in itself. Third, they show an interaction between principles, for we see that to be treated unequally or inequitably is to be disrespected, and to be disrespected can lead to unequal or inequitable treatment. From this study and from our microanalysis of these story lines, *"no es justo"* seems to include honor/dignity violations we have not seen in our schema for type of unfairness, as well as honor/dignity violations interacting with equity violations.

Honor and Dignity in America

Our findings that honor and dignity violations loom large in Spanish participants' unfairness or *"no es justo!"* claims dovetails with other research findings. Research into Spanish emotions confirms that, at least in metropolitan Spain, the traditional basis of everyday moral order is very much alive, and central in that tradition are matters of honor and dignity.[7] This contrasts with the basis of equity and equality that seem to dominate the local moral orders of much of American society and Japan as well. When we examine honor and dignity more closely and contrast it with equity and equality, there are a number of differences worth noting. For one, equity and equality are more abstract principles, whereas honor and dignity may be personal: It is typically *my* honor and *my* dignity that are at stake. For another, equity and equality concepts are usually symmetrical, whereas honor concepts rarely are. For example, although professors determine the students' grades based on equity, students, at the end of the semester, evaluate professors on some equity basis as well. If we assert our own equality then, we must grant it to others. But in regard to honor, you may owe me respect by virtue of who and what I am, but I may owe you only polite condescension;[8] this asymmetry is recorded in the grammars of second-person pronouns in most European languages, where I may be *vous* to you, while you are *tu* to me.

When we turn this examination of honor back to the United States, there are signs, historic and current, that this honor code is not only Hispanic. An honor morality survives in parts of the indigenous American culture, most dramatically at certain social levels and in certain ethnic groups. Butterfield described the honor code among the white southerners of the antebellum period this way:

> Honor meant reputation; a man's worth resides in the opinions of others. Honor also meant valor; a man had to be prepared to fight to defend his honor if challenged or insulted ... honor became a compelling passion, an overwhelming concern with one's reputation and manliness.[9]

In their work, *Culture of Honor*,[10] Nisbett and Cohen turned to the South, where they argue and document that such a culture is strongly rooted in and connected to violence. It is an "*honor* not in the sense of probity of character but in the sense of status and power,"[11] where a male

> must constantly be on guard against affronts that could be construed by others as disrespect. When someone allows himself to be insulted, he risks giving the impression that he lacks the strength to protect what is his. Thus the individual must respond with violence or the threat of violence to any affront.[12]

A violation of honor was an insult, indignity, and humiliation, and whether it was focused on manliness or dignity or both, it nonetheless called for action and redress. In our current culture, particularly among the young, the word "dissing" is now quite salient, as "disrespect violations" trigger claims of unfairness and oftentimes violence as well; unlike Peter Pan, many youths of today, perceiving to be "dissed," will pick up the knife or gun and take a life rather than take the insult.

Once upon a time in Spain one would have said the same. The cult of the *hidalgo* or gentleman and the widespread conception of *machismo* and so on were linked in various ways such that *dignidad* was defended. We have seen, in our Spanish study, that *dignidad* survives. If anecdotal accounts from the antebellum South and our current mean streets are any indications, then disrespect may be a type of unfairness that we have missed. It is likely that some honor violations were in our data from the studies, rather than absent entirely, but we may have missed these as a distinct type group for three reasons. First, given the population we have been working with, which is underrepresented along geographic and socioeconomic lines that would most likely produce disrespect unfairnesses, we simply may have gotten too few for a separate category. Second, having gotten some, coders, not seeing a category that directly captures these, may have put them in the miscellaneous category. A third possibility is that coders put them in the "lack of due process category" as the best fit. Thus without a separate identifiable category to house them, and with a population that may evoke fewer such instantiations, we have no estimates on their frequency and severity.

UNFAIRNESS VERSUS MISFORTUNE VERSUS INJUSTICE: AN EXPERIMENT

When Hook put the bite on Peter and J. M. Barrie cried "unfair," a question arose about this instance in the light of the American, Japanese, and Spanish studies: What type of unfairness was this? Was it an inequitable outcome complaint, was it a violation of the fair fighting process, or was it about equity at all? If Peter Pan was Spanish, would he be complaining about honor and dignity violations, or if he was an urban American youth, would he be complaining about being "dissed"? This question not only takes us into the details of types, but it moves us toward the essence of unfairness and how it is different from related concepts. Using the Peter Pan example again, we can ask, was it "But it's not fair!" or was it *"No es justo!"* or is there any difference? We can expand the question by considering a different jolt: What if Peter Pan had been hit by a bolt of lightning rather than bitten by Hook? Would this be an unfairness or simply a misfortune (i.e., an impersonal act of nature) and is there a difference?

We found in our first experiment with exclusively American participants that there are significant differences among misfortune, injustice, and unfairness, and that "unfairness" turns out to be the broadest term, with an ambit most inclusive. We also saw, from the Japanese study, that those participants regard misfortune cases quite differently from Americans. Now, we pose the question to a Spanish sample.

We went back to the data set from the original American experiment to create an appropriate comparison group for our Spanish student participants and selected nine vignettes.[13] The vignettes fell into one of three type categories. The first category (A) involves "when no work is rewarded," a standard inequity complaint, and there were three vignettes in this category, one where the complainant is a teenager (AT), a second where the complainant is a college student (AS), and the third involving an adult (AA) complainant. The other six vignettes are category D types, "when innocence is punished." These fall within the equity sphere, but with a difference around who or what is to blame. There were three vignettes that we called D1 types (D1T, D1S, D1A), where the blame seemed to lie with nature or life, thus being misfortune cases. The three remaining vignettes (D2 types, D2T, D2S, and D2A) were injustice cases, as a human agent is responsible for bringing about the harm. The specific vignettes are shown in Appendix 15A.

RESULTS AND DISCUSSION

The quantitative severity ratings for the nine vignettes were analyzed.[14] We tested the unfairness/misfortune/injustice variable (which we dubbed umi) to see if these three ratings for each vignette and across all vignettes were significantly different. Going further, we also did two preplanned comparisons, testing whether there was an unfairness + injustice versus misfortune (U + I versus M) distinction and an unfairness versus injustice (U versus I) distinction.

The second independent variable involved the two samples (American versus Spanish), and this variable was dubbed culturetype. We also examined the umi × culturetype interaction effect. Finally, we assessed the vignettes themselves, in two ways. In the first way, we broke the vignettes into three conceptually different type categories (A, D1, and D2), dealing with "reward-to-effort" inequities (A), and into "innocence being punished" cases, where the latter was further divided into those involving misfortune, where no human agent was at fault (D1) and those where a human agent was at fault (D2). In the second way of dividing the vignettes, we looked at the age of the complainant, whether it was a teenager (T), a student (S), or an adult (A), and this variable was dubbed subjecttype.

The mean severity ratings are shown in Table 15-1, and the analyses

TABLE 15-1
The Mean Severity Ratings of Unfairness (U), Misfortune (M),
and Injustice (I) (umi) by Vignette (type and claimant), for the subjecttypes
(American and Spanish)

umi/subjecttypes	Vignettes—by type (A, D1, D2) and by claimant (T, S, A)								
	AT	AS	AA	D1T	D1S	D1A	D2T	D2S	D2A
U/Americans	75	64	74	68	67	69	89	80	86
U/Spanish	58	86	84	68	69	63	86	74	94
U/Overall	67	75	79	68	68	66	87	77	90
M/Americans	15	18	19	96	93	93	74	87	67
M/Spanish	22	26	23	92	86	95	88	87	73
M/Overall	19	22	21	94	89	94	81	87	70
I/Americans	79	60	74	32	29	27	87	65	89
I/Spanish	66	82	84	38	40	38	67	63	72
I/Overall	73	71	79	35	34	33	77	64	81
Means across umi									
Americans	57	48	56	65	63	63	83	77	81
Spanish	49	64	64	66	65	65	80	75	80

revealed significant main effects for umi and culturetype, a significant interaction effect for umi × culturetype, and significant differences for both preplanned comparisons (U + I versus M, and U versus I).[15] Overall, then, the participants' significantly different ratings for "unfairness," "misfortune," and "injustice" tell us that these concepts are distinct. But the significant culturetype and culturetype × umi interaction effects tell us that there are differences in the way the Spanish and American samples judge these cases.

To bring out the subtler details, the overall umi effect turns out to be significant on eight of the nine vignettes, and marginally significant on the other (D2T); moreover, the same eight of nine significant results repeat for the U + I versus M preplanned comparisons. What this tells us is that misfortune ratings are clearly different than unfairness or injustice ratings, and they were most dramatically different for the A type cases involving inequities in reward to effort. This is confirmed by the U versus I preplanned comparisons, which are significant on only six of the nine vignettes, but not on any of the A cases; said another way, the A cases are seen as either unfairness or injustice cases, but not as misfortune cases. The misfortune ratings turn out to be highest on the D1 type cases, which we expected because here life or nature delivers the suffering; however, these D1 types are seen secondarily as unfairnesses, but not at all as injustices, and these are the cases that most sharply differentiate unfairness from injustice. For the third type (D2), where innocence is punished by human agents, all three ratings are high, with a tighter variance than the other two types (A or D1), yet significant differences still emerge: Overall, these cases are primarily seen as unfairnesses, secondarily as misfortunes, and lastly as injustices, and thus these D2 types further sharpen the unfairness versus injustice distinction. Summing up, of the three constructs, unfairness has the widest orbit.

As for our cross-cultural analysis, the results show nuances that are missed in the overall analyses of the culturetype main effect and the culturetype × umi interaction effect. As for a general trend, the Spanish participants give both higher and lower unfairness ratings than do American participants, but the significant results only occur for the A type inequity cases. For case AT, involving a teenager, the Spanish participants rate this as less severe than do Americans, but when the subjecttype is a student (AS) or an adult (AA), they rate the unfairness as more severe than the Americans. Do the Spanish participants tend to discount the unfairnesses of the younger complainants as they boost the worthiness of adult complaints? The answer is "not across the board," for when the case is D1 or D2 and the complainant is a teenager, the ratings are as high as for student and adult complainants. Thus this interaction effect for culturetype × umi and the main effect for culturetype are restricted to A type inequity cases.

Although the significant results accent differences, some of them subtle, the overall results must be seen in the broad context. In that context, the American and Spanish participants' perspectives are fairly similar. Specifically, if one group sees a particular case as a misfortune or unfairness or injustice, so will the other group.

LOOKING BACKWARD, LOOKING FORWARD

What this cross-cultural investigation has shown is that the concept of unfairness cuts deeply and broadly through the thinking of both American and Spanish samples, as it did through the American and Japanese samples. Once again, now through the instances of unfairness that the Spanish give, a consistent finding is that these unfairness complaints signal something substantive rather than ephemeral, something weighty rather than petty. Although "But it's not *fair!*" may not be a perfect word-for-word translation of *"No es justo!"* instantiations of each clearly translate into the other, transcending the particular language and the particulars of culture. *Fair* and *justo* turn out to be polysemic, and our unfairness concept is the central core of each, rather than injustice or misfortune, which have lesser orbits. In regard to the misfortune cases, the Spanish are much closer to the Americans than to the Japanese in seeing these as unfairnesses and not as bad luck.

In looking back, fairness appears to be a foundational concept, and a sweeping one. Looked at from the other end, unfairness can be leveled anywhere across the social, societal, and cultural sweep, signaling something deep. It turns out to be a claim that is heard in all sorts of relationships, quite apart from how individuals align in those relationships (e.g., equals, parent-to-child, spouse-to-spouse, boss-to-employee). Broader still, the claims are heard in regard to how society and its governmental and regulatory institutions deal with its people, and going higher still, claims relate to our relationships with life, nature, and God as well. In its breadth across the landscape, and in its passion and primacy, the import of unfairness is clearly established as foundational.

Yet our cross-cultural work marks out some differences. The American and Spanish cultures examined here accent some different types of unfairness in part. Whereas equality and equity concerns are very evident in the narratives of participants from both countries, concerns over honor and dignity are weighted more heavily in the Spanish sample. Moreover, these equality, equity, and honor and dignity principles are not necessarily independent: We saw, for example, how honor violations can trigger equality or equity issues, and vice versa, indicating new complexities for a type of unfairness analysis.[16]

In the cross-cultural direction, we are still a long way from establishing if there are universal types of unfairness and what their local acculturation may be. Yet at a basic level, we have learned that "unfairness" appears to be the right term: It is the term with the widest orbit, for it covers the injustice cases and many of the misfortune cases as well. What we are sure about is another certainty: That along with death and taxes, we can count on new instances of "But it's not fair!" The research findings make it clear that these claims cannot be dismissed as narcissistic whines and petty complaints. The complainants' cries, coupled with their blame judgments, are warning signals to relationships, society, and culture, and as their severity ratings show, their anger does not go away easily or quickly. Yet these cries contain an obvious hope—that tomorrow will be a fairer day.

Although much more cross-cultural research could be done, we have gone as far as we will in that direction. In looking forward, we begin our concluding Part V (Consistencies, Contradictions, Conundrums, and Common Sense) by returning to another study, this one done very differently, to bring to light "low-level unfairnesses," to more adequately assess the petty whines challenge, and to find out more about getting over unfairnesses or transforming them into "not an unfairness." This study leads to the concluding chapter.

APPENDIX 15A

CASE VIGNETTES

AT. A high school coach told the players of the girl's soccer team that the starters for next week's game would be determined by who comes to all the practices and who works the hardest during practice. Sara, one of the players, missed most of the practices, and when she was there, fooled around and did not work hard, yet she got to start in the next game.

AS. In a particular college course, the professor assigned a 20-page paper, which counted for 50% of the grade. The professor expected to see many sources cited. Students had most of the semester to work on the paper, but one student did no work on it; rather, he stayed up all night the night before it was due and turned in 20 pages of trash, with no references. Yet he got an A.

AA. At a particular computer company, the policy was that promotions go to those who show the most initiative and make the greatest efforts toward developing new software. Despite this policy, one worker, who made the least effort and showed almost no initiative, received a promotion.

D1T. An infant who seemed perfectly healthy suffocated and died in the crib at night.

D1S. A college student who was driving home for the weekend got caught in a tornado that lifted and tossed his car. He was killed.

D1A. A 40-year-old man, in good health, died in an earthquake as a building fell in on him.

D2T. A crack baby born with many problems including the likelihood of retardation because his parent was a crack addict, died from the complications in the first week of life.

D2S. A student learned that lightning struck her mother as she was stepping out a car, and when her father called 911, the operator made a tragic mistake by sending the ambulance to the wrong address. Her father's frantic phone calls were too late, and her mother died on the way to the hospital.

D2A. A parent with a history of violence and physical abuse shook a child who was crying and the child died.

ENDNOTES

1. I wish to thank my coauthors on this work, Rom Harré, of Georgetown University; Lincacre College, of Oxford University; and Jose-Luis Rodriguez Lopez, of the Departmento de Psicologia, Universidad Complutense, Madrid. *See* N. J. Finkel, R. Harré, and J. R. Lopez, "Commonsense Morality Across Cultures: Notions of Fairness, Justice, Honor and Equity," *Discourse Studies* 3 (2001): 31–53.

2. L. L. Weinreb, *Natural Law and Justice* (Cambridge, MA: Harvard University Press, 1987).

3. Regarding the divergence possibility, let us recall our earlier experiment that addressed a similar question with an American population. In that experiment, we found that unfairness was not the same as either injustice or misfortune, and "unfairness" turned out to be the wider construct.

4. After all, unfairness can be seen as polysemic, for sometimes it is used to cover injustice cases, other times to cover misfortune cases, and at still other times it means something different.

5. The same story line was used by English schoolchildren to explain attacks on incompetent teachers. *See* P. Marsh, E. Rosser, and R. Harré, *The Rules of Disorder* (London: Routledge and Kegan Paul, 1977).

6. F. Diaz-Plaja, *The Spaniard and the Seven Deadly Sins*, trans. J. I. Palmer (New York: Scribner, 1967).

7. R. Harré, "Emotion Across Cultures," *Innovation* 11 (1998): 43–52.

8. E. Goffman, *Interaction Ritual: Essays on Face-to-Face Behavior* (Garden City, NY: Anchor, 1967).

9. F. Butterfield, *All God's Children: The Bosket Family and the American Tradition of Violence* (New York: Knopf, 1995), pp. 10–11.

10. R. E. Nisbett and D. Cohen, *Culture of Honor: The Psychology of Violence in the South* (Boulder, CO: Westview Press, 1996).

11. *Id.*, p. xvi.

12. *Id.*, p. xv.

13. To fairly compare the two cultural groups, we eliminated the adults from the data set. Second, because our Spanish group was small, we would use a within-subject design as a way of increasing the power of the test, where participants would make severity ratings on three scales for each vignette, scales that would be labeled "misfortune," "injustice," and "unfairness." Thus, we eliminated all of the between-subject groups from the original American data set. The final reduction of the original data set involves the number of cases. Originally, the American participants had 33 case vignettes to make ratings on, but we selected only 9 of those vignettes, which were given to the Spanish sample. Thus in terms of case materials, their order, the essential design, and the likeness of participants, we created comparability.

14. These results were obtained using MANOVA and ANOVA analyses.

15. The MANOVAs showed significant differences for umi (F [18, 394] = 18.3, $p < .0001$), for subjecttype (F [9, 197] = 4.1, $p < .0001$), for the umi $\times$ subjecttype interaction effect (F [18, 394] = 2.5, $p = .0007$), for the U + I versus M distinction (F [9, 197] = 40.0, $p < .0001$), and for the U versus I distinction (F [9, 197] = 4.96, $p < .0001$).

16. An implication for future research is apparent: To add this "honor and dignity" category to the American schema and further test whether this addition pulls some instances out of our miscellaneous category or pulls from other categories; adding a sample that crosses both cultures, such as a Spanish sample living in the United States, could produce further nuances.

V

CONSISTENCIES, CONTRADICTIONS, CONUNDRUMS, AND COMMON SENSE

Then the Unnamable Asked Job:
Has God's accuser resigned?
Has my critic swallowed his tongue?
. . . .
Do you dare to deny my judgment?
Am I wrong because you are right? (p. 84)

From Stephen Mitchell's *The Book of Job* (1987)

16

RECTIFYING, NULLIFYING, AND SOFTENING UNFAIRNESSES: TO ERR IS HUMAN

To this point, participants of various ages, and now nationalities, have reported thousands of unfairness instances, which have been deconstructed, categorized, and analyzed in different ways and along different dimensions. Overall, the findings are consistent, and from these we have made a number of generalizations. Our confidence in both the findings and the generalizations grows—in part because they recur and in part because the experimental results, deriving from a more controlled methodology, converge with them.

A GENERALIZING LIMITATION?

However, amid the consistency and confidence, questions arise and a doubt grows. In branching out to tap other cultures, we were responding to a doubt that grew out of sample limitations, having only American participants limited the findings to that sample. Now we respond to another limitation that prevents generalizations in a different direction, a limitation that challenges the fairness of our rebuttal of the critics' "narcissistic petty whines" claim.

287

To explain the problem, we begin with a consistent finding: In study after study, we find that participants' severity ratings generally fall in the "high" (51–75) or "severe" (76–100) categories, and this is so whether we look at each individual's set of instances, a particular age group, across age groups or cultural groups, or across the entirety. Thus what we have on the average are "hot" unfairnesses that are not exaggerations, because independent raters judge them "hot" as well. Where the uncertainty arises is over the distribution of unfairnesses, a distribution that is neither normal (i.e., bell-shaped) nor rectilinear in shape, but skewed left, having most of the instances near the "severe" right end of the continuum. The question is this: Is this skewed shape the natural distribution, where severe-end unfairnesses dominate over low-end unfairnesses in actuality, or do we have a skewed picture because we have miss the low-end unfairnesses in our research?

The importance of this question for the critics' claims of petty whines grows obvious. The critics would argue that it is precisely at the low-end where petty whines would show. Second, they would argue that we should see a much higher percentage of Y instances at the low-end, and the intersection of Y and low-end is where we would get the narcissistic focus. Thus to the critics, our research to this point has stacked the deck against finding and validating the narcissistic petty whines thesis because we have tapped severity levels where *petty whines* would not manifest. We take this point and its underlying question about the distribution quite seriously, as they become focal in this chapter.

Let us look at some assumptions, the facts as we know them, and some conservative inferences. If we make the questionable assumption that unfairnesses fall equally or normally across the severity scale, then low-level unfairnesses would indeed be underrepresented. We cannot dismiss this assumption by arguing that our skewed shape is in fact the natural shape, because we do not know that. In fact, from our facts, we ourselves have legitimate doubts about the distribution being skewed in that way.

Some of our doubts stem from our "getting over" study (chapter 8), where we found that rate of change scores were greatest when unfairnesses were personal, of a certain type, where blame was directed at individuals, and where severity was less to begin with. These findings suggest that low-level unfairnesses existed but now have faded from mind, and thus fail to appear in research booklets. Anecdotal evidence also suggests the same conclusion, for we, as parents, may remember particular "But it's not fair!" claims our children once uttered but have now forgotten, although we have forgotten similar claims we uttered as children, though our parents remember them well.

This forgetting, we can assume, is more likely to happen with low-level unfairnesses. We can call this the differential processing hypothesis, which posits differences in memory and recollections for low versus hot unfairnesses and explains why we see so many of the latter but not the former. We can also generate a second hypothesis, which, like the first, also holds that the skewed distribution is not the natural one, but this one holds that the distortion results from social desirability operating to suppress low-level unfairnesses. This hypothesis notes that as we try to manage our social relations, we typically put on our best face, presenting ourselves in the most desirable light, and if this is so then participants may not want to reveal their petty whines, trivial concerns, or small-mindedness to experimenters and independent raters. If social desirability is the operative factor, then participants may generate a higher percentage of the more acceptable, unarguable high-end unfairnesses, while suppressing the petty, the trivial, and the narcissistic.

A third hypothesis, like the previous two, rejects the claim that the true population distribution is bunched upward but argues that the cause of the distortion involves the task of instantiating unfairnesses, coupled with the prototypes participants carry, both of which lead to high-end instances. The argument is that our very task instructions—with "But it's not fair!" boldly accented and exclaimed—make high-level unfairnesses far more salient in the minds of participants, along with inferences they may make, such as "the experimenter wants me to recall high-enders." Regarding the prototypes participants carry in mind and bring with them to the task, "hot" instantiations may already be front and center, salient and accessible, poised anxiously to spring from memory to booklet pages as soon as the task instructions fire the trigger, or as soon as they "figure out" that this is what we want.

Whether it is a differential processing, social desirability, or the task instructions coupled with prototypes, or some combination, the unfairness distribution may be missing the petty whines. If any one of these hypotheses is true, then the unfairness picture we have been constructing may be askew. If this is so, then maybe it is we who have been unfair to the critics who have argued right from the beginning that unfairnesses would reveal the narcissistic and the petty.

In the following research, we have made a substantial change in our methodology in an effort to bring low-level unfairnesses to light. Then, by having independent coders making categorizations and ratings, we can assess whether these low-level unfairnesses are the suspected petty whines or the narcissistic petty whines that some allege.

Learning From Low-Level Unfairnesses

There is another reason to focus on the low-enders. They afford us an opportunity to ask and answer the following question: What separates an "unfairness" from "not an unfairness"? At the high end, there is little disagreement about its unfairness, as both participant and independent rater concur, but this may not be true for a low-end instance, where there may be more disagreement over its status as an unfairness. More disagreement may result because people have criterion or threshold differences about where a "not an unfairness" ends and where an "unfairness" begins. In this chapter, we put the question this way: What turns an experience that the participant regards as an "unfairness"—into one the participant subsequently regards as "not an unfairness"?

Our type data suggest answers. To explicate, in the "no work is rewarded" (I/A) category, the instance can turn into a "not an unfairness" if the "no work" is either not rewarded or if the person actually did work. Similarly, in the "hard work is not rewarded" (I/B) category, this can become a "not an unfairness" if the "hard work" is rewarded or if the work done was neither hard nor good work. By altering a key fact in this fashion, we can go through the rest of the type categories and turn those into "not an unfairness."

In the previous examples, two types of changes are evident, which we dub rectifying and nullifying changes. In the rectifying type, someone corrects an unfair outcome or process by making it fair, and thus the claim evaporates. So if a "discriminatory treatment" claim alleges that an "illegitimate factor" led to the reward or punishment (IV/F), then turning this illegitimate factor into a legitimate one eliminates the claim. Less evident than rectifying is the nullifying type. Both types were illustrated in the "hard work not rewarded" (I/B) category mentioned above: Such an "unfairness" became a "not an unfairness" when "hard work" was rewarded (rectifying) or when the work was neither hard nor good work (nullifying). In the nullifying type, the claimant's own faults, flaws, or mistakes may undermine his or her claim.

This nullifying process, which turns a low-level unfairness into "not an unfairness," meshes with what we found in chapter 11 (When the Victim Is Flawed or Bears Fault). In that experiment, when the victim was flawed or committed a fault, and when the flaw or fault was relevant to the claim, the severity rating significantly lowered; in reverse, when the fault was with the one who perpetrated the unfairness, the severity increased. If we relate these findings to the hypothesized threshold for unfairness, "other's fault" can turn an ordinary act into an "unfairness," whereas claimant's fault can mitigate or nullify an unfairness.

The rectifying change is self-evident. The nullifying change is backed by related findings suggesting that it is on point. But both rectifying and nullifying are still speculative, awaiting the empirical test. The question is this: Will we find these two types of changes when we test, and will we find other types that are not so apparent?

To get at what types of change turn low-level unfairnesses into "not an unfairness," we first had to change our usual methodology to increase the probability that sufficient numbers of low-level unfairnesses would be reported. We did this by asking a group of students ($N = 88$) to keep an unfairness journal for 6 weeks. These participants were free to recall unfairness instances from their past or "any you notice occurring during this six week period." They were asked to record, for each instance, whether this was an old or recent event (O/R), as well as making our familiar designations, categorizations, and ratings.[1]

Changing the basic task (and the time to complete it) from a research booklet (one week) to keeping an unfairness journal (6 weeks) ought to increase the total number of instances participants report; more to our point, recent, everyday instances ought to increase, and these ought to contain more low- and moderate-level occurrences. If the predictions are accurate, then sevnow and sevthen scores ought to be significantly lower than we found in previous studies.[2]

In addition to changing the task methodology, we also made two modifications of the type schema, based on what we now know from prior studies. First, based on consistent findings from the misfortune versus injustice versus unfairness experiment (chapter 9), coupled with the 10:1 ratio over "misfortune" cases in the Japanese study (chapter 14), we broke the "innocence is punished" category into two categories, one called "innocence is punished by human agents" and the other called "innocence is punished by life, nature, or God," a distinction participants make and which cluster analysis separated. The second change, based on the Spanish study (chapter 15), was that we now added a category called "when the respect deserved is not forthcoming, and you are 'dissed,'" to see if these unfairnesses would surface if the category became available.[3]

Participants Creating Experimental Vignettes

Increasing low-level unfairnesses was the initial step for evaluating the narcissistic, petty whines claim, but another step was needed for assessing what types of change turn low-level unfairnesses into "not an unfairness." To accomplish the latter, we asked participants, after the 6-week journal task was complete, to create vignettes for a simple one-variable design experiment (one variable, two levels of the variable). The instructions were as follows:

> You are to go back to your Unfairness Journal instances to find an instance that reflects, in your rating of its severity—a "low level" unfairness, one that might be marginal or questionable in the mind of another. I want you to modify the instance, creating two very similar

vignettes (cases). One case should be such that you believe it is an unfairness, even though it is a low one. The second case, made by changing something in the "fact pattern" of the instance, should be one that you believe just fails to amount to an unfairness. Designate the first one with a U (for unfairness), and designate the second with an N (for not an unfairness).

Our task was then to reliably categorize what those fact pattern changes signified and then to analyze those changes across our key variables.

RESULTS AND DISCUSSION

Our change from the research booklet format to a journal task produced the changes we had hoped for. There were many more unfairnesses per participant, with an average of 17.7.[4] Recent unfairnesses were more plentiful, accounting for 46.2% of the instances. The percentage of Y instances was higher than previous studies (50.3%), and it was slightly higher for recent (51.6%) versus old (49.2%) experiences, making the overall distribution pattern a bit more personal than in previous studies; on the other hand, the percentage of U experiences, many of them very salient in the media, also increased for recent (15.2%) versus old (9.0%), making the distribution more impersonal as well. As we hoped, the percentages of "low" (20.2%) and "moderate" (25.9%) level unfairnesses increased over previous work, with the "low" plus "moderate" percentage at 46.1%; these changes were reflected in the significantly lower mean sevnow (52.3) and sevthen (57.8) ratings for "recent," whereas the ratings for "old" were 58.1 and 71.1, respectively. This fact is confirmed by the significantly lower sevnow scores from the independent raters as well (e.g., 52.8).[5]

With low-level unfairnesses in abundance, we could assess the critics' claim that at this level we would find the narcissistic, the petty, and the trivial, and this is where independent raters would more likely disagree with participants claims. But this is not what we found. Independent raters see these low-level unfairnesses as "low-level unfairnesses," rather than petty, trivial, questionable, or bogus, and the correlation between participants' ratings and independent coders' ratings is quite high.[6]

With this new sample, containing more recent instances and a higher percentage of low- to medium-level unfairnesses, the basic findings replicate. For example, the distribution, severity ratings, and rate of change scores for specific and major categories of type look quite familiar (see Table 16-1), as do the measures for blame (see Table 16-2). As for the two changes we made in our categorization schema (see Table 16-1), the results were as follows: When we separated the "innocence punished" cases into those caused by "human agents" and those caused by "life, nature, or God,"

TABLE 16-1
The Frequencies (*n*), Percentages (%), Sevnow, Sevthen, and Rate of Change Ratings for Specific and Major Type Categories

Major/Specific Category	*n*	%	Sevnow	Sevthen	RateChange
I—Reward to effort	108	13.7	50.3	60.8	10.7
A. No work rewarded	31	4.1	48.2	59.2	13.3
B. Hard work not rewarded	81	10.6	51.8	62.0	9.6
II—Wrongful behavior	48	6.1	56.1	65.9	7.7
C. Wrongful	48	6.3	56.1	65.9	7.7
III—Punishment to behavior	283	36.0	66.9	74.7	7.7
D. Punished by human agents	128	16.8	62.3	69.4	9.3
L. Punished by life, nature, God	125	16.4	73.3	81.0	5.3
E. Disproportionate	31	4.1	59.8	70.8	10.6
IV—Discriminatory treatment	162	20.6	49.5	60.4	10.5
F. Unfair advantages	122	16.0	48.1	59.9	10.3
G. Equal treatment	30	3.9	49.3	60.5	13.0
V—Lacking process and/or respect	185	23.5	47.6	56.5	8.7
H. Arbitrary rules	100	13.1	49.0	62.4	14.9
I. No respect	64	8.4	47.4	50.1	6.5

the former accounted for 16.8% of the total number of unfairnesses, and the latter accounted for 16.4% of the total number; and when we separated the "disrespect" instances from our "due process" category, the former accounted for 8.4%, not an insignificant amount. Overall, then, with a better distribution across severity, these findings are quite consistent with earlier results, and they again rebut the critics' claims.

Analyzing the Change Reasons

As we anticipated, many participants turned an "unfairness" (U) into a "not an unfairness" (N) by rectifying—simply reversing the unfairness. If the outcome was unfair, the participant's change made the outcome fair and appropriate. If the punishment was disproportionate, it now becomes proportionate and appropriate. If an illegitimate factor was used in making some discrimination, then a legitimate factor is now used. If an authority blamed all for the actions of a few, then the authority now blames only

TABLE 16-2
The Frequencies (*n*), Percentages (%), Sevnow, Sevthen, and Rate of Change Ratings for Major Blame Categories

Major Category	*n*	%	Sevnow	Sevthen	RateChange
I—Authority (boss, parent)	265	33.0	53.1	65.3	10.0
II—Equal	209	26.0	48.1	57.6	11.2
III—Society	174	21.6	59.6	64.4	8.2
IV—Life, nature, heredity	117	14.6	61.9	71.7	8.3
V—God	39	4.9	72.6	84.0	5.9

the guilty. If there was lack of due process, then it now has due process. If there was lack of respect shown, now respect is shown.

Rectifying is the type that occurs most often, but only 38.7% of the time. Thus other types of change must also occur to turn a U into an N. The second is the nullifying type (this occurs 32.0% of the time), where the participant (in the Y instances) or the alleged victim (in the K or U instances) makes a mistake that nullifies the claim. To illustrate and contrast the rectifying and nullifying types, here is a low-level unfairness that was reported. A student, running to a class, drops 75 cents in a candy machine and presses E-5 for his favorite choice; but the machine "eats" his 75 cents. After class, he goes and complains to someone in authority, seeking to get his money back, but is told that there is nothing that can be done. In the rectifying solution, the authority takes his name and address, and his money is mailed back to him. In the nullifying solution, the student returns to the candy machine and sees what he did not see the first time—a sign saying that "E-5 does not work." Thus his own mistake negates his claim.

Beyond rectifying and nullifying, we found a third type, which we call softening. Softening occurs 29.3% of the time, and it involves a fairer process. In these instances, the outcome unfairness still remains, but the participant feels that she has a voice, has some input, is given choices or alternatives, is being listened to, and that her voice has some effect on the authority, who shows flexibility around the rules or gives her reasons (an explanation) for why something has happened.[7] Finally, in this fairer process, she is being treated with respect and being dealt with honestly.

In contrast to what happens in rectifying, for softening the outcome remains unchanged but a fairer, more considerate process tames the ire and mends the wound. In contrast to nullifying, the participant is not at fault in softening; rather, the one who has perpetuated the unfairness (or the authority) goes to certain lengths to explain and to listen to the claimant and does so with respect. The claimant does not get all she wants in softening (unlike rectifying), but she does not have her claim undercut and dismissed, as in nullifying. Thus if rectifying and nullifying represent "all or none" solutions to unfairnesses, softening is a midrange solution, muting the unfairness with a soothing process.

These three different solutions do not occur equally across personal, recent, and type unfairnesses. For the personal variable, Y (43.9%) instances are higher than U + K (28.6%) in the rectifying type of change: When the unfairness occurs to us, we are more apt to want it reversed. For the nullifying type of change, the percentage is higher for U + K (46.9%) than Y (24.6%), where participants are more apt to find fault with the claimant when the claimant is someone else.

Here we can ask, Is this the "blaming of the victim" strategy that the just-world view predicts? Or is it a modification of "blaming of the victim," where we do so as long as the victim is not me? If we turn these questions to our exemplar, do Eliphaz et al. blame Job and nullify his claim as long as the unfairness hits Job, whereas they would demand a rectifying change if they were on the receiving end?

In trying to answer the general question, we run into a confound: The U + K instances involve different types of unfairnesses than the Y, and the former types may be difficult or impossible to rectify. Because the types of unfairnesses are not equivalent in Y versus U + K conditions, we cannot say for sure why this difference occurs. However, while we do see participants applying the nullifying type of solution more frequently in the U + K conditions, they also apply it to their own (Y) unfairnesses, 24.6% of the time, which is not insignificant.

For the recent variable (recent versus old), the rectifying solution is favored in the old instances more than the recent (32.7% versus 52%), whereas nullifying (34.7% versus 24%) and softening (32.7% versus 24%) solutions increase in recent. For the type variable, the rectifying solution dominates in "no work is rewarded" (I/A), "hard work is not rewarded" (I/B), "wrongful behavior is rewarded or not punished" (II/C), and in "equal treatment when it should be individualized" (IV/G). The nullifying solution is prominent in "punishment is disproportionate to the act and intent" (III/E) and in "unfair advantages or connections" (IV/F). The softening solution is prominent in "innocence is punished by human agents" (III/D), "unfair advantages or connections" (IV/F), "lack of due process" (V/H), and "respect not forthcoming" (V/I).

A Conundrum: Where Successes Lead to Skewed Pessimism

We now know what we have long suspected—that low-level unfairnesses are there—and these can be brought out by keeping a journal. With daily time, and extended time to reflect, and with the focus on recent as well as old events, the distribution pattern, which had been consistently skewed left, begins to unskew. If low-level unfairnesses are always with us, they are more likely to be Y instances, as the data show, and these are the ones previous findings show are the most likely to be forgotten. It is likely they are forgotten because they are less hot to begin with, because, as Y instances, we have greater control over these and process them relatively quickly and because they are more likely to be of types that are processed more successfully. Another factor that crowds these low-level Y instances out are newer and hotter U instances that come so regularly by way of the media. But when all is said and done, these low-level claims should be our success stories: They should lead to optimistic feelings about ourselves, as they enhance our sense of efficacy, as the positive outcomes result from our own actions, actions that counteract "learned helplessness."[8]

Yet we find a conundrum. A number of participants commented that this daily journal task made them "more sensitive" to unfairnesses, and some noted (with parenthetical pessimism) that they were seeing far more unfairnesses than they were ordinarily aware of. A few said that they were seeing life—as a student, roommate, friend, family member, citizen of this country, and human being in this world—as filled with unfairnesses. If that is their perception, then pessimism is understandable. But is their perception distorted and their pessimism unwarranted? Why was it that their "getting over" successes, which ought to add optimism, did not counteract their pessimism?

Our analysis of this conundrum begins with a question: Do we even remember our successes, or do we quickly forget them? If we forget quickly, what then? Then comes to mind the prototypical, severe unfairnesses,[9] and these Jobian, media prototypes are the intractable ones. Also arriving are a new bumper crop of low-level unfairnesses, as the journals illustrate. In some ways then "our plate" of unfairnesses always seems full. But with the processing and forgetting of the "easy ones" and the addition of "hard ones" (some severe U unfairnesses occurred during this 6-week interval), the contents on our full plate appear to skew toward the constant stream of horror stories. We see the faces of the victims of violence, war, hurricanes, earthquakes, famine, and genocide; the faces of the surviving family members of the victims of plane crashes, shootings, and atrocities are shown; we see faces of the perpetrators, hardened criminals, the acts of insane or antisocial minds, those acting out of hatred and passion, juveniles who take guns to school and fire; and we hear Job's lament about wrongdoers going unpunished. The net effect may be a plate containing a growing percentage of intractable, unforgettable unfairnesses, and this could well bring on pessimism.

When Fairnesses Are Not Registered

These reasons suggest why perceptions may be skewed in the pessimistic direction and why the unfairness picture may be seen through a glass darkly. With U experiences growing in our memories, about which we lack control, the sense of impotence and pessimism can increase, along with the conclusion that society and the world community have lost control. Still, there is something else that is generally omitted from the picture, which by its absence may distort the picture even more. We asked participants to keep an unfairness journal—but they were not asked to see and record instances of fairness, kindness, or generosity shown to them daily. Acts of this sort are not generally reported on the front page of our newspapers, nor are they the likely lead-in story on the news. If these "routine" instances of kindness and civility go relatively unnoticed, pessimism may weigh heavy on our balance scale, without any counterweight.

Let us consider a few possibilities. In our own lives, we may have a roommate or spouse who shuts the radio alarm quickly so that we might sleep undisturbed, who fixes us coffee, who hands us our favorite section of the newspaper when we stagger to the kitchen, or who toasts our bagel for us while we sit—when we may register none of it, save for the "un-fairness" that he or she left crumbs on the counter. We may have a pro-fessor who grades papers quickly and conscientiously to get them back to the students while the task is still fresh, or who extends office hours to tutor students on tough material or to counsel students when their personal life turns rough—yet we may register only how difficult and hence how unfair the last exam was. We may have a parent who provides for us in countless ways—who cooks, cleans, and chauffeurs us about, is ready to assist with homework, stands on the sidelines of our soccer games, and attends to our needs and wants before we even recognize we have them—yet we only register how unfair it is that the parent will not let us get a tattoo. Parents understand about unfairness and what is not recognized with even a "thanks," but what do participants register? If we fail to register these not-so-routine courtesies and civilities, our picture may be skewed.

In looking back, we can now see that our unfairness topic represents but one side of a bigger picture. The picture not only stretches from 0 to 100 (our unfairness severity scale), but it goes left as well, all the way through fairness, kindness, and generosity. We have not tapped that left end of the continuum directly, as our task consistently points participants toward the right end. It is only a guess, but we surmise that a task asking participants to give instantiations of fairness, kindness, and generosity would be harder to do and would yield fewer instances. If that guess turned out to be true, that would be a commentary. This possibility suggests that it may not be the task instructions, or just task instructions, for we may have predilections to see and store unfairnesses such that our vision and vista seldom embrace the whole. If we are predisposed by history and pro-totypes to look right (and to the far right at that), if our successes with low-level unfairnesses are quickly forgotten, and if we overlook fairnesses, then all of these factors taken together may lead us to see darkness over the deep.

A Conundrum About Blame

Throughout our earlier research studies, we found blame to be en-demic to unfairnesses, and there was no exception when low-level unfair-nesses were in focus. Moreover, from the earlier studies, we found that the severity that attaches to who or what we blame reveals not some equiva-lency, but an ordinal relationship: In general, we blame equals and parents the least, particularly when the latter are our parents; we blame bosses more, and society even more; and we also blame life at high levels, and blame God at the highest level.[10]

Now, let us consider our findings in an even broader light, where an assertion about the nature of human nature, and an ideal about human nature, provide the comparative context. Here the contextual phrase was penned by the poet Alexander Pope—"to err is human; to forgive, divine." When we apply its first part to our results, we find that our participants do not accept certain errs. If error is part and parcel of the human condition, as the poet has it, then our human participants do not fully embrace this, for they point their finger of blame with each unfairness. But the key distinction is "certain errs." We know that many individuals do forgive many small infractions, and as a professor I know that students, for example, want to be forgiven as well, as they forgive me for most of my faults, foibles, and follies. Said another way, most are not nit-pickers. Yet once we have made the designation that something is an unfairness, we have put the "error" into a different class, above a certain threshold such that it cannot be easily brushed off with a "whatever" or some "part and parcel of the human condition" whitewash. Some human errors, then, though they may derive in part from our human nature, should not be made, and the judgment of "unfairness" indicates that the maker of the error could have done otherwise and better, and should have.

If participants do not fully embrace the poet's "err is human" claim but rather have some subjective forgiveness/blaming threshold, they do not seem to manifest the poet's ideal about forgiveness being "divine." The charitable exceptions seem to be those errs below the threshold. But once participants make the judgment that an instance is an unfairness, they do not excuse, and mitigate very little. When a longer time duration is brought into the picture (chapter 8, Do We Ever Get Over Unfairnesses?), we saw that forgiveness was neither an easy matter nor an instant (divine) process. Furthermore, we have seen over and over again in the studies that our human charitableness does not extend to the divine God, when the latter is held responsible for the unfairness, for here the participants' blame is hottest and the forgiveness is least. Thus regarding the poet's "to err is human; to forgive, divine" message, we do not readily accept errs above a threshold, nor do we divinely forgive them.

LOOKING BACKWARD, LOOKING FORWARD

In looking back, now at a data set containing numerous low-level unfairnesses, we can finally reject the critics' claims of petty whines. In the eyes of the independent coders, they turn out to be what their designation states, merely low-level unfairnesses. Moreover, despite the fact that low-level unfairnesses tend to be more Y experiences, that does not mean that they are narcissistic in some exaggerated or distorted way. Rather, the outside coders see these as unfairnesses that just happen to happen to the participant. What we have learned is that the unfairness distribution is different than we previously have seen, particularly on the severity dimension but also on the personal dimension, and these differences affect type and blame as well. These low-level unfairnesses are there, and these are the ones most easily gotten over, though our successes at processing these do not automatically translate into a greater sense of efficacy or optimism about ourselves or life.

In looking back, we asked our participants to do a new task—creating a "not an unfairness" from what had been a low-level unfairness. Here, blame comes to the fore, along with apparent conundrums and inconsistencies. Yet in the end, it is consistency that rules. Blame, in one form or another and in various degrees, is involved in rectifying, nullifying, and softening. To rectify this, others who bring about the unfairness must explicitly recognize that they are to blame and that restitution on their part is called for. To nullify this, victims must explicitly recognize that it is they who stand with "black hands" rather than a Jobian clean heart and must come to own the blame that they have previously laid at the doorstep of the other; by putting blame on themselves, the unfairness evaporates, or where self and other both bear blame, the claim is mitigated and muted. Nullifying, then, is more complex and perspectival than rectifying, for in the latter process it is simply the case that someone is right and someone is wrong. When the Unnamable asks Job, "Am I wrong because you are right?" we hear that the matter may be anything but simple.

Softening is even more complex. It begins, like rectifying, with others recognizing that the participant's unfairness claim has some merit, but others do not necessarily accept that they are to blame or have a duty to reverse it. Rather, others give the victim an ear, listening to the victim's voice, claims, and feelings about what has happened. It is "procedural fairness" from one view, or old-fashioned considerateness, caring, kindness, and respect from an interpersonal perspective. This softening response appears to work therapeutically in that the victim comes to feel better even though the unfairness is not necessarily made any better (as in rectifying). A further differentiation is that softening is less confrontational than the other two processes, for it does not push the blaming finger into someone's chest or eye, as in rectifying, and it does not ping-pong the blaming, which may occur in nullifying, where the other who was blamed now turns on the victim. In softening, blame itself is softened, receding more into background. If blame is recognized, it is typically implicit, a phenomenological truth rather than an objective truth, whereby the other acknowledges that the victim believes he or she has a claim, and that this belief warrants listening to. In a way, it is a strategy that seems to reduce blame from both the other and the victim and seems to reframe the issue as other than blame.

Softening thus advances nullifying by several steps. In nullifying, a new fact comes to light that shifts the perspective and conclusion about who is in the wrong, as the blame moves from the other to the victim. In rectifying, victims somehow get the wrongful others to see that they are wrong and make restitution, as blame stays where it was laid. In softening, perspectives shift, such that the other hears and responds to the victim's cry and gives respect on procedural and interpersonal levels. This is not the divine intervention that many modern-day Jobs hope for, where the unfairness is reversed. Rather it turns out to be a very human response, and for many people it seems to be enough.

But the three, rectifying, nullifying, and softening, when taken together, reflect a consistency. Of course, if we had our druthers, our first choice is likely to be rectifying, a reversal and undoing of the unfairness. This can be viewed pejoratively, as a primitive, childlike wish. Moreover, on the practical level, many unfairnesses cannot be undone. Yet the underlying wish is that unfairnesses not be perpetrated in the first place. In this sense, the cry of unfairness is not a cry of anarchy and disorder, nor is it a call for rudeness and incivility, for it is, at base, a cry to preserve the order and to uphold the standards. When we add nullifying to the picture, it strongly counters victimology claims. Participants are quick to see relevant fault on the part of the claimant, and if they find such fault, they are unwilling to buy "blaming the other" when it is not warranted. Said another way, participants turn out not to be just worlders in the Eliphaz et al. sense, for they are not willing to blame the victim when there is no blame. Instead, when there is no blame, and no easy restitution, what they want, as softening reveals, is understanding, empathy, compassion, and to be treated in a civic and civilized way.

In looking forward to the concluding chapter, it is time to put these findings into context, to see the broad picture. It is also time to return to the early issues that set us on this journey, to evaluate unfairness claims and the challenges to them. Finally, it is time to take a fair reading of commonsense unfairness and to see what it says about commonsense fairness.

ENDNOTES

1. They were asked to record what is now standard information: when each instance occurred (agewhen) and their own age (so we could compute an agediff score), and whether the instance was personal or not (Y, K, or U). We also repeated what are now familiar tasks in a familiar sequence: They made sevnow and sevthen ratings (so we could compute sevdiff and then rate of change scores) and type and blame categorizations; a week later, an independent rater made a sevnow rating for these instances and categorized each for type and blame; finally, the participant and independent rater had to sit

down and try to reconcile differences regarding their type and blame judgments when they disagreed.

2. If participants do in fact report a higher percentage of more recent events, we would expect higher agewhen and lower agediff scores. If unfairnesses are more recent, we might expect, on the personal dimension, a higher percentage of Y instances and thus differences for type and blame as well.

3. Our assumption is that such "disrespect" instances have been there all along (although we do not know to what extent), but that they were either lumped under the "miscellaneous" category or grouped with "lack of due process" instances.

4. The standard deviation was 3.6, and the range was from 10 to 29. In subsequent analyses, to weight each participant equally, we used only the first 10 instances for each participant.

5. When we categorize unfairnesses into low (1–25), medium (26–50), high (51–75), and severe (76–100), we found the percentage of instances in these four categories to be 20.2, 25.9, 27.4, and 26.4, indicating that this journal methodology was producing more low- and medium-rated unfairnesses than earlier studies.

6. $R = .45$.

7. These findings accord with procedural justice findings. *See, e.g.*, E. A. Lind and T. Tyler, *The Social Psychology of Procedural Justice* (New York: Plenum Press, 1988).

8. M. E. P. Seligman, *Helplessness: On Depression, Development, and Death* (San Francisco: Freeman, 1975).

9. This is not quite "learned helplessness," but a forgetting of the fact that one is not helpless.

10. Even at the low levels, we see this consistent trend.

17

TOWARD A FAIR READING OF COMMONSENSE UNFAIRNESS AND FAIRNESS

At the very beginning of this work, a chorus of social critics decried "the whining and narcissism" of unfairness claims and claimants.[1] Pontificating without the sanctity of evidence, the critics held these claims to be bogus or petty whines, while alleging that the claimants were in the throes of narcissism, delusional expectations, and childish wishes. Yet here is the rub: This critical conclusion, despite its unison, is sharply and consistently refuted by our findings.[2]

The most obvious rebuttal evidence comes from independent raters, who overwhelmingly agree with the participants that their instances are unfairnesses, and they further agree with the participants' type and blame categorizations and their severity ratings; this is agreement at general and specific levels, across thousands of unfairness instantiations, across age groups, and across some cultural groups. Furthermore, as we saw in the previous chapter, this agreement now extends to low-end unfairnesses, just the end of the continuum where the critics' narcissistic petty whine charge is most likely to stick. But it did not. Finally, the participants' claims were not dominated by narcissistic "self-as-victim" instances, for the claims of others they know and others they do not know actually predominate, showing an empathetic concern, which is yet another rebuttal of narcissism and victimology assertions.

We thus have a contradiction: Our empirical assessment of "common-sense unfairness" and the critics' assessment of citizens' "common sense" unfairness claims are miles apart. Our data strongly suggest that the critics are significantly off the mark, because these narratives turn out to be substantive plaints, wherein echoes from Job and Greek and Shakespearean tragedies are heard. This contradiction leaves us with a conundrum: How is it possible, in this information age, where pollsters tap community sentiment so regularly, for the views of the critics to be so far off base?

On the Flowering of Outliers and the Withering of Prototypes

We must consider context. Pundits write for newspapers or news magazines, and some do regular stints as talking heads on television news/analyses shows. As a group, they follow media reports religiously, for this is habit and hallowed ground from which comes their daily bread. In many ways, they are the media, even when their screeds spotlight the media. If this is a reasonable surmise, then pundits more than most may believe that media presentations represent orthodoxy. If this is so, they may be the victims of the very prototypes they rail against or help to shape.

The findings from commonsense unfairness suggest how this might be. In study after study, we find basic agreement between participants and raters regarding whether these instances are unfairnesses, an agreement that extends to their type and blame categorizations and severity ratings. However, although agreement is the rule, there are also disagreements over the few outlier instances that are situated at the questionable edge of the categories. Regarding outliers, we find that independent coders are more likely to view these through differing perspectives, focus on different aspects of the event, or construe different victims than the participants who offer these. More to the point, the coders are more likely to see these outliers as falling into the "not an unfairness" at all category.

If critics not only see these outliers as our coders do, but focus on these at the expense of the vast majority where agreement is common, then their picture of commonsense unfairness can indeed become distorted. Although outliers are rarities in our studies, they are staples in the media fare, and it is the steady diet that distorts.

Three media outliers illustrate how this distortion may come about, and all three examples fall within the "disproportionate punishment" type category. Citing an editorial from *The Washington Post* titled "Killing Babies,"[3] the first outlier begins this way: "The combined lesson of two court decisions Thursday—one in Maryland and one in Delaware—is that killing one's baby will, first, bring scant punishment and, second, will not be deemed subsequently to preclude future custody over children." In this editorial, two legal cases became transformed into media cases, which were used to underscore the conclusion that punishments and consequences were too light. In short sound bites, the long and checkered history of infanticide law is absent, the fuller context of current cases is not presented, and citizens' perceptions may become distorted. This can happen if citizens come to believe that these rare cases occur more frequently than they do, in more heinous form than they actually do, or that extreme leniency is the typical consequent. Thus what starts as a very rare phenomenon now is seen as an epidemic as outliers push the prototype further from the center of its type category.

Disproportionate punishment outliers also come in excessive varieties. One that we examined experimentally (see chapter 10) was a punitive damages case brought in Alabama by Ira Gore Jr. against BMW of North America. That an Alabama jury awarded Gore $4 million in punitive damages was but one high-profile media case that was seized on to allege that punitive damage awards had run amok and to argue that awards ought to be capped or taken out of the jury's province entirely. Another such high-profile media outlier case involved Stella Liebeck,[4] who sued McDonald's after being burned by hot coffee; if the compensatory damages award of $160,000 did not raise heat, the $2.7 million for punitive damages certainly put the issue on the boil, as many in the media concluded, with many citizens following, that civil juries were "out of control."[5] The impressions of excess and of being out of control were largely based on outliers. Once again, an outlier, presented out of context, is touted as typical when it is anything but.

The final illustration of this outlier effect comes from the world of sports. In an article titled "What Is Fair for Carlesimo?" Tony Kornheiser wrote,

> Nobody's talking about choking the coach anymore, are they?
> Now they're talking about "fundamental fairness" for the player.
> Latrell Sprewell's appearance in Oakland on Tuesday afternoon was terrifically effective in changing the dialogue on what had been an open and shut case of assault.
>
> Now the focus will go to fairness and due process and the uncomfortable presence of race. The possibility of defining what's "appropriate behavior" for a coach will be on the table. Choking that coach will be in the background.[6]

The Golden State Warriors, Sprewell's team at the time of the incident, terminated his 4-year contract, worth $7.7 million in salary that year, and the National Basketball Association suspended him for a year. Sprewell appealed his punishment, which had only been monetary. As columnist Michael Kelly pointed out,[7] "If I tried to strangle my boss in front of a dozen witnesses, I would expect to lose not merely my job but my freedom."

Both Kelly and Kornheiser recognized that from Sprewell's vantage point, Sprewell claimed to be the victim, but this was not as the columnists saw it. Viewers who watch the news and read their sports pages are likely to form perceptions from the outliers and may generalize to "prima donna athletes out of control," "punishments woefully out of tune with offenses," or "due process as an obfuscation for turning a defendant into the victim."

These may be the sort of generalizations people make when they hear or read that Amy Grossberg and her former boyfriend, Brian Peterson—who killed their baby, dumped it in a trash bin, and sought to conceal it—are sentenced to 2½ years and 2 years, respectively. Furthermore, when the Amy Grossberg and Brian Peterson story is coupled with that of La-trena Pixley—who smothered her infant daughter Nakya (who ended up in a dumpster) and who received a sentence of weekends in detention for three years and was then granted custody of her 2-year-old son[8]—what are we to think? Some might well conclude that these individuals "got away with murder," and others might conclude that most infanticide defendants "get off" light. Taking these outliers together, one might conclude that criminal, family, and civil court decisions bear no proportional relationship to the offense, a sweeping conclusion again based on outliers, which ends up sharply skewing the picture toward the outliers.

A Conundrum Without Context

Every parent who has separated two quarreling children, or every marital therapist listening to two quarreling adults, is reminded of the old adage—there are two sides to every story. These stories begin with a different "who started it," cite different facts, or put different spins to the same facts. The parent or therapist earnestly listening for the "truth," hears the latter dissolving into some Rashomon of noisy perspectivalism. But there is another side to this. We also know that there are times and situations were two stories can be an advantage, each acting as a ballast for the other, dragging extremist claims toward the center. For example, our legal system turns this "two sides" adage into a fairness principle: The truth will emerge where two equally matched adversaries have it out before an impartial jury, it is held. Two sides, then, can create a context where outliers can be exposed, cross-examined, and weeded with facts. Without context and cross-examination, outliers will loom larger in foreground than their substance and frequency warrants, whereas prototypes will be pulled toward *extremis*.

A Blaming Conundrum

At the very beginning of this work, some critics put the blame on blaming, which they connected to victimology,[9] the pointing toward others as responsible while simultaneously denying their own responsibility. This victimology was also connected to impairments of one's mental health (most prominently, narcissism) and sense of civic virtue (most notably, when rudeness and incivility rise).[10] Putting the blame on blame has become the fashionable if not facile answer, repeated so often that the allegation moves to a conviction. But this broad-brush negative view of blame is sharply contradicted by our findings, which leads to another conundrum. What accounts for this disconnect between our results and the allegation?

The answer, in part, comes about because the positive side to the blame story is all too often missed, and it is missed most when necessary distinctions are not made, when outliers rule, and when screeds and jeremiads substitute for facts. To unravel this, let us start with consistent finding from our research—that participants blame some *who or what* for the unfairness and seldom blame themselves. This finding appears to give credence to blaming as victimization, as avoiding responsibility, as reflecting a narcissistic view. Yet we offer a different interpretation, for if these claims were just the negative, then outside coders should disagree with participants far more than they did; to the contrary, the interrater reliability for blame was quite high, higher, in fact, than it was for type. Thus to the disinterested outsiders, who presumably have no victimization to grind, participants' blame designations seem appropriate to the unfairness.

This finding suggests that we ought to make a differentiation between "blaming as in victimization" and "blaming as an appropriate response," which Shaver called an appropriate response for moral affronts and misfortunes.[11] From our data, there is other evidence that supports making discriminations. For example, participants will direct their blame at themselves or the victim of the unfairness when flaw or fault are germane.[12] Blame, then, is not always negative nor always pointing outward.

Let us consider its positive ends. Blame conveys an angry yet moral message to an equal, parent, boss, society, or even to God that they have erred, failed, or fallen below some acceptable fairness standard. Blame also conveys, implicitly or quite explicitly, that we expect better from them. When it is aimed at a claimant who is perceived to be at fault (nullifying), the blame is put on the claimant for inappropriately blaming (victimization) and claiming an unfairness when he or she has no case.

Continuing with the positive face, blame not only reminds others of our values and expectations, it is also a reminder to ourselves of what we value and hold dear: It reaffirms the moral order, the fairness standards, and the expectations of civic virtue. This is neither a retreat from civic virtue nor a retreat into victimhood and narcissism, but quite the opposite. For example, our familiar, Peter Pan, wants his Neverland to be a fair one, where even a grownup like Captain Hook sustains the principle of fighting fair, while our exemplar, Job, fervently wants a world where even God acts fairly and does not dodge blame that ought to be owned. Our first conclusion is an obvious one: There are cases where blame is appropriate, and blurring distinctions by casting them as "blame as bad" would be severely distorting the facts.

From the negative view of blaming, it is all too easy to caricature claimants as noisy children, rebellious teenagers, and grownups who have not grown up, and to allege that their cries and claims contribute to a climate of rudeness and incivility. From the negative view, images of claimants manifesting rudeness, incivility, and anarchy can follow. But images and allegations need to be deconstructed before they take on a life of their own, and in the light of our data and what we know from other sources, we must differentiate appropriate blaming from this nexus of rudeness, incivility, and anarchy.

Neither we nor our coders find these images fitting the participants' unfairness instances and their blame designations. Far from promoting disharmony in the social fabric, participants tend to be "conservatives," valuing the legal and social rules that make for fairness and civility, and they react when these rules are violated. Hence, far more often than it is apparently acknowledged, *unfairness claims are a condemning reaction to rudeness and incivility*, rather than the cause of it, and thus many of the critics appear to have cause and effect backward.

In Caldwell's A *Short History of Rudeness*,[13] he presented the complexities that are so often missed or reduced to stereotypes. For example, Caldwell pointed out that rudeness has served a positive function throughout history, particularly in confronting social and legal rules and restrictions that no longer seem fair. To illustrate, consider the civil rights era in the 1950s and 1960s in the southern United States, when an African American tried to enter a desegregated school, sit at a lunch counter or at the front of a bus, or drink from a water fountain "For Whites Only." Surely there were many who saw these as acts of rudeness, incivility, and anarchy, though history would characterize them otherwise. Thus some claims of unfairness, and the blaming that goes with it, do challenge the status quo, because it is unfair. So there is another set of claims that are not conservative and do not call for the restoration of the accepted norms, but call for change and new norms in the name of fairness.

If blaming gets a bad rap because it is seen as negative, there is a positive factor that comes into play that reaches the level of a religious tenet: that getting over and letting go of blame is both the right and therapeutic thing to do. Traditional religions preach forgiving or letting go of blame, whereas psychotherapists, today's "secular priesthood,"[14] generally reaffirm this view. Holding on to anger over past grievances is likely to harm us psychologically, so the call-in-radio shrinks say; self-help literature tells us that blaming is destructive for relationships and for enjoying life, then offers us 12-step approaches for overcoming these "negative" feelings. Hollywood movies of heinous crimes and crazed killers portray the latter as fixated and obsessed over past inequities, unable to conquer or quell blame, thereby showing us all too graphically the moral of the story—what happens if we do not get over it.

Our evidence (chapter 8, Do We Ever Get Over Unfairnesses?) does show that some people retain unfairnesses for decades. But before concluding that this is unhealthy or a failing on their part, we must cross-examine "getting over" more closely—by contemplating a universe where there is no blame—where no one blames anybody for anything. In this new world, "12-step, self-help prescriptions" always do the trick, positive affirmations unfailingly eliminate the negative, managed care cures the client in one session, and psychiatry's potent drugs "chill us out"—all to the insurance carriers' delight.

If we could let go of unfairnesses (and the blame that attaches) that easily, would this new world be closer to civic virtue? If parents could instantly let go of their anger or irritations, such that children no longer get sent to "time out" and teenagers are no longer "grounded," what will we be begetting? If we nurture nothing but "forgiving and getting over," leaving blame as some psychic and religious relic in the past, this will not lead to moral behavior and civic virtue being taught or modeled. Elevating an isolated therapeutic value above all else is not likely to curb narcissism nor rein in unwarranted entitlement claims. To the contrary, it is the very climate in which such excesses flower. Thus there is nothing divine about this sort of forgiving, for in its unbounded charitableness, in the speed in which the grace is granted, and in its very omnipresence, it is indiscriminate.

Holding on to blame holds to those standards and values we want in our community, our consciousness, and for our children; to swiftly "forgive and get over" reduces their importance to a "whatever." A one-sided blame-as-bad view is likely to leave the positive face unseen, such that appropriate discriminations are lost, a false nexus is created, and the interesting complexities of blame reduce to a one-sided prototype.

UNFAIRNESS AS FOUNDATIONAL

In a quote cited earlier, Craig Haney argued that the Constitution "serves as the basis for our expectations about legal fairness and justice . . . [and] as it is publicly understood and discussed, stands as a major source of our *symbolic legality*."[15] Although I do not disagree with Haney's ground-floor placement of the Constitution, I wish to add a basement: that the Constitution itself rests on a foundational level of fairness and unfairness. Some founding fathers recognized this,[16] Jefferson's Declaration of Independence reveals it, and our research findings affirm that symbolic legality is rooted in ordinary citizens' notions of what is fair and unfair. Thus the assertion that constitutional law "serves as the basis for our expectations about legal fairness and justice" needs to be modified, at least in this sense: Constitutional law cannot be *the* basis but only *a* basis—for citizens' commonsense notions derive from an earlier time, long before the Constitution's enumerated rights and the Supreme Court's 200 years of constitutional rulings became known to us.[17] Our participants, the vast majority of whom are old enough and educated sufficiently to cite constitutional law, seldom do: When asked to explain why an instance is an unfairness, they invoke commonsense unfairness and not the legal cite.[18]

There is deeper and older ground beneath the law, as our data show. It follows, then, that a relationship must exist between this foundational level of commonsense fairness and the constitutional ground floor. We can find this acknowledged in many Supreme Court decisions, sometimes where "great cases" or "hard cases," as Justice Holmes put it,[19] or the "trouble cases," as Llewellyn and Hoebel put it,[20] have been before the Court; sometimes it comes in cases that sharply divide the Court, where majority and dissenting opinions, and their acerbic footnotes, will oftentimes invoke basic fairness principles, community sentiment, and the view that the law must rest and square with that sentiment and the underlying fairness principles.[21] We oftentimes hear such an acknowledgment following an alleged case of "nullification," where the jurors appear to have disregarded the law,[22] or reconstrued the legal instructions,[23] to bring their underlying, basement-level fairness principles to weigh in. Social scientists and scholars who investigate "institutional legitimacy"[24] are in fact dealing with the ground floor-to-foundational level relationship, and the consequences for the Court and the nation if the two levels disconnect.

Our data support this foundational-level view and its connectedness with the edifice above. In bringing the unfairness foundation to light, we have exposed its forms (types), its intensity (severity), its staying power (rate of change), and its connections to people, society, life, and God (blame). Further, this level is not just foundational for justice and formal law, but for a much wider landscape that takes in everyday life concerns and relationships. Specifically, "unfairness" is applied more to human relationships than "injustice," to cases, situations, and events that never come to court. It is applied to equals, be they siblings, spouses, roommates, neighbors, coworkers, or complete strangers, for we carry our fairness expectations into such relationships and interactions. Expectations about equity and equality (in its many forms), procedural due process, and basic respect are significant principles, although these may differ in degree with the closeness of the relationship, among other factors. When the relationship is hierarchical (i.e., where the other is our parent, teacher, coach, or boss), we have expectations, although these may change in degree as we acknowledge the other's authority. When the authority is society, represented by its officials or institutions, the expectations are with us yet again, sometimes lessening or rising, depending on the action and the issue.

Our foundational notions show constancy and variation, as severity findings for type, blame, and type × blame effects reveal. On the side of constancy, these expectations are not gossamer; on the variation side, they are not cast in stone. They end up being neither simplistic prototypes nor black-and-white caricatures, but finely graded constructs with highly nuanced discriminations that appear reasonable to outsiders as well.

Yet as we explore the unfairness foundation, we also find that it extends to expectations about life, nature, and even God, those "misfortune" instances, and this foundational area is oftentimes disputed. Americans show considerable disagreement over these: Some consign them to "misfortune" whereas others consign them to "unfairness." We also found that these cases sharply divide the American from the Japanese participants: The latter find these not to be unfairnesses but rather instances of bad luck. Many Americans want luck, along with heredity, to be equitably if not equally distributed, and many want nature to be less unruly and life itself to be less unpredictable.

Undoubtedly, it would be a safer, more predictable world if hurricanes and earthquakes did not produce death and destruction, or if birth defects and diseases did not lead to parents burying their children ahead of time. Our world would no doubt be more understandable, with less anguish, if God gave answers, or straight answers, or found other ways to place a bet. Some hold that the wish to reduce life's "error variance" is a childish wish and argue that we would be better off if we accepted a world that guarantees nothing and accepted that life is not supposed to be fair. But if wishing to reduce life's error variance is a childish wish or a trumped-up entitlement claim we lay before life out of our narcissism or naiveté, and if turning misfortunes into unfairnesses is but a primitive conceptual error, then this argument has much to explain.

How, for example, do we explain why many respected adults, working in the various sciences, seek to promote safety, security, and order in a world, thereby reducing error variance, and do so with government funding and with society's hopes for their success? To see this as either childish or pathological seems ludicrous. Some "misfortunes" of 50 or 100 years ago (e.g., certain diseases and inherited conditions) have already moved into "unfairnesses," for knowledge has superceded ignorance. Similarly, within nature, although there will always be hurricanes and earthquakes, there may come a day where scientists can better predict their occurrence, or engineers can better design structures that withstand them, or emergency planning can be more efficient, such that human lives could be saved. Thus misfortunes may have a human factor to them, such that unfairness judgments may turn out to be apt, as well as blame designations when humans fail to do what could have been done.

PERSPECTIVES AND PRINCIPLES CLASHING

Apart from the outliers and the problematic misfortune cases (particularly the subset where God is blamed), broad agreement about unfairness is the rule. But if agreement is the general rule, why does it seem as if disagreements abound? I have already argued that media presentations may distort our perceptions, and that prototypes pushed by outliers to *extremis*, particularly when context is absent, may distort further. Yet there must be more to it, for there are legitimate disagreements, typically at a higher level, that involve a clash of perspectives and principles. We turn to a variety of large and small examples to bring this to light.

Affirmative Action and Reaction

In 1954, in *Brown v. Board of Education*,[25] the Supreme Court constitutionally struck down the "separate but equal" system of segregation in public schools, as it had previously struck down the segregated policy of some law schools in not admitting African Americans. The Court and most of the country recognized that segregation was an unfairness that denied equal opportunity for all and thereby limited opportunities. Desegregation was an immediate answer. More heated disagreements subsequently arose, not over the basic principle, but over a key implementation strategy, court-ordered school busing, that set opponents of the latter to cite other unfairness principles.

Two decades later, another legal remedial was affirmative action. At its outset, community sentiment varied, but with legislative and legal backing, public university admissions were opened wider, as were hiring practices in industries and occupations that had been formerly closed. Over time, though, its justifying rationale began to change, with "redressing past wrongs" giving way to the "creating diversity" rationale. With the rationale changing, community sentiment began shifting against affirmative action, and this became nationally evident in Proposition 209 in California and Initiative 200 in Washington, both of which banned affirmative action.[26] Other states have followed, and the courts seem to be doing so as well. The affirmative action claims run throughout our data, with participants citing unfairness on both sides of the issue. Of note in this larger dispute is the fact that opponents and proponents of affirmative action cite the same unfairness principle—discriminatory treatment and failure to provide equal opportunity—but, from the opponents' perspective the principle is applied to individuals and groups who lose out to affirmative actions. This sort of clash, where differing perspectives are brought to bear on the same alleged unfairness, recurs in our work and accounts for a sizable percentage of disagreements.

Hoop Dreams and Playing Below the Rim

Although some disputes involve the same unfairness principle applied to different victims, other disputes result from a clashing of two different unfairness principles. This clashing of principles also recurs in our work and accounts for a substantial number of disagreements over type of unfairness. Here is a local matter that illustrates this point: The issue is basketball court time in Fairfax County, Virginia, where, according to an article in *The Washington Post*,[27] too many children want to play basketball and there are not enough gyms to accommodate. Fairfax County Youth Basketball League officials decided that the "select teams," made up of the more talented players, should be given the advantage. Although league officials decided that this was an "equitable" solution, some would-be players, their parents, and a few league officials cried "foul" and "unfair," for equality was sidelined in favor of differential treatment.

Though this local issue appears small, the larger equality-versus-equity controversy is not, and this can be seen when we move from the gym to the classroom. In an article by Benbow and Stanley,[28] the authors focused on the past three decades of educational treatment, where equality trumped equity and where, in their analysis, inequity resulted. The authors wrote,

> Over the past three decades, the achievement of waves of American students with high intellectual potential has declined as a result of inequity in educational treatment. This inequity is the result of an extreme form of egalitarianism within American society and schools, which involves the pitting of equity against excellence rather than promoting both equity *and* excellence, anti-intellectualism, the "dumbing down" of the curriculum, equating aptitude and achievement testing with elitism . . . and the insistence of schools to teach all students from the same curriculum at the same level.[29]

These scholars are not alone. Sternberg has questioned whether equality ("equal protection") leaves many students playing below the rim and their potential.[30] This "equality" is troubling when "students could achieve at higher levels if they were instructed and assessed in ways that at least partially matched their patterns of analytical, creative, and practical abilities,"[31] and Sternberg backed up his argument with data that appear to confirm his position. But if we assess differences in abilities and make differential educational decisions based on those differences, we are no longer in the land of strict equality, and this is troubling to others.

Take the assessment and placement in classes for the "educable mentally retarded" (EMR) as the example, a practice that has gone on for a generation and where "Black children have been scandalously overrepresented" in such classes.[32] However, as Buss noted, "identifying exactly what makes this a scandal and whom we should blame is not so obvious."[33] What

Buss had misgivings about is the transformation of an issue that was educational in origin into a legal one, now to be decided by legal policy making: Is "a problem of biblical proportions"[34] more likely to be resolved when judges try "to make it fit available legal concepts"[35] or not? Seeking justice in the courts for an educational fairness issue in the schools may not necessarily promote the latter. If justice concepts are too few when the fairness issue is individualized and complex, then the former must squeeze the latter into a rule that is too tight, too broad, or just lacking fit.

Equal and Individualized Justice: Handicaps and Golf Handicaps

In the preceding discussion, two time-honored fairness principles—equality and equity—lead to inequities in the eyes of some. Now we meet two more time-honored principles clashing. Juxtaposed against the principle of equal justice is the principle of individualized justice. From the individualized principle, we assess each case on its merits and each defendant on his or her merits, rather than treating them uniformly. But from the equal justice principle, if defendants who commit the same crime get wildly different punishments, an "unequal treatment" claim results. However, from the individualized principle, if all defendants who commit the same crime get exactly the same punishment, where no individualized assessment of aggravating and mitigating factors is conducted, an "equal treatment when it should be individualized" unfairness results.[36]

This particular clash of principles plays out in participants' narratives. We know that youngsters cry "unfair" when a teacher punishes the whole class or when a parent punishes both siblings for the actions of the one guilty party; yet we also know, from a different set of instances, what happens when all parties are guilty but only one is punished. These two fairness principles, both honored in the abstract and in their particulars, nonetheless may clash.

Now let us add "handicaps" to this discussion. Many are born with disabilities and handicaps of one sort or another, or become disabled through accident, trauma, or disease, and we find such instances cited by participants under the "innocence punished" category. Those who succeed despite their disabilities are oftentimes exemplars of will, determination, and the best of the human spirit. As our civilization advances in its sensibilities, we have come to recognize that many with disabilities can do the job, and that barring them from the opportunity is another sort of unfairness. This recognition is codified in the Americans With Disabilities Act (ADA). Whether it is the force of law or just fundamental fairness (fairness as need), we are apt to give that individual a chance, even if it means making certain adjustments and accommodations. What do we do, for example, if disabilities leave individuals blind, deaf, or wheelchair bound, yet they believe they can succeed at college if one gets an oral testing situation, another gets a sign language interpreter, and the third gets a wheelchair ramp to gain access? We are apt to make it so, not just because the ADA says to make it so but because bending the customary for the individualized principle seems the fair thing to do.[37]

Professional sports, on the other hand, generally do not bend their strict rules for a particular person's disability, opting instead for another principle—to keep the playing field level. Nonprofessional golfers have their handicaps, but at the professional level, the rules are the rules, uniform for all. As sportswriter Thomas Boswell stated,

> Pro golfers often say, with pride, their sport is not fair. The perfect drive that ends in a divot, the fatal gust of wind, the diabolical spike mark on the 18th green is part of the game's lore. Surmounting such mishaps, or enduring them, is recalled with relish.[38]

Casey Martin was born with Klippel Trenaunay Weber Syndrome; by talent and hard work, he has become a golfer, a very good one. The circulatory problems in his right leg are severe, and to compete with the best he needs a cart; but the pros who play the game on the PGA circuit do not use carts, unlike the millions of hacks who play *at* the game. Boswell stated,

> With a cart, he could probably play on the PGA Tour. His game's that good. Without a cart, he hasn't got a prayer. His leg's that bad. The Tour said: "No cart."[39]

Casey Martin went to court, using the ADA, to use a cart. Many golfers and sportswriters, though personally sympathetic to Martin's case, nonetheless felt that his having a cart put them at an unfair disadvantage. This case then jumped from the sports pages and the court to the court of public opinion, as the media brought this case to national attention. That this case so grabbed our attention while dividing sentiments illustrates what happens when equally compelling fairness principles are at odds. Many opined on both sides of the issue, as did participants in our most recent "But it's not fair!" study. Even though sides were taken, many acknowledged that there seemed to be "no happy solution" that resolves the controversy and no rule that could be applied steadfastly to all variants that can come to mind, or to courts in the future.

A President Is Impeached, But Has the Governing Fairness Principle Been Found?

Although the Martin case made headlines in January of 1998, the dominant story of the year, which reached its high- or low-water mark (depending on one's perspective) on December 19, 1998, was "Clinton Impeached." This is a story that historians and political scientists will write about for years to come, a story far too large and complex to tell in this space, but far too important to completely ignore given our topic of unfairness.

As members of the House of Representatives rose to give their brief speeches, the words "fair" or "unfair" tumbled out frequently, but they were applied differently by Democrats and Republicans—to different actors and actions, to different outcomes and processes, and to different legal issues and moral values. There were disagreements over what alleged harms occurred, and who or what was victimized (e.g., the Republic, its laws, the Constitution, the office of the presidency, Monica Lewinsky, the president's wife, daughter, friends, cabinet members, the citizens of the nation, its dead citizens [in particular, who gave their lives for the country on foreign battlefields] or our young children, in particular). Although almost all acknowledged error (i.e., that some unfairness had happened), clarity quickly shattered into cubist-like perspectives. But it did not stop there. There were disagreements of what types of culpability were involved (e.g., personal, familial, ethical, moral, legal, constitutional), their degree (i.e., does it rise to the impeachable level where reasonable doubt is erased), whether the offenses were established by fair due process, and what would be the proportional punishment. Clearly, judgments on these questions, some factual, others value laden, and still others mixing fact and value, were at odds, with biases confounding.

In the end, the partisan disconnect was stark, although unsurprising to many: 98% of the Republicans voted for two articles of impeachment, 98% of the Democrats voted against. More surprising was the disconnect between the polls voting for impeachment and the polls recording the views, values, and votes of citizens. Even under the quieter, more dignified Senate trial, the absence of agreed upon rules for resolving the clash of fairness principles made it extraordinarily difficult to determine which principle or value warranted hegemony.[40]

The noise, partisanship, and confoundings that surround and taint the matter make seeing the core fairness issue difficult and make us yearn, perhaps, for a simplified experimental vignette that controls the extraneous while reducing the matter to its essentials. But sometimes life is noisy, and vignettes oversimplify far too much. Still, by a change of venue—moving down the block—we might at least remove the partisanship.

Down the block from the Capitol is the Supreme Court, where justices, inoculated by a life appointment, are more immunized to political pressures and public sentiment than members of the House and Senate, who must face an electorate on a regular basis. If the rules for deciding fairness cases are anywhere, they should be here, and there are reasons for hopefulness. For one, the cases the Court chooses to hear have been scrutinized at lower levels, where parsing and filtering through rigorous processes have distilled wheat from chaff. For another, the issues have been thoroughly briefed, with briefs responding to briefs. Yet in evaluating this more objective way of sifting and deciding, there is reason to conclude that the Court's decisions do not yield *the answer:* If Supreme Court justices had agreed upon rules for resolving the collision of clashing fairness principles, there ought to be far more 9–0 decisions than are actually obtained.

CONCLUSIONS

If "hard cases make bad law," as the legal aphorism has it, then this is also the controlling adage when fairness principles clash. Be it in the aerie of the High Court, in the partisan trenches of Congress, or on the ground of public opinion, we see division over hard cases. In fact, we seem to find it almost everywhere we look. In school classrooms and on school boards we find division over equity and equality, and it is there in school gymnasiums, where youngsters, parents, and a County Recreational League clash over basketball court time. In colleges and universities, and in state-wide referendums, there is division over continuing affirmative action. Even from tee to green, handicaps and golf carts end up in court.

Clearly, the divine rules are not at hand. Job's Answer answers very little, and when we move to earthly substitutes—be they from black-robed brethren on the High Court or our first gods (parents)—they, too, fall all too humanly short. But we should not be discouraged by the hard cases, nor should we be blinded by them, for this would be the same sort of error we began this chapter with—mistakenly seeing the outlier for the common and failing to take context into our picture.

From our work, a simpler and more optimistic conclusion results: Most often there is agreement over unfairness, and most cases are not hard cases. Given our findings, we are much further along at identifying commonsense fairness and unfairness principles.[41] Building relationships, a society, a world based on fairness principles, which holds together and to civic virtues, remains unfinished work, a dream in progress. But from our work, we know something about the basis of the dream and its connection to reality. We know that it is not just a childish, Peter Pan dream, nor the dream of just narcissists, nor propped up straw men, such as baby boomers with bogus entitlement claims. To the contrary, it is the dream of those who empathize with the unfairnesses of unknown others, whose writing is laced with insistence and blame. In its most positive face, the judgment of unfairness acts as a motivating force—driving us and others to do better —to owning responsibilities and accepting our duties.

The dream of a society based on fairness is common and broad based, uniting ordinary citizen, politician, and justice; it unites Founding Fathers, the homeless, and the poets who walk half-deserted streets. However, hard cases create divisions, because the principles do not order neatly nor logically, and thus finding which fairness principle best resolves hard cases troubles the highest jurists. This very dilemma was addressed at an American Bar Association conference in December of 1998 by Justice Kennedy, who spoke about, of all things, fairness.[42] He said, "each judge each day must renew her oath, must renew his oath of fairness." He went on to say that "after 20 years on the bench, it surprises me how often I have to examine myself for any biases or prejudice that might creep into an opinion." Perhaps this "oath to fairness," though it is not chiseled atop the Supreme Court building, may be found in the basement, at the foundational level. This justice, who is not alone, does not find fairness by looking solely at law or logic.[43] He tells us that he looks inward—perhaps to that place where commonsense fairness resides.

Not Fair! began not in the lofty reaches of theory or philosophy, nor in sacred texts, nor in Supreme Court decisions, though all have been cited along the way. We began at the foundational level, with ordinary people's unfairness instantiations, and in closing we return to there, where the ground has been dug and fundamental findings unearthed.

"Commonsense unfairness" turns out to be quite stable: The basic types of unfairness, these fairness building blocks, are held in solid agreement by participants and outsiders, whereas the outlier exceptions turn out to be far fewer than a "media read" would suggest. Though the findings can be simply stated, the import is considerable. The overall accord around type and severity is promising; so too is the accord around blame and how blame is used in understanding unfairnesses, insisting on fairness, and separating the unfair from the not unfair. Had we found, to the contrary, great rifts in the foundation, where the essential substance of unfairness had no consensual basis, then these narratives would amount to no more than braying babble. Had we found an indiscriminate and avoidance-like blaming, then the story we build on such a foundation would surely topple, as they would be but subjective, fairy-tale fluff with neither moral bite nor claim to our attention.

But the cry, "But it's not fair!" is far more often than not, a claim with moral bite and with substance that warrants our attention. We may try to respond to the claimant by rectifying or nullifying, though in some cases we cannot do either; in those cases, we may try to understand the claim and ease the pain, though this may not erase it. Then again, we may respond with jeremiads and rants, particularly when we choose to hear only the cries but not its substance and are thus mistakenly moved to dismiss the claim and diagnose the claimant. But such a response cannot claim the civic virtue high ground, for it displays no empathy for the other and fails to square with the facts.

In everyday life, most choose to respond to claimants, which makes life better for each of us. Yet in responding to the other, we are also responding to ourselves and responding from our fundamental values—

affirming our sense of what is the right and fair thing to do. The claim of unfairness is a reaction to wrong, but it also a desire for better, which is not just for the self but for others and for the world we live in. Once we penetrate the cry of "But it's not fair!" and unearth its essence, we end up finding a common ground.

ENDNOTES

1. *See, e.g,* G. F. Will, "Really 'Risky' Times," *Washington Post* (January 11, 1998), p. C9. In his article, Will connected television news with "the whining and narcissism of baby boomers" and "fairness," when he stated, "Furthermore, television news is produced largely by and for baby boomers, who in their narcissism constantly congratulate themselves on discovering new things (sex, cigars, injustice, martinis, risks). Now they are turning 50 and discovering a cosmic injustice: They are going to die. Is this *fair?* Can't Congress produce just one more entitlement. If this generation of whiners had been born just 50 years earlier, many of its members would have died before learning how to whine."

2. There is much more evidence on this point from the area of commonsense justice. *See, e.g.,* N. J. Finkel, *Commonsense Justice: Jurors' Notions of the Law* (Cambridge: Harvard University Press, 1995); N. J. Finkel, "Culpability and Commonsense Justice: Lessons Learned Betwixt Murder and Madness," *Notre Dame Journal of Law, Ethics & Public Policy* 10 (1996): 11–64; N. J. Finkel, "Commonsense Justice, Psychology, and the Law: Prototypes Common, Senseful, and Not," *Psychology, Public Policy, and Law* 3 (1997): 461–489; N. J. Finkel, "But It's Not Fair!: Commonsense Notions of Unfairness," *Psychology, Public Policy, & Law* (in press); N. J. Finkel, "Commonsense Justice and Jury Instructions: Instructive and Reciprocating Connections," *Psychology, Public Policy, & Law* (in press); N. J. Finkel and J. L. Groscup "Crime Prototypes, Objective Versus Subjective Culpability, and a Commonsense Balance," *Law and Human Behavior* 21 (1997): 209–230; N. J. Finkel and J. L. Groscup, "When Mistakes Happen: Commonsense Rules of Culpability," *Psychology, Public Policy, and Law* 3 (1997): 1–61; N. J. Finkel and B. D. Sales, "Commonsense Justice: Old Roots, Germinant Ground, and New Shoots," *Psychology, Public Policy, and Law* 3 (1997): 1–15.

3. "Killing Babies," *Washington Post* (July 11, 1998), p. A18.

4. Leibeck v. McDonald's Corp., No. CV-93-2419, 1995 WL 360309 (N.M. Dist. Ct. 1994).

5. *See, e.g.,* J. K. Robbennolt and C. A. Studebaker, "Anchoring in the Courtroom: The Effects of Caps on Punitive Damages," *Law and Human Behavior* 23 (1999): 353–373.

6. T. Kornheiser, "What Is Fair for Carlesimo?" *Washington Post* (December 11, 1997), pp. D1, D8.

7. M. Kelly, "The Sprewell Saga." *Washington Post* (December 11, 1997), p. A27.

8. K. Shaver, "Pixley Custody Decision Sent Back." *Washington Post* (February 18, 1999), pp. A1, A14. Maryland's highest court ruled that Judge Mason's

decision, which gave Pixley custody of her son "without determining whether she was likely to abuse or neglect him," was a mistake. Although the ruling was unanimous, Judge Cathell "chastised his colleagues in a separate concurring opinion for not using their "collective common sense" and saying flat out that anyone convicted of killing a child "should be presumed an unfit parent," regardless of any other consideration. Whether this appellate ruling reaches the public's perceptions, and affects their prototypes of this and other such cases, is an empirical question.

9. *See, e.g.,* "To top it off, our kids are imbued with victimology, which today has become the American way of blame. It is too routine for adults and their kids to explain all their problems as victimization." M. E. P. Seligman, "The American Way of Blame," *Monitor* 29 (July 7, 1998), p. 2, president's column; *See also* S. Martin, "Seligman Laments People's Tendency to Blame Others," *Monitor* 29 (October 10, 1998), p. 50.

10. J. Kadlecek, "Mourning a Loss of Civic Morality: Symposium Addresses 'Main Challenge' in U.S.," *Washington Post* (May 30, 1998), p. B9.

11. K. G. Shaver, *The Attribution of Blame: Causality, Responsibility, and Blameworthiness* (New York: Springer-Verlag, 1985).

12. We learned in chapter 16, Rectifying, Nullifying, and Softening Unfairness: To Err Is Human, how blame directed inward can nullify an unfairness claim; and in that chapter, as well as in chapter 11, When the Victim Is Flawed or Bears Fault, we saw the "two-way-street" nature of participants' blame; when it is directed back at the participant it mitigates or undercuts the claim, or when directed outward, it can enhance a claim.

13. M. Caldwell, *A Short History of Rudeness: Manners, Morals, and Misbehavior in Modern America* (New York: Picador, 1999).

14. P. London, *The Modes and Morals of Psychotherapy* (New York: Holt, Rinehart, & Winston, 1964).

15. C. Haney, "The Fourteenth Amendment and Symbolic Legality: Let Them Eat Due Process," *Law and Human Behavior* 15 (1991): 183.

16. G. Wills, *A Necessary Evil: A History of American Distrust of Government* (New York: Simon & Schuster, 1999).

17. The matter is actually more complex, for the ground floor can come to influence the foundation. *See, e.g.,* S. E. Merry, *Getting Justice and Getting Even: Legal Consciousness Among Working-Class Americans* (Chicago: University of Chicago Press, 1990). Merry wrote, "Law works in the world not just by the imposition of rules and punishments but also by its capacity to construct authoritative images of social relationships and actions, images which are symbolically powerful. Law provides a set of categories and frameworks through which the world is interpreted. Legal words and practices are cultural constructs which carry powerful meanings not just to those trained in the law or to those who routinely use it to manage their business transactions but to the ordinary person as well. Law in this ideological sense can be described as a discourse, a way of talking about actions and relationships" (pp. 8–9).

18. This does not mean that their commonsense notions are not influenced by the legal concepts. *Id.*

19. Northern Securities Company v. United States, 193 U.S. 197 (1904); R. A. Posner, ed. *The Essential Holmes* (Chicago: University of Chicago Press, 1992).

20. K. Llewellyn and E. A. Hoebel, *The Cheyenne Way* (Norman: University of Oklahoma Press, 1941).

21. Finkel, *Commonsense Justice*.

22. *Id.*

23. *Id.*

24. J. L. Gibson, "Understandings of Justice: Institutional Legitimacy, Procedural Justice, and Political Tolerance," *Law & Society Review* 23 (1989): 469–496; J. L. Gibson, "Institutional Legitimacy, Procedural Justice, and Compliance with Supreme Court Decisions: A Question of Causality," *Law & Society Review* 25 (1991): 631–635; T. R. Tyler, "Governing Amid Diversity: The Effect of Fair Decisionmaking Procedures on the Legitimacy of Government," *Law & Society Review* 28 (1994): 809–831.

25. 347 U.S. 483 (1954).

26. *See, e.g.*, R. Sanchez, "Washington's New Affirmative Action Question: How to End It," *Washington Post* (November 13, 1998), p. A2; N. Hentoff, "Rocky Road to Equality," *Washington Post* (July 27, 1998), p. A23.

27. E. Lipton, "Youth Basketball's Squeeze Play: Some Cry Foul Over Fairfax Plan to Allot Court Time," *Washington Post* (July 15, 1997), p. A1.

28. C. P. Benbow and J. C. Stanley, "Inequity in Equity: How 'Equity' Can Lead to Inequity for High-Potential Students," *Psychology, Public Policy, and Law* 2 (1996): 249–292.

29. *Id.*, p. 249.

30. R. J. Sternberg, "Equal Protection Under the Law: What Is Missing in Education?" *Psychology, Public Policy, and Law* 3/4 (1996): 575–583.

31. *Id.*, p. 575.

32. W. G. Buss, "Intelligence Testing and Judicial Policy Making for Special Education," *Psychology, Public Policy, and Law* 3/4 (1996): 584–602.

33. *Id.*, p. 584.

34. *Id.*

35. *Id.*, p. 602.

36. This was the Supreme Court's argument in striking down North Carolina's death penalty statute, which made the death penalty mandatory following conviction for certain crimes. *See* Woodson v. North Carolina, 428 U.S. 280 (1976), and Roberts v. Louisiana, 428 U.S. 325 (1976).

37. This is not always the case. For example, people suffering from depression have argued in court, schools, and the workplace about being penalized unfairly, yet these individuals typically lose in court. B. A. Masters, "Depression Gets Its Day in Court," *Washington Post* (March 27, 1998), pp. B1, B8.

38. T. Boswell, "The Rules Are Still the Rules," *Washington Post* (January 14, 1998), pp. D1, D2.

39. *Id.*, p. D1.

40. A survey on values, done by *Washington Post*, the Henry J. Kaiser Family Foundation, and Harvard University, documents the clash of values and changing values over the past 30 years. D. S. Broder and R. Morin, "Struggle Over New Standards," *Washington Post* (December 27, 1998), pp. A1, A18.

41. J. Rawls, "Justice as Fairness," *The Philosophical Review* LXVII (1958):164–

194; but see J. W. Chapman, "Justice and Fairness." In *Nomos VI: Justice*, ed. C. J. Friedrich and J. W. Chapman (New York: Atherton Press, 1963), 147–169.

42. J. Biskupic, "In Rare Appearance, 2 Justices Concur Against Threats to Neutrality," *Washington Post* (December 6, 1998), p. A2.
43. *See, e.g.*, O. W. Holmes, *The Common Law* (Cambridge, MA: Harvard University Press, 1963/1881); R. Dworkin, *Law's Empire* (Cambridge, MA: Harvard University Press, 1986); R. A. Posner, *The Problems of Jurisprudence* (Cambridge, MA: Harvard University Press, 1990).

AUTHOR INDEX

SUBJECT INDEX

325

Blame (*continued*)
  misfortune and, 56–57, 165
  prevalence of, 297–298
  recognized as variable, 71
  religious variables and, 98–99, 308
  severity correlated with, 116–118,
    135–136, 147, 149
  victim blamed, 24, 28, 219, 294. *See
    also* Fault of victim or flawed vic-
    tim
  victimology distinguished from blam-
    ing, 16
BMW of North Am., Inc. v. Gore, 188,
  190–198, 305
Bosses, assigning blame to, 93, 99–101,
  114–118, 135–136
  passage of time's effect on, 144–152
Brown v. Board of Education, 312

California Proposition 209, 312
"Cause and effect" arguments, 11
Central tendency measure, 36
Cheating, 73, 113, 210–211, 214
Children. *See also* Parents, assigning
    blame to
  assessing blame (study 2 participants),
    94
  assessing victim of unfairness (study 4
    participants), 130
  blaming themselves for parents' di-
    vorce, 91
  death of. *See* Death
  egocentrism of, 138
  first unfairnesses, 4, 8, 10
  parental-child exchanges on fairness,
    25–27
  victimology and, 16
Chronology of reported unfairnesses, 115
Clinton, Bill, impeachment of, 315–316
Coding of types of unfairness, 77–80,
    86–89, 95–98
  difficulty with categorizing arbitrary
    rules, 110
  disagreement between coder and par-
    ticipant, 114, 130, 137, 174, 237,
    304
  outcome versus process disagreements,
    187
  participants doing coding, effect of,
    101, 110

perspective on blame, 92, 136–137
perspective on unfairness/misfortune/in-
    justice distinctions, 174
severity as factor, 117
Cognitive balance, 24
Collectivism versus individualism, 240–
    241, 243, 249, 260, 261–263
College students as study participants
  assessing ability to get over unfairness
    (Study 5), 144
  assessing blame (Study 2), 77
  assessing severity (Study 3), 111
  assessing victim of unfairness (Study
    4), 130
  distinguishing misfortune versus injus-
    tice versus unfairness, 167–168
  fault of victim, 210
  Japanese versus American students,
    250, 255–256
  low-level unfairnesses, 291–292
  open-ended, narrative, and deconstruc-
    tive approach (Study 1), 66–68
  Spanish versus American culture, 272
Commonsense justice, 155
Commonsense unfairness, 4, 77, 78, 304,
    318
  Japanese, 249–267
  Spanish, 269–284
  versus legal unfairness factors, 192–194
Communal sharing, 243–244
Comparative standards, 229
Comparisons that give succor, 36–38
Concern for others. *See* Empathy
Connections. *See* Advantages or connec-
    tions that are unfair
Constitution, U.S., 309–310
Contributory negligence, 208. *See also*
    Fault of victim or flawed victim
Criminal law, 206–207. *See also* Supreme
    Court cases
Critics
  academic critics, 13–16
  off base in assessment of unfairness
    claims, 304
  social critics, 10–13, 303
Cross-cultural studies, 233–284
  elementary forms of human relations,
    243–244
  fundamental attribution error, 241

homogeneity of study participants creating need for, 236–238
India and collectivism, 240–241
Japanese versus American culture, 240–241, 249–267
justice and fairness as subjects of prior studies, 238–239
Spanish versus American culture, 269–284
universals about unfairness, 238
value dimensions, 240–243
Culpability, 241. *See also* Fault of victim or flawed victim; Guilt of victim
legal analysis and, 206–207
Cultural variables, 8

Daytime talk shows, 11, 12
Death
as factor in classifying as unfairness/misfortune/injustice, 173
babies killed by parents and disproportionate punishments, 306
fault/flaw manipulation in instances of, 213–214
Death penalty case, 188, 190–198
Declaration of Independence, 13, 309
Defendant's rights, 191, 195, 196, 197
Desegregation, 308, 312
Dignity, 45, 77
Discriminatory treatment. *See also* Individualized discriminatory treatment as desirable
as part of schema, 69–70, 83, 122–123
blame correlated with, 95–101, 116–118
equality as underlying principle involved, 74–75, 78
fault/flaw manipulation, 215
frequency of occurrence in studies, 71–72, 95–98, 111–114, 133–135, 144–151, 251–259
Japanese versus American culture, 251–263
low-level unfairnesses, 290, 292–295
outcome versus process unfairness, 71
passage of time correlated with, 144–151
severity correlated with, 111–114, 116–118, 257–258

Disproportionate or displaced punishment
American view of, 238
as part of schema, 70, 84, 122
blame correlated with, 95–98
cluster analysis of unfairness/misfortune/injustice, 173
equity theory and, 77–78, 186
frequency of occurrence in studies, 72, 95–98, 111–114, 144–151, 251–259
Japanese versus American culture, 251–259
low-level unfairnesses, 292–295
outliers skewing picture and media reporting, 305–306
passage of time correlated with, 144–151
severity correlated with, 76, 101, 111–114
Distributive justice, 23, 49, 50–55, 77, 186, 243
Due process. *See also* Lack of due process; Process and fairness
punishment requiring, 186
views of ordinary citizens on, 166
Duty failure and classifying unfairness/misfortune/injustice, 173
Duty to obey the law, 54–55

Education and equality, 313–314
Effort to reward. *See* Reward to effort
Egocentrism. *See* Narcissism
Elderly persons
assessing victim of unfairness (Study 4 participants), 130
concern for others expressed by, 127–128
Emotions affecting judgments of fairness, 226–227
Empathy, 138, 304
increase with age, 132
versus narcissism, 127–141
"Equal justice under law," 45, 78, 185, 207
Equality matching, 243–244
Equals, assigning blame to, 99–101, 114–118, 135–136
getting over unfairness of, 144–152

Heredity as basis for inequality claims, 75–76, 260
Hindsight bias, 175
Honor
    in American culture, 277–278
    in Spanish culture, 274–276
Human agency as source of unfairness, 92, 96, 103
    cases involving, 228–230
    fault of victim, 210–212
    injustice versus misfortune versus unfairness, 173, 209
    just-world views and, 228
    Spanish versus American culture, 279–281

Imbalance, 15
Impeachment of President Clinton, 315–316
Impersonal agency as source of unfairness, 92, 96, 102, 115, 154, 164
    acts of nature and, 228
    misfortune versus unfairness, 209, 223
    Spanish versus American culture, 279–281
Incompetent counsel, 191, 195, 197
India and collectivism, 240–241
Individualism, 14–15
    American versus Japanese culture, 240–241, 249, 261–263
Individualized discriminatory treatment as desirable, 71, 186
    as part of schema, 83, 123
    cluster analysis of unfairness/misfortune/injustice, 173
    needy as beneficiaries of, 75, 78
    severity correlated with, 111
Individualized punishment, 190, 196, 197, 314
Inheritance as basis for inequality claims, 75–76, 260
Injustice distinguished from misfortune and unfairness, 56, 223, 278–279. See also Misclassification of unfairness/misfortune/injustice (umi)
Innocence punished
    age affecting view of, 102
    as part of schema, 84, 122

blame and, 92, 95–98, 102, 118
consensus in studies about, 73, 238
frequency of occurrence in studies, 71–72, 95–98, 111–114, 133–135, 144–151, 251–259
Japanese versus American culture, 251–259, 262
Job's story, 80–81
low-level unfairnesses, 292–295
misfortune and, 164
no accommodation made for, 112
passage of time correlated with, 144–151
severity correlated with, 101, 111–114, 118, 257–258
Spanish versus American culture, 279–281
Institutional legitimacy, 310

Japanese versus American culture, 249–267
    age as factor, 256, 258, 259
    categories of unfairness, 251–259
    collectivism versus individualism, 240–241, 243, 249, 260, 261–263
    differences found, 258–263
    discriminatory treatment, 251–263
    "fairness" in Japanese language, 239–240
    gender effects, 256, 260
    Japanese schema for types of unfairness, 251, 264–266
    power distance, 242
    research design, 250–251
    results and discussion, 251–259
    severity ratings, 257–258
Job's story, 27–38, 66
    claim and blame, 27–38
    desire for fairness, 307
    dispositional factors affecting Eliphaz et al., 225
    exemplar of unfairness, 38
    legacies of, 30–31
    punishment undeserved, 72, 118, 230, 299
    theodicy, 31–34
    translated into modern terms, 103
Just-world belief, 23–42
    comparisons that give succor, 36–38

Just-world belief (*continued*)
  delusion of, 26
  dispositional factor of, 225, 228–230
  flawed victims and, 207–208, 216
  goodness and work should be rewarded,
    73–76, 96
  Job and, 27–38
  research findings on, 23–24
Justice and fairness, 43–62. *See also* Dis-
    tributive justice; "Equal justice
    under law"
  conjugate use of the two terms, 43, 44,
    46, 55
  distinguishing the two terms, 44
  legal and political nature of justice, 48
  outcome and, 49, 54
  overlapping and separate use of the
    two terms, 44, 55
  process and, 48, 54
  reciprocity and, 47, 49, 55, 77
  relationship of the two terms, 43–56
  social, informal nature of fairness, 48
  subset use of the two terms, 44, 46, 55
  synonymous use of the two terms, 43,
    44, 46, 55

Koon v. United States, 188, 190–198

Labeling reason for unfairness, 230
Lack of due process, 77
  as part of schema, 70, 85, 123–124
  blame correlated with, 95–101, 116–
    118
  cluster analysis of unfairness/misfor-
    tune/injustice, 173
  frequency of occurrence in studies, 72,
    95–98, 111–114, 133–135, 144–
    151, 251–259
  Japanese versus American culture,
    251–259, 260–261
  low-level unfairnesses, 292–295
  passage of time correlated with, 144–
    151
  punishment handed out and, 186
  severity correlated with, 111–114,
    116–118, 257–258
Law. *See also* Punishment and process ex-
    periment; Supreme Court cases

commonsense unfairness versus legal
    unfairness, 192–194
  culpability and legal analysis, 206–207
  duty to obey, 54–55
  fairness and, 26, 306
  outcome bias of judges, 176
  process and fairness in, 77
Lawsuits, 9, 26, 53
  excessive punitive damages, 188, 190–
    198, 305
  whiplash cases, 156
Legal and political nature of justice, 48
Legitimacy of unfairnesses, 128
Life, assigning blame to, 99–101, 114–
    115, 116–118
  getting over unfairness of, 144–152,
    155–156
  randomness of life, 230
Low-level unfairnesses, 287–301
  converting into "not an unfairness,"
    291–292, 299
  design of study, 291–292
  effect of fairnesses not being equally
    registered, 296–297
  fault of victim or flawed victim as fac-
    tor, 290, 300
  pessimism and, 295–296
  reasons for converting into "not an un-
    fairness," 293–295
  reasons to study, 289–290
  rectifying or nullifying by claimant,
    294–295, 299–300
  results and discussion, 292–298
  severity ratings, 290, 292
  softening of claimant, 294–295, 299–
    300
  underrepresentation in studies, 288

Market pricing, 243–244
Media's effect on assessment of unfair-
    nesses, 304–306, 313
Memory of unfairnesses, 95
  severity as gauge of, 103–104, 110–111
Misclassification of unfairness/misfortune/
    injustice (umi), 163–184
  age of study participants, 167
  cluster analysis, 172–174
  distinguishing injustice versus misfor-
    tune versus unfairness, 165

ABOUT THE AUTHOR

Norman J. Finkel is professor of psychology of Georgetown University. He received his PhD in clinical psychology from the University of Rochester in 1971, and since coming to Georgetown he has served as director of undergraduate studies, director of graduate studies, and as chair of the department. He has also been in private practice for 20 years. His research in the area of psychology and law focuses on how community sentiment and jurors' views of law and justice, what he calls "commonsense justice," may affect, nullify, and perfect black-letter law. His book with Harvard University Press (1995), *Commonsense Justice: Jurors' Notions of the Law*, brings empirical findings of how jurors construe both facts and legal concepts and weave them, along with their prototypes, into views of what is fair and just. He has done empirical work in a number of criminal and civil law areas, involving insanity, infanticide, self-defense, capital felony-murder, the juvenile death penalty, the right to die, euthanasia, manslaughter, impossible-act cases, and mistake-of-law and mistake-of-fact cases, where commonsense notions are elucidated and then compared to black-letter law. He is a coeditor of *Law and Public Policy/Psychology and the Social Sciences (Forensic Studies)*, a book series published by the American Psychological Association (APA), and has served on the editorial boards of various journals, such as *Psychology, Public Policy, and Law, Law and Human Behavior*, and *Behavioral Sciences & the Law*. He is currently an at-large member of the American Psychology-Law Society (Division 41 of the APA). Some of his other books include *Insanity on Trial* (Plenum Press), *Therapy and Ethics: The Courtship of Law and Psychology* (Grune & Stratton), and *Mental Illness and Health: Its Legacy, Tensions, and Changes* (Macmillan).

Evaluating Job-Related Training